D0301759

A PRACTICAL GUIDE TO

Security Engineering and Information Assurance

A PRACTICAL GUIDE TO

Security Engineering and Information Assurance

DEBRA S. HERRMANN

AUERBACH PUBLICATIONS

A CRC Press Company

Boca Raton London New York Washington, D.C.

Library of Congress Cataloging-in-Publication Data

Herrmann, Debra S.
A practical guide to security engineering and information assurance / Debra S. Herrmann.
p. cm.
Includes bibliographical references and index.
ISBN 0-8493-1163-2 (alk. paper)
1. Computer security. 2. Data Protection. I. Title.

QA76.9.A25 H47 2001
005.8—dc21 2001037901
CIP

This book contains information obtained from authentic and highly regarded sources. Reprinted material is quoted with permission, and sources are indicated. A wide variety of references are listed. Reasonable efforts have been made to publish reliable data and information, but the author and the publisher cannot assume responsibility for the validity of all materials or for the consequences of their use.

Direct all inquiries to CRC Press LLC, 2000 N.W. Corporate Blvd., Boca Raton, Florida 33431.

Auerbach is an imprint of CRC Press LLC

No claim to original U.S. Government works
International Standard Book Number 0-8493-1163-2
Library of Congress Card Number 2001037901
Printed in the United States of America 1 2 3 4 5 6 7 8 9 0
Printed on acid-free paper

Abstract

This book is a comprehensive yet practical guide to security engineering and the broader realm of information assurance (IA). This book fills an important gap in the professional literature. It is the first book to:

1. Examine the impact of both accidental and malicious intentional action and inaction on information security and IA
2. Explore the synergy between security, safety, and reliability engineering that is the essence of IA
3. Introduce the concept of IA integrity levels
4. Provide a complete methodology for security engineering and IA throughout the life of a system

The relationship between security engineering and IA and why both are needed is explained. Innovative long-term vendor, technology, and application-independent strategies demonstrate how to protect critical systems and data from accidental and intentional action and inaction that could lead to a system failure/compromise. These real-world strategies are applicable to all systems, from small systems supporting a home-based business to those of a multinational corporation, government agency, or critical infrastructure system. Step-by-step, in-depth solutions take one from defining information security/IA goals through performing vulnerability/threat analyses, implementing and verifying the effectiveness of threat control measures, to conducting accident/incident investigations, whether internal, independent, regulatory, or forensic. A review of historical approaches to information security/IA puts the discussion in context for today's challenges. Extensive glossaries of information security/IA terms and 80 techniques are an added bonus.

This book is written for engineers, scientists, managers, regulators, academics, and policy-makers responsible for information security/IA. Those who have to comply with Presidential Decision Directive (PDD-63), which requires all government agencies to implement an IA program and certify mission-critical systems by May 2003, will find this book especially useful.

Dedication

This book is dedicated to the memory of Harry E. Murray, Edward P. Herrmann, and Chet and Telma Cherryholmes.

Other Books by the Author

Software Safety and Reliability: Techniques, Approaches, and Standards of Key Industrial Sectors, IEEE Computer Society Press, 1999.

Contents

List of Exhibits

Chapter 2

Chapter 3

Chapter 4

Chapter 5

Chapter 6

Chapter 7

Chapter 8

Appendix B

Appendix D

Chapter 1

Introduction

It is often said that "information is power." This is true because information, correctly integrated, analyzed, and synthesized, leads to knowledge and informed decision-making. Today, the vast majority of the world's information resides in, is derived from, and is exchanged among multiple automated systems. Critical decisions are made (to place an order to buy or sell stocks) and critical actions are taken (to administer a transfusion of a certain blood type, or to change runways during a landing) based on information from these systems. For information to become power, the information must be accurate, correct, and timely, and be presented, manipulated, stored, retrieved, and exchanged safely, reliably, and securely. Information assurance (IA) is the enabler of this power.

1.1 Background

The twentieth century began with the industrial revolution and ended with rapid technological innovation that heralded the information revolution of the twenty-first century. The information revolution has brought many advantages to individuals and organizations. Vast quantities of information are available at incredible speeds to a multitude of people worldwide. E-Commerce is a catalyst for rapid business growth, particularly the development of small and home-based businesses.

The information revolution has also brought its share of risks. For example, millions of dollars were spent globally to prepare for and prevent major Y2K-related hazards. As a result of the time and resources applied, these efforts were highly successful. This exercise made modern society realize, in some cases for the first time, our near total dependence on the safe, reliable, and secure operation of interconnected computer technology from multiple industrial sectors; in particular, the eight critical infrastructure systems:

1. Telecommunications systems
2. Banking and financial systems
3. Power generation and distribution systems
4. Oil and gas distribution and storage systems
5. Water processing and supply systems
6. Air, water, and ground transportation systems
7. Emergency notification and response systems
8. Systems supporting critical government services

Preparations for Y2K were limited to transactions based on a single-date event: the transition from December 31, 1999, to January 1, 2000. In contrast, the infrastructure systems mentioned above operate, for the most part, 24 hours a day, 7 days a week, and perform critical transactions continuously. In addition, they interact with every segment of our society: manufacturing, wholesale and retail businesses, the media, hospitals, schools, and postal/package services, not to mention our homes. Consequently, infrastructure systems must operate safely, reliably, and securely at all times to avoid major disruptions to modern society. Ensuring this capability, even in the presence of accidental errors and intentional attacks, is the domain of IA.

1.2 Purpose

This book is a comprehensive yet practical guide to information security and the broader realm of information assurance (IA). This book fills an important gap in the professional literature. It is the first book to:

1. Examine the impact of both accidental and malicious intentional action and inaction on information security and IA
2. Explore the synergy between security, safety, and reliability engineering that is the essence of IA
3. Introduce the concept of IA integrity levels
4. Provide a complete methodology for information security/IA throughout the life of a system

The relationship between information security and IA and why both are needed is explained. Innovative long-term vendor, technology, and application-independent strategies demonstrate how to protect critical systems and data from accidental and intentional action and inaction that could lead to a system failure/compromise. These real-world strategies are applicable to all systems, from small systems supporting a home-based business to those of a multinational corporation, government agency, or critical infrastructure system. Step-by-step, in-depth solutions take one from defining information security/IA goals through performing vulnerability/threat analyses, implementing and verifying the effectiveness of threat control measures, to conducting accident/incident investigations, whether internal, independent, regulatory, or forensic. A review of historical approaches to information security/IA puts the discussion in context for today's challenges. Extensive glossaries of information security/IA terms and 80 techniques are an added bonus.

Many information security/IA techniques are borrowed from other engineering disciplines. In some cases, these techniques are used "as is." In others, the techniques or the interpretation of the results obtained from using them have been adapted specifically for information security/IA. In addition, there are several new and hybrid techniques. To help make order out of chaos, this book consolidates and organizes information about the information security/IA techniques, approaches, and current best practices.

IA is a new and dynamic field. Widespread use of the term IA, in particular as it relates to protecting critical infrastructure systems, dates back to the late 1990s. A series of events took place in the United States that helped propel the demand for IA. In 1996, the National Information Infrastructure Protection Act, Title 18 U.S.C. Section 1030, was passed.[178] In October 1997, the President's Commission on Critical Infrastructure Protection issued its final report and recommendations.[176] This led to the issuance of Presidential Decision Directive-63 (PDD-63) on May 22, 1998. PDD-63 established the nation's initial goals, many of which are set for the years 2003 to 2005, for IA and a cooperative framework between industry, academia, and local and national governments. As a result, a lot of people have suddenly inherited responsibility for information security/IA and are learning of its importance for the first time. Consequently, this book provides concrete guidance for those new to the field of information security/IA and those who wish to update the depth and breadth of their skills.

1.3 Scope

This book is limited to a discussion of information security/IA. Information security/IA is a global concern; it is not limited to a single industrial sector, economic segment, or legal jurisdiction. As a result, this book looks at the information security/IA challenges and opportunities from a global perspective.

Electronic privacy rights, intellectual property rights in regard to cryptographic algorithms, and national security concerns about exporting encryption technology are the subject of lively debates. This book acknowledges that these debates are ongoing, but does not participate in them. Instead, the reader is referred to Schneier and Banisar,[408,*] which provides an excellent treatment of these subjects.

The psychological motivation behind computer crime is not within the scope of this book, nor are general-purpose software engineering issues.

1.4 Intended Audience

This book is written for engineers, scientists, managers, regulators, academics, and policy-makers responsible for information security/IA. Readers will

* Schneier, B. and Banisar, D. *The Electronic Privacy Papers: Documents on the Battle for Privacy in the Age of Surveillance*, John Wiley & Sons, 1997.

find the abundant practical "how-to" information, examples, templates, and discussion problems most useful. This book assumes a basic understanding of software engineering; however, no previous background in information security/IA is expected.

1.5 Organization

This book is organized in eight chapters. This chapter puts the book in context by explaining the rationale and purpose for which the book was written. It defines limitations on the scope of the book's subject matter, identifies the intended audience for whom the book was written, and discusses the organization of the book.

Chapter 2 sets the stage for the remainder of the book by providing an introduction to and overview of the basic concepts related to information security/IA. The use of information security/IA principles in different application and technology domains and its importance to a variety of stakeholders are explored.

Chapter 3 examines the historical precedents and changes in technology that necessitated the development of information security/IA. Specifically, techniques and approaches employed in physical security, communications security (COMSEC), computer security (COMPUSEC), information security (INFOSEC), system safety, and system reliability are reviewed. The benefits, limitations, and weaknesses of these approaches are analyzed relative to today's technology.

Chapters 4 through 8 define the five major components of a comprehensive and effective information security/IA program and the activities involved in each:

1. Defining the boundaries of the system
2. Performing vulnerability and threat analyses
3. Implementing threat control measures
4. Verifying the effectiveness of threat control measures
5. Conducting accident/incident investigations

As will be seen, there is considerably more to information security/IA than firewalls, encryption, and virus protection.

Four informative annexes are also provided. Annex A presents a glossary of acronyms and terms related to information security/IA.

Annex B presents a glossary of 80 information security/IA analysis, design, verification, and accident/incident investigation techniques. A description of each technique is given in the following format:

- **Purpose:** summary of what is achieved by using the technique; why the technique should be used
- **Description:** a summary of the main features of the technique and how to implement it

- **Benefits:** how the technique enhances IA integrity or facilitates assessment; any cost benefits derived from using the technique
- **Limitations:** factors that may limit the use of the technique, affect the interpretation of the results obtained, or impact the cost-effectiveness of the technique
- **References:** sources for more information about the technique

Annex C lists the sources that were consulted during the development of this book and provides pointers to other resources that may be of interest to the reader. Annex C is organized in three parts: standards, publications, and online resources.

Annex D summarizes the components, activities, and tasks of an effective information security/IA program.

Chapter 2

What Is Information Assurance, How Does It Relate to Information Security, and Why Are Both Needed?

This chapter explains what information assurance (IA) is, how it relates to information security, and why both are needed. To begin, IA is defined in terms of what it involves and what it accomplishes. Next, the application and technology domains in which information security/IA should be implemented are explored. Finally, the benefit of information security/IA to individuals and organizations is illustrated from the perspective of the different stakeholders. The interaction between information security/IA and infrastructure systems is illustrated throughout the chapter.

2.1 Definition

The first standardized definition of IA was published in U.S. DoD Directive 5-3600.1 in 1996:

> Information operations that protect and defend information and information systems by ensuring their availability, integrity, authentication, and nonrepudiation; including providing for restoration of information systems by incorporating protection, detection, and reaction capabilities.

This definition provided a good starting point in that it recognized the need for protection, detection, reaction, and restoration capabilities. However, it is too narrow in scope.

This book proposes a broader definition of IA:

> An engineering discipline that provides a comprehensive and systematic approach to ensuring that individual automated systems and dynamic combinations of automated systems interact and provide their specified functionality, no more and no less, safely, reliably, and securely in the intended operational environment(s).

A broader definition of IA is needed for the following reasons. First, the definition proposed by this book uses the term "automated systems" rather than "information systems." Automated systems encompass a broader range of systems and technology, consistent with the infrastructure systems identified in Chapter 1 and later in this chapter. Automated systems include systems employing embedded software or firmware and performing critical control functions. In this context, information can take many forms beyond the alphanumeric information associated with information systems; for example, a control sequence that stops a subway train, opens a bridge, or shuts down a power distribution hub. All types of information and systems need the protection provided by IA.

Second, the definition of IA proposed in this book incorporates individual systems and dynamic combinations of systems. Many automated systems are dynamically connected and configured to operate in tandem, series, or parallel, to accomplish specific tasks. This combination of systems may include traditional information systems as well as other types of automated systems. The specific systems connected, the duration of the connection, the operational modes, scenarios, and dependencies change frequently. The dynamic reconfiguration can occur as part of a new capability or service or in response to the execution of a contingency plan. Dynamic combinations of disparate geographically dispersed systems is the norm rather than the exception in today's technology landscape.

The 1991 Gulf War has often been called the first information war. In many ways, the Gulf War was the harbinger of IA. The ability to rapidly integrate commercial and military information technology from multiple companies and countries and the ability to dynamically reconfigure it was critical to the success of the Allies. As Toma[430] reports:

> *The communication network that supported Operation Desert Storm was the largest joint theater system ever established. It was built in record time and maintained a phenomenal 98 percent availability rate. At the height of the operation, the system supported 700,000 telephone calls and 152,000 messages per day. More than 30,000 radio frequencies were managed to provide the necessary connectivity and to ensure minimum interference.*

The Gulf War also presented another unique technological situation. It was the first time journalists (audio, video, and print) provided near-real-time reporting. This led to competition between the military and the journalists for the (fixed) capacity of commercial satellite networks and the intrinsic security vulnerabilities of this arrangement.[235]

Third, more robust properties are needed than availability, integrity, authentication, and nonrepudiation if a system is to meet its IA goals. These properties by themselves are important but incomplete. A more complete set of system properties is provided by combining safety, reliability, and security. For example, authentication and nonrepudiation are two of many properties associated with system security. Likewise, availability is one of many properties associated with system reliability. A safe, reliable, and secure system by definition has proactively built-in error/fault/failure (whether accidental or intentional) prevention, detection, containment, and recovery mechanisms.

IA is a three-dimensional challenge; hence, the problem must be attacked from all three dimensions — safety, reliability, *and* security. Safety and reliability vulnerabilities can be exploited just as effectively, if not more so, as security vulnerabilities, the results of which can be catastrophic. As Neumann[362] notes:

> *…many characteristic security-vulnerability exploitations result directly because of poor system and software engineering. … Unfortunately, many past and existing software development efforts have failed to take advantage of good engineering practice; particularly those systems with stringent requirements for security, reliability, and safety.*

Historically, safety, reliability, and security engineering techniques have been applied independently by different communities of interest. The techniques from these three engineering specialties need to be integrated and updated to match the reality of today's technological environment and the need for IA. As Elliott states[256]:

> *…although safety-related systems is a specialized topic, the fruits from safety-related process research could, and should, be applied to support the development of system engineering and the management of other system properties, such as security and reliability.*

It is the synergy of concurrent safety, reliability, and security engineering activities, at the hardware, software, and system levels, that lead to effective information security/IA throughout the life of a system. Gollmann[277] concurs that:

> *…similar engineering methods are used in both areas. For example, standards for evaluating security software and for evaluating safety-critical software have many parallels and some experts expect that eventually there will be only a single standard.*

2.2 Application Domains

Information security/IA is essential for mission-critical systems, business-critical systems, and infrastructure systems. In fact, there are very few automated systems today that do not require some level of information security/IA. The decade following the Gulf War led to an awareness of the all-encompassing nature of information security/IA. As Gooden[279] observes:

> *Today we see a reach for maximum bandwidth to support a global telecommunications grid, moving terabits of voice, data, images, and video between continents. But in many cases, the grid has a foundation of sand. It continues to be vulnerable to service disruption, malicious destruction or theft of content by individuals, criminal cabals, and state-sponsored agents. The threat is as real as the growing body of documentation on bank losses, service disruptions, and the theft of intellectual property.*

An infrastructure system is defined as[176,178]:

> A network of independent, mostly privately owned, automated systems and processes that function collaboratively and synergistically to produce and distribute a continuous flow of essential goods and services.

As mentioned in Chapter 1, the eight categories of infrastructure systems identified in PDD-63 are:

1. Telecommunications systems
2. Banking and financial systems
3. Power generation and distribution systems
4. Oil and gas distribution and storage systems
5. Water processing and supply systems
6. Water, air, and ground transportation systems
7. Emergency notification and response systems
8. Systems supporting critical government services

These eight categories represent a wide range of technology. Each of the eight infrastructure systems is critical. Furthermore, there is a high degree of interaction and interdependence among the eight, as shown in Exhibit 1. For example, banking and financial systems are dependent on telecommunications and power generation and distribution, and interact with emergency systems and government services. It is interesting to note that all infrastructure systems: (1) are dependent on telecommunications systems, and (2) interact with emergency systems and government services.

Exhibit 2 illustrates the interaction and interdependency between infrastructure systems, mission-critical systems, and business-critical systems. Together, these sets of systems constitute essentially the whole economy. Again, there is a high degree of interaction and interdependence. All of the mission-critical systems and business-critical systems are dependent on telecommunications,

Exhibit 1 Interaction and Interdependency Among Infrastructure Systems

Infrastructure System	*1*	*2*	*3*	*4*	*5*	*6*	*7*	*8*
1. Telecommunications	—	I	D	I	I	I	I	I
2. Banking and finance	D	—	D				I	I
3. Power generation and distribution	D	I	—	I	D	I	I	I
4. Oil and gas distribution and storage	D	I	D	—		D	I	I
5. Water processing and supply	D		D		—		I	I
6. Transportation systems	D	I	D	D	I	—	I	I
7. Emergency systems	D	I	D	D	D	D	—	I
8. Government services	D	D	D	D	D	D	I	—

Note: D - dependent on infrastructure system; I - interacts with infrastructure system.

Exhibit 2 Interaction and Interdependency Between Infrastructure Systems, Mission-Critical Systems, and Business-Critical Systems

Mission-Critical/Business-Critical Systems	*1*	*2*	*3*	*4*	*5*	*6*	*7*	*8*
9. Wholesale/retail business systems	D	D	D	D	D	D	I	
10. Manufacturing systems	D	D	D	D	D	D	I	
11. Biomedical systems	D	D	D		D	D	I	I
12. Postal/package systems	D	D	D	D		D	I	I
13. Food production and distribution systems	D	D	D	D	D	D	I	I
14. Entertainment, travel systems	D	D	D		D	D	I	
15. News media, broadcast, and publishing systems	D	D	D			D	I	I
16. Housing industry systems	D	D	D	D	D	D	I	
17. Education, academic systems	D	D	D		D	D	I	I

Note: D - dependent on infrastructure system; I - interacts with infrastructure system.

banking and financial, power generation and distribution, and transportation systems. They all interact with emergency systems. Campen[231] notes some the ramifications of this interdependency:

> *Major reorganizations are taking place within the (U.S.) Departments of Defense and Justice to provide policy and leadership to defend critical infrastructures. The White House describes these infrastructures as essential to the minimum operations of the economy and the government.*

2.3 Technology Domains

Information security/IA applies to all technology domains; in fact, it is difficult to talk about a technology domain to which information security/IA does not apply. In terms of hardware, information security/IA is applicable to computer hardware, communications equipment, communications lines — terrestrial and wireless, power grids, and other connected equipment within the operational environment. In terms of software, information security/IA is applicable to all layers of the International Organization for Standardization (ISO) open systems interconnection (OSI) and TCP/IP communications reference models, from the physical layer through the application layer. Common examples of information security/IA technology domains include military computer communications command control and intelligence (C^4I) systems, manufacturing process control systems, decision support systems, e-Commerce, e-mail, biomedical systems, and intelligent transportation systems (ITS). To illustrate, Barber[208] has identified the following information security/IA concerns related to medical informatics:

1. Clinical implications of data reported
2. Loss of medical records, subrecords, or data items
3. Unauthorized or accidental modifications of data
4. Privacy of medical records
5. Misidentification — wrong record, person, treatment profile
6. False positive or false negative test results
7. Wrong treatment delivered
8. Malicious errors (nonprescribed/bogus therapies)
9. Accuracy and currency of information reported

In today's technological environment, it is rare for an individual or organizational user to own all of the equipment involved in a transaction. Instead, they own some basic equipment but rely on service providers from the infrastructure systems to do the rest. Consider when an item is purchased online. The purchaser owns the computer/modem, pays for local telephone service, and pays for an Internet service provider. The online business pays for the same equipment and services on their end. Both the purchaser and the online business are relying on the: (1) telecommunications systems to make the purchase possible; (2) banking and financial systems to approve/authenticate the purchase and payment; and (3) transportation systems to deliver the item(s) purchased to the purchaser and provide proof of delivery to the seller. The reliable and secure exchange of critical information, across many systems, in a timely manner is required to complete this transaction.

This scenario, which is depicted in Exhibit 3, illustrates some of the challenges for information security/IA. First, all of the systems within each of the four domains involved in the transaction (purchaser, online business, financial, and transportation) must function correctly. This may involve one or more geographically dispersed systems/components. Second, the transactions among these four domains must work correctly. Eleven high-level transactions are identified in the figure. However, this is only a subset of the total transactions involved. Other transactions include wholesale/retail exchanges, ordering packing materials, etc. Underpinning all of these transactions is reliable and secure telecommunications. To grasp the scope of the IA challenge, one needs to multiply the transactions involved in this one example by the total number of online purchases made simultaneously each day and each week. McGraw[349] sizes up the e-Commerce information security/IA challenge:

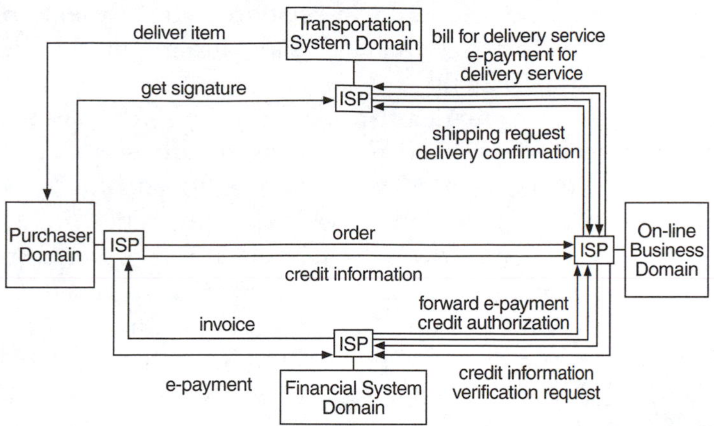

Exhibit 3 Illustration of the Technology Domains Involved in Information Assurance Using an Online Purchase as an Example

> *Data from Forrester Research indicates that e-Commerce, which totaled about $8 billion in 1998, will reach more than $327 billion in the U.S. by 2002 and will be four times that amount globally.*

2.4 Importance

IA affects nearly all aspects of the everyday life of individuals and organizations. As reported by Wood[442]:

> *The Presidential Decision Direction - 63 (PDD-63) ... notes that infrastructures — energy, banking, finance, transportation, water systems, etc. — have historically been 'physically and logically separate with little interdependence.' Now they are increasingly linked together by, and absolutely dependent on, an information infrastructure that is vulnerable to technical failure, human error, natural causes, and physical and cyber attacks.*

IA has a pervasive role in today's technological society. This role can be divided into seven categories:

1. Human safety
2. Environmental safety
3. Property safety
4. Economic stability and security
5. Social stability
6. Privacy, both individual and corporate
7. National security

Exhibit 4 examines the role of IA in relation to the benefits provided, the beneficiaries, and the infrastructure systems that are required to be functioning correctly to achieve this benefit.

IA protects humans from death and injury by preventing accidental or intentional equipment failures and minimizing the consequences of potential failures. (The term "equipment" is used broadly to encompass anything that is automated or under computer control.) This protection benefits the individual, their family, and employer. The manufacturers, seller, and operator of the equipment also benefit because they avoid liability lawsuits.

Consider the following example. Three hundred and fifteen people were scheduled to board a flight to Chicago at 9 a.m. Due to a mechanical problem, the plane scheduled for that flight had to be unloaded immediately before takeoff. The airline had to:

1. Query its fleet database to locate a new plane that is available in the immediate vicinity.
2. Check the new plane's maintenance records/status to verify that it is air worthy and has adequate fuel and supplies.
3. Verify that the new plane will accommodate this number of passengers.
4. Verify that the original flight crew is trained/certified for this type of plane.
5. Coordinate with the local air traffic control system to bring the new plane to the gate and have the defective one removed.
6. Arrange to have baggage moved from the first plane to the second.
7. Coordinate with air traffic control systems locally and in Chicago to develop a new flight plan/schedule.
8. Update departure/arrival monitors at both airports.
9. Book passengers on later connecting flights, if necessary.
10. Accomplish all of this very quickly and pleasantly so that the passengers do not get rowdy and create another hazard.

Each of these steps depends on the accurate and timely processing of correct information across multiple systems, from the initial detection of the problem through booking new connecting flights. In this scenario, IA played a role in protecting human safety, environmental safety, and property safety. It also prevented economic disruption for the airline, passengers, and their employers.

This example is not far from reality. On January 6, 2000, WTOP News and National Public Radio reported that the air traffic control (ATC) system serving Washington National Airport and Dulles Airport was inoperative for three hours in the morning due to an "unknown" problem. Because no flights could land or take off at these two airports, all East Coast air traffic was essentially shut down. An additional four hours were required to clear the backlog. Apparently, a similar problem was experienced at Boston Logan Airport earlier that week. The Chicago example only involved one flight. The shutdown on January 6, 2000, involved several hundred flights.

Representatives to the U.S. Congress frequent Washington National and Dulles airports. As a result, any shutdown at these airports has visibility. That

Exhibit 4 The Importance of IA in the Real World

Information Assurance Role	*Benefit*	*Who Benefits*	*Infrastructure Systems Required*
Human safety	Protection from accidental and malicious intentional death and injury	Individuals Their families Their employers Manufacturer of equipment Seller of equipment Operator of equipment	Telecommunications Power generation Oil & gas Water supply Transportation Emergency
Environmental safety	Protection from accidental and malicious intentional permanent or temporary damage and destruction	Individuals Society as a whole Manufacturer, distributor, and operator of equipment	Telecommunications Power generation Oil & gas Water supply Transportation Emergency Government
Property safety	Protection from accidental and malicious intentional permanent or temporary damage and destruction	Property owner Property user Manufacturer Distributor	Telecommunications Power generation Oil & gas Water supply Transportation Emergency
Economic stability and security	Protection from economic loss, disruption, lack of goods and services	Individuals Society as a whole Financial institutions Wholesale, retail businesses Manufacturing Local, national, global trade	Telecommunications Banking & finance Power generation Oil & gas Water supply Transportation Emergency Government

Exhibit 4 The Importance of IA in the Real World (continued)

Information Assurance Role	*Benefit*	*Who Benefits*	*Infrastructure Systems Required*
Social stability	Protection from social chaos, violence, loss of way of life, personal security	Individuals Society as a whole	Telecommunications Banking & finance Power generation Oil & gas Water supply Transportation Emergency Government
Privacy a. Individual b. Corporate	a. Protection from identify theft, financial loss, intrusion into private life, character assassination, theft of intellectual property rights b. Protection from financial loss, loss of customers, theft of intellectual property rights	a. Individuals, their family, their employer b. Corporation employees, stockholders, business partners	Telecommunications Banking & finance Power generation Oil & gas Water supply Transportation Emergency Government
National security	Access to and disclosure of sensitive economic and other strategic assets is safeguarded	Individuals Society as a whole Neighboring countries Global trading partners Multinational corporations	Telecommunications Banking & finance Power generation Oil & gas Water supply Transportation Emergency Government

evening, one Representative asked, "How could this happen? — the air traffic control system is brand new." How? Because newness does not mean a system is safe, reliable, or secure; in fact, the opposite often is true.

IA plays a role in protecting the environment from accidental or intentional damage and destruction. An example is the nuclear power plant control and protection systems that notify operators of any anomalies and prevent the release of radiation into the atmosphere. IA also plays a role in protecting property, for example, monitoring equipment that prevents water or fire damage and notifies emergency response teams.

IA plays a critical role in maintaining economic stability and security. Business, industry, the financial markets, and individuals are dependent on the near-instantaneous, accurate, and secure processing and exchange of correct information across multiple systems worldwide. This capability sustains the global economy.

Human safety, environmental safety, property safety, and economic stability and security are all precursors for social stability. Hence, IA contributes to social stability. Given the vast quantity of information stored electronically about individuals and organizations and the advent of data mining techniques, IA plays a critical role in protecting privacy. Likewise, national security organizations, whether operating alone or within the context of multinational alliances, are totally dependent on the safety, reliability, and security provided through the discipline of IA.

2.5 Stakeholders

As one can see from the discussion above, all of us are stakeholders when it comes to IA, whether one is acting as an individual or as a member of an organization. This highlights the fact that the benefits of IA (or the vulnerabilities and threats encountered when IA is not implemented or implemented ineffectively) accrue from many different perspectives, including:

- Individuals and organizations
- Financial institution a, buyer, seller, financial institution b
- Equipment owners, operators, and manufacturers

In contrast, there are the (illegal or, at a minimum, unethical) benefits that an individual or organization accrues when they exploit vulnerabilities in a system.

Consider the purchase of this book. Exhibits 5 and 6 illustrate all the possible ways in which this book could be purchased — the potential transaction paths. In other words, the book could be purchased in person at a bookstore, over the Internet, over the phone, by mail, or by fax. These are the only five purchase options. Payment options are limited to cash, credit card, debit card, check, gift certificate, previous store credit, or corporate purchase order. (In this example, the cash must be obtained from an ATM.) The combination of a possible purchase method with a feasible payment mode results in a transaction path. Exhibit 7 correlates these transaction paths to

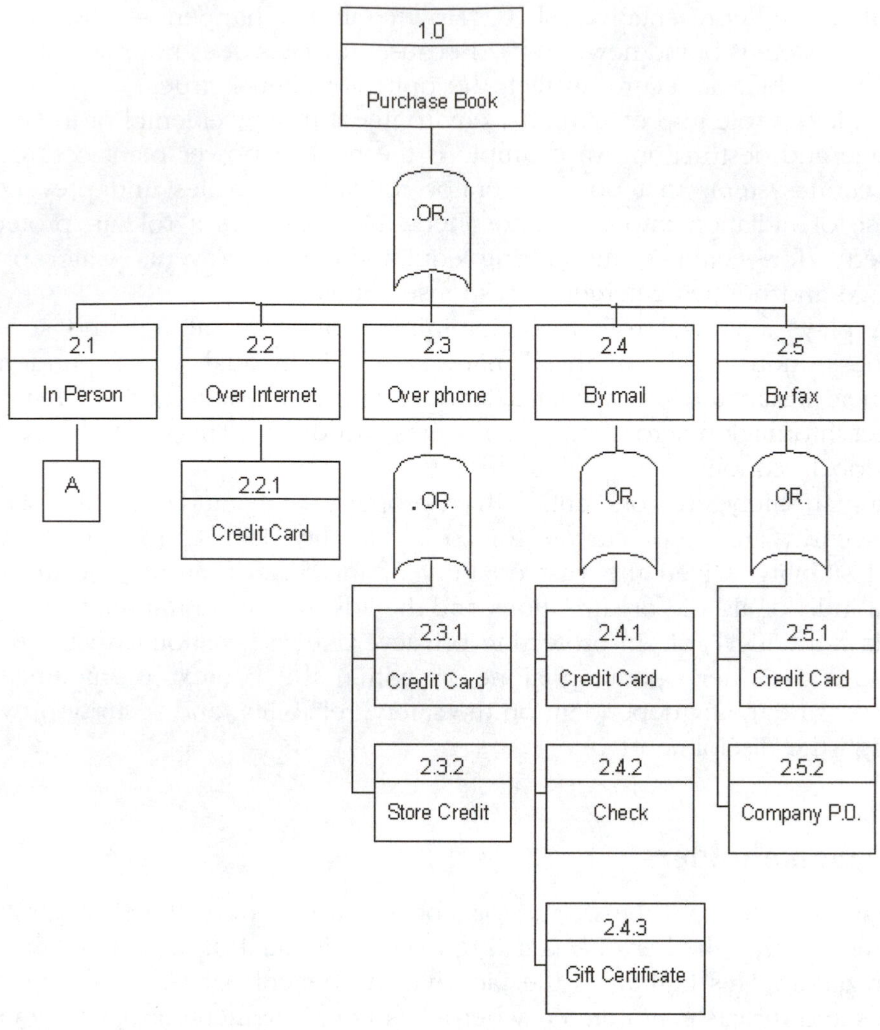

Exhibit 5 Sample Identification of Transaction Paths

vulnerabilities and threats, and identifies potential consequences to the different stakeholders. Different transaction paths may have the same or similar vulnerabilities, threats, and consequences. Hence, the set of transaction paths for which threat control measures are implemented represents a reduction of the original set. Likewise, the likelihood and severity associated with specific transaction paths must be analyzed prior to developing threat control measures. The process of analyzing transaction paths to identify critical threat zones is explained in Chapter 5.

This is a hypothetical example and for illustrative purposes, worst-case scenarios are developed. Many of these events may seem far-fetched. However, several similar events have actually occurred in recent years; examples include:

1. Examine the vulnerability/threat scenario for transaction path 1.0 ← 2.1.6.1a. In 1996 following an "upgrade" to ATM software, a major East

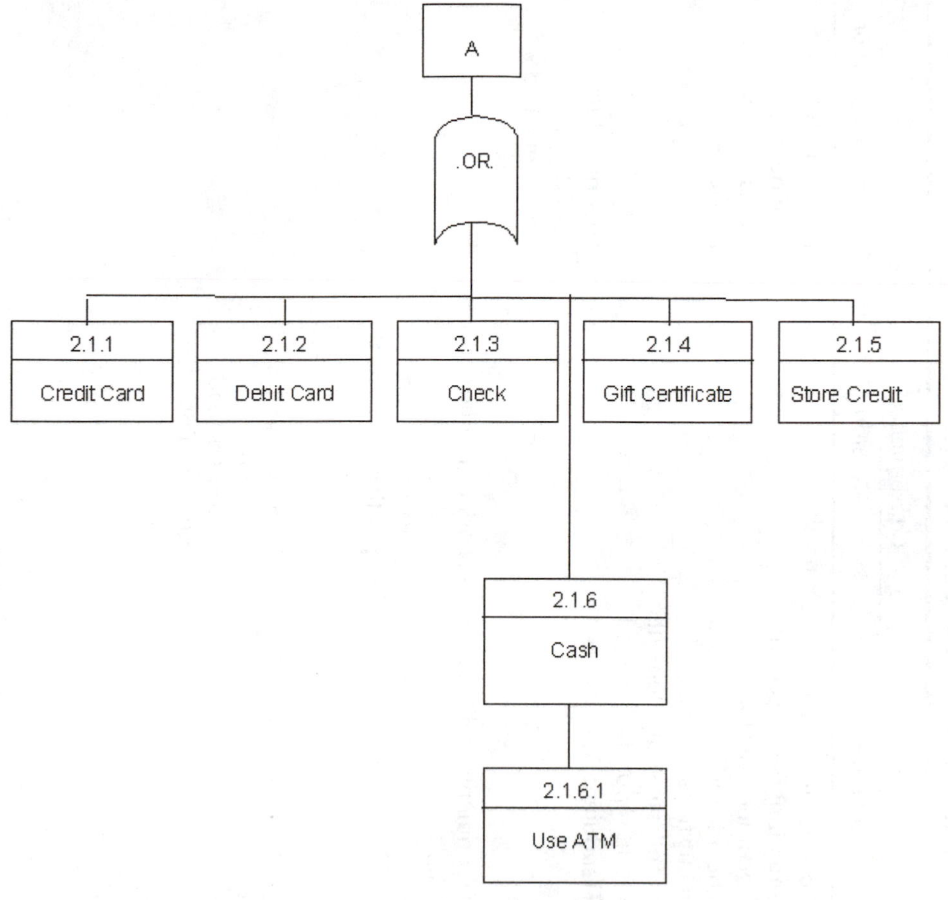

Exhibit 6 Sample Identification of Transaction Paths (continued)

Coast bank actually deducted twice the cash amount withdrawn from customer accounts. Needless to say, the customers were not happy.

2. The vulnerability/threat scenario for transaction paths 1.0 ← 2.1.4 and 1.0 ← All is similar to the Jewell situation following the 1996 Atlanta Olympics in which profiling resulted in erroneous information being reported to the news media, which then quickly spread worldwide. Jewell subsequently won several lawsuits related to character defamation.
3. The vulnerability/threat scenario for transaction path 1.0 ← 2.2.1.2a is similar to that reported by WTOP News and National Public Radio on January 10, 2000. In this incident, the credit card information, names, and addresses of 200,000 customers of an online business were stolen by a hacker. When the extortion payment was not made, information about 25,000 of the customers was posted on a Web site.
4. The vulnerability/threat profiling scenario (1.0 ← All) relates to the Monica Lewinsky affair. During the investigation/trial, a local Washington, D.C., bookstore was asked to provide a list of the books purchased and videos rented by Ms. Lewinsky. The bookstore admitted that it had the information but, despite the legal pressure, declined to provide it.

Exhibit 7 Sample Correlation of Vulnerabilities, Threats, Transaction Paths, and Consequences

Transaction Path	*Vulnerability*	*Threat*	*Consequences*		
			To Individual	*To Store*	*To Financial Institution*
1.0 ← 2.1.6.1	a. ATM software error	a. ATM returns correct amount of cash, but deducts twice the amount from your account.	a. You are unaware of the situation; bank account becomes overdrawn, checks bounce, and you incur fines; it takes 3 months to straighten out; credit report is damaged.		a. Loss of public confidence, customers; bad publicity.
	b. Remote ATM network has limited security.	b. ATM account and PIN numbers are intercepted.	b. Fraudulent ATM use.		b. Loss of public confidence, customers; bad publicity.
1.0 ← 2.1.1	a. Credit card number is stored in store's computer with your name and address.	a. Misuse of credit card information by store employee.	a. Fraudulent credit card use.	a. Loss of public confidence, customers; bad publicity; potential lawsuit.	
	b. Credit card information transferred over unsecured line for verification.	b. Credit card information intercepted and misused.	b. Fraudulent credit card use.	b. Loss of public confidence, customers; bad publicity. Potential lawsuit.	

	c. Software error in reconciling purchase.	c. You are billed for 9 other purchases that were made after yours.	c. Difficulty in proving you did not make these purchases; credit is tied up while situation is resolved; potential damage to credit history.	c. Unhappy customer notifies others; bad publicity.	c. Unhappy customer notifies others; bad publicity.
1.0 ← 2.1.2	a. Debit card information is stored in store's computer with your name and address.	a. Misuse of debit card information later by store employee.	a. Fraudulent debit card use.	a. Loss of public confidence, customers; bad publicity; potential lawsuit.	
	b. Debit card information is transferred over unsecured line for verification.	b. Debit card information intercepted.	b. Fraudulent use of credit card.	b. Loss of public confidence, customers; bad publicity; potential lawsuit.	b. Loss of public confidence, customers; bad publicity; potential lawsuit.
	c. Software error in reconciling purchase.	c. You are billed for 9 purchases that were made after yours.	c. Difficulty in proving you did not make purchases; account is tied up during resolution; possible damage to credit history.	c. Loss of public confidence, customers; bad publicity; potential lawsuit.	c. Loss of public confidence, customers; bad publicity.
1.0 ← 2.1.3; 1.0 ← 2.4.2	a. Unsecured line used to send/ receive information to check verification service	a. Account number and balance intercepted; account is drained.	a. You are unaware of the situation; bank account becomes overdrawn; checks bounce; you incur fines; it takes 3 months to straighten out; credit history is damaged.	a. Loss of public confidence, customers; bad publicity; potential lawsuit.	a. Loss of public confidence, customers; bad publicity; potential lawsuit.

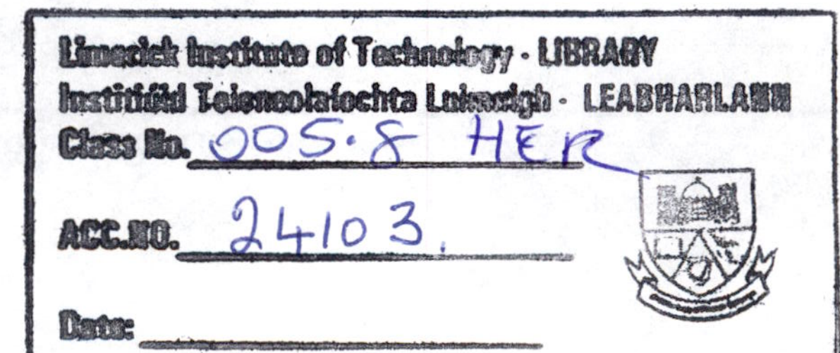

Exhibit 7 Sample Correlation of Vulnerabilities, Threats, Transaction Paths, and Consequences (continued)

Transaction Path	Vulnerability	Threat	Consequences: To Individual	Consequences: To Store	Consequences: To Financial Institution
1.0 ← 2.1.4; 1.0 ← 2.4.3	a. Gift sales clerk preparing gift certificate makes a typo in the "from" section, typing XZY instead of XYZ.	a. Retail sales clerk notices that certificate is from XZY, a terrorist organization that has been in the news recently, and tells store manager, who calls the police.	a. You spend a few days in the clink because the person who can straighten this out is away on business; in the meantime, you lose your security clearance and hence your job; your name is all over the news media.	a. Store, media, and law enforcement officials face potential character defamation and other related lawsuits; bad publicity.	
	b. Gift sales clerk preparing gift certificate makes a typo in the "to" section, misspelling your last name.	b. Retail sales clerk thinks you are attempting to use the gift certificate fraudulently.	b. You endure a major hassle and/or end up forfeiting the value of the gift certificate.	b. Unhappy customers tell others; bad publicity.	
	c. Sales clerk preparing gift certificate makes a typo in the year.	c. Gift certificate was only good for one year; because it is "expired," you cannot use it.	c. You lose the value of the gift certificate.	c. Unhappy customers tell others; bad publicity.	
1.0 ← 2.1.5; 1.0 ← 2.3.2	a. Database containing store credit has been corrupted.	a. Your $50 store credit has been reduced to $5.00.	a. You have to prove the $50 credit or forfeit the $45.	a. Loss of public confidence, customers; bad publicity.	

	b. Database containing store credit is "busy" and not accessible right now.	b. Customers become annoyed and leave.	b. You have to come back later or use another payment option.	b. Loss of business.	
1.0 ← 2.2.1; 1.0 ← 2.3.1; 1.0 ← 2.4.1	a. Credit card number is stored in store's computer with your name and address.	a. Misuse of credit card information by store employee.	a. Fraudulent credit card use.	a. Loss of public confidence, customers; bad publicity; potential lawsuit.	
	b. Credit card information transferred over unsecured line for verification.	b. Credit card information intercepted and misused.	b. Fraudulent credit card use.	b. Loss of public confidence, customers; bad publicity; potential lawsuit.	
	c. Software error in reconciling purchase.	c. You are billed for 9 other purchases that were made after yours.	c. Difficulty in proving you did not make these purchases; credit is tied up while situation is resolved; potential damage to credit history.	c. Loss of public confidence, customers; bad publicity; potential lawsuit.	c. Loss of public confidence, customers; bad publicity.
	d. Order entry processing error.	d1. You receive and are billed for 100 copies of the book. d2. Your order is shipped to Hawaii while you receive the order that should have gone to Hawaii.	d. Major inconvenience; credit is tied up pending resolution.	d. Loss of public confidence, customers; bad publicity.	

Exhibit 7 Sample Correlation of Vulnerabilities, Threats, Transaction Paths, and Consequences (continued)

Transaction Path	*Vulnerability*	*Threat*	*Consequences*		
			To Individual	*To Store*	*To Financial Institution*
1.0 ← 2.5.1	a. Unsecured line is used during fax transmission either to place or verify the order.	a. Credit card information is intercepted and misused.	a. Fraudulent use of credit card.	a. Loss of public confidence, customers; bad publicity; potential lawsuit.	
	b. Credit card number is stored in store's computer with your name and address.	b. Misuse of credit card information by store employee.	b. Fraudulent credit card use.	b. Loss of public confidence, customers; bad publicity; potential lawsuit.	
	c. Credit card information is transferred over unsecured line for verification.	c. Credit card information intercepted and misused.	c. Fraudulent credit card use.	c. Loss of public confidence, customers; bad publicity; potential lawsuit.	
	d. Software error in reconciling purchase.	d. You are billed for 9 other purchases that were made after yours.	d. Difficulty in proving you did not make these purchases; credit is tied up while situation is resolved; potential damage to credit history.	d. Loss of public confidence, customers; bad publicity.	d. Loss of public confidence, customers; bad publicity.

	e. Order entry processing error.	e1. You receive and are billed for 100 copies of the book. e2. Your order is shipped to Hawaii while you receive the order that should have gone to Hawaii.	e. Major inconvenience; credit is tied up pending resolution.	e. Loss of public confidence, customers; bad publicity.
1.0 ← 2.5.2	a. Order entry processing error.	a1. You receive and are billed for 100 copies of the book. a2. Your order is shipped to Hawaii while you receive the order that should have gone to Hawaii.	a. Major inconvenience; credit is tied up pending resolution.	a. Loss of public confidence; bad publicity.
1.0 ← All	a. Retail store maintains a database of all books purchased by you.	b. Profiles of your book-buying habits are exchanged with other sources.	c. Law enforcement officials notice that you have been buying many books related to computer security, encryption, etc. and determine you are a potential cyber terrorist; you have to explain that you are doing research for your Ph.D. in Computer Science.	c. Customer sues store for breach of privacy, among other things.

2.6 Summary

This chapter demonstrated why the discipline of IA must be applied to all categories of automated systems and dynamic combinations of these systems. The need for safe, reliable, and secure functionality is near universal in terms of today's application and technology domains. The benefit of IA, to a variety of stakeholders, individuals, organizations, and the environment, is manifest.

President Clinton acknowledged the importance of and benefits from IA in an address he made January 8, 2000. As reported by Babington[207] in the *Washington Post*, Clinton announced plans for a $2 billion budget to meet the nation's security challenges related to high technology. Part of the funding will go toward the establishment of a new research Institute for Information Infrastructure Protection. Babington[207] quoted Clinton as saying:

> *Our critical systems, from power structures to air traffic control, are connected and run by computers. ... There has never been a time like this in which we have the power to create knowledge and the power to create havoc, and both these powers rest in the same hands. ... I hope that ... we will work together to ensure that information technology will create unprecedented prosperity ... in an atmosphere and environment that makes all Americans more secure.*

Next, Chapter 3 examines the historical approaches to information security/IA.

2.7 Discussion Problems

1. Why is IA important to the biomedical industry?
2. What infrastructure systems do law enforcement officials: (a) depend on and (b) interact with?
3. Which of the eight infrastructure systems is more important than the rest? Why?
4. Why is IA concerned with more than information systems?
5. What does software safety contribute to IA?
6. What does software reliability contribute to IA?
7. Who is responsible for IA?
8. Develop a diagram illustrating the technology domains in the news media that are dependent on IA.
9. What benefit do individuals derive from IA programs implemented by banking and financial systems?
10. What additional vulnerabilities and threats could be associated with Exhibits 5 and 7?
11. What is the relationship between IA and infrastructure systems?
12. Exhibit 3 illustrates the transactions that must take place to complete an online purchase. Identify the vulnerabilities associated with these transactions.

Chapter 3

Historical Approaches to Information Security and Information Assurance

Safety, reliability, and security concerns have existed as long as there have been automated systems. The first standards for software safety* and software security** were developed in the late 1970s; the first software reliability*** standards followed a decade later. These standards represented a starting point for defining safety, security, and reliability design, development, assessment, and certification techniques. Implementation, however, was fragmented because safety, security, and reliability were handled by different communities of interest and there was little communication or coordination between them. These techniques were appropriate for the technology and operational environments of their time. A time when computers and telecommunications were separate entities; computer networks consisted of dedicated lines; and textual, image, audio, and video data were isolated. Distributed processing had just begun, but portable computers and media remained unknown. Many of these techniques assumed that the computer was in one room or, at most, a few local buildings.

This chapter reviews the historical approaches to information security and information assurance, specifically the approaches to system security, safety, and

* MIL-STD-882A, System Safety Program Requirements, U.S. Department of Defense (DoD), June 28, 1977.

** DoD 5200.28-M, ADP Computer Security Manual — Techniques and Procedures for Implementing, Deactivating, Testing, and Evaluating Secure Resource-Sharing ADP Systems, with 1st Amendment, U.S. Department of Defense (DoD), June 25, 1979.[140]

***IEEE Std. 982.1-1989, IEEE Standard Dictionary of Measures to Produce Reliable Software.[42]

reliability; what these approaches accomplished; and their limitations relative to today's technology. These historical approaches fall into seven main categories:

1. Physical security
2. Communications security (COMSEC)
3. Computer security (COMPUSEC)
4. Information security (INFOSEC)
5. Operations security (OPSEC)
6. System safety
7. System reliability

Many of these approaches originated in the defense and intelligence communities. At the time, only national security information was considered worth protecting. Gradually, these approaches spread to the financial community and others. The limitations of traditional security standards reflect their origin. As Underwood[434] notes:

- They only assess products, not the development processes.
- They evaluate components, not systems.
- They required a specialized skill set by the assessor or the results were invalid.
- They focus on correct solutions, not necessarily cost-effective ones.

3.1 Physical Security

Physical security is defined as:

> the protection of hardware, software, and data against physical threats to reduce or prevent disruptions to operations and services and/or loss of assets.

In summary, the purpose of physical security is to protect physical system resources (as opposed to logical system resources) from (1) physical damage that could impair operations and (2) theft.

Historically, physical security plans focused on four major challenges:

1. Protecting computer and communications resources from damage due to fire, water, radiation, earthquake, or other natural disaster
2. Maintaining appropriate temperature, humidity, dust, and vibration levels
3. Providing sustained power levels despite transient spikes, brownouts, and power failures
4. Controlling physical access to computer and communications resources to known authorized personnel

The primary emphasis was on protecting the central computer facility or computer center that housed the mainframe computer, operator console(s), disk packs, tape drives, and high-speed printers. Secondary emphasis was

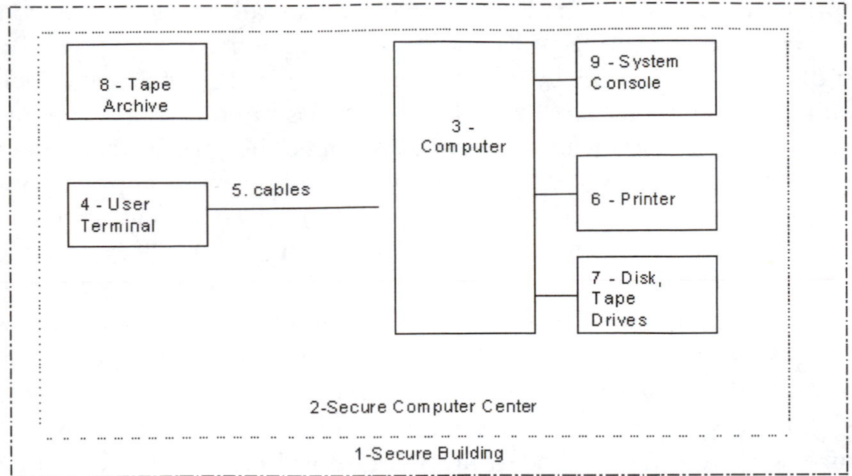

1. Controlled access to building, badge/visual recognition required.
2. Controlled access to computer center, badge, combination lock, fingerprint scanner, visual recognition required. UPS. Specialized HVAC. Protection from fire, flood, radiation, earthquake, natural disasters.
3. Only local equipment and remote equipment connected by dedicated lines. Only known authorized users allowed in Computer Center. Center staffed 24 hours/day. Memory overwritten before reuse.
4. Controlled access to user terminals. Use of shielded terminals.
5. Use of shielded cables, locked cable ducts.
6. Controlled access to printers and printouts. Sensitive printouts packaged in opaque plastic. Old unneeded printouts shredded, placed in burn bags.
7. Controlled access to disk and tape drives. Magnetic media overwritten before reused, degaussed before disposal.
8. Controlled access to tape archive. Tapes stored in locked cabinet.
9. Controlled access to operator console.

Exhibit 1 Traditional Physical Security Perimeters

placed on protecting remote "dumb" terminals, printers, and modems. Archives and documentation relating to the design and operation of the mainframe were generally protected in the same manner as the computer center (see Exhibit 1).

The computer center was located in a dedicated room, usually the first floor or basement of a building because of the weight involved. The room was constructed with flame-retardant raised floor panels and ceiling tiles, and water sprinklers or chemical fire suppressants. Specialized heavy-duty cooling and air filtering systems were installed to keep the computer center cool, usually 68°F. Specialized flooring was installed to absorb vibration. Robust surge protection and ambient power sources were provided by high-capacity uninterrupted power supplies (UPS) and motor generators (MGs). In some circumstances, computer equipment was designed to be resistant to radiation (Rad Hard). In short, not much was left to chance in terms of the computer facility itself.

Likewise, a variety of measures were employed to control physical access to computer and communications resources. Access to the computer center and rooms containing remote equipment was restricted by badge readers, combination locks, fingerprint scanners, and visual recognition to known authorized operations staff, users, and maintenance staff. People without the appropriate identification had to be escorted at all times. Some computer centers activated a flashing red light to alert staff when an uncleared person was in the room. Occasionally, the "two man rule" was implemented whereby a minimum of two people had to staff the computer center at any time. Depending on the classification level of printouts, they were sealed in opaque plastic and had to be signed for. Equipment leaving the computer room had to be signed for and accompanied by an authorized property pass. Video surveillance cameras kept track of people and equipment entering and leaving the computer center.

Communications traffic was isolated on different channels according to classification level (red/black separation). Cables, and sometimes peripherals and computer centers, were shielded (Tempest technology) to prevent emanations that could be intercepted and interpreted. To prevent or at least minimize wire tapping, dedicated lines connected remote floors and facilities to the computer center and cable ducts were locked. DoD 5300.28-M[140] required that each remote physical device and location have a unique ID. Prior to establishing a session, the CPU would verify that the device was legitimate and had the proper authorization for the requested classification level; if not, the connection was dropped.

Disk mirroring helped prevent the loss of critical data and the associated downtime. During one phase, removable hard drives were in vogue. At the end of a work day or shift, the hard drives were removed and locked in safes. Locks of various types were used to prevent the theft of computers, disks, tapes, archival media, and printouts. Off-site storage provided continuity of operations in the event of a natural disaster or intentional sabotage.

The safe and reliable disposal of obsolete, unneeded, or inoperable classified resources remains a perennial problem. In the early days, elaborate schemes were developed to erase, degauss, and destroy tapes, disks, hard drives, and memory. For example, DoD 5200.28-M[140] required:

- Using a bulk tape degausser that performed a triple overwrite procedure: first all binary 1's, then all binary 0's, followed by repeating a single random alphanumeric character
- Transitioning core memory from a binary 1 to 0 to 1 again, 1000 times
- Exposing inoperable equipment to a magnetic field of 1500 Oersted three times

Equivalent procedures were specified for destroying nondigital information, such as an analog audio recording, that was recorded on magnetic media. Paper resources were shredded and placed in burn bags. Today, volatile memory should be overwritten before it is reused or powered down, much like the above precautions taken to protect magnetic storage media, because the contents can be reconstructed. As Gollmann[277] notes, "The content loss of volatile memory is neither instantaneous nor complete."

In the past, significant emphasis was placed on physical security — protecting the computer center. It was assumed that (1) an intruder had to be on the premises; and (2) if a security perimeter were compromised, the system would quickly shut down or switch to only unclassified processing. Some historical physical security paradigms are still valid; however, many are not. The computer is no longer in one room. For example, in the client/server environment, processing power, memory, and disk storage are distributed. Computer and communications equipment are no longer separate; rather, they are integrated. Remote access is the norm rather than the exception, whether through mobile computing, telecommuting, home offices, or remote diagnostics/help. Although some PC CPU chips and operating systems have unique identifiers, not all do; nor is a user tied to a single desktop system. The days of dedicated lines are gone, particularly with the advent of wireless and other high-bandwidth services. Today, physical security must consider the ramifications of LANs, WANs, VPNs, and the Internet. CD-R disks have created a new challenge for disposing of obsolete sensitive material. Finally, intruders are rarely on the premises.

3.2 Communications Security (COMSEC)

Communications security, or COMSEC, is a collection of engineering activities that are undertaken to protect the confidentiality, integrity, and availability of sensitive data while it is being transmitted between systems and networks. Confidentiality ensures that only the intended recipients receive and are able to interpret the transmitted data. As a result, potential losses from theft of information are minimized, including financial loss, loss of competitive advantage, loss of public confidence, loss of privacy, character defamation, national security compromises, and loss of intellectual property rights.[248] Integrity ensures that the data received is an accurate representation of the data sent. In other words, the data has not been accidentally or intentionally altered, corrupted, destroyed, or added to. Availability ensures that the data is received within the specified transmission time(s), plus or minus a reasonable tolerance factor. DoD 5200.28-M[140] required that COMSEC principles be applied to all: communications lines and links, multiplexers, message switches, telecommunications networks and interfaces, and emanations control. In the past, COMSEC focused on protecting end-to-end data transmission across dedicated lines from one secure facility to another, as shown in Exhibit 2. Data leaving a computer center was multiplexed and encrypted, sometimes more than once. A secret key system was used, and the keys were changed simultaneously on both ends of the communications link on a regular basis.

Spectrum management and encryption were the primary means of providing confidentiality. Spectrum management attempted to prevent or at least minimize the ability to intercept, interpret, or block data transmissions through spectrum planning and interference and jamming countermeasures. In some cases, this involved regular changing of call signs, words, suffixes, and frequencies. In addition, switches that permitted users to access systems at different security levels had to do so while ensuring that an electrical connection did not exist between the two systems or networks.

Encryption, assuming that spectrum management and other security measures are not 100 percent foolproof, makes data and messages unintelligible to all

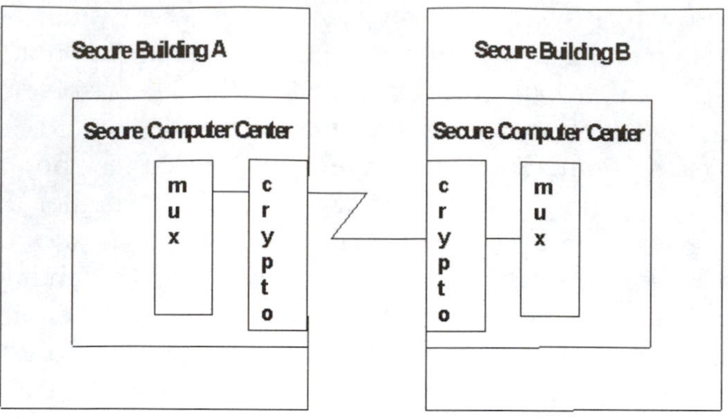

Exhibit 2 Historical COMSEC Architecture

but the intended recipient(s). This is accomplished through a systematic method of scrambling the information. A mathematically based encryption algorithm specifies the steps involved in transforming the data. Encryption algorithms can operate on a single bit or byte (stream ciphers) or a fixed number of bits of data at a time (block ciphers). Encryption algorithms can be implemented in hardware or software.

A key represents a specific instance of the encryption algorithm. Keys can be public, private, or secret and are changed frequently. In contrast, the algorithm remains constant. Both or all parties to a transaction must use the same encryption algorithm and know which type of key scheme is being used. With secret keys, the same key is used for encryption and decryption. More recently, public/private key schemes were developed in which one key is used for encryption and another for decryption. Public/private keys only work in designated pairs. Historically, both the encryption algorithm and the key were safeguarded. Today, a variety of encryption algorithms are publicly available and only private and secret keys are protected. (This arrangement assumes that the private key cannot be determined from the public key.)

Cryptography predates computers and probably has been around as long as humans have had the need to send/receive secret messages.[316] Knott[318] reports on the use of cryptography during the American Revolution:

> *Throughout the American Revolution, General Washington placed great importance on learning British intentions and shielding his own army's activities. Elaborately coded communications were used by the general to communicate with his spy network through a system implemented by staff officers such as Alexander Hamilton. … In 1779, Tallmadge added to this layer of protection by developing a cipher and code that used codebooks available only to himself, Townsend, and Washington.*

Exhibit 3 Simple Illustration of the Steps Involved in Encryption

Step 1: English language, Roman alphabet
Step 2: Block cipher, 128-bit, 16-byte block size
Step 3: a. Move blanks (x+1) spaces to the right.
b. Move vowels (x–1) spaces to the left.
c. Replace consonants with the consonant that is x places after it in the alphabet. Loop around the alphabet if necessary.
d. Enter the message in reverse order.
Step 4: Secret key, (x) = 2
Step 5: ASCII

Plaintext message:	Happy Birthday.
Blocked message:	Happy Birthday.^
Intermediate messages:	a. happybir thday.^
	b. ahppyib rthady.^
	c. ajqqzic tvjafz.^
	d. ^.zfajvt cizqqja
Cipher text:	^.zfajvt cizqqja

The following simple example, that of sending a secret message between two parties, illustrates some of the basic principles involved in cryptography. The first step is to determine what language and alphabet the message is to be sent in. This is important because of the different number of letters in each alphabet, the fact that some languages are written right to left while others are written left to right, and the fact that in some alphabets the same character can represent a letter and a number — they have a dual meaning. The second step is to determine whether a block cipher or stream cipher will be used; if a block cipher, define the blocksize of data that the encryption algorithm operates on; that is, how many 8-bit bytes. The third step is to specify the shift/substitution/manipulation algorithm. The fourth step is to define the key type and length. The fifth step is to specify the code in which the data will be represented to the computer, for example, ASCII. Exhibit 3 illustrates these principles.

This simple example starts out with an English language message: Happy Birthday. This is the message the sender wants to send the recipient; it is referred to as the plaintext message. First, the message is blocked to fit the specified encryption block size of 16 bytes. Because the message is only 15 bytes long, it is padded with a blank space (^). (Note that some encryption algorithms pad on the left, and others pad on the right.) Next, the message goes through the four transformations specified by the encryption algorithm. Note that x is the key and in this instance x = 2. The final transformation results in the cipher text, which is transmitted to the recipient. To read or decrypt the message, the recipient goes through the same steps in reverse order using the same key. The sender and the receiver know the encryption algorithm and the key; that information does not have to be transmitted. This is how a secret key encryption system works.

In 1976, the U.S. National Bureau of Standards (NBS), now the National Institute of Standards and Technology (NIST), published the Data Encryption

Standard (DES).[153] DES was developed to protect the transmission of unclassified data by government agencies. The algorithm operated on 64-bit blocks of data with a 56-bit key. In summary, the algorithm consisted of two steps that were repeated 16 times[409]:

1. Exchange the left half of the 64-bit message with the right half.
2. Replace the right half of the message with the bitwise exclusive OR of the right half and a 32-bit word (a complicated function (f) of the left half, the key, and the iteration number).

Since then, many publicly available encryption algorithms have been developed.

The concept of using a pair of keys — one to encrypt and the other to decrypt — began in the late 1970s. This concept became known as public/private keys. The two keys are mathematically related; however, in *theory*, it is infeasible to derive one key from the other. RSA* was the first public key encryption system sufficiently robust to use for both encryption and digital signatures. The following steps summarize the RSA algorithm[409]:

1. Choose two, large random prime numbers (p, q) of equal length.
2. Compute $n = p * q$.
3. Choose a random prime number e, such that e has no factors in common with $((p-1)(q-1))$; e with n comprise the public key.
4. Compute the private key, $d = e^{-1} \bmod ((p-1)(q-1))$.
5. Choose a binary block size that equals the largest power of 2 that is less than n.
6. Break the plaintext message into blocks (m_i); pad if necessary.
7. Generate the cipher text, $c_i = m^e_i \bmod n$.
8. Recover the plaintext, $m_i = c^d_i \bmod n$.

Note that p and q are destroyed, only the public key (e, n) is distributed, and the private key (d) is protected.

The key to the acceptance and widespread use of public key encryption has been the public key infrastructure (PKI) made possible through a set of public key cryptography standards known as PKCS.[179–191] RSA Laboratories has been the driving force behind the development and promulgation of the PKCS suite since the early 1990s. They understood early on that the way to achieve interoperability in a multi-vendor environment is through the use of commercial consensus standards. Most PKCSs exhibit a reasonably high degree of compatibility with the corresponding ISO/IEC standards. The current set of PKCSs at the time of writing are listed below. The latest information on PKCS developments can be found at: www.rsa.com[489]:

- PKCS #1 v2.1 — RSA Cryptography Standard, (draft) September 17, 1999
- PKCS #3 v1.4 — Diffie-Hellman Key Agreement Standard, November 1, 1993

* The algorithm is named for its three inventors: Ron Rivest, Adi Shamir, and Leonard Adleman.

- PKCS #5 v2.0 — Password-based Cryptography Standard, March 25, 1999
- PKCS #6 v1.5 — Extended Certificate Syntax Standard, November 1, 1993
- PKCS #7 v1.5 — Cryptographic Message Syntax Standard, November 1, 1993
- PKCS #8 v1.2 — Private Key Information Syntax Standard, November 1, 1993
- PKCS #9 v2.0 — Selected Object Classes and Attribute Types, February 25, 2000
- PKCS #10 v1.7 — Certification Request Syntax Standard, May 26, 2000
- PKCS #11 v2.11 — Cryptographic Token Interface Standard, (draft) November 2000
- PKCS #12 v1.0 — Personal Information Exchange Syntax, June 24, 1999
- PKCS #13 (proposal) — Elliptic Curve Cryptography Standard, October 7, 1998
- PKCS #15 v1.1 — Cryptographic Token Information Syntax Standard, June 6, 2000

A newer type of public key cryptosystems is referred to as elliptic curve cryptosystems (ECCs). Lee[330] reports that:

> *Protocols based on ECCs are becoming the standard for the information authentication step for wireless devices. ... Breaking an ECC requires determining the number of times that a seed value, a known point on an elliptic curve, is multiplied to get to another point on the same elliptic curve.*

Encryption algorithms involve complex mathematical specifications of the transformations performed on the data, such as hashing functions. Often, the entire algorithm is repeated two, three, or more times. Key lengths range from 56 to 128 bits or higher. For a complete discussion of current cryptographic algorithms, see Schneier,[409] Menezes,[353] Kippenhan,[316] and Stallings.[419]

Historically, the primary means of providing integrity was by implementing error detection/correction algorithms on the communications links. This included longitudal and vertical parity checks, cyclical redundancy checks, Hamming codes, convolutional codes, recurrent codes, and checksums. These algorithms verified that the data had not been accidently or intentionally corrupted during transmission, including the deletion of data or insertion of bogus data, and that the packets were reassembled in the correct order. When errors were detected, they were corrected or a request was sent to retransmit the packet.

Historically, the primary means of providing availability was through redundant communications equipment (hot standby) and having alternative communication paths available in case the primary path was not available. For the data to be available when needed, the communications equipment and links had to be engineered to meet reliability requirements.

In the past, COMSEC principles were primarily applied to end-to-end communication links that transmitted textual, voice (STU technology), and image data separately. Today, COMSEC principles are applied to audio, video, image, and textual data that are transmitted together across a variety of network types and topologies, such as ISDN, ATM, SONET, Frame Relay, VPNs, and wireless. The need for data confidentiality, integrity, and availability during transmission remains; what has changed are the implementation strategies. Encryption is applied to data that is stored (files, e-mail, voice mail) as well as data that is transmitted (Internet and cell phone traffic). Data integrity concerns have been expanded to include verifying the true sender of files or e-mail through the use of digital signatures. Likewise, the distribution of public keys is verified. Because dedicated lines are rarely used anymore, firewalls are employed to block unknown and unauthorized people and processes from accessing network resources.

Encryption is not a perfect solution to data confidentiality; instead, it should be considered a temporary solution. All cryptographic algorithms can be broken just like shredder remnants can be pieced together; the variable is the amount of time it takes. Schneier[411] notes the limitations of commercial encryption products:

> *Most cryptography products on the market are insecure. Some don't work as advertised. Some are obviously flawed. Others are more subtly flawed.*

Schneier[410] cites several common weaknesses in implementing encryption algorithms, including:

- Not destroying the plaintext after encryption
- Use of temporary or virtual swapping files
- Buffer overflows
- Weak error detection/correction
- Key escrow accounts
- Use of default parameters
- Ability to reverse-engineer the product

In short, cryptography should be considered only one component of an overall comprehensive security program.[248,277,410]

Three concerns must be addressed when implementing encryption:

1. The time and system resources consumed to perform encryption and decryption
2. When to perform encryption; that is, what layer in the communications protocol suite
3. What encryption algorithm to use or what encryption strength/level of protection is needed

Encryption consumes time and processing power for both the sender and receiver. The more complex the encryption algorithm, the more system resources are consumed. To address the first item, Sandia National Laboratories has developed an ASIC that implements the DES algorithm. It is targeted for use in unclassified networks, digital cell phones, and high-definition television

(HDTV). The ASIC can also support triple-DES. As reported by Hankins,[283] the nominal encryption rate is 6.7 billion bps with a theoretical limit of 9.28 billion bps. The next step is to commercialize the product.

The level of encryption strength needed will depend on what type of information is being protected, for example, national security information, financial transactions, corporate research, or general-purpose e-mail. To address the third item, in 1997, NIST made a formal announcement of its intent to sponsor the development of an advanced encryption standard (AES). NIST chose to engage the resources of the international cryptographic community to develop the new AES algorithm, rather than develop it in-house as had been done with other cryptographic algorithms in the past. The goal of the AES project was to develop a replacement for DES, which is no longer considered sufficiently robust. The basic requirements were that AES support a block size of 128 bits, and key lengths of 128, 192, and 256 bits. Fifteen algorithms from twelve countries were submitted for the initial selection process. In October 2000, Rijndael was selected "as the best overall algorithm for AES".[173] The next step is to issue Rijndael as the approved AES federal (U.S.) information processing standard (FIPS); this is scheduled to occur in the summer/fall of 2001. Commercial products will follow thereafter. For a complete discussion of the new algorithm and the selection process, see Reference 173.

The second item must be addressed on a case-by-case basis within the context of the overall security program, network, system, and application architectures. Chapter 6 provides guidance in this area.

3.3 Computer Security (COMPUSEC)

Computer security is defined as:

> preventing, detecting, and minimizing the consequences of unauthorized actions by users (authorized and unauthorized) of a computer system.

In this case, the term "users" includes authorized users, or insiders, who are attempting to do something for which they lack permission, as well as unauthorized users, or outsiders, who are attempting to break into a system. The term "computer system" applies to any type or configuration of hardware and software, including distributed processing, client/server applications, embedded software, and Internet applications. COMSEC is primarily concerned with protecting data during transmission. COMPUSEC is primarily concerned with protecting data while it is processed and stored. Some of the threats to stored data include[249]:

Active Threats	*Passive Threats*
Overwriting	Browsing
Modifying	Aggregation and inference
Inserting	Replaying
Deleting	Leakage
Blocking access to	Copying and distributing

Primarily defense and intelligence systems employed COMPUSEC in the past. The intent was to prevent deliberate or inadvertent access to classified material by unauthorized personnel, or the unauthorized manipulation of the computer and its associated peripheral devices that could lead to the compromise of classified information.[140] COMPUSEC principles were applied to the design, development, implementation, evaluation, operation, decommissioning, and sanitization of a system.

A secure system operated in one of four modes: controlled, dedicated, multilevel, or system high. Occasionally, a system was designed so that it could be shut down and restarted in a different security mode. These four modes are defined as follows[140]:

1. Controlled security mode. Some users with access to the system have neither a security clearance nor a need-to-know for all classified material contained in the system. The separation and control of users and classified material on the basis of security clearance and security classification are not under operating system control.
2. Dedicated security mode. The computer system and all of its peripherals are exclusively used and controlled by specific users or groups of users who have a security clearance and need-to-know for the processing of a particular category and type of classified material.
3. Multi-level security mode. The system permits various categories and types of classified materials to be concurrently stored and processed and selective access to such material concurrently by uncleared users and users having differing security clearances and need-to-know. Separation of personnel and material on the basis of security clearance and need-to-know is accomplished by the operating system and related system software.
4. System high security mode. All system components are protected in accordance with the requirements for the highest classification category and type of material contained in the system. All personnel having access to the system have a security clearance but not necessarily a needs-to-know for all material contained in the system. The design and operation of the system must provide for the control of concurrently available classified material on the basis of need-to-know.

Each of these four security modes represented a different approach to the control and separation of dissimilar combinations of user clearances, needs-to-know, and level(s) of classified material handled by the system.

DoD 5200.28-M*, one of the first COMPUSEC standards, levied the following requirements on computer systems[140]:

* DoD 5200.28-M, ADP Security Manual — Techniques and Procedures for Implementing, Deactivating, Testing, and Evaluating Secure Resource-Sharing ADP Systems, with first amendment, U.S. Department of Defense (DoD), June 25, 1979.

1. Ensuring that two or more independent controls would have to malfunction simultaneously for a breach of system security to occur (defense in depth)
2. Monitoring protection state variables to control execution of operations and prevent illegal operations
3. Controlling access to memory locations
4. Ensuring predictable translation into object code
5. Protecting registers through error detection and redundancy checks
6. Performing parity checks and address bound checks of all operands/operators
7. Using interrupts to control operator malfunction
8. Verifying read, write, edit, and delete privileges
9. Labeling classified material
10. Clearing memory residue, overwriting memory before reuse
11. Logging attempts to circumvent system security measures
12. Implementing security safeguards during scheduled and unscheduled system shutdown, restart, and start-up
13. Maintaining an audit trail of security-related transactions, such as log on/log off attempts and times, information about resources accessed, created, changed, deleted, outputs generated, etc.
14. Employing user and terminal IDs as part of the access control and authentication system
15. Controlling access to system resources, utilities, and data through the operating system

The purpose of these measures was to prevent accidental or malicious intentional violations of system security and provide historical records of such transactions.

DoD 5200.28-M specified the implementation of COMPUSEC features. The next logical development was a standard that specified how to evaluate the effectiveness of the implementation of these features. The result was CSC-STD-001-83, the Trusted Computer System Evaluation Criteria (TCSEC)*, commonly known as the *Orange Book*, issued by the U.S. DoD in 1983. A second version of this standard was issued in 1985**.

The *Orange Book* proposed a layered approach for rating the strength of COMPUSEC features, similar to the layered approach used by the Software Engineering Institute (SEI) Capability Maturity Model (CMM) to rate the robustness of software engineering processes. As shown in Exhibit 4, four evaluation divisions composed of seven classes were defined. Division A class A1 was the highest rating, while division D class D1 was the lowest. The divisions measured the extent of security protection provided, with each class and division building upon and strengthening the provisions of its predecessors.

* CSC-STD-001-83, Trusted Computer System Evaluation Criteria (TCSEC), National Computer Security Center, U.S. Department of Defense (DoD), August 15, 1983.

** DoD-5200.28-STD, Trusted Computer System Evaluation Criteria (TCSEC), National Computer Security Center, U.S. Department of Defense (DoD), December 1985.

Exhibit 4 Summary of *Orange Book* Trusted Computer System Evaluation Criteria (TCSEC) Divisions

Evaluation Division	*Evaluation Class*	*Degree of Trust*
A - Verified protection	A1 - Verified design	Highest
B - Mandatory protection	B3 - Security domains	
	B2 - Structured protection	
	B1 - Labeled security protection	
C - Discretionary protection	C2 - Controlled access protection	
	C1 - Discretionary security protection	
D - Minimal protection	D1 - Minimal protection	Lowest

Twenty-seven specific criteria were evaluated. These criteria were grouped into four categories: security policy, accountability, assurance, and documentation, as shown in Exhibit 5.

Most often, a basic capability was established at C1, and then new requirements were added at each of the seven layers. Security testing is a good example of this, as illustrated in Exhibit 6. (It is interesting to note that although the *Orange Book* was published in the early 1980s, it required security testing to evaluate the ability of a system to withstand denial-of-service attacks at level B1.) In other cases, a criterion was only required at the higher layers, such as trusted recovery.

The *Orange Book* introduced the concepts of a trusted computing base (TCB) and security kernel or reference monitor. A TCB represents the combination of hardware, firmware, and software that is responsible for enforcing a security policy. A security kernel or reference monitor is the combination of hardware, firmware, and software that mediates all access to system resources while protecting itself from modification. A security kernel enforced the access control portion of a system security policy. The *Orange Book* required that a security model be verified through a formal mathematical proof at class A1. Today, formal mathematical proofs are also used to verify the correctness of requirements and designs for safety-critical systems.

The Honeywell Secure Communications Processor (SCOMP) Trusted Operating Program (STOP) Release 2.1 was the first product to be rated A1/B3. The final evaluation report,[138] issued September 28, 1985, noted that product ratings had to be tied to operational missions and environments. By October 1997, 106 commercial products appeared on the National Computer Security Center TCSEC evaluated products list, including three at A1 and three at B3.[248]

Access control, authentication, and audit trail were the three cornerstones of COMPUSEC in the early days. For example, the majority of the features listed in Exhibit 5 relate to access control and authentication, especially those listed under Security policy and Accountability. The assurance features correspond to software integrity — ensuring that the software not only functions correctly but that it correctly and reliably enforces the security policy. This differs from COMSEC, which promoted data confidentiality.

Exhibit 5 Summary of *Orange Book* Trusted Computer System Evaluation Criteria (TCSEC)

Category	*Feature Evaluated*	*A1*	*B3*	*B2*	*B1*	*C2*	*C1*
Security policy	Discretionary access control	x	+	x	x	+	+
	Sanitize storage before reuse	x	x	x	x	+	
	Security labels	x	x	+	+		
	Label integrity	x	x	x	+		
	Export labeled information	x	x	x	+		
	Export to multi-level secure devices	x	x	x	+		
	Export to single-level secure devices	x	x	x	+		
	Labeling human-readable output	x	x	x	+		
	Mandatory access controls	x	x	+	+		
	Subject sensitivity labels	x	x	+			
	Device labels	x	x	+			
Accountability	Identification and authentication	x	x	x	+	+	+
	Audit trail	x	+	+	+	+	
	Trusted communications path	x	+	+			
Assurance	System architecture	x	+	+	+	+	+
	System integrity	x	x	x	x	x	+
	Security testing	+	+	+	+	+	+
	Design specification verification	+	+	+	+		
	Covert channel analysis	+	+	+			
	Trusted facility management	x	+	+			
	Configuration management	+	x	+			
	Trusted recovery	x	+				
	Trusted distribution	x					
Documentation	Security features users' guide	x	x	x	x	x	+
	Trusted facility manual	x	+	+	+	+	+
	Testing documentation	+	x	+	x	x	+
	Design documentation	+	+	+	+	x	+

Note: x, no additional requirements for this class; +, new or enhanced requirements for this class; (blank), no requirements for this class.

Access control is defined as:

> design features that protect IA-critical and IA-related systems, applications, and data by preventing unauthorized and unwarranted access to these resources.

Access control can be implemented to control access to networks, computer systems, individual software applications, data, utilities, and shared resources such as printers. Access control consists of two main components: (1) access control rights that define which people and processes can access which system resources, and (2) access control privileges that define what these people and processes can do with or to the resources accessed.[248,357] Examples of access privileges include: read, write, edit, delete, execute, copy, print, move, forward,

Exhibit 6 *Orange Book* Testing Requirements

Class	*Reqt. Type*	*Requirement*
C1	New	The security mechanisms shall be tested and found to work as claimed in the system documentation. Testing shall be done to ensure that there are no obvious ways for an unauthorized user to bypass or otherwise defeat the security protection mechanisms.
C2	Add	Testing shall include a search for obvious flaws that would allow violation of resource allocation, or that would permit unauthorized access to the audit trail or authentication data.
B1	Add	A team of individuals who thoroughly understand the specific implementation of the security protection mechanisms shall subject its design, documentation, source code, and object code to thorough analysis and testing. Their objectives shall be: to uncover all design and implementation flaws that would permit a subject external to the security protection mechanism to read, change, or delete data normally denied under the mandatory or discretionary security policy; as well as to ensure that no subject (without authorization to do so) is able to cause the system to enter a state such that it is unable to respond to communications initiated by other users. All discovered flaws shall be removed or neutralized, and the system retested to demonstrate that they have been eliminated and that new flaws have not been introduced.
B2	Change	All discovered flaws shall be *corrected* and the system retested to demonstrate that they have been eliminated and that new flaws have not been introduced.
	Add	The security protection mechanism shall be found relatively resistant to penetration. Testing shall demonstrate that the security protection mechanism implementation is consistent with the descriptive top-level specification.
B3	Change	The security protection mechanism shall be found *resistant* to penetration.
	Add	No design flaws and no more than a few correctable implementation flaws may be found during testing and there shall be reasonable confidence that few remain.
A1	Change	Testing shall demonstrate that the security protection mechanism implementation is consistent with the *formal top-level specification*.
	Add	Manual or other mapping of the formal top-level specification to the source code may form a basis for penetration testing.

Source: From CSC-STD-001-83, Trusted Computer System Evaluation Criteria (TCSEC), National Computer Security Center, U.S. Department of Defense, August 15, 1983; DOD-5200.28-STD, Trusted Computer System Evaluation (TCSEC), National Computer Security Center, U.S. Department of Defense, December 1985.

distribute, etc. Access control rights and privileges can be defined on a need-to-know basis or a security classification scheme. Access control rights and privileges are generally defined in a matrix format by user name, user roles, local or global user groups. Access control is usually implemented through a combination of commercial operating system utilities and custom code. Access control provides a first layer of defense in protecting IA-critical and IA-related system resources; it enforces authorization policies.[248] Effective implementation of access control depends on:

1. Taking the time to define a comprehensive set of access control rights and privileges, including permissions to create/change these definitions
2. Protecting the table containing these definitions from unauthorized manipulation and corruption
3. A robust authentication capability

As Denning[248] points out, "Access controls are no better than the authentication mechanism on which they are based."

One area that is often overlooked, to the detriment of security, is inferred access control privileges. Inferred access control privileges are implied subsets or extensions to discrete access control privileges. For example, if someone has the discrete privilege to edit a file, that person also has the inferred privilege to read the file. In contrast, does someone who has the discrete privilege to read a file have the inferred privilege to print it? Perhaps not. Inferred access control privileges can occur by accident if sufficient care is not taken in defining discrete access control rights and privileges. Inferred access control privileges apply to processes as well as data. A determination should be made whether or not a user or process should inherit the privileges of an invoked process.[277] This needs to be decided on a case-by-case basis; however, the operating system should always be protected. Users should rarely have direct access to the operating system. In fact, Gollmann[277] recommends: (1) using status flags to distinguish between user, administrative, and operating system function calls; and (2) applying access controls to specific memory locations to prevent illegal modification of the operating system, application programs, and data. He gives a good illustration of the latter — the need to remove the NT registry editor from all user PCs.[277]

Authentication is defined as:

> establishing, verifying, or proving the validity of a claimed identity of a user, process, or system.

Authentication is a design feature that permits the claimed identity of a user, process, or system to be proven to and confirmed by a second party. Authentication is invoked prior to access control rights and privileges. A combination of parameters can be used to establish an identity, such as user name, password, biometric information, and traffic source. There are weaknesses associated with each of these parameters; thus, it is best to use a combination of parameters and not rely on any one of them alone. For example, Gollmann[277] cites common password vulnerabilities, including:

- Password guessing
- Password spoofing
- Use of default passwords

- Compromised password file
- Web browsers that store previous screens which contain user name and password

Chapter 6 discusses the strengths and weaknesses of different authentication methods.

To protect the user and the system, authentication should be bidirectional; that is, the user should be authenticated to a system and a system should be authenticated to a user. The latter is an important step in preventing site switching and other security compromises while connected to the Internet. A strong authentication strategy is essential for implementing effective access control rights and privileges. The effectiveness of an authentication strategy is determined by: (1) the selection of parameters to be verified, and (2) how stringent the verification process is. The goal is to minimize the number of false positives and false negatives.

An audit trail is defined as:

> a set of records that collectively provide documentary evidence of system resources accessed by a user or process to aid in tracing from original transactions forward and backward from records and reports to their component source transactions.

An audit trail is a design feature that provides an ongoing system monitoring and logging function. An audit trail serves four purposes. First, it captures information about what people and processes accessed what system resources and when they did so. Second, it captures information about system state transitions, the availability and loading of system resources, and the general "health" of the system. When abnormal events are logged, they trigger warnings and alarms so that action can be taken to prevent or minimize the effects of hazardous events. For example, an alarm may trigger the shutdown of an unstable nuclear power plant or the blocking of an intrusion attempt. The alarms may trigger a combination of automatic processes and operator alerts. Third, audit trail data is used to develop normal system and user profiles as well as attack profiles for intrusion detection systems. Fourth, audit trails are used to reconstruct events during accident/incident investigations.

An audit trail provides real-time and historical logs of system states, transitions, and usage. It is essential for safe, secure, and reliable system operation and for performing trend analysis and pattern recognition of anomalous events. The completeness of the events/states recorded and the timeliness in responding to the anomalous events determines the effectiveness of the audit trail. An audit trail consumes system resources; thus, care should be exercised when determining what events to record and how frequently to record them. A determination must also be made about the interval at which audit trails should be archived and overwritten.

Historically, COMPUSEC focused on protecting defense or national security information that was stored, processed, and generated on mainframe computers.

Today, COMPUSEC principles have been extended to a wide range of applications and system architectures, including client/server applications operating across LANs, WANs, VPNs, and the Internet. The rapid expansion of and interest in computer security is due to the sensitivity and volume of legal, financial, medical, business, and government data that is stored and processed today. In addition, as Denning[248] notes:

> *Almost any illegal activity that can be committed can be accomplished through the use of a computer, or at a minimum, with the computer as a willing accomplice.*

In the past, access control features were concerned with mediating access to a single system and its resources. Today, firewalls are used to mediate access between networks and the multiple systems and processors connected to them, while intrusion detection systems help prevent attempts to bypass security mechanisms. The audit trail now serves a new purpose — the development of normal system and user profiles as well as attack profiles for use by intrusion detection systems.

3.4 Information Security (INFOSEC)

The *Orange Book* was oriented toward custom software, particularly defense and intelligence applications, operating on a mainframe computer that was the predominant technology of the time. Guidance documents were issued*; however, it was difficult to interpret or apply the *Orange Book* to networks or database management systems. When distributed processing became the norm, additional standards were issued to supplement the *Orange Book*, such as the Trusted Network Interpretation** and the Trusted Database Management System Interpretation***. Each standard had a different color cover and collectively they became known as the rainbow series.

---

* (a) CSC-STD-003-85, Guidance for Applying the Trusted Computer System Evaluation Criteria (TCSEC) in Specific Environments, National Computer Security Center, U.S. Department of Defense (DoD), June 1985.[136]
(b) CSC-STD-004-85, Technical Rationale Behind CSC-STD-003-83, National Computer Security Center, U.S. Department of Defense (DoD), 1985.[137]
(c) NCSC-TG-025 version 2, A Guide to Understanding Data Remembrance in Automated Information Systems (AIS), National Computer Security Center, U.S. Department of Defense (DoD), September 1991.[147]

** (a) NCSC-TG-005 version 1, Trusted Network Interpretation of the TCSEC, National Computer Security Center, U.S. Department of Defense (DoD), July 1987.[144]
(b) NCSC-TG-011 version 1, Trusted Network Interpretation of the TCSEC, National Computer Security Center, U.S. Department of Defense (DoD), August 1, 1990.[145]

***NCSC-TG-021 version 1, Trusted DBMS Interpretation of the TCSEC, National Computer Security Center, U.S. Department of Defense (DoD), April 1991.[146]

At the same time, similar developments were proceeding outside the United States Between 1990 and 1993, the Commission of the European Communities*, the European Computer Manufacturers Association (ECMA)**, the Organization for Economic Cooperation and Development (OECD)***, and the Canadian System Security Centre**** all issued computer standards or technical reports. These efforts and the evolution of the rainbow series were driven by three main factors:

1. The rapid change in technology, which led to the need to merge COMSEC and COMPUSEC
2. The more universal use of information technology (IT) outside the defense and intelligence communities
3. The desire to foster a cost-effective commercial approach to IT security that would be applicable to multiple industrial sectors

The new paradigm combines COMSEC and COMPUSEC and is known as INFOSEC. INFOSEC is defined as:

> the protection of information against unauthorized disclosure, transfer, or destruction, whether accidental or intentional.

The emphasis is on protecting information, which is more refined than data, from accidental *and* intentional malicious actions. This is a broader scope than either COMSEC or COMPUSEC. INFOSEC can be applied to any type of software application, system architecture, or security need.

The current internationally recognized approach to INFOSEC is known as the Common Criteria*****. The Common Criteria are the result of a cooperative effort by Canada, France, Germany, the Netherlands, the United Kingdom, and the United States. The first version was published in January 1996, the second in May 1998. The next step was to promulgate the criteria via an international standard, ISO/IEC 15408 (Parts 1–3), which was approved in 1999******. The goal was to develop a standard by which the security of IT products, systems, and networks could be evaluated such that the evaluation would receive mutual

---

* (a) Information Technology Security Evaluation Criteria (ITSEC), Commission of the European Communities, Provisional Harmonised Criteria, version 1.2, June 1991.
(b) Information Technology Security Evaluation Manual (ITSEM), Commission of the European Communities, 1992.

** Secure Information Processing versus the Concept of Product Evaluation, Technical Report ECMA TR/64, European Computer Manufacturers Association (ECMA), December 1993.

***Guidelines for the Security of Information Systems, Organization for Economic Cooperation and Development (OECD), November 1992.[54]

****The Canadian Trusted Computer Product Evaluation Criteria, Canadian System Security Centre, version 3.0e, 1993.

*****Common Criteria for Information Technology (IT) Security Evaluation, version 2.0, Common Criteria Editing Board (CCEB), May 1998.[52]

******(a) ISO/IEC 15408-1(1999-12) Information Technology — Security Techniques — Common Criteria for IT Security Evaluation (CCITSE) — Part 1: General Model.[120]
(b) ISO/IEC 15408-2(1999-12) Information Technology — Security Techniques — Common Criteria for IT Security Evaluation (CCITSE) — Part 2: Security Functional Requirements.[121]
(c) ISO/IEC 15408-3(1999-12) Information Technology — Security Techniques — Common Criteria for IT Security Evaluation (CCITSE) — Part 3: Security Assurance Requirements.[122]

recognition across national borders. At the same time, system developers gain insight into what features and techniques are important through the publication of the evaluation criteria.

The Common Criteria separate functional security requirements from security assurance requirements.[248] As Caplan and Sanders[238] point out:

> *Functional requirements represent a statement of the security functionality or features a product is intended to provide. Satisfying assurance requirements gives you confidence that the functional requirements have been met.*

This is similar to the distinction between functional safety requirements and safety integrity requirements found in many international standards, for example, IEC 61508-3.[65]

ISO/IEC 15408 is written for use by three different communities: customers, developers, and evaluators. Customers define their IT security requirements, in an implementation-independent fashion, in what is referred to as a protection profile (PP). Developers respond to the PP with an implementation-dependent design, referred to as a security target (ST). Evaluators assess the conformance of the as-built system or product, referred to as the target of evaluation (TOE), to requirements stated in the PP*. Many U.S. government agencies are required to follow the Common Criteria methodology; PPs are often included in procurement announcements and offerors are required to submit an ST in response as part of their proposal.

ISO/IEC 15408 defines a standard set of functional security classes, families, and components, as shown in Exhibit 7. A customer selects the appropriate items from this set to define their functional security requirements.

Likewise, a standard set of security assurance classes, families, and components are defined, as shown in Exhibit 8. Security assurance requirements are grouped according to evaluation assurance levels (EALs). A customer specifies the required EAL.

Security assurance provides grounds for confidence that an IT product or system meets its security objectives. The Common Criteria philosophy is to provide assurance based on an evaluation (active investigation) of the IT product or system that is to be trusted. Evaluation techniques can include, but are not limited to[120–122]:

- Analysis and checking of processes and procedures
- Checking that processes and procedures are being applied
- Analysis of the correspondence between TOE design representations
- Analysis of the TOE design representation against the requirements
- Verification of proofs
- Analysis of guidance documents
- Analysis of functional tests developed and the results provided
- Independent functional testing

* Sample PPs are posted on the NIAP and IATF Web sites.[451,471]

Exhibit 7 ISO/IEC 15408-2 Functional Security Classes and Families

Class	*Family*
Security audit (FAU)	Security audit automatic response (FAU_ARP)
	Security audit data generation (FAU_GEN)
	Security audit analysis (FAU_SAA)
	Security audit review (FAU_SAR)
	Security audit event selection (FAU_SEL)
	Security audit event storage (FAU_STG)
Communication (FCO)	Nonrepudiation of origin (FCO_NRO)
	Nonrepudiation of receipt (FCO_NRR)
Cryptographic support (FCS)	Cryptographic key management (FCS_CKM)
	Cryptographic operation (FCS_COP)
User data protection (FDP)	Access control policy (FDP_ACC)
	Access control functions (FDP_ACF)
	Data authentication (FDP_DAU)
	Export to outside TSF control (FDP_DAU)
	Information flow control policy (FDP_ITC)
	Information flow control functions (FDP_IFF)
	Import from outside TSF control (FDP_ITC)
	Internal TOE transfer (FDP_ITT)
	Residual information protection (FDP_RIP)
	Rollback (FDP_ROL)
	Stored data integrity (FDP_SDI)
	Inter-TSF user data confidentiality transfer protection (FDP_UCT)
	Inter-TSF user data integrity transfer protection (FDP_UIT)
Identification and authentication (FIA)	Authentication failures (FIA_AFL)
	User attribute definition (FIA_ATD)
	Specification of secrets (FIA_SOS)
	User authentication (FIA_UAU)
	User identification (FIA_UID)
	User-subject binding(FIA_USB)
Security management (FMT)	Management of functions in TSF (FMT_MOF)
	Management of security attributes (FMT_MSA)
	Management of TSF data (FMT_MTD)
	Revocation (FMT_REV)
	Security attribute expiration (FMT_SAE)
	Security management roles (FMT_SMR)
Privacy (FPR)	Anonymity (FPR_ANO)
	Pseudonymity (FPR_PSE)
	Unlinkability (FPR_UNL)
	Unobservability (FPR_UNO)

- Analysis for vulnerabilities (including flaw hypothesis)
- Penetration testing

The validity of documentation and the resulting IT product or system is measured by expert evaluators with increasing emphasis on scope, depth, and rigor. Greater assurance results from the application of greater evaluation

Exhibit 7 ISO/IEC 15408-2 Functional Security Classes and Families (continued)

Class	*Family*
Protection of the TSF (FPT)	Underlying abstract machine test (FPT_AMT)
	Fail secure (FPT_FLS)
	Availability of exported TSF data (FPT_ITA)
	Confidentiality of exported TSF data (FPT_ITC)
	Integrity of exported TSF data (FPT_ITI)
	Internal TOE TSF data transfer (FPT_ITT)
	TSF physical protection (FPT_PHP)
	Trusted recovery (FPT_RCV)
	Replay detection (FPT_RPL)
	Reference mediation (FPT_RVM)
	Domain separation (FPT_SEP)
	State synchrony protocol (FPT_SSP)
	Timestamps (FPT_STM)
	Inter-TSF TSF data consistency (FPT_TDC)
	Internal TOE TSF data replication consistency (FPT_TRC)
	TSF self-test (FPT_TST)
Resource utilization (FRU)	Fault tolerance (FRU_FLT)
	Priority of service (FRU_PRS)
	Resource allocation (FRU_RSA)
TOE access (FTA)	Limitation on scope of selectable attributes (FTA_LSA)
	Limitation on multiple concurrent sessions (FTA_MCS)
	Session locking (FTA_SSL)
	TOE access banners (FTA_TAB)
	TOE access history (FTA_TAH)
	TOE session establishment (FTA_TSE)
Trusted path/channels (FTP)	Inter-TSF trusted channel (FTP_ITC)
	Trusted path (FTP_TRP)

effort, and the goal is to apply the minimum effort required to provide the necessary level of assurance. This increasing level of effort is based on[120–122]:

1. **Scope:** the portion of the IT product or system included in the evaluation
2. **Depth:** the level of design and implementation detail evaluated
3. **Rigor:** the application of effort in a structured, formal manner

ISO/IEC 15408 defines seven evaluation assurance levels (EALs), as shown in Exhibit 9. EALs represent the degree of confidence that functional security requirements have been met, with EAL 7 being the highest rating and EAL 1 the lowest. Depending on how a product or system is designed, built, and evaluated, it could be rated anywhere from EAL 1 to EAL 7. However, it is unlikely that a product or system could be rated EAL 4 or higher without prior planning and preparation to receive such a rating. It is possible for variations of a product, targeted for diverse customers, to receive different ratings.

Exhibit 8 ISO/IEC 15408 Security Assurance Classes and Families

Class	*Family*
Protection profile evaluation (APE)	TOE description (APE_DES) Security environment (APE_ENV) PP introduction (APE_INT) Security objectives (APE_OBJ) IT security requirements (APE_REQ) Explicitly stated IT security requirements (APE_SRE)
Security target evaluation (ASE)	TOE description (ASE_DES) Security environment (ASE_ENV) ST introduction (ASE_INT) Security objectives (ASE_OBJ) PP claims (ASE_PPC) IT security requirements (ASE_REQ) Explicitly stated IT security requirements (ASE_SRE) TOE summary specification (ASE_TSS)
Configuration management (ACM)	CM automation (ACM_AUT) CM capabilities (ACM_CAP) CM scope (ACM_SCP)
Delivery and operation (ADO)	Delivery (ADO_DEL) Installation, generation, and start-up (ADO_IGS)
Development (ADV)	Functional specification (ADV_FSP) High-level design (ADV_HLD) Implementation representation (ADV_IMP) TSF internals (ADV_INT) Low-level design (ADV_LLD) Representation correspondence (ADV_RCR) Security policy modeling (ADV_SPM)
Guidance documents (AGD)	Administrator guidance (AGD_ADM) User guidance (AGD_USR)
Life-cycle support (ALC)	Development security (ALC_DVS) Flaw remediation (ALC_FLR) Life-cycle definition (ALC_LCD) Tools and techniques (ALC_TAT)
Tests (ATE)	Coverage (ATE_COV) Depth (ATE_DPT) Functional tests (ATE_FUN) Independent testing (ATE_IND)
Vulnerability assessment (AVA)	Covert channel analysis (AVA_CCA) Misuse (AVA_MSU) Strength of TOE security functions (AVA_SOF) Vulnerability analysis (AVA_VLA)
Maintenance of assurance (AMA)	Assurance maintenance plan (AMA_AMP) TOE component categorization report (AMA_CAT) Evidence of assurance of maintenance (AMA_EVD) Security impact analysis (AMA_SIA)

Exhibit 9 Summary of Common Criteria for IT Security Evaluation Assurance Levels (EALs)

Level	*Evaluation Mode*	*Use Scenario*	*Degree of Confidence*
EAL 7	Formal design verification and testing	Suitable for extremely high-risk scenarios; highest security	Highest
EAL 6	Semi-formal design verification and testing	Suitable for high-risk loss scenarios; very high security	
EAL 5	Semi-formal design and testing process	High security	
EAL 4	Methodical design, testing, and review process; independent security evaluation	Medium security	
EAL 3	Methodical testing	Moderate security	
EAL 2	Structural testing	Minimal security	
EAL 1	Functional testing; no security evaluation	No security	Lowest

Sources: Adapted from Caplan, K. and Sanders, J., *IT Professional*, 1(2), 29–34, 1999; Denning, *Information Warfare and Security*, Addison-Wesley, 1999; ISO/IEC 15408-1, 15408-2, 15408-3 (1999-12), Information Technology — Security Techniques — Common Criteria for IT Security Evaluation (CCITSE) — Parts 1, 2, and 3.

ISO/IEC 15408[120–122] permits tailoring of functional security and security assurance requirements through a standard three-step process. This is the decision-making process a customer or developer will follow when developing their proposed approach:

1. Standard classes, components, and activities are identified. This information is derived from ISO/IEC 15408 Parts 2 and 3.[121,122]
2. Each of these classes, components, and activities is examined to determine if they are directly applicable to the specific project. This analysis is strictly a yes/no function. The project team may decide that a component or an activity is not applicable because of the nature of the project. If so, an adequate rationale for deleting a component or activity should be provided. In summary, this step analyzes how *explicit* requirements could be satisfied using standard components and activities.
3. Potential areas for augmenting or extending standard requirements are analyzed. The customer or developer may propose additional components or activities to meet project specific requirements. Augmentation refers to adding standard components to an EAL that are normally associated with a higher EAL. Extension refers to adding new project-specific components to a standard functional security or security assurance class. This step focuses on meeting *implied* requirements, which unfortunately are often overlooked.

A parallel effort, known as the systems security engineering capability maturity model or SSE-CMM*,**, was initiated by the U.S. National Security Agency (NSA), Office of the (U.S.) Secretary of Defense (OSD), and the Communications Security Establishment (Canada) in April 1993. ISO/IEC 15408 is primarily an assessment of a product's (or system's) functional security. In contrast, SSE-CMM is primarily an assessment of the security engineering process used to develop a product or system. The intent is to provide a standardized assessment that assists customers, such as NSA, DoD, and CSA, determine the ability of a vendor to perform well on security engineering projects.

SSE-CMM was derived from the systems engineering capability maturity model (SE-CMM). Additional specialized security engineering needs were added to the model so that it incorporates the best-known security engineering practices.[148] SSE-CMM follows the same philosophy as other CMMs, by identifying key process areas (KPAs) and five increasing capability levels:

0 — not performed
1 — performed informally
2 — planned and tracked
3 — well defined
4 — quantitatively controlled
5 — continuously improving

SSE-CMM identifies eleven security engineering key process areas, as summarized below. Each process area is further subdivided into base practices.

Security Engineering KPAs

PA01 — administer security controls
PA02 — assess impact
PA03 — assess security risk
PA04 — assess threat
PA05 — assess vulnerability
PA06 — build assurance argument
PA07 — coordinate security
PA08 — monitor security posture
PA09 — provide security input
PA010 — specify security needs
PA011 — verify and validate security

Method, version 2.0, April 16, 1999.[149]

In summary, a potential vendor is rated 0 to 5 in each of the eleven security engineering KPAs. An overall rating is given based on the security engineering KPAs and other organizational and project management factors. The customer then determines if the vendor's rating is appropriate for their specific project.

* Systems Security Engineering Capability Maturity Model (SSE-CMM) Model Description Document, version 2.0, April 1, 1999.[148]

** Systems Security Engineering Capability Maturity Model (SSE-CMM) Appraisal Method, version 2.0, April 16, 1999.[149]

Version 2.0 of the SSE-CMM and the associated appraisal method were issued in April 1999. The next step is to promulgate SSE-CMM as an ISO/IEC standard. The latest information about the SSE-CMM can be found at www.sse-cmm.org or www.issea.org.[500,501]

3.5 Operations Security (OPSEC)

Operations security or OPSEC is defined as:

> the implementation of standardized operational procedures that define the nature and frequency of interaction between users, systems, and system resources, the purpose of which is to: (1) maintain a system in a known secure state at all times, and (2) prevent accidental or intentional theft, destruction, alteration, or sabotage of system resources.

As the name implies, OPSEC addresses security concerns related to the operation of a system. OPSEC is more involved with personnel issues, staff responsibilities, and duties than other security measures. OPSEC considers both insider and outsider threats. To illustrate, one historical OPSEC requirement was known as "man-in-the-loop." This operational requirement stated that electronic messages (and sometimes hardcopy printouts) had to be reviewed by a person, to verify that security markings were correct, before they could be released or forwarded. The information was considered too sensitive to rely on automatic processing alone.

Exhibit 10 lists examples of items that should be considered when developing OPSEC procedures. These items fall into three categories: personnel operations, software/data operations, and administrative operations. These procedures should be well-defined, communicated to all stakeholders, and in place before a system is initialized. Note that this list is not exhaustive; there are also many site-specific issues to consider.

In addition to security clearances and background checks, it is important to ensure that staff members have the appropriate education and experience to perform their assigned duties. A person who has little or no understanding of security is unlikely to take it seriously, recognize or respond to potential security problems correctly. This need was recognized in the *Orange Book*, which specified requirements for personnel who conducted security testing. Increasing requirements were specified for each division. For example, the requirements for Division B were[135]:

> The security testing team shall consist of at least two individuals with Bachelor degrees in Computer Science and at least one individual with a Master's degree in Computer Science. Team members shall be able to follow test plans prepared by the system developer and suggest additions, shall be conversant with the flow hypothesis or equivalent security testing methodologies, shall be fluent in the TCB implementation language(s), and shall have assembly-level programming experience. Before testing begins, the team members shall have functional knowledge of, and shall have completed the system developer's internals course for the system being evaluated. At least one team member shall have previously completed a security test on another system.

Exhibit 10 Examples of Items to Address in OPSEC Procedures

1. Personnel Operations (user, system administrator, trainee, maintenance staff, visitors, etc.)
   a. Security clearances, background checks, badges
   b. Proof of staff competence
   c. Searching briefcases, purses, backpacks, etc. when entering/leaving building
   d. Training staff on security features and responsibilities
   e. Defining policy on working alone, after hours, from home, or while traveling (remote access)
   f. Defining policy for taking computers, reports, electronic files out of the office
2. Software/Data Operations (text, image, audio, video)
   a. Schedule for performing system and data integrity checks, backups, generating archives
   b. Schedule and procedures for deleting and disposing of sensitive material, electronic and hardcopy
   c. Procedures for off-site storage
   d. Labeling classified or sensitive data while it is stored, processed, displayed, transmitted, or printed
   e. Defining policy for storing diskettes and other media
   f. Controlling access to archives
   g. Defining audit trail archival and overwrite procedures and schedule
   h. Defining policy for reusing electronic storage media
   i. Procedures and schedule for executing virus scan software on servers and user workstations
   j. Procedures and schedule for updating virus scan software
   k. Site and application specific software and data operations
3. Administrative Operations
   a. Defining hours system can be accessed, and types of transactions that can be done during those hours
   b. Scheduling preventive maintenance
   c. Defining conditions that should trigger an emergency shutdown, automatic or operator assisted, of a communications node, system resource, or the entire system
   d. Defining policy on whether or not PCs should be turned off while someone is away from their desk, at lunch, overnight, and the use of screen savers and privacy screens
   e. Defining how often passwords and other authentication data should be changed and verified
   f. Defining how often access control rights and privileges should be reviewed and updated
   g. Defining procedure for terminating user accounts normally and on an emergency basis
   h. Schedule and procedures for performing security inspections, security assessments, and safe checks
   i. Schedule and procedures for changing combinations
   j. Property pass procedures
   k. Schedule and procedures for managing the distribution, generation, update, storage, replacement, and revocation of cryptographic material and other security tokens

In other words, general-purpose software engineering skills alone were considered inadequate.

OPSEC was relatively straightforward in the days of mainframes and computer centers; it has become much more complex today given mobile computing, telecommuting, client/server applications, and Internet applications.

3.6 System Safety

System safety is defined as[143]:

> *the application of engineering and management principles, criteria, and techniques to achieve acceptable mishap risk, within the constraints of operational effectiveness, time, and cost, throughout all phases of the system life cycle.*

The term "mishap risk" is used to distinguish between type of risk of concern to system safety and that of schedule or cost risk. Mishap risk is defined as[143]:

> *an expression of the possibility and impact of an unplanned event or series of events resulting in death, injury, occupational illness, damage to or loss of equipment or property (physical or cyber), or damage to the environment in terms of potential severity and probability of occurrence.*

As shown in Exhibit 11, system safety is composed of several components. The exact combination of components will vary from system to system. For this book, software safety is the primary component of concern. Software safety is defined as[288]:

> *design features and operational procedures which ensure that a product performs predictably under normal and abnormal conditions, and the likelihood of an unplanned event occurring is minimized and its consequences controlled and contained; thereby preventing accidental injury or death, environmental or property damage, whether intentional or accidental.*

Software is generally categorized as being safety-critical, safety-related, or nonsafety-related. These terms are defined as follows[288]:

- **Safety-critical software:** Software that performs or controls functions which, if executed erroneously or if they failed to execute properly, could directly inflict serious injury to people, property, and/or the environment or cause loss of life.
- **Safety-related software:** Software that performs or controls functions which are activated to prevent or minimize the effect of a failure of a safety-critical system.
- **Nonsafety-related software:** Software that performs or controls functions which are not related to safety.

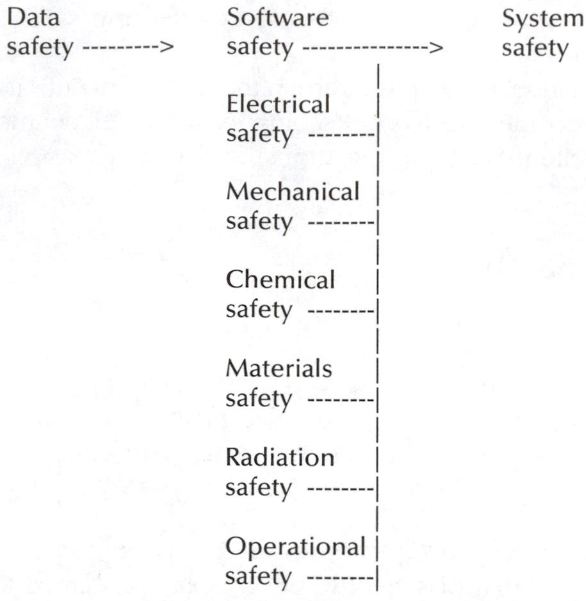

Exhibit 11 Software as a Component of System Safety. (*Source:* Herrmann, D., *Software Safety: The Medical Perspective*, Invited Tutorial, 16th International System Safety Society Conference, September 14–19, 1998, Seattle, WA.)

To illustrate, a software-controlled automobile braking system is classified as safety-critical. A software-controlled air bag deployment system is classified as safety-related. And a software-controlled automobile sound system is classified as nonsafety-related.

The discipline of system safety and software safety originated in the defense and aerospace industries. MIL-STD-882 has been the foundation of system safety for the U.S. military. The original standard was issued in 1969. Revision A was published in 1977, revision B in 1984, and revision C in 1993. MIL-STD-882D,[143] the current version, was adopted in 1999. MIL-STD-882D and its predecessors focus on mishap risks associated with the development, test, acquisition, use, and disposal of DoD weapon systems, subsystems, equipment, and facilities.[143] These standards assigned three types of tasks and activities: safety program management, risk analysis, and risk control, as shown in Exhibit 12.

MIL-STD-1574A (USAF)*, a tailored version of MIL-STD-882A, was developed especially for space and missile systems. Although issued in 1979, MIL-STD-1574A made some observations that are equally applicable today:

> Accident prevention is of major concern throughout the life cycle of a system. Planning and implementation of an effective system safety program, commensurate with the requirements of each phase in the acquisition process, is of prime importance in minimizing risk of accidents and their associated cost impacts during the systems test and

* MIL-STD-1574A, System Safety Program for Space and Missile Systems, U.S. Air Force (USAF), August 15, 1979.

Exhibit 12 System Safety Tasks and Activities Required by MIL-STD-882D

Safety Program Management
- 102 System Safety Program Plan
- 104 Safety Reviews and Audits
- 105 Safety Working Group
- 106 Hazard Tracking

Risk Analysis
- 201 Preliminary Hazard List
- 202 Preliminary Hazard Analysis, Functional FMECA
- 204 Subsystem Hazard Analysis, Design FMECA
- 205 System Hazard Analysis, Interface FMECA
- 206 HAZOP Studies

Risk Control
- 203 Safety Requirements
- 301 Safety Assessments
- 302 Safety Testing
- 303 Safety Review of ECRs and SPRs
- 401 Safety Verification
- 402 Safety Compliance Assessment

Source: From MIL-STD-882D, Mishap Risk Management (System Safety), U.S. Department of Defense (DoD) Standard Practice (draft), October 20, 1998.

> operational phases. System safety responsibilities shall be an inherent part of every program and the implementation of the complete system program requires extensive participation and support by many disciplines and functional areas.

In other words, prior planning is necessary if safety is to be achieved. Second, safety tasks and activities are ongoing throughout the system life cycle. Third, safety engineering should be an integral part of the system engineering process. Finally, effective safety engineering requires an interdisciplinary approach. These four principles are true for reliability engineering and security engineering as well.

The purpose of safety engineering is to manage mishap risks. This is accomplished through a combination of analysis, design, and verification activities, such as those discussed in Annex B, as well as operational procedures. A series of hazard analyses are performed throughout the life cycle to identify risks, their causes, the severity of the consequences should they occur, and the likelihood of them occurring. Risks are then eliminated or controlled through inherent safe (re)design features, risk mitigation or protective functions, system alarms and warnings, and comprehensive instructions for use and training that explain safety features, safety procedures, and the residual risk.

As the quote above stated, the first step is to develop a system safety plan and a corresponding software safety plan. The plan explains the tasks and activities to be performed, the schedule with key milestones and decision points, and the roles and responsibilities of the different stakeholders and the coordination of their efforts. At the same time, a system safety case and a software safety case are begun. A safety case is a systematic means of gathering and reporting the data needed by contractual, regulatory, and certification authorities to certify that a system has met specified safety requirements and is safe for use in the intended operational environment. Assumptions, claims, evidence, and arguments form the basis of a safety case. A safety plan and a safety case complement each other; the plan states what is intended to be done while the case proves that it was done. A safety case is a living document throughout the system life cycle.

To be achieved, safety requirements must be specified — both the functional safety requirements and the safety integrity requirements. These requirements explain how a system should prevent, detect, respond to, contain, and recover from hazards so that the system remains in a known safe state at all times. This involves specifying must work functions (MWFs) and must not work functions (MNWFs),[126,127] under what conditions a system should fail safe or fail operational, and the time required to safe or shutdown a system before corrective action can be taken.[439]

Since its beginning in the defense and aerospace industries, the need for software safety has expanded to most industrial sectors, including the railway, automotive, power generation, commercial aircraft, air traffic control systems, process control, and biomedical industries. A new application is intelligent transportation systems (ITS). As Jesty[308] points out, software will play a major role in:

- Providing pre-trip information
- Providing route guidance
- Performing demand management and traffic control functions
- Assisting emergency vehicle management
- Monitoring the transportation of HAZMAT

Another reasonably new application is marine navigation systems in which software is responsible for integrating and supplying correct, current, and understandable real-time information from multiple sources. Mills[356] notes the concomitant challenges:

> *In safety-critical situations, the information must be correct and readily available in an instantaneously understandable form. ... this is not always the case if cycling through screens is necessary or information such as symbols has to be interpreted. However, there is another problem in that when information is integrated the choice of which information is redundant is often made at the system/chip level so that the user has no idea what has been discarded.*

There are many parallels between safety and security engineering. Security engineering speaks in terms of vulnerabilities and threats, while safety engineering speaks in terms of risks and hazards. In both instances, the intent is to: (1) prevent accidental or malicious intentional actions that could have negative consequences; (2) minimize or eliminate the probability of unintended or unspecified functionality; and (3) keep the system in a known safe or secure state at all times. Many of the same techniques are used for both safety and security engineering, as shown in Annex B; the difference is the perspective from which the techniques are applied and the results interpreted. For example, access control can be employed to restrict access to sensitive information *and* to prevent unauthorized users from initiating safety-critical functions.[333,422] The concept of defense in depth is employed in both safety and security engineering. The dual usage of Formal Methods was mentioned earlier. There are also many parallels between physical security and physical safety; operational security and operational safety.

3.7 System Reliability

System reliability is the composite of hardware and software reliability predictions or estimations for a specified operational environment. Hardware reliability is defined as:

> the ability of an item to correctly perform a required function under certain conditions in a specified operational environment for a stated period of time.

Software reliability is defined as[288]:

> *a measure of confidence that the software produces accurate and consistent results that are repeatable, under low, normal, and peak loads, in the intended operational environment.*

Hardware is primarily subject to random failures, failures that result from physical degradation over time and variability introduced during the manufacturing process. Hardware reliability is generally measured quantitatively. Software is subject to systematic failures, failures that result from an error of omission, an error of commission, or an operational error during a life-cycle activity.[288] Software reliability is measured both quantitatively and qualitatively. To illustrate, a failure due to a design error in a memory chip is a systematic failure. If the same chip failed because it was old, that would be considered a random failure. A software failure due to a design or specification error is a systematic failure. Hence, system reliability measurements combine quantitative and qualitative product and process assessments.

Reliability engineering emerged as an engineering discipline in earnest following World War II. The defense and aerospace industries led this development; other industries such as the automotive, telecommunications, and consumer electronics became involved shortly thereafter. Initial efforts were focused on components, then subsystems, and systems. A variety of statistical techniques were developed to predict and estimate system reliability. Failure data was collected, analyzed, and shared over the years so that the techniques could be improved. The notion of software reliability did not begin until the late 1970s.

Early software reliability models tried to adapt hardware reliability models. They applied statistical techniques to the number of errors found during testing and the time it took to find them to predict the number of errors remaining in the software and the time that would be required to find them. Given the difference in hardware and software failures, the usefulness of these models was mixed. The limitations of early software reliability models can be summarized as follows[288]:

1. They do not distinguish between the type of errors found or predicted to be remaining in the software (functional, performance, safety, reliability, etc.).
2. They do not distinguish between the severity of the consequences of errors (insignificant, marginal, critical, catastrophic) found or predicted to be remaining in the software.
3. They do not take into account errors found by techniques other than testing (e.g., static analysis) or before the testing phase.

These limitations led to the development of new software reliability models and the joint use of qualitative and quantitative assessments.

The purpose of reliability engineering is to ensure that a system and all of its components exhibit accurate, consistent, repeatable, and predictable performance under specified conditions. A variety of analysis, design, and verification techniques, like those discussed in Annex B, are employed throughout the life cycle to accomplish this goal. Current and thorough user documentation is an important part of this process because it will explain the correct operation of a system, applications for which the system should and should not be used, and procedures for preventive, adaptive, and corrective maintenance.

As in safety engineering, the first step is to develop a system reliability plan and a corresponding software reliability plan. Similarly, a system reliability case and a software reliability case are begun. A reliability case demonstrates that a system has met specified reliability requirements and is fit for use in the intended operational environment.

Reliability requirements are specified at the system level, then allocated to system components such as software. A series of analyses, feasibility studies, and trade-off studies are performed to determine the optimum system architecture that will meet the reliability requirements. A determination is made about how a system should prevent, detect, respond to, contain, and recover from errors, including provisions for degraded mode operations. Progress toward meeting reliability goals is monitored during each life-cycle phase.

One of the more interesting and promising new developments in this field is the application of Bayesian Belief networks (BBNs) to model system and software dependability. BBNs are graphical networks that represent probabilistic relationships among events or propositions. Bouissou, Martin, and Ourghanlian[221]; Niel, Littlewood, and Fenton[361]; and Neil and Fenton[360] describe several advantages of BBNs:

1. They can be used as a decision aid in the context of uncertainty.
2. They have the ability to combine different types of information: inference, evidence, and expert judgment.
3. They improve communication among different stakeholders.
4. They address known risks, unexpected and unknown results and effects.
5. The probabilities are updated as new knowledge or uncertainty is propagated through the network.

Agena, Ltd., has reported several successful BBN projects. In one project, BBNs were used to predict software defects in consumer digital electronic products[387]:

> The defect prediction BBN models the process of defect insertion and discovery at the software module level. It will be used to predict the number of residual defects, and defect densities, at various life-cycle phases and with various different types of assumptions about the design and testing process.

A second project involved assessing the reliability of military vehicles during all life-cycle phases. A tool composed of five modular BBNs was developed for this project[431]:

1. A Bayesian updating BBN to predict the reliability of subsystems using failure data from historically similar subsystems
2. A recursive BBN used to combine subsystem reliability probability distributions together to achieve a vehicle-level prediction
3. A design-quality BBN used to estimate design unreliability caused by a variety of design process factors
4. A manufacturing-quality BBN used to estimate unreliability caused by poor-quality manufacturing processes
5. A vehicle testing BBN that uses failure data gained from vehicle testing to infer vehicle reliability

Other applications of BBNs reported by Agena, Ltd., include[431]:

1. Assessing risks associated with specific new programmable electronic system components for the transportation industry
2. Modeling risk in air traffic control systems
3. Automated test case generation and software reliability forecasting for the telecommunications industry
4. Operational risk forecasting for the financial and insurance industries
5. Modeling expected jury reasoning for criminal trials

In addition, research is underway to determine if BBNs can be used effectively to predict intrusion-detection profiles prior to an attack.

There are several parallels between reliability engineering and safety or security engineering. Reliability engineering speaks in terms of failure modes and failure rates. In this instance, the term "failure" encompasses all types of failures, including security compromises and safety violations. The goal of all three disciplines is to prevent, detect, contain, and recover from erroneous system states and conditions. However, reliability engineering does not place as much emphasis on intentional malicious actions as safety or security engineering. Integrity and availability are major concerns of reliability engineering, just as they are for safety and security engineering. Reliability engineering activities are performed throughout the life cycle at the system and software level. As shown in Annex B, many of the same analysis, design, and verification techniques are used by safety, reliability, and security engineering. For example, a combined FTA/FMECA can be used by a reliability engineer to determine failure modes and rates. A safety engineer can use the same analysis to identify potential hazardous failures and the risk mitigation/control measures needed. A security engineer can use the same analysis to identify potential failures that could lead to security compromises. Again, the difference is the perspective from which the techniques are applied and the results interpreted. This concept is developed further in Chapters 4 through 8.

3.8 Summary

This chapter reviewed the seven historical approaches to information security/IA: physical security, communications security (COMSEC), computer security (COMPUSEC), information security (INFOSEC), operations security (OPSEC), system safety, and system reliability. Each of these seven approaches served a different purpose, as summarized in Exhibit 13. A variety of techniques were used by these historical approaches to achieve and maintain information confidentiality, data and system integrity and availability. Some techniques were used by multiple approaches, as shown in Exhibit 14. Although many parallels existed between these approaches, there was a lack of formal coordination and communication among them. For the most part, these activities were performed in isolation; at best, there was limited ad hoc coordination.

All of the approaches have had to evolve and need to continue evolving to correspond to changes in technology and operational environments, profiles, and missions. In the early days, physical security, COMSEC, COMPUSEC, and OPSEC were designed around the concept of a mainframe computer in a secure computer center. The advent of distributed processing, PCs, and LANs led to the initiation of INFOSEC, which merged/superseded COMSEC and COMPUSEC. Originally, system safety and system reliability gave nominal consideration to software. Today, software is a major component of safety engineering and reliability engineering.

At present, almost all systems, particularly infrastructure systems, mission-critical systems, and business-critical systems, have a combination of safety, reliability, and security requirements. A system may have high security, medium reliability, and no safety requirements, or a system may have high safety, high reliability, and medium security requirements. To illustrate:

Exhibit 13 Summary of the Different Roles Played by Historical Approaches to Information Security/IA

Type of IA Activity	*Role or Purpose*
Physical security	Protect system resources from physical damage that could impair operations and services. Protect physical system resources from theft.
Communications security (COMSEC)	Protect the confidentiality, integrity, and availability of sensitive data while it is being transmitted between systems and networks.
Computer security (COMPUSEC)	Prevent, detect, and minimize the consequences of unauthorized actions by users (authorized and unauthorized) of a computer system.
Information security (INFOSEC)	Protect information against unauthorized disclosure, transfer, or destruction, whether accidental or intentional.
Operations security (OPSEC)	Implement standardized operational procedures that define the nature and frequency of interaction between users, systems, and system resources; the purpose of which is to: (1) maintain a system in a known secure state at all times, and (2) prevent accidental or intentional theft, destruction, alteration, or sabotage of system resources.
System safety	Achieve acceptable mishap risk, within the constraints of operational effectiveness, time, and cost throughout all phases of the system lifecycle.[143]
System reliability	Achieve correct functional performance under certain conditions in a specified operational environment for a stated period of time.

- A financial system has high security, medium reliability, and no safety requirements.
- A database of medical records has medium safety, reliability, and security requirements.
- A spy satellite has high security and reliability requirements and low safety requirements. (It should not be able to malfunction and crash in an inhabited area.)
- An air traffic control system has high safety and reliability requirements and medium security requirements.
- An automobile has high safety, high reliability, and low security requirements. (An unauthorized person should not be able to tamper with the onboard PLCs or embedded software.)

Hence, it is essential that safety, reliability, and security engineering efforts be systematically coordinated and integrated. This is the realm of information security/IA.

Next, Chapter 4 explains how to identify what systems and data need to be protected and why.

Exhibit 14 Summary of the Techniques Used by Historical Approaches to Information Security/IA

Type of IA Activity	*Confidentiality Measures*	*Integrity Measures*	*Availability Measures*
Physical security	Isolating data of different classification levels on different channels Shielding equipment and cables Controlling physical access to equipment Remote equipment identified by location		Specialized HVAC UPS Protecting equipment from natural disasters Disk mirroring Off-site storage
Communications security (COMSEC)	Encryption Spectrum management Secure switch isolation	Error detection/ correction algorithms Formal proofs of correctness	Redundant communication equipment Alternate communication paths
Computer security (COMPUSEC)	Access control Authentication Audit trail Process isolation Labeling	Partitioning Information hiding	Trusted recovery
Information security (INFOSEC)	Encryption Spectrum management Secure switch isolation Access control Authentication Audit trail Process isolation Labeling Protection against accidental and intentional actions	Error detection/ correction algorithms Formal proofs of correctness Partitioning Information hiding Protection against accidental and intentional actions EALs	Redundant communication equipment Alternate communication paths Trusted recovery
Operations security (OPSEC)	Personnel operations Data operations Administrative operations	Data operations Administrative operations	Data operations Administrative operations
System safety	Access control	Error detection/ correction algorithms Plausibility checks Defensive programming Hazard analyses Formal proofs of correctness Partitioning Information hiding SILs	Defense in depth Block recovery Fail safe or fail operational

Exhibit 14 Summary of the Techniques Used by Historical Approaches to Information Security/IA (continued)

Type of IA Activity	*Confidentiality Measures*	*Integrity Measures*	*Availability Measures*
System reliability		Error detection/ recovery algorithms Fault tolerance FTA/FMECA Reliability allocation	Reliability block diagrams Reliability estimation and prediction Block recovery Degraded mode operations

3.9 Discussion Problems

1. What role does intrusion detection play in physical security?
2. Describe the role software reliability serves in protecting data confidentiality and availability.
3. Develop a physical security plan for a home-based online business. The business has three mini-tower computers in two different geographic locations, one printer, and a notebook computer that is taken to trade shows. There are five employees, two of which live in the house. The house has two phone lines. The online business is run out of the lower level of the house.
4. What different or additional physical security measures, if any, should be taken for home offices and mobile computing compared to a business office, and vice versa?
5. The XYZ company uses online e-forms to capture, update, and store personnel records, such as address, title, salary, bonuses, and performance appraisals. Develop an access control strategy that accommodates these five user groups: employee, first level supervisor, second level supervisor, personnel officer, and marketing manager.
6. How is the strength of an encryption algorithm measured?
7. What kind of authentication is needed for the following scenarios: remote access, mobile computing, distributed work groups, remote help/diagnostics?
8. What is the difference, if any, between security classification schemes based on security levels and those based on need-to-know? Which of these two approaches accommodates compartmentalization?
9. Describe the role encryption serves in protecting data integrity.
10. Why should or should not access control features be implemented for safety-critical software? For reliability-critical software?
11. What role does an audit trail play in protecting: (a) security-critical software, (b) safety-critical software, and (c) reliability-critical software? What role does an audit trail play in investigating an incident related

to the failure or compromise of: (a) security-critical software, (b) safety-critical software, and (c) reliability-critical software?

12. What are the major components of an OPSEC plan? What does each address?
13. What parallels exist between: (a) safety and reliability engineering, (b) safety and security engineering, and (c) security and reliability engineering?
14. Which of the seven historical approaches to IA considered: (a) accidental actions, and (b) malicious intentional actions?
15. Describe the differences and similarities between the Common Criteria and the SSE-CMM.
16. What benefit does a customer gain by requiring a vendor to be rated at a specific SSE-CMM level? What competitive advantage or disadvantage does a vendor gain by obtaining an SSE-CMM rating?

Chapter 4

Define the System Boundaries

To be effective, an information security/IA program must correspond to the reality of today's technology: distributed processing; client/server applications; mobile code; integrated audio, video, image, and textual data; PLCs; ASICs; embedded systems; wireless communications; and, of course, the Internet. An integrated methodical approach is needed: one that is comprehensive in scope, encompassing safety, reliability, and security engineering. Information security/IA is not just a software challenge; rather, it involves dynamic interactions within and among a multitude of hardware, software, telecommunications, and people.

Many organizations take a haphazard approach to information security/IA. If for no other reason than listening to the evening news, they are cognizant of the fact that something should be done to protect their IT base. So a firewall and virus scanner are installed, users are assigned passwords, and possibly e-mail is encrypted. However, the effectiveness of these measures is quite limited due to the lack of planning, analysis, and coordination that preceded them; a solution was implemented without defining the problem.

This chapter describes the initial component of an information security/IA program — defining the boundaries of the system to be protected. This component is comprised of four activities:

1. Determining what is being protected and why
2. Identifying the system
3. Characterizing system operation
4. Ascertaining what one does and does not have control over

These activities are straightforward. It is essential that they be performed — one must know what one is protecting before an effective strategy for doing so can be developed. As Jesty[308] reports, one of the first challenges in certifying the safety, reliability, or security of a system — particularly intelligent transportation systems (ITS) — is to define the boundaries and components of a system. Likewise, the first step in the U.K. Central Computing and Telecommunications Agency (CCTA) Risk Analysis and Management Methodology (CRAMM), developed in 1991, and its successors BS 7799[20,21] and ISO/IEC 17799(2000-12),[123] is to define the boundaries of a system.[208]

4.1 Determine What is Being Protected and Why

Webster's dictionary defines *protect* as:

> vt. (1) to cover or shield from exposure, injury, or destruction, guard; (2) to maintain the status or integrity of.

The purpose of information security/IA is to protect critical systems and data. Before this can be accomplished, the systems and data being protected need to be identified. Not all systems or system components may need to be protected; nor will they all need the same level of protection. Therefore, the first step is to define what is being protected:

- Systems that process or generate data?
- Systems that display data?
- Backup, archival, or online storage systems?
- Control systems that act on real-time data?
- Communications systems?
- Voice, video, image, or textual data?
- Hardcopy output?
- Input devices?

The next step is to define why these items need to be protected. The specific rationale and purpose for protecting each system and component should be explained. Information security/IA activities should not be undertaken just because "everyone else is doing it." Rather, information security/IA activities should be undertaken with the intent of accomplishing specific goals for specific reasons. This is common sense because goals must be articulated before they can be achieved. It also ensures that systems and components are not over- or under-protected. A clear, concise, unambiguous statement of the IA goals (what is being protected) and a justification for those goals (why these items are being protected) are needed. This statement should focus on what is to be accomplished — not how it is accomplished. The "how" is determined later. The goals should be stated succinctly and in a manner such that their achievement can be easily verified. For large systems, it may be useful to express these goals hierarchically, with a limit of three or four levels of detail (see Exhibit 1).

Exhibit 1 Sample Statement of IA Goals

Goal	Justification
1. Protect the privacy and integrity of customer records from accidental or malicious intentional unauthorized disclosure, manipulation, alteration, abuse, corruption, and theft.	1.a Customer loyalty depends on sound business ethics.
1.1 Protect personal identifying information: name, address, phone number, e-mail address, account number, and fax number.	1.b Local (or national) regulations require privacy protections.
1.2 Protect customer payment information and history.	1.c Liability lawsuits may result from a failure to protect customer records.
1.3 Protect customer purchase history and preferences.	1.d Fraud lawsuits may result from a failure to protect customer records.
1.4 Protect customer online, voice, fax, and hardcopy transactions.	

4.2 Identify the System

Webster's dictionary defines a system as:

> *a regularly interacting or interdependent group of items forming a unified whole.*

Similarly, IEEE Std. 610.12-1990* defines a system as:

> *a collection of components organized to accomplish a specific function or set of functions.*

The common theme between these definitions is that a system is composed of smaller parts that cooperate to accomplish something. Within the IT domain, systems are generally considered to be composed of subsystems, components, and subcomponents, as shown in Exhibit 2. However, what constitutes a system is relative to one's vantage point. What one person considers a system, another person might consider a subsystem or a collection of systems. In other words, abstractions about systems and their constituent components can go to very high and very low levels, depending on one's perspective and the purpose of the abstractions. The lack of specificity in terminology defining what is a system versus a subsystem or component is one reason why all stakeholders should be involved in defining the boundaries of a system.

In the IT world, it is common to think of systems as consisting of only hardware, software, and telecommunications equipment. Information security/IA takes a much broader view of systems, adding items such as people,

* ANSI/IEEE Std. 610.12-1990, Standard Glossary of Software Engineering Terminology.[44]

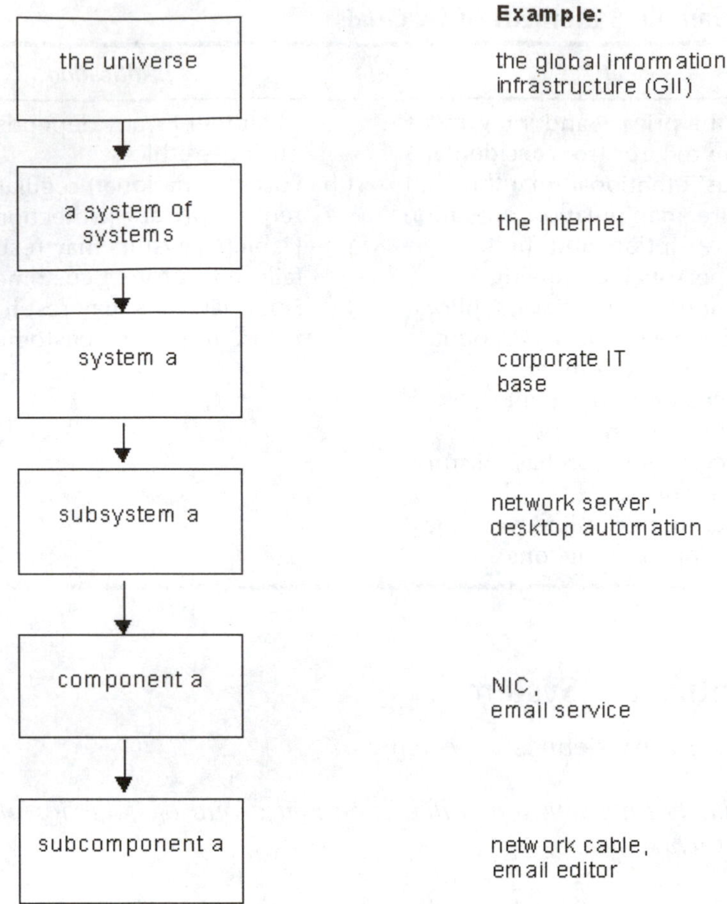

Exhibit 2 Standard Hierarchy Used in System Definition

operational procedures, and the supporting infrastructure systems to the equation. As such, systems include logical and physical, animate and inanimate, primary and support, dynamic and static entities. The following are examples of each type of system entity:

- **Logical:** Software is a logical entity.
- **Physical:** Software executes and is stored on physical entities such as computers, hard drives, floppy drives, PROMs, PLCs, and ASICs.
- **Animate:** Human users, system administrators, trainers, and maintenance staff are the animate entities within a system.
- **Inanimate:** All other system entities are inanimate; for example, system archives.
- **Primary:** Primary entities are those that contribute directly to accomplishing a system's function; for example the CPU, operating system, applications software, and end users.
- **Support:** The electric power grid and the telecommunications backbone are examples of support entities, as are most infrastructure systems.

They are essential but contribute indirectly to the accomplishment of a system's function.

- **Dynamic:** System configurations and operational procedures are dynamic entities. Both tend to evolve or be modified frequently over the life of a system, due to enhancements, maintenance, and changes in technology. A change in a dynamic entity should trigger the revalidation of protection strategies.
- **Static:** The entities that are static will vary from system to system. In one case, a maintenance schedule may be static; in another, the electromechanical components may be static.

Note that an item may fall into more than one entity type. For example, an item could be logical, primary, and dynamic. Only the pairs are mutually exclusive: logical/physical, animate/inanimate, primary/support, and dynamic/static. In general, different protection strategies are needed for different entity types.

To identify the boundaries of a system, one must first pick a starting point or prime entity from which to work upward to identify the outer limits of the system and downward to identify the constituent subsystems, components, and subcomponents. These are the two end points. To illustrate, suppose one is trying to define a demographic system in order to perform an epidemiological study. One picks the people living in city C as the starting point:

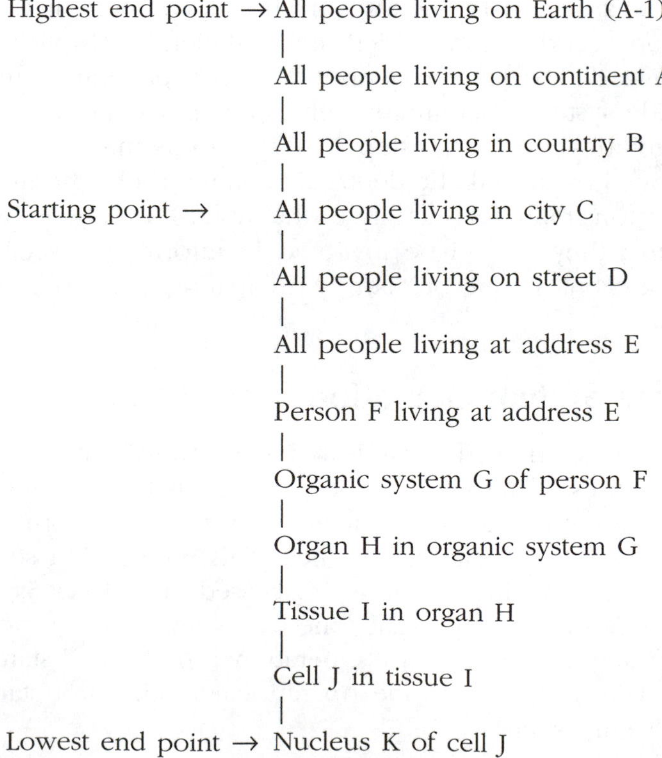

On a case-by-case basis, a determination is made about the level to which it is meaningful to carry the identification process, both upward and downward.

For example, epidemiological studies require a statistically significant group of people. Hence, items E–K, A-1, and A would not be considered meaningful.

Once the upper and lower limits of the system have been established, the system definition should be formally documented as shown in Exhibits 3 and 4. In this example, the boundaries of a radiation therapy system are being defined. The graphical system definition in Exhibit 3 helps establish which entities are inside and outside the system boundary. External entities may be optional or mandatory; hence, it is important to capture them. Often, but not always, links to external entities such as infrastructure systems will be through internal support entities. Some sources talk about unbounded systems, especially when discussing Internet applications or interaction between mission- or business-critical systems and infrastructure systems. The concept of an unbounded system is useful to denote the interaction and interdependency between systems. However, information security/IA activities must be focused on a system that has defined boundaries and distinguishes between internal and external entities.

The tabular system definition in Exhibit 4 captures a lower level of detail about the system and characterizes the entities. These two charts reinforce each other and promote a thorough system definition. The formal process of documenting the system definition ensures that entities are not left out or overlooked. Defining the boundaries of a system also helps to designate organizational responsibility for information security/IA activities. In this way, responsibility can be assigned to the organizational component that can carry out information security/IA activities most efficiently. Duplication of effort is also minimized. For large organizations with geographically dispersed enterprisewide systems, defining system boundaries and information security/IA responsibilities is a crucial step. The system definition should be reviewed and approved by all stakeholders. It is common today to automatically assign total responsibility for security to the system or network administrator. By all means, they should be involved in information security/IA activities and analyses, but as one of many participating stakeholders.

4.3 Characterize System Operation

Thus far, we have (1) determined what is being protected and why, and (2) defined the boundaries of the system. The next step is to characterize the system operation. A system operation characterization takes two forms: operational modes or states and operational profiles. This information serves as input to the vulnerability and threat analyses discussed in Chapter 5.

An operational mode or state represents one of several states or modes in which a system or system entity can exist. Operational modes and states may or may not be mutually exclusive. Some operational modes and states are common to most systems, such as:

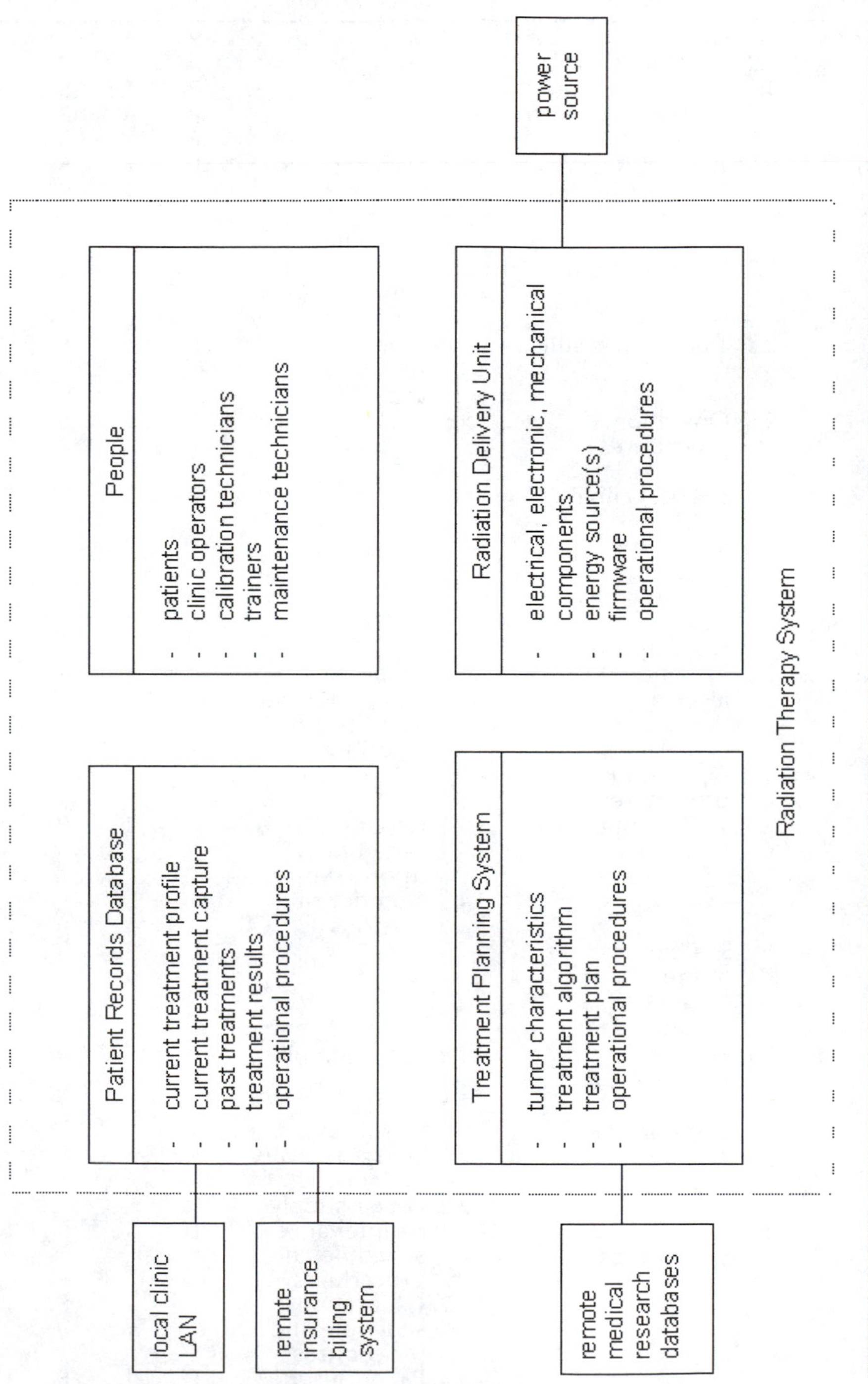

Exhibit 3 Sample High-Level System Definition

Exhibit 4 Sample High-Level System Definition

System: Radiation Therapy System as of: 20 March 2000

Subsystem	*Component*	*Subcomponent*	*L/P*	*A/I*	*P/S*	*D/S*
1. People	1.1 Patients	—	P	A	P	D
	1.2 Clinical operators	—	P	A	P	D
	1.3 Calibration staff	—	P	A	S	D
	1.4 Maintenance staff	—	P	A	S	D
	1.5 Training staff	—	P	A	S	D
2. Patient records DBMS	2.1 Treatment profile	2.x.1 Data records	L	I	S	D
	2.2 Current treatment capture	2.x.2 Record management capability	L	I	S	D
	2.3 Past treatments	2.x.3 Report generation capability	L	I	S	S
	2.4 Treatment results	2.x.4 Query/ response capability	L	I	S	D
	2.5 Operational procedures	2.x.5 Backup/archive capability	L	I	S	D
	**2.6 Local clinic LAN	—	P	I	S	D/S
	**2.7 Remote insurance/ billing system	—	L	I	S	D/S
3. Treatment planning system	3.1 Tumor characteristics	—	L	I	P	D/S
	3.2 Radiation therapy algorithm	3.2.1 Optional components or variations of algorithm	L	I	P	S
	3.3 Operational procedures	—	L	I	S	D/S
	3.4 Treatment plan x	3.4.1 Dosage 3.4.2 Targeting information 3.4.3 Number of sessions	L	I	P	D/S
	**3.5 Remote medical research databases	—	L	I	S	D/S
4. Radiation delivery system	4.1 Electrical, electronic, and mechanical components	4.1.x Subassemblies	P	I	P	S
	**4.2 Energy source(s)	4.2.1 Energy delivery system 4.2.2 Power supply	P	I	P	S
	4.3 Operational procedures	4.3.1 Maintenance schedule and procedures	L	I	S	D/S
		4.3.2 Calibration schedule and procedures	L	I	S	D/S
		4.3.3 Patient use procedures	L	I	P	D/S

Note: L/P, logical or physical entity; A/I, animate or inanimate entity; P/S, primary or support entity; D/S, dynamic or static; and **, external entity.

- Normal operations:
  - start-up
  - shutdown
  - reconfiguration
  - restart/reset
  - backup
  - standby
  - maintenance
  - decommission
  - perform normal system-specific functions

- Abnormal operations:
  - failure of system hardware
  - failure of system or application software
  - operator error
  - degraded mode operations
  - shutdown under abnormal conditions (e.g., an attack)

Operational modes and states can be further characterized by performance and reliability constraints, such as response times, processor load/capacity, bandwidth requirements, sequencing of state transitions, etc. The level and type of information that is useful is decided on a case-by-case basis.

Operational profiles are a direct corollary to operational modes and states. Operational profiles or scenarios represent the set of operations that a system can execute.[343] While operational modes and states only consider the inanimate entities of a system, operational profiles also take into account the human component. Operational profiles depict how humans interact with a system to accomplish tasks, through an analysis of operational scenarios, user views, and system events. They capture domain knowledge about how a system can be (and in reality is) used.

Operational profiles are often developed to support reliability engineering analyses. These operational profiles focus on end users. For information security/IA purposes, operational profiles should also be developed for maintenance staff, trainers, system administrators, super-users, testers, and potential intruders. Sometimes it is helpful to devise operational profiles graphically, using a tree notation. Operational profiles developed for reliability purposes often assign a probability that each action will be performed, or alternatively prorate a user's time among all possible activities. Whether or not this additional level of detail is useful is decided on a case-by-case basis.

Exhibit 5 presents a sample high-level system operational characterization, continuing the radiation therapy system example. The operational modes and states are listed. An indication is given as to whether or not a mode occurs before, after, or during another mode. Constraints associated with activating or transitioning to a mode and what agents can initiate a mode are identified. Next, operational profiles are developed by type of operator. In this example, there are three types of end users, maintenance staff, a system administrator, trainers, and potential intruders. The primary activities performed by each

Exhibit 5 Sample High-Level System Operation Characterization

System: Radiation Therapy System as of: 30 March 2000

I. Operational Modes and States

Mode/State	*Occurs Before*	*Occurs After*	*Occurs During*	*Constraints*	*Initiated by*
Normal Operations					
Start-up	All other modes	—	—	Power availability, absence of system fault	System administrator, maintenance staff
Shutdown	—	All other modes	—	System has been safed, records saved	System administrator, maintenance staff
Reconfiguration	Shutdown	Start-up	—	No end users active	System administrator, maintenance staff
Restart/reset	Shutdown	Start-up	—	No end users active	System administrator, maintenance staff
Backup	Shutdown	Start-up	—	No end users active	System administrator, maintenance staff
Standby	Shutdown	Start-up	—	No end users active	System administrator, maintenance staff
Maintenance	Shutdown	Start-up	—	No end users active	System administrator, maintenance staff
Decommission	Shutdown	Start-up	—	System has been safed, no end users active	System administrator, maintenance staff
Perform normal system-specific functions	Shutdown	Start-up	Varies	System resources are available	All except intruders
Abnormal Operations					
Failure of patient records database	Shutdown	Start-up	—	Failure must not cause safety and/or security violation	Operator error, system HW/SW fault
Failure of treatment planning system	Shutdown	Start-up	—	Failure must not cause safety and/or security violation	Operator error, system HW/SW fault

Exhibit 5 Sample High-Level System Operation Characterization (continued)

Mode/State	*Occurs Before*	*Occurs After*	*Occurs During*	*Constraints*	*Initiated by*
Failure of radiation treatment unit	Shutdown	Start-up	—	Failure must not cause safety violation	Operator error, system HW/SW fault
Degraded mode operations	Shutdown	Start-up, system failure	—	Criteria for transferring to degraded mode operations must be defined and met	System software and/or system administrator

II. Operational Profiles

Operator	*Primary Activities*	*Time Distribution*	*Sequencing, Timing, or Other Restrictions*
End user a	Logon	5%	Patient records must be initialized before any other transactions can take place
	Access, enter, store, forward patient records	90%	
	Logoff	5%	

operator are discerned. Time on the system is allocated among these activities. Any restrictions related to performing these activities are noted.

4.4 Ascertain What One Does and Does Not Have Control Over

The final activity in defining the boundaries of a system is to ascertain what system entities one does and does not have control over. This information is crucial input to the vulnerability and threat analyses discussed in Chapter 5.

The level of control the system owner has over each entity is determined using the system definition charts (Exhibits 3 and 4) as input. The level of control is determined for all identified internal and external entities. The level of detail for which control status is identified corresponds to the level of detail in the system definition charts. As shown in Exhibit 6, the first three columns of the system entity control analysis are taken directly from the system definition charts. Two new columns are added: control status and explanation. The control status records the degree of control or responsibility a system owner has over the accurate functioning of an entity. The control status can be either total, partial, or none. These terms are defined as follows:

- **Total control:** System owner has total control over and responsibility for an entity, the correctness and performance of its actions.
- **Partial control:** System owner shares control over and responsibility for an entity, the correctness and performance of its actions with one or more second parties, usually through a legal mechanism such as a contract.
- **None:** System owner has no control over or responsibility for an entity, but is dependent on the services it provides. One or more third parties have this responsibility and control. Infrastructure systems are a good example.

A brief rationale for the assigned control status is given in the explanation column. Most system owners are surprised to discover how few entities they have total control over. This discovery has a significant impact on the vulnerability and threat analyses, as well as the development of contingency plans.

4.5 Summary

The first component of an effective information security/IA program is to define the boundaries of a system. There are four activities involved in defining the boundaries of a system, as listed below and summarized in Exhibit 7:

- Determining what is being protected and why
- Identifying the system
- Characterizing system operation
- Ascertaining what one does and does not have control over

Exhibit 6 Sample High-Level System Entity Control Analysis

Subsystem	Component	Subcomponent	Control Status	Explanation
1. People	1.1 Patients	—	None	Patients are not employees or otherwise under contract to the clinic.
	1.2 Clinical operators	—	Total	All legitimate operators are clinic employees.
	1.3 Calibration staff	—	Partial	Calibration staff are under contract to the clinic.
	1.4 Maintenance staff	—	Partial	Maintenance staff are under contract to the clinic.
	1.5 Training staff	—	Partial	Trainers are under contract to the clinic.
2. Patient records DBMS	2.1 Treatment profile	2.x.1 Data records	Total	Clinic owns patient records.
	2.2 Current treatment capture	2.x.2 Record management capability	None	DBMS application software is provided and maintained by vendor.
	2.3 Past treatments	2.x.3 Report generation capability		
	2.4 Treatment results	2.x.4 Query/ response capability		
	2.5 Operational procedures	2.x.5 Backup/ archive capability	Partial	Clinic owns backup/archive records. Vendor owns software that generates backups.
	**2.6 Local clinic LAN	—	Partial	Clinic contracts for LAN services.
	**2.7 Remote insurance/ billing system	—	None	Third party maintains insurance/billing databases.

Exhibit 6 Sample High-Level System Entity Control Analysis (continued)

Subsystem	*Component*	*Subcomponent*	*Control Status*	*Explanation*
3. Treatment planning system	3.1 Tumor characteristics	—	Total	Clinic owns patient records.
	3.2 Radiation therapy algorithm	3.2.1 Optional components or variations of algorithm	Partial	Clinic implements specific instance of algorithm. Vendor owns application software.
	3.3 Operational procedures	—	Partial	Clinic is responsible for enforcing operational procedures. Vendor is responsible for developing operational procedures.
	3.4 Treatment plan x	3.4.1 Dosage 3.4.2 Targeting information 3.4.3 Number of sessions	Total	Clinic employee develops specific treatment plan.
	**3.5 Remote medical research databases	—	None	Clinic neither creates or maintains research databases; a third party does.
4. Radiation delivery system	4.1 Electrical, electronic, and mechanical components	4.1.x Subassemblies	None	Vendor has total responsibility.
	**4.2 Energy sources	4.2.1 Energy delivery system 4.2.2 Power supply	None	Power company and vendor have responsibility.
	4.3 Operational procedures	4.3.1 Maintenance schedule and procedures 4.3.2 Calibration schedule and procedures 4.3.3 Patient use procedures	Partial	Clinic is responsible for enforcing procedures. Vendor is responsible for developing accurate procedures.

Note: **, external entity.

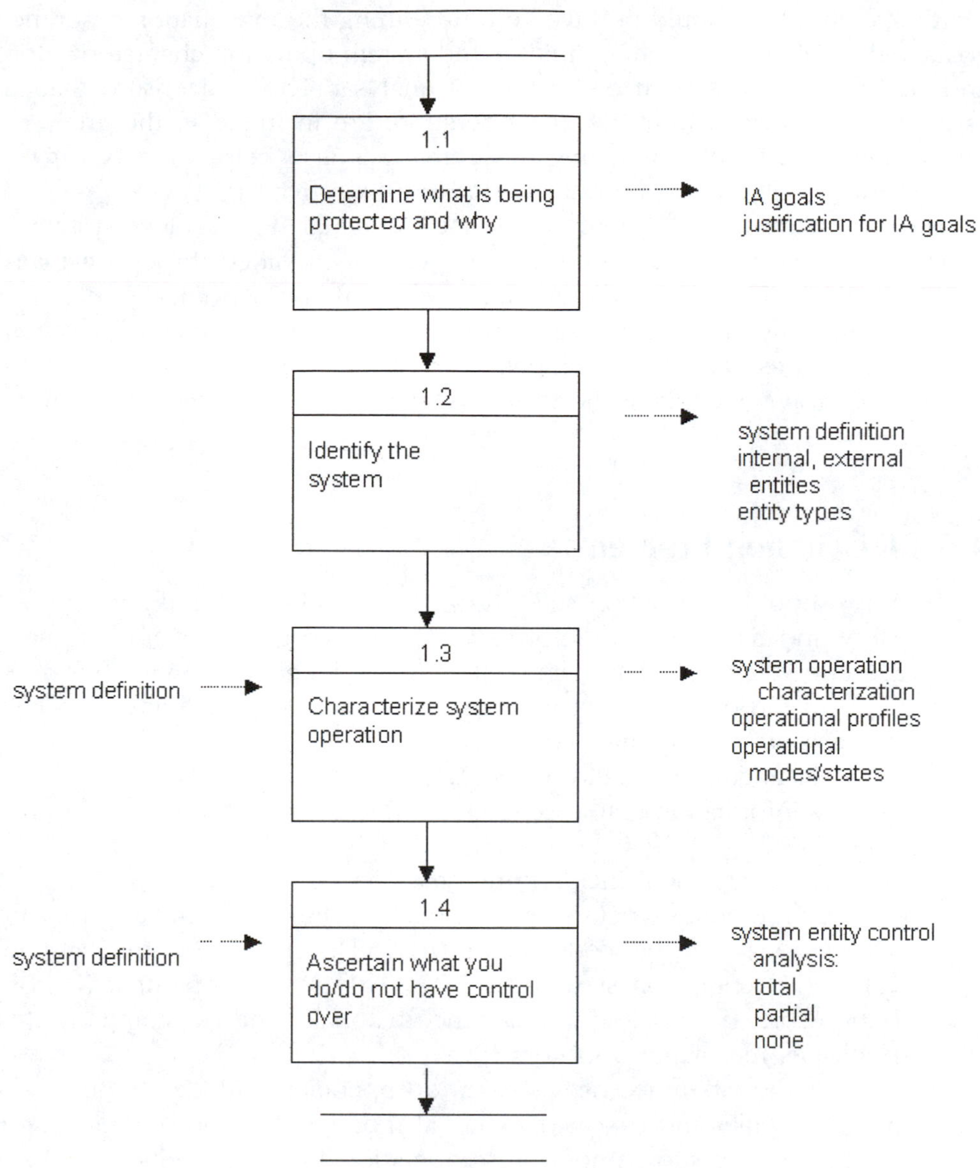

Exhibit 7 Summary of Activities Involved in Defining System Boundaries

This component is crucial; one must know what one is protecting and why before effective protection strategies can be developed. Expressed another way, an organized attack begins with a specific target in mind; hence, it is only logical that protection strategies should also be developed with specific targets in mind.

The results of the analyses conducted while defining the boundaries of a system provide essential input to other components of an information security/IA program. For example, the system definition, system operation characterization, and system entity control analysis are input to the vulnerability and threat analyses, while the information assurance goals are input to implementing threat control measures.

All stakeholders should be involved in defining the information assurance goals, developing the system definition and system operation characterization, and performing the system entity control analysis. This will ensure that all aspects of a system, its entities and operation, are included in the analyses. The formal process of conducting these analyses also helps identify organizational responsibility for information security/IA activities.

The boundaries of a system should be defined before a new system is deployed and whenever a system is enhanced or modified through a maintenance activity. The results of these analyses should be periodically reviewed to ensure that they remain accurate. In addition, the boundaries of a system are (re)defined as part of an accident/incident investigation.

Next, Chapter 5 explains how and why to conduct vulnerability/threat analyses.

4.6 Discussion Problems

1. Why should information security/IA activities be undertaken?
2. How and by whom are information assurance goals developed?
3. Describe the internal and external entities for a generic online business.
4. Why would or would not it be useful to include probability of occurrence in an operational profile?
5. What distinguishes quality IA goals?
6. How is information that is generated while defining the system boundaries used?
7. When is an accident/incident investigation performed?
8. Identify the entity type(s) for each of the following items and explain your rationale: (a) bar code reader, (b) DVD, (c) ISP, (d) e-mail system, (e) credit verification system, (f) WAN, (g) UPS, (h) antenna, (i) fiber optic cable, (j) user and maintenance manuals, and (k) company that publishes the manuals in item (j).
9. What is the difference between: (a) an operational mode and an operational profile; and (b) an operational mode and an operational state?
10. Why should or should not system operational characterizations include interaction with external entities?
11. What is the purpose of performing the system entity control analysis?
12. What commonalities exist between the development of protection strategies and an organized attack?
13. Discuss the fringe benefits of defining system boundaries.
14. Why is it possible for different people to define the boundaries of a system differently? How should these differences be resolved?

Chapter 5

Perform Vulnerability and Threat Analyses

This chapter describes the second component of an effective information security/IA program — performing vulnerability and threat analyses. Outputs from the previous component, defining the system boundaries, are used during the vulnerability and threat analyses. To conduct vulnerability and threat analyses, the following activities are performed:

- IA analysis techniques are selected and used.
- Vulnerabilities, their type, source, and severity are identified.
- Threats, their type, source, and likelihood are identified.
- Transaction paths, critical threat zones, and risk exposure are evaluated.

These activities are conducted in a sequential and iterative manner, as explained in the following discussion. Again, all stakeholders should be involved in these activities.

5.1 Definitions

On occasion, the terms "vulnerability" and "threat," "hazard," and "risk" are used interchangeably. These terms are related; however, they have distinct meanings. Vulnerability is defined as[362]:

> *a weakness in a system that can be exploited to violate the system's intended behavior relative to safety, security, reliability, availability, integrity, and so forth.*

Vulnerabilities are inherent in the design, operation, or operational environment of a system. They accrue as a result of errors of omission, errors of commission, and operational errors that occur during the life of a system.

Threat is defined as:[362]

> *the potential danger that a vulnerability may be exploited intentionally, triggered accidentally, or otherwise exercised.*

In other words, a vulnerability is a weakness that can be taken advantage of to violate system safety, reliability, and/or security, while a threat represents the potential to exploit that weakness.

Hazard is defined as:[56]

> *a source of potential harm or a situation with potential to harm.*

A hazard represents potential injury or death to humans, or damage or destruction to property or the environment.

Risk is defined as:[143]

> *(1) A combination of the likelihood of a hazard occurring and the severity of the consequences should it occur; (2) an expression of the possibility and impact of an unplanned event or series of events resulting in death, injury, occupational illness, damage to or loss of equipment or property, or damage to the environment in terms of potential severity and probability of occurrence.*

A hazard is an undesirable event with negative consequences, while risk represents the likelihood that the hazard will occur and the severity of the consequences thereof.

These four concepts are closely related, as shown in Exhibit 1. A vulnerability, or inherent weakness in a system, leads to one or more potential hazards. Hazards represent potential sources of harm or injury to individuals, property, or the environment. It is important to note that the harm or injury caused by a hazard may or may not be physical. For example, a system weakness that allows credit card information to be stolen results in financial harm. A hazard occurs when a threat is instantiated accidentally or intentionally. It is possible for more than one threat to trigger the same hazard. For example, the same hazard could be triggered accidentally or intentionally through different mechanisms. Risk is the composite of the likelihood of a threat being instantiated and the worst-case severity of the hazard consequences.

The use of the terms "severity" and "likelihood" also needs clarification. Severity characterizes the consequences of a potential hazard, the extent of harm or injury that could be inflicted. Following standard risk management practices, the worst-case scenario is evaluated. Most international standards[24,57,63,129–130,143] recognize four levels of severity:

- **Catastrophic:** fatalities or multiple severe injuries; loss of one or more major systems
- **Critical:** single fatality or severe injury; loss of a major system

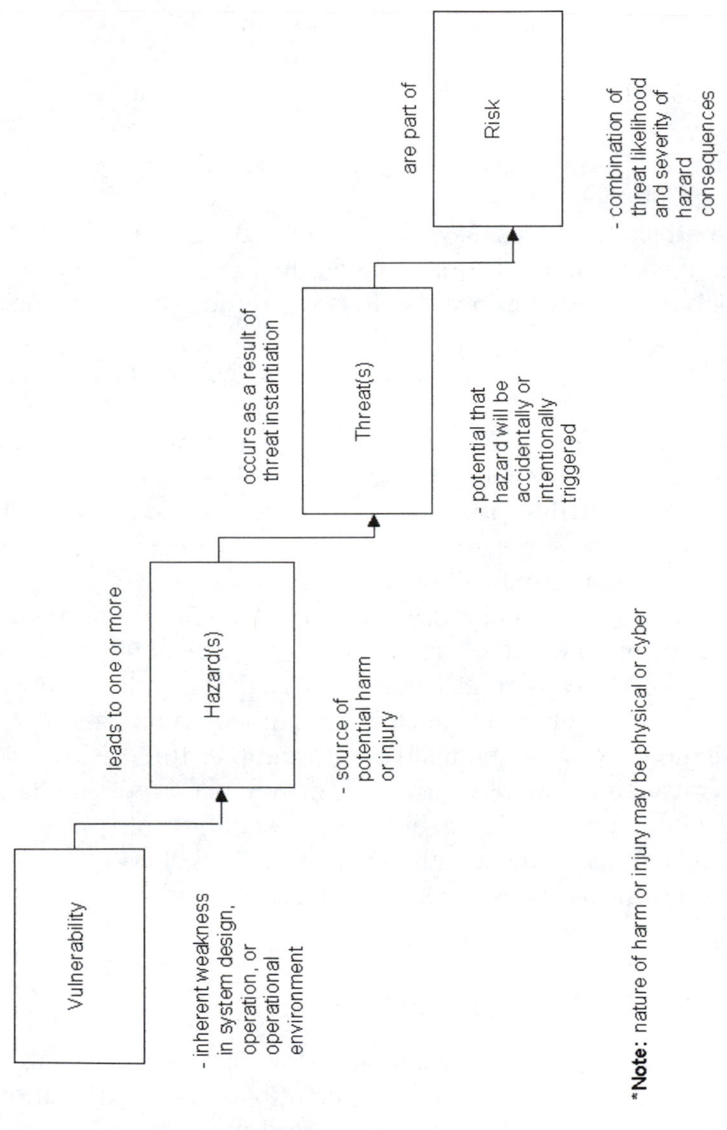

Exhibit 1 Interaction Between Vulnerabilities, Hazards, Threats, and Risk

- **Marginal:** minor injury; severe system(s) damage
- **Insignificant:** possible single minor injury; system damage

Remembering that injury refers to potential harm that may or may not be physical in nature, severity levels can be applied to the full range of IA safety, reliability, and security concerns.

Likelihood characterizes the probability of threat instantiation, that is, a hazard being effected. The most likely scenario is evaluated. Many international standards[24,57,63,129–130,143] recognize six levels of likelihood:

1. **Frequent:** likely to occur frequently; the hazard will be experienced continually (10^{-2})
2. **Probable:** will occur several times; the hazard can be expected to occur often (10^{-3})
3. **Occasional:** likely to occur several times over the life of the system (10^{-4})
4. **Remote**: likely to occur at some time during the life of the system (10^{-5})
5. **Improbable:** unlikely but possible to occur during the life of the system (10^{-6})
6. **Incredible:** extremely unlikely to occur during the life of the system (10^{-7})

Likelihood can be assessed qualitatively or quantitatively, depending on the nature of a system. Most international standards support both types of assessments. The quantitative assessment of random hardware failures is straightforward. Systematic software failures, operational errors, and malicious intentional acts lend themselves to qualitative assessments.

As noted earlier, risk is the composite of threat likelihood and the severity of the consequences of a potential hazard should a vulnerability be exploited. Risk is evaluated for every potential vulnerability/threat pair. Vulnerabilities are often exposed as a result of an unusual unplanned combination of events occurring simultaneously or sequentially. For example, three isolated events could each be considered low risk; however, if they occurred simultaneously or immediately after one another, a high-risk scenario could result. Consequently, a system risk assessment must evaluate the likelihood and severity of individual events and combinations of events.

5.2 Select/Use IA Analysis Techniques

A variety of analytical techniques are employed to discover vulnerabilities in the specification, design, implementation, operation, and operational environment of a system, the potential hazards associated with these vulnerabilities, and the threat that these hazards will be triggered accidentally or with malicious intent. Some vulnerabilities can be identified through informal brainstorming sessions. However, a comprehensive exploration of vulnerabilities, hazards, and threats requires the use of more formal techniques.

Exhibit 2 lists 19 current proven IA analysis techniques. A description of each technique is provided in Annex B, which discusses the purpose, benefits,

Exhibit 2 Information Assurance Analysis Techniques

I. IA Analysis Techniques	*C/R*	*Type*	*Life-Cycle Phase in which Technique is Used*		
			Concept	*Development*	*Operations*
Bayesian Belief networks (BBNs)[b]	C1	All	x	x	x
Cause consequence analysis[a,b]	R1/C1	SA, SE	x	x	x
Change impact analysis	C1	All		x	x
Common cause failure analysis[a]	C1	All	x	x	x
Develop operational profiles, formal scenario analysis	C1	All	x	x	x
Develop IA integrity case	C1	All	x	x	x
Event tree analysis[a,b]	R1/C1	All	x	x	x
Functional analysis	C1	SA, SE	x	x	x
Hazard analysis	C1	SA, SE	x	x	x
HAZOP studies[a,b]	C1	SA, SE	x	x	x
Highlighting requirements likely to change	C1	All	x		
Petri nets[a,b]	C1	SA, SE		x	x
Reliability block diagrams	C1	RE	x	x	x
Reliability prediction modeling	C1	RE	x	x	
Response time, memory, constraint analysis	C1	All		x	x
Software, system FMECA[a,b]	C1	All	x	x	x
Software, system FTA[a,b]	R1/C1	SA, SE	x	x	x
Sneak circuit analysis[a,b]	C1	SA, SE		x	x
Usability analysis	C1	SA, SE	x	x	x

[a] These techniques can also be used during verification of the effectiveness of threat control measures.

[b] These techniques can also be used during accident/incident investigations.

Source: Adapted from Hermann, D., *Software Safety and Reliability: Techniques, Approaches and Standards of Key Industrial Sectors,* IEEE Computer Society Press, 1999.

Legend for Exhibit 2

Column	*Code*	*Meaning*
Type	SA	Technique primarily supports safety engineering
	SE	Technique primarily supports security engineering
	RE	Technique primarily supports reliability engineering
	All	Technique supports a combination of safety, security, and reliability engineering
C/R	Cx	Groups of complementary techniques
	Rx	Groups of redundant techniques; only one of the redundant techniques should be used

and limitations of each technique, and provides pointers to references for further information.

IA analysis techniques uncover safety, reliability, and security vulnerabilities. Some IA analysis techniques focus on one aspect, such as safety; others evaluate a combination of safety, reliability, and security concerns, as noted in Chapter 3. The type column in Exhibit 2 indicates the primary focus of each technique.

IA analysis techniques are employed iteratively throughout the life of a system: when a new system concept is being defined, during design and development, when a system is deployed and becomes operational, and as part of system upgrades or other maintenance activities. IA analysis techniques are also undertaken following a system failure/compromise and as part of a periodic reassessment of IA strategies. Vulnerabilities, hazards, and threats are monitored throughout the life of a system because of the potential for new vulnerabilities, hazards, and threats to be introduced or the status of known vulnerabilities, hazards, or threats to change at any point. The last three columns in Exhibit 2 indicate the generic life-cycle phase(s) in which a technique can be used most effectively.

Not all techniques are used at one time or for one system. Rather, a complementary set of techniques are employed that: (1) evaluate all aspects of a system's design, operation, and operational environment; and (2) comprehensively assess safety, reliability, and security issues. The set of techniques employed will vary, depending on the life-cycle phase. The C/R column in Exhibit 2 identifies groups of complementary and redundant techniques.

After the IA analysis techniques have been selected and the phase(s) when they will be used identified, the next step is to train the team that will use the techniques. It is essential that all team members thoroughly understand how to use the techniques and correctly interpret the results obtained from using them. Again, it is imperative to have all stakeholders participate; not all stakeholders will perform the analysis, but they should participate and review the results. Exhibit 3 cites the IA analysis role of each technique.

A high-level example is developed next that illustrates how to identify vulnerabilities using the input from the system boundary definition (Chapter 4). Exhibit 4 summarizes this process. An online banking system is evaluated in this example.

Input from System Boundary Definition

1. IA goals:
   Protect the privacy and integrity of customer records from accidental or malicious intentional unauthorized disclosure, manipulation, alteration, abuse, corruption, and theft. Protect personal identifying information: name, address, phone number, e-mail address, account number, and fax number. Protect customer account balance and transaction information.

2. System entity definition:
   Internal: Web servers
   Local LAN, workstations, printers
   Bank employees
   External: Links to other financial systems
   Links to other financial institutions
   Customers, their workstations, and ISPs
   Telecommunications backbone
   Power, environmental controls
   Maintenance and vendor staff
3. System operation characterization:
   normal modes and states:

Online	Offline
Start-up	Shutdown
Application-specific functions:	Reconfiguration
Customer logon/logoff	Restart/reset
Check account balance	Backup
Move funds between accounts	Standby
Pay bills	Maintenance
Order stocks or insurance	Decommission
Check if transaction has cleared	
Open CD	
Process and post customer transactions	
Charge fees for online banking services	

   Operational profiles (developed for):
   Customers
   Bank employees
   System administrator
   Vendor and maintenance staff
   Potential intruders
4. System entity control analysis:
   Total control: Bank employees
   Partial control: Web servers
   Local LAN, workstations, printers
   Links to other financial systems
   Links to other financial institutions
   Maintenance and vendor staff
   None: Customers, their workstations, ISPs
   Potential intruders
   Power, environmental controls
   Telecommunications backbone, ISP

The set of IA analysis techniques corresponds to IA goals and system specifics. In this example, the IA goals concern protecting the privacy and integrity of customer records. The emphasis is on information security and reliability; no safety goals are stated. From these goals it can be inferred that

Exhibit 3 Analysis Role of IA Techniques

Analysis Technique	*IA Analysis Role*
Bayesian belief networks (BBNs)	Provide a methodology for reasoning about uncertainty as part of risk analysis and assessment.
Cause consequence analysis	Enhance IA integrity by identifying possible sequences of events that can lead to a system compromise or failure.
Change impact analysis	Analyze *a priori* the potential local and global effects of changing requirements, design, implementation, data structures, or interfaces on system performance, safety, reliability, and security; prevent errors from being introduced during enhancements or maintenance.
Common cause failure (CCF) analysis	Enhance IA integrity by identifying scenarios in which two or more failures or compromises occur as the result of a common design defect.
Develop operational profiles, formal scenario analysis	Identify operational profiles, capture domain knowledge about MWFs and MNWFs; understand human factors safety, reliability, and security concerns.
Develop IA integrity case	Collect, organize, analyze, and report information to prove that IA integrity requirements have been (or will be) achieved and maintained.
Event tree analysis	Enhance IA integrity by preventing defects through analysis of sequences of system events and operator actions that could lead to failures, compromises, or unstable states.
Functional analysis	Identify safety and security hazards associated with normal operations, degraded mode operations, incorrect usage, inadvertent operation, absence of function(s), and accidental and intentional human error.
Hazard analysis	Enhance IA integrity by identifying potential hazards associated with using a system so that appropriate mitigation features can be incorporated into the design and operational procedures.
HAZOP studies	Prevent potential hazards (accidental and intentional, physical and cyber) by capturing domain knowledge about operational environment, parameters, modes/states, etc. so that this information can be incorporated in the requirements, design, and operational procedures.
Highlighting requirements likely to change	Enhance the maintainability of threat control measures and IA integrity.
Petri nets	Identify potential deadlock, race, and nondeterministic conditions that could lead to a system compromise or failure.
Reliability block diagrams	Enhance IA integrity by identifying diagrammatically the set of events that must take place and the conditions that must be fulfilled for a system or task to execute correctly[69,131]; support initial reliability allocation, reliability estimates, and design optimization.

Exhibit 3 Analysis Role of IA Techniques (continued)

Analysis Technique	*IA Analysis Role*
Reliability prediction modeling	Predict future reliability of a software system.
Response time, memory, constraint analysis	Ensure that the operational system will meet all stated response time, memory, and other specified constraints under low, normal, and peak loading conditions.[333]
Software, system FMECA	Examine the effect of accidental and intentional, random and systematic failures on system behavior in general and IA integrity in particular.
Software, system FTA	Identify potential root causes of undesired system events (accidental and intentional) so that mitigating features can be incorporated into the design and operational procedures.
Sneak circuit analysis	Identify hidden unintended or unexpected hardware or software logic paths or control sequences that could inhibit desired system functions, initiate undesired system events, or cause incorrect timing and sequencing, leading to a system compromise or failure.
Usability analysis	Enhance operational IA integrity by ensuring that software is easy to use so that effort by human users to obtain the required service is minimal[18]; prevent induced or invited errors that could lead to a system failure/compromise.

the primary transactions involve the acquisition, manipulation, storage, retrieval, and display of information and that the system is data (text) intensive with active user involvement.

Next, the system entity definition is used to identify high-level potential failure points. Both internal and external entities are considered. Failure points represent potential attack points. In this example, that would include:

- Web server failures
- Local LAN, workstation, or printer failures
- Failure of links to other financial systems
- Failure of links to other financial institutions
- Telecommunications backbone or ISP failures
- Faulty power source or environmental controls
- User actions (customers, bank employees, maintenance or vendor staff, potential intruders)

Failure scenarios are postulated for each potential failure point, using the system operational characterization and entity control analysis as input. The intent is to premise all the ways in which an entity could fail or be induced to fail, that is, perform contrary to specified intended functionality. In other words, what could go wrong with a system? How could a system "break" or be broken? Failure scenarios include safety and security compromises, and

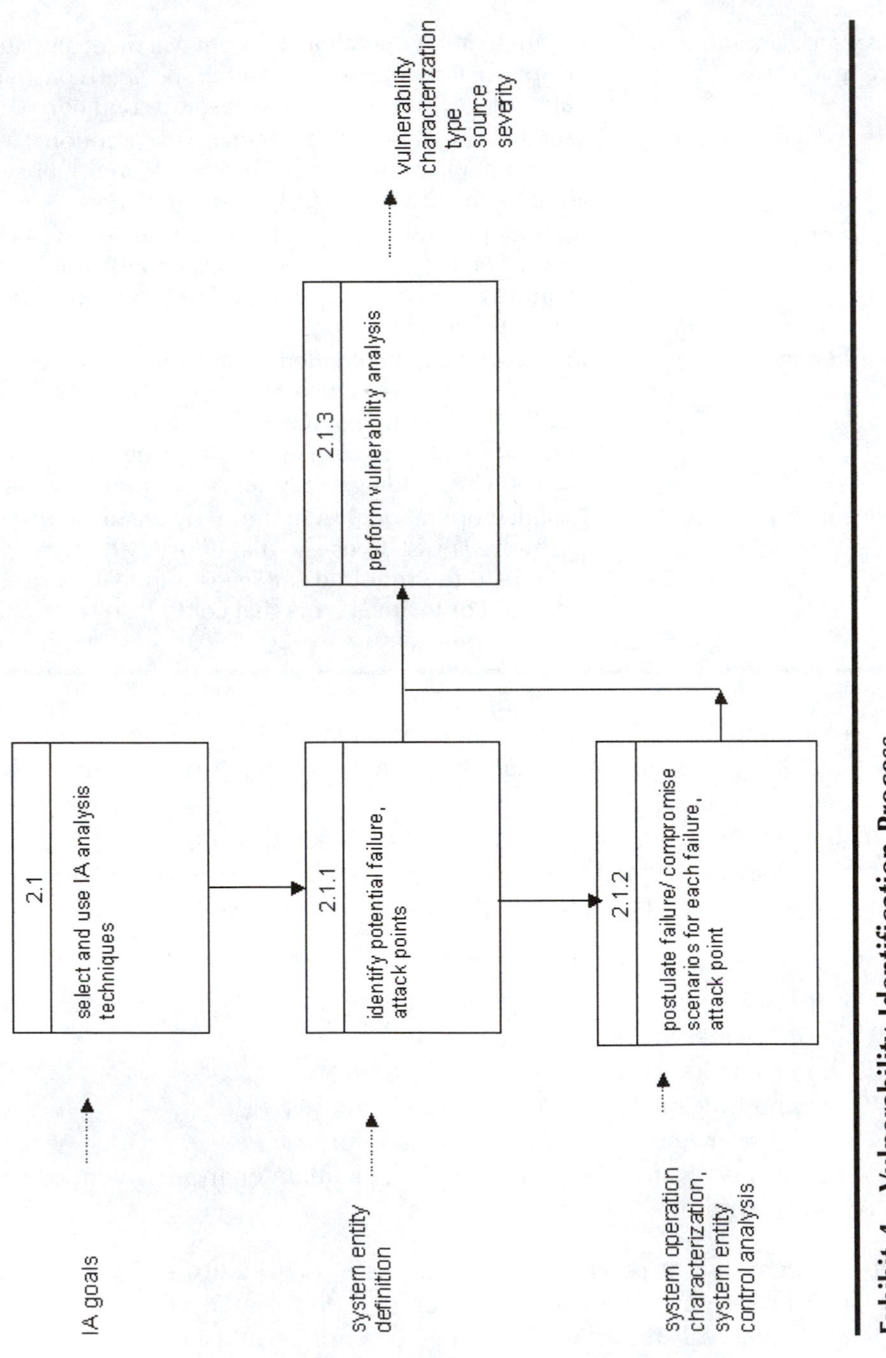

Exhibit 4 Vulnerability Identification Process

reliability degradation, in addition to the more well-known system unavailability, slowness, and crashes. Induced failures are the outcome of malicious intentional action. Other failures are the consequence of accidental errors or inaction during the specification, design, development, operation, or maintenance of a system.

In our example, failure scenarios are postulated for each of the seven potential failure points. For the sake of brevity, only the Web server failure scenarios are expanded. The Web server could fail or be induced to fail through a failure in the: server hardware, communications equipment and software, operating system, applications software, or DBMS. The server hardware could fail or be induced to fail through a fault/failure in: memory, the CPU, hard drive, power supply, back plane, bus, etc., as well as incorrect environmental controls or a faulty power source. The communications equipment and software could fail or be induced to fail through a fault/failure in the: gateway hardware and interfaces, communications protocols, routing table, etc. The Web server operating system could fail or be induced to fail through a fault/failure that: causes the system to become saturated, interferes with interrupt handling, corrupts the registry, causes buffer overflows, corrupts file and directory structures, overwrites user accounts and privileges, initiates conflicts between different software applications, etc. The web server application software could fail or be induced to fail through a fault/failure resulting from: functional errors, the inability to access the resources needed, erroneous command sequences, illegal data input, incompatibility with a new version of the server operating system or DBMS, etc. The server DBMS could fail or be induced to fail through a fault/failure which causes: data files to become corrupted, errors in query/retrieval functions, errors in display functions, errors when data is entered, modified, or deleted, etc. The crashing, slow operation, or unavailability of any of these five components also constitutes a failure scenario.

IA analysis techniques are used to further decompose failure scenarios to identify and characterize vulnerabilities. Exhibit 5 demonstrates the link between failure points, failure scenarios, and nine of the many potential vulnerabilities for the hypothetical high-level online banking example.

5.3 Identify Vulnerabilities, Their Type, Source, and Severity

IA vulnerabilities are classified three ways, as shown in Exhibit 6:

- The type of action that caused the vulnerability to manifest itself: accidental action (or inaction) or intentional malicious action or inaction
- The method by which the vulnerability is exploited: direct or indirect involvement on the part of the perpetrator
- The nature of the vulnerability or weakness: safety, reliability, security, or some combination thereof

A vulnerability may be the result of accidental or intentional human action. An accidental vulnerability is the result of an error of commission or an error

Exhibit 5 Correlation of Failure Points, Failure Scenarios, and Vulnerabilities

System: online banking

Failure Point	*Failure Scenario*	*Vulnerability*
Web server	Application software not protected	Little or no error detection/ correction or fault tolerance
Web server	Operating system saturated	If number of simultaneous users exceeds x, system becomes unstable and exhibits unpredictable behavior
Web server	DBMS data files corrupted	Data files can be accessed directly without going through DBMS applications software
Web server	Sporadic system shut down or unpredictable behavior	Server hardware subjected to extreme environmental conditions
User action	User authorizations not checked in order to speed up system response times; security compromised	End users and system administrator lack sufficient training, limited understanding of system security features and procedures
User action	Backups and archives generated sporadically or not at all; backups and archives not verified and are unreliable	Unsecure backups, archives
User action	Hardcopy printouts thrown in open trash bins; security compromised	Careless disposal of hardcopy printouts
User action	Portable equipment and storage media taken out of facility, occasionally lost or stolen; files from unknown/untrusted sources loaded onto system	No control over portable equipment or storage media
Web server	Conflicts between COTS applications cause unpredictable behavior; unauthorized user can access COTS applications	COTS components installed with default values, guest accounts, possible trap doors

of omission; that is, something was done wrong or not done during the specification, design, development, or operation of a system. Failing to specify illegal or incompatible system modes and states, so that the system is not prevented from entering them, is an example of a vulnerability that results from an error of omission. If the illegal and incompatible system modes and states were specified, but incorrectly, leaving the system unprotected, that would result in a vulnerability from an error of commission. As Lindquist and Jonsson[335] note:

> *Vulnerabilities may also be introduced by changes in the system environment or the way the system operates.*

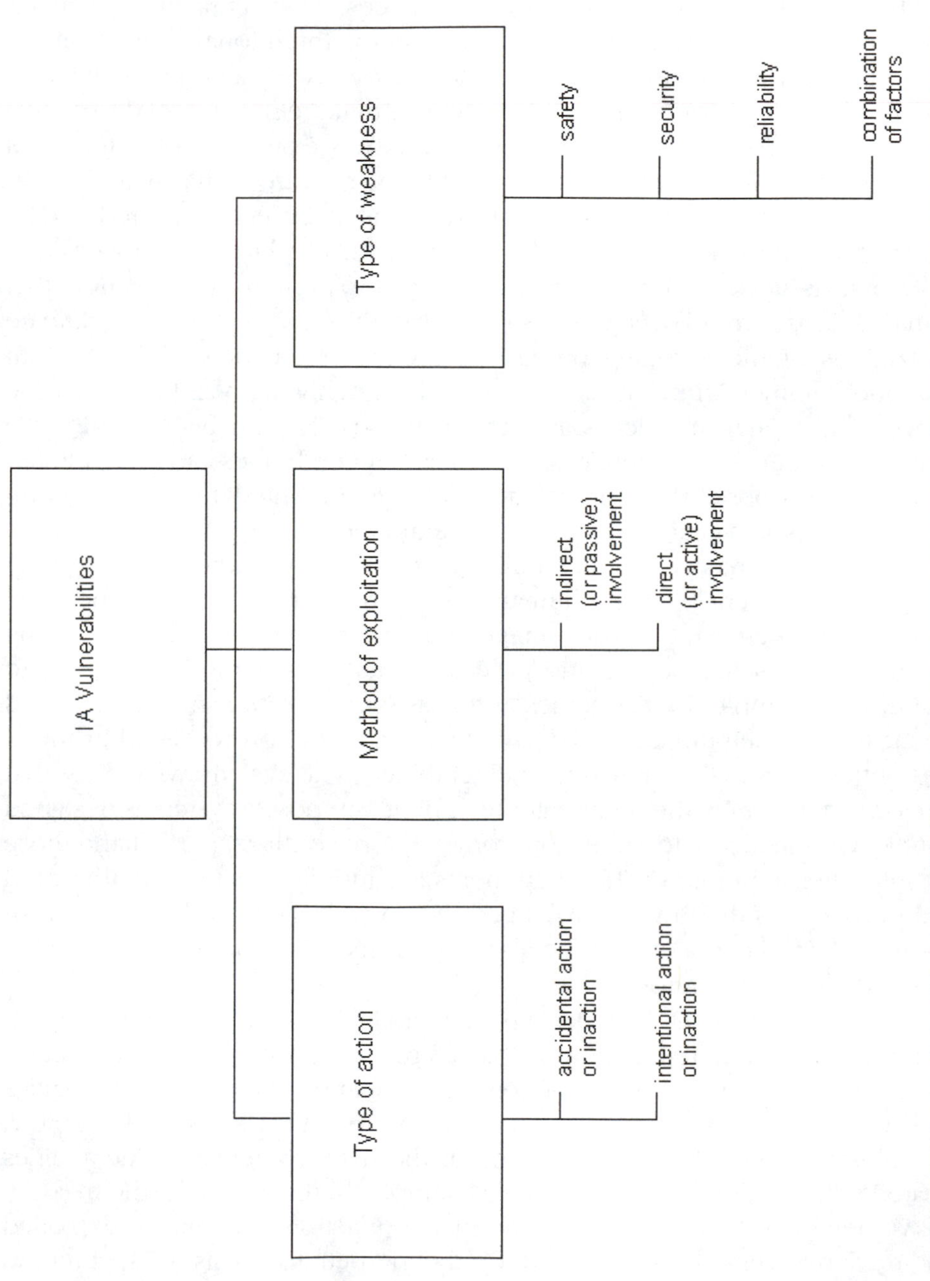

Exhibit 6 Classification of IA Vulnerabilities

As a result, the vulnerability analyses should be reviewed, updated, and revalidated frequently.

An intentional vulnerability is the result of preplanned action — something was done on purpose or deliberately not done. An intentional vulnerability allows features that control system integrity to be bypassed. Intentional vulnerabilities may be created for beneficial purposes, such as facilitating maintenance activities or remote diagnostics and help. Intentional vulnerabilities may be created for malicious purposes, such as allowing certain individuals or organizations to perform unauthorized actions that are illegal and destructive in nature. Trap doors and Trojan horses are two examples of intentional malicious vulnerabilities. A trap door is a hidden software or hardware mechanism that permits system protection mechanisms to be circumvented.[135] The inventor of the trap door is the only one who knows how to activate it. A Trojan horse is a computer program with an apparent useful function that contains additional (hidden) functions that surreptitiously exploit the legitimate authorizations of the invoking process to the detriment of security.[135] Both custom and commercial products should be thoroughly analyzed to detect the presence of potential trap doors and Trojan horses. The analysis should also determine whether or not intentional beneficial vulnerabilities can be exploited for malicious purposes. The prevalence of undocumented features in commercial products is a major source of vulnerabilities.

An indirect (or passive) vulnerability is a system weakness that can be exploited independent of direct human action on the part of the perpetrator. Most often, a perpetrator takes advantage of an indirect vulnerability by relying on the actions of other people and processes, that is, waiting for an error to be made. For example, if user names and passwords are transmitted or stored in the clear, a perpetrator does not have to exert any effort to decipher them.

In contrast, a direct (or active) vulnerability is a system weakness that requires direct action by the perpetrator to exploit. Suppose a system is designed without or with inadequate protection from memory conflicts, particularly those that result when multiple COTS components are installed. A perpetrator could initiate transactions that trigger prolonged memory conflicts and thereby crash the system. Exploitation of a vulnerability such as this requires direct action on the part of a perpetrator.

The third way to classify types of vulnerabilities is by the nature of the system weakness. A system might exhibit safety vulnerabilities, security vulnerabilities, reliability vulnerabilities, or some combination thereof. Vulnerabilities may be related; a security vulnerability may give rise to a safety vulnerability, etc. To illustrate, Exhibit 7 classifies nine of the many potential vulnerabilities associated with the online banking system example. In this example, the majority of the vulnerabilities were caused by accidental inaction and can be exploited by indirect involvement on the part of the perpetrator. This is a common situation. Online banking systems do not have safety concerns; consequently, the vulnerabilities are a mixture of security and reliability weaknesses.

A vulnerability may be present in hardware, software, communications equipment, operational procedures for end users, system administrators, and

Exhibit 7 Identification of Vulnerability Types

System: online banking

Vulnerability	*Vulnerability Type*		
	Type of Action	*Method of Exploitation*	*Type of Weakness*
Little or no error detection/ correction or fault tolerance	Accidental inaction	Indirect	Security, reliability
If number of simultaneous users exceeds x, system becomes unstable and exhibits unpredictable behavior	Accidental inaction	Indirect	Security, reliability
Data files can be accessed directly without going through DBMS applications front-end	Accidental inaction	Direct	Security
Suboptimal operational environment, sporadic system shutdown or unpredictable behavior	Accidental inaction and intentional action	Indirect	Security, reliability
End users and system administrator lack sufficient training, understanding of system security features and procedures	Accidental inaction	Indirect	Security
Unsecure backups, archives	Accidental inaction	Indirect	Security, reliability
Careless disposal of hardcopy printouts	Accidental inaction	Indirect	Security
No control over portable equipment or storage media	Accidental inaction	Direct	Security, reliability
COTS components installed with default values, guest accounts, possible trap doors	Accidental inaction and intentional action	Direct	Security, reliability

maintenance staff, and the operational environment. The source of a vulnerability refers to the point in time when the vulnerability was introduced into the system. Some concrete action was taken or left undone to manifest the vulnerability. Exhibit 8 identifies the source of the online banking system example vulnerabilities.

Next, the severity of the consequences of a hazard, resulting from a vulnerability being exploited, is estimated. As previously mentioned, there are four levels of severity: catastrophic, critical, marginal, and insignificant. The primary difference between catastrophic and critical hazards is that critical hazards affect one person/system, while catastrophic hazards affect multiple people/systems. As an example, Exhibit 9 assigns a severity to the potential worst-case hazard consequences for the nine online banking system vulnerabilities. Note that in some cases a range of severities is assigned.

COTS products represent a potential source of vulnerabilities for a variety of reasons, such as the prevalence of undocumented features and functionality,

Exhibit 8 Identification of Vulnerability Sources

System: online banking

Vulnerability	*Source of Vulnerability*
Little or no error detection/correction or fault tolerance	Failure to specify and implement requirements so that system remains in known safe and secure state at all times IA goals not defined
If number of simultaneous users exceeds x, system becomes unstable and exhibits unpredictable behavior	Failure to perform response time, memory, constraint analysis
Data files can be accessed directly without going through DBMS applications front-end	Limited/weak access control and authentication mechanisms
Suboptimal operational environment, sporadic system shutdown or unpredictable behavior	Failure to perform HAZOP studies Vendor recommendations for operational environment ignored or incorrect
End users and system administrator lack sufficient training, limited understanding of system security features and procedures	Failure to develop operational profiles and scenarios Inadequate operational procedures Poor planning and training prior to system deployment
Unsecure backups, archives	Inadequate operational procedures Physical security issues not considered
Careless disposal of hardcopy printouts	Inadequate operational procedures Physical security issues not considered
No control over portable equipment or storage media	Inadequate operational procedures Physical and operational security issues not considered
COTS components installed with default values, guest accounts, possible trap doors	Inadequate analysis of COTS vulnerabilities prior to installation Failure to confine COTS products

maintenance or diagnostic trapdoors, default settings, conflicts with other COTS products, etc. As Lindquist and Jonsson[335] state:

> *Any type of COTS component might have an impact on the overall system security, depending on how it is used in a system. Therefore, every type of COTS product could be security-related.*

Zhong and Edwards[446] cite specific vulnerabilities associated with unexpected/undocumented COTS behavior:

- The component may access unauthorized resources or services.
- The component may access a resource in an unauthorized way.
- The component may abuse authorized privileges.

Concerns about vulnerabilities inherent in COTS products are not limited to software; hardware is included as well. Given the emphasis on using COTS

Exhibit 9 Identification of Vulnerability Severity

System: online banking

Vulnerability	*Hazard Consequences*	*Severity*
Little or no error detection/ correction or fault tolerance	Transactions posted to wrong accounts; interest payable, interest due calculated incorrectly; automatic deposits and payments lost; etc.	Critical - catastrophic
If number of simultaneous users exceeds x, system becomes unstable and exhibits unpredictable behavior	Screens are displayed very slowly; wrong screens are displayed; screens are displayed in wrong sequence; customer A sees customer B's transaction; etc.	Marginal - critical
Data files can be accessed directly without going through DBMS applications front-end	Critical/sensitive data can be maliciously altered, deleted, copied, and/or stolen with ease.	Critical - catastrophic
Suboptimal operational environment, sporadic system shutdown or unpredictable behavior	Customers cannot access the system; system crashes in the middle of a transaction; partial posting of transactions.	Marginal
End users and system administrator lack sufficient training, limited understanding of system security features and procedures	System security features are routinely disabled and/or bypassed.	Critical - catastrophic
Unsecure backups, archives	Critical/sensitive data can be maliciously altered, deleted, copied, and/or stolen with ease.	Critical - catastrophic
Careless disposal of hardcopy printouts	Critical/sensitive data can be stolen, copied, and/or distributed.	Critical - catastrophic
No control over portable equipment or storage media	Critical/sensitive data and applications can be stolen, copied, altered, or given to a third party.	Critical
COTS components installed with default values, guest accounts, possible trap doors	COTS components perform incorrectly, however, error is not overtly obvious; system security authorizations can be bypassed for malicious purposes.	Critical

products to (supposedly) deploy systems faster and cheaper, the concern about COTS products is likely to increase in the future. The same holds true with regard to software reuse. Exhibit 10 summarizes potential hardware and software COTS vulnerabilities that may manifest themselves at any time during the life of a system.

Vulnerability analyses evaluate internal and external entities. Like most systems, Internet-based applications rely on external entities to accomplish their mission. Each external entity is a potential source of additional vulnerabilities. To illustrate, Bradley et al.[223] have identified several potential vulnerabilities associated with routers, including:

Exhibit 10 Potential COTS Vulnerabilities

1. Component design:
   - Inadvertently flawed component design
   - Intentionally flawed component design
   - Excessive component functionality
   - Open or widely spread component design
   - Insufficient or incorrect documentation
2. Component procurement:
   - Insufficient component validation
   - Delivery through insecure channel
3. Component integration:
   - Mismatch between product security levels
   - Insufficient understanding of integration requirements
4. System Internet connection:
   - Increased external exposure
   - Intrusion information and tools easily available
   - Executable content
   - Outward channel for stolen information
5. System use:
   - Unintended use
   - Insufficient understanding of functionality
6. System maintenance:
   - Insecure updating
   - Unexpected side effects
   - Maintenance of trap doors

Source: Summarized from U. Lindquist and E. Jonsson, *Computer,* 31(6), 60–66, 1998. With permission.

- Dropping packets
- Misrouting packets
- Intelligent network sinks cooperating to conceal evidence of dropping or misrouting packets
- Altering contents of a packet, message, or destination address, copying to other addresses
- Sending false topology/routing table updates to bypass good routers and target malicious routers
- Injecting bogus packets
- Inspecting packet contents

Note that this list is a combination of accidental and intentional malicious action.

It is essential that vulnerability analyses be performed because all systems have vulnerabilities. As Neumann[362] succinctly states, "There is never an absolute sense in which a system is secure or reliable." Identifying vulnerabilities is the first step along the road to determining threats and risk exposure. Without this first step, effective threat control measures cannot be implemented.

Vulnerabilities can exist in a system's hardware, software, communications equipment, operational procedures, and operational environment. Vulnerabilities can be related to system safety, reliability, and security. Vulnerabilities can result from accidental or malicious intentional action or inaction. Historically, the safety and reliability communities focused on accidental vulnerabilities, while the security community focused on malicious intentional vulnerabilities. Information security/IA brings these different perspectives together. As Jackson[304] notes:

> *Hazard analysis of potentially safety-critical systems has evolved on the assumptions that hardware suffers from wear and tear in normal use, that [software] logic contains accidental design errors made in good faith, and that all systems are subject to environmental occurrences. The notion of malicious interference or sabotage is not generally considered, but it puts a very different complexion on hazard analysis. … Malicious interference is normally the parallel province of security, and in some sectors, such as the nuclear sector, safety and security are inseparable.*

It is important to be thorough when performing vulnerability analyses; the effectiveness of the threat control measures depends on it. Certain kinds of vulnerabilities are often overlooked. For example, vulnerabilities related to inadvertently revealing data through ignorance, naivete, over-confidence, negligence, or other operational errors are often ignored.[357] This highlights the need to consider human factors and operational procedures when performing vulnerability analyses, not just hardware and software. Another category that is often overlooked is lateral hazards that result from vulnerabilities. Lateral hazards are unique to each system and are difficult to analyze. They generally result from an unusual unplanned combination of events, the composite of which has potential hazardous consequences. The following situation illustrates this concept. During the winter, a water pipe freezes in a high-rise condominium. The pipe bursts and floods several floors. Water seeps into the elevator shaft, causing it to malfunction. Water also leaks into the building's automatic fire alarm system, causing it to cease functioning. In this case, the vulnerability was a water pipe freezing and the hazard was water damage from a flood. However, the hazard (flood) caused other lateral hazards to occur: the elevator and automatic fire alarm malfunctions.

Vulnerabilities need to be not only identified, but also characterized according to type, source, and severity so that: (1) appropriate threat control measures can be developed, and (2) resources can be effectively applied to the most critical vulnerabilities. This is common sense because the weakest link in a system will be attacked. Exhibit 11 provides a system vulnerability characterization for the online banking example. A common misperception in the information security world is that most vulnerabilities are caused by intentional action and require direct exploitation. In contrast, in this example, 82 percent of the vulnerabilities are caused accidentally and can be exploited indirectly. Equally alarming is the fact that 56 percent of the vulnerabilities are catastrophic.

Exhibit 11 Vulnerability Characterization Summary: Online Banking System

as of date:______________

I. Vulnerability Type Summary

	Cause				*Exploitation*			
	Accidental		*Intentional*		*Indirect*		*Direct*	
Vulnerabilities	#	%	#	%	#	%	#	%
Safety	—		—		—		—	
Reliability	—		—		—		—	
Security	3	27%	—		2	18%	1	9%
Combination	6	55%	2	18%	6	55%	2	18%
Total	9	82%	2	18%	8	73%	3	27%

II. Vulnerability Source Summary

	Lack of Control				*Operational*				*System Error*			
	Internal Entity		*External Entity*		*Environment*		*Procedures*		*Specification*		*Design, Integration*	
Vulnerabilities	#	%	#	%	#	%	#	%	#	%	#	%
Safety	—		—		—		—		—		—	
Reliability	—		—		—		—		—		—	
Security	—		—		—		2	18%	—		1	9%
Combination	—		—		1	9%	2	18%	2	18%	3	27%
Total	—		—		1	9%	4	36.5%	2	18%	4	36.5%

III. Vulnerability Severity Summary

	Catastrophic		*Critical*		*Marginal*		*Insignificant*	
Vulnerabilities	#	%	#	%	#	%	#	%
Safety	—		—		—		—	
Reliability	—		—		—		—	
Security	3	33%	1	11%	—		—	
Combination	2	22%	2	22%	1	11%	—	
Total	5	56%	3	33%	1	11%	—	

Note: A vulnerability may have multiple causes and multiple exploitation methods; there is not a one-to-one correspondence. Similarly, a vulnerability may have multiple sources. Likewise, vulnerability severity can be expressed as a range (see Exhibit 5.9). In this case, the worst-case scenario is used to characterize the vulnerabilities.

5.4 Identify Threats, Their Type, Source, and Likelihood

Information security/IA threats are characterized in three ways, as shown in Exhibit 12:

- Type of action that can instantiate the threat
- Source of the action that can trigger the threat
- Likelihood of the threat occurring

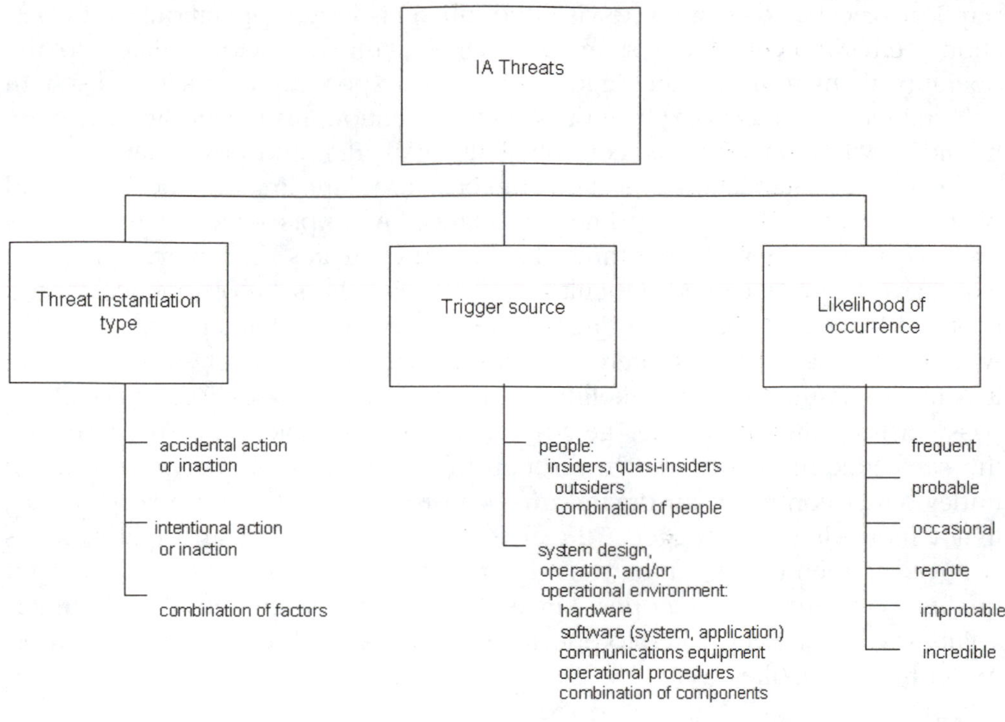

Exhibit 12 Characterization of IA Threats

It is important to maintain the distinction between vulnerabilities (weaknesses in system design, operation, or operational environment that can be exploited) and threats (the potential that a weakness will be exploited). Otherwise, the results from the vulnerability and threat analyses will be confusing and misleading.

A threat can be instantiated by accidental or intentional action or inaction, or a combination of factors. This is different than the accidental action or inaction and intentional action or inaction that are the cause of vulnerabilities. In that case, the accidental action or inaction, or intentional action or inaction, caused the vulnerability to be manifest. In this case, accidental action or inaction, or intentional action or inaction, will cause a threat to be instantiated and a vulnerability to be exploited. In addition, a combination of accidental and/or intentional action and/or inaction may trigger a threat. This is why it is important to analyze combinations of events and not just single events.

A threat can be triggered by people or system entities. People who can trigger a threat include insiders (people employed by an organization), quasi-insiders (people under contract to provide certain services to an organization), visitors (customers, vendors, meeting attendees, etc.), and outsiders (people who have no formal relationship to an organization). Most sources[248,277,362,399] consider insiders and quasi-insiders to be as likely a threat source as outsiders. Then again, insiders may collude with outsiders to trigger a threat. As Jajodia[305] points out, it may be difficult to determine if a threat is in fact originating from an insider or an outsider due to masquerading. Outsiders can include individuals, groups, or state-sponsored organizations whose goal is to inflict physical or cyber damage. Likewise, the inherent design, operation, and operational environment of a system can trigger a threat. Factors related to the operational environment can trigger a threat and expose an unanticipated system vulnerability, such as unexpected resource contention, insufficient temperature, humidity, vibration, and dust controls, EMC, EMI, RFI, and power faults.

Once the instantiation type and trigger source are known, the likelihood of a threat occurring is of prime importance. Attempts have been made to produce precise quantitative threat likelihood estimates[375]; however, they are expensive to produce and difficult to defend. For the sake of practicality and reasonableness, qualitative estimates are sufficient. The intent is to predict whether or not a threat is likely to occur; and if so, how likely. For example, it is fair to assume that the likelihood of virus, denial-of-service, IP spoofing, password stealing, and other generic attacks is probable if not frequent. By the same token, entities shown through the entity control analysis not to be under direct control of an organization can reasonably be assumed to be as, if not more, likely to trigger a threat than an entity under an organization's control. As mentioned earlier, most international standards[57,65,129,130,143] use six qualitative likelihood categories. Once assessed, threat likelihood and vulnerability severity are correlated to prioritize resources for threat control measures. As Rathmell[391] makes clear:

> *InfoSec resources can best be applied **only** if guided by a structured threat assessment process.*

Exhibit 13 identifies the threats for the nine vulnerabilities associated with the online banking system example. This process links the vulnerabilities and threats. As Rathmell[391] notes:

> *An overall risk assessment must overlay identified or potential threats onto the vulnerabilities of the defenders' information activities in order to determine the degree of risk and so plan responses.*

The threat instantiation type is determined for each vulnerability in the first column. It can be accidental action, accidental inaction, intentional action, intentional inaction, or a combination of factors. For example, the threat instantiation type for Vulnerabilities 2 and 5 is a combination of factors. The threat trigger source for each vulnerability is fixed in the second column. The trigger source can be various groups of people, other system entities, or a combination of people and system entities, as cited for Vulnerability 2. The likelihood of the threat occurring is estimated in column three. Following standard risk management practices, likelihood estimates are developed for worst-case scenarios. Denning[248] and Rathmell[391] observe that threat likelihood is a dynamic index because it results from a combination of capability, motive, and resources available. Hence, likelihood estimates should be reviewed, updated, and revalidated frequently.

Exhibit 14 presents the system threat characterization for the online banking example. The majority of the threats are intentionally instantiated (56 percent)

Exhibit 13 Threat Identification: Online Banking System

as of date:____________

Vulnerability	*Instantiation Type*	*Trigger Source*	*Likelihood of Occurrence*
1. Little or no error detection/ correction or fault tolerance	Accidental inaction	System design: system will corrupt itself	Frequent
2. If number of simultaneous users exceeds x, system becomes unstable and exhibits unpredictable behavior	Accidental or intentional action	System design: system will corrupt itself (accidental) People: insiders or outsiders who become aware of this design flaw may purposely exploit it (intentional)	Probable Occasional
3. Data files can be accessed directly without going through DBMS applications front-end	Intentional action	People: insiders or outsiders who become aware of this design flaw may purposely exploit it	Occasional
4. Suboptimal operational environment, sporadic system shutdown or unpredictable behavior	Accidental inaction	System design: system will corrupt itself	Occasional
5. End users and system administrator lack sufficient training, limited understanding of system security features and procedures	Accidental or intentional action	People: insiders, by not understanding or following security procedures, create opportunities for outsiders to trigger more serious threats	Probable
6. Unsecure backups, archives	Intentional action	People: insiders or outsiders who become aware of this operational weakness may purposely exploit it	Occasional
7. Careless disposal of hardcopy printouts	Intentional action	People: insiders or outsiders who become aware of this operational weakness may purposely exploit it	Occasional
8. No control over portable equipment or storage media	Intentional action	People: insiders, or insiders colluding with outsiders, could purposely exploit this operational weakness	Occasional
9. COTS components installed with default values, guest accounts, possible trap doors	Intentional action	People: system components create the vulnerability, but it takes deliberate action on the part of insiders or outsiders to exploit it	Occasional

Exhibit 14 Threat Characterization Summary: Online Banking System

as of date:____________

I. Threat Instantiation Type Summary

	Accidental		*Intentional*		*Combination*	
Threats	#	%	#	%	#	%
Safety	—		—		—	
Reliability	—		—		—	
Security	—		2	22%	1	11%
Combination	2	22%	3	33%	1	11%
Total	2	22%	5	56%	2	22%

I. Threat Trigger Source Summary

	People		*Systems*		*Combination*	
Threats	#	%	#	%	#	%
Safety	—		—		—	
Reliability	—		—		—	
Security	3	33%	—		—	
Combination	3	33%	2	22%	1	11%
Total	6	67%	2	22%	1	11%

III. Threat Likelihood Summary

	Frequent		*Probable*		*Occasional*		*Remote*		*Improbable*		*Incredible*	
Threats	#	%	#	%	#	%	#	%	#	%	#	%
Safety	—		—		—		—		—		—	
Reliability	—		—		—		—		—		—	
Security	—		1	11%	2	22%	—		—		—	
Combination	1	11%	1	11%	4	45%	—		—		—	
Total	1	11%	2	22%	6	67%	—		—		—	

and triggered by people (67 percent). However, that does not mean that the other ~30 percent of the threats should be ignored, that is, those that are instantiated accidentally or triggered by inherent flaws in a system design, operation, or operational environment.

Exhibit 15 depicts the initial correlation of vulnerability severity and threat likelihood for the online banking example. Using this information, priorities can be established for threat control measures. One possible grouping would be:

- High priority: vulnerabilities 1, 3, 5, 6, 7
- Medium priority: vulnerabilities 2, 8, 9
- Low priority: vulnerability 4

Priorities are decided on a case by case basis, taking into account a variety of parameters such as: laws and regulations, liability and other legal concerns,

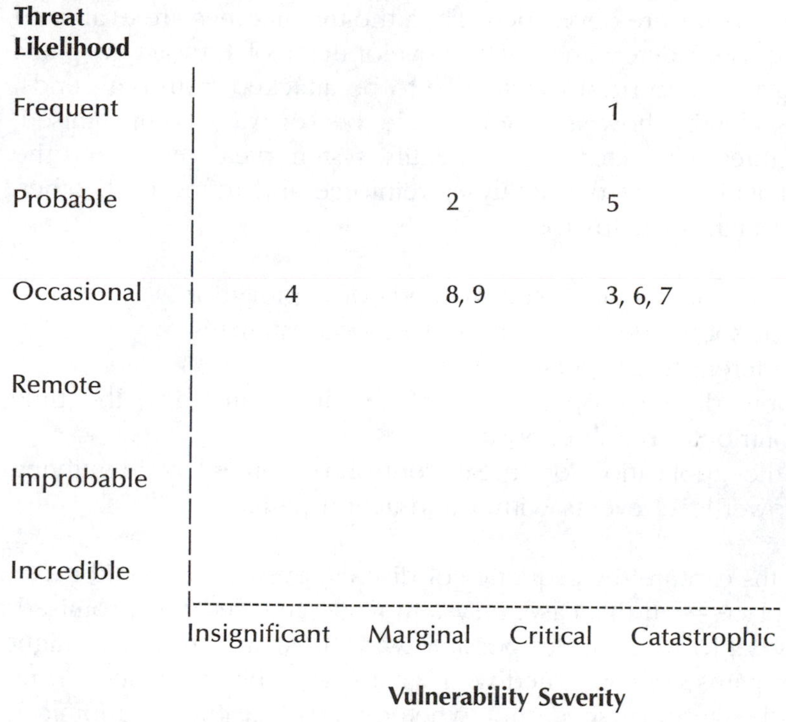

Exhibit 15 Correlation of Threat Likelihood and Vulnerability Severity to Prioritize Threat Control Measures. *Note:* numbers shown on the graph represent the vulnerability number.

organizational goals and ethics, and of course cost and schedule. A decision could be made not to do anything about vulnerabilities that are of marginal severity or lower in one instance. In another situation, a decision may be made that all (known) vulnerabilities must be eliminated or mitigated to the extent that they become insignificant.

5.5 Evaluate Transaction Paths, Threat Zones, and Risk Exposure

For the hypothetical high-level online banking example: (1) vulnerabilities, their type, source, and severity have been identified; (2) threats, their type, source, and likelihood have been determined; and (3) the vulnerability severity and threat likelihood have been correlated to prioritize threat control measures. The next step is to implement the threat control measures, right? For a very simplistic system perhaps. However, in the real world, systems are complex and as a result there are more parameters to consider. Hence, the threat and vulnerability analyses need to be refined; otherwise, a lot of the time and resources spent on threat control measures could be wasted. Consequently, the next step is to ascertain all logically possible combinations of discrete activities that could cause a system to be compromised; in other words, potential transaction paths are developed. Then the threat zones are evaluated and initial risk exposure determined. The development of transaction paths permits the information security/IA challenge to be attacked from both ends. Transaction paths identify how a system could be (or was) compromised. Vulnerability and threat characterizations identify system weaknesses and the potential for exploitation. The two analyses reinforce and refine each other. This extra level of analysis helps to:

- Uncover new vulnerabilities and methods of exploitation
- Refine threat source definitions and likelihood estimates
- Examine different threat perspectives
- Evaluate how different operational modes and states and the time element contribute to risk exposure
- Optimize the application of threat control resources by identifying common lower-level events within transaction paths

Transaction paths capture the sequence of discrete events that could cause an event to take place — in this case, a system to be attacked/compromised. Transaction paths depict all logically possible ways in which an event might occur. Transaction paths are concerned with what is logically possible — how something could be accomplished, not whether it is feasible, economical, probable, etc. That aspect of the analysis comes later. As Sherlock Holmes repeatedly reminds Dr. Watson, "When the possible has been eliminated, consider the impossible." The rationale is that what is often considered impossible is not really impossible, but rather improbable, like an unusual combination of events. Rabbi Levi Shem Tov expressed the same idea in a different manner, "Persistence is what makes the impossible possible, the possible probable, and the probable definite."

All possible paths are shown in one diagram. Each discrete event is numbered hierarchically. An individual path represents a unique route from the top event to a bottom event. Logic symbols define the relationship between alternative events. Paths are developed to the level to which it is meaningful to carry the analysis. As explained in Chapter 8, transaction paths can also be developed *a posteriori* to reconstruct how an accident/incident occurred.

To illustrate, potential transaction paths that could lead to the compromise of a hypothetical air traffic control (ATC) system will be developed. First, the boundaries of the system are defined. As shown in Exhibit 16, the three main system entities are the aircraft/pilot, radar, and ATC system/controller. At a high level, the logical operation of the ATC system can be summarized as follows. All aircraft in airspace x continuously send a location signal that is monitored by radar x. The radar links the location information to specific aircraft and forwards it to the ATC system. The ATC system maintains real-time information about the location of airborne aircraft, aircraft on the ground, status of runways, taxiways, and gates, and projected flight plans and schedules. At the same time, voice communication takes place between the pilot and the assigned air traffic controller. Depending on the size of an airport and the volume of traffic, the responsibility for flights may be distributed

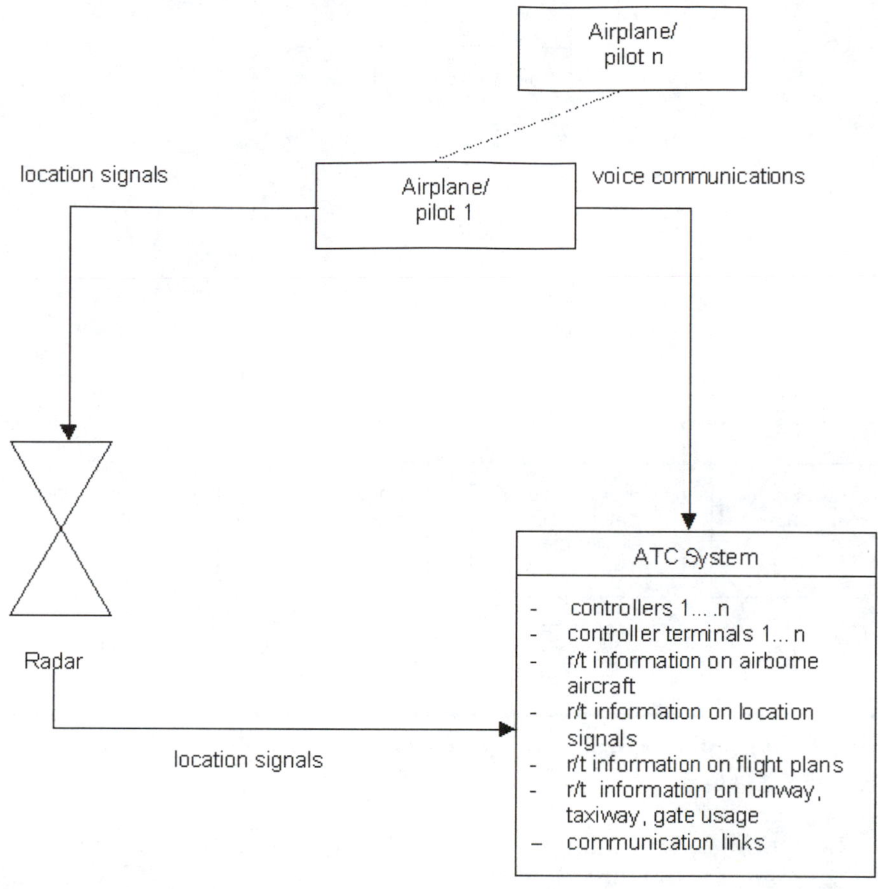

Exhibit 16 High-Level Depiction of the Logical Operation of an ATC System

among several air traffic controllers or assigned to a single person. The operation of this system depends on several assumptions, including:

- The pilot assumes that he or she is communicating with the real air traffic controller.
- The air traffic controller assumes that he or she is communicating with the real pilot.
- The radar assumes that the signal is coming from the identified aircraft.
- The ATC system assumes the signal received is from radar x.

Exhibits 17 through 25 illustrate the potential transaction paths that could lead to a compromise of the hypothetical ATC system example. At the first level, there are four possible ways in which the hypothetical ATC system could be compromised (Exhibit 17):

- Tampering with communication from the radar to the ATC system
- Tampering with voice communications between the ATC controller and pilot

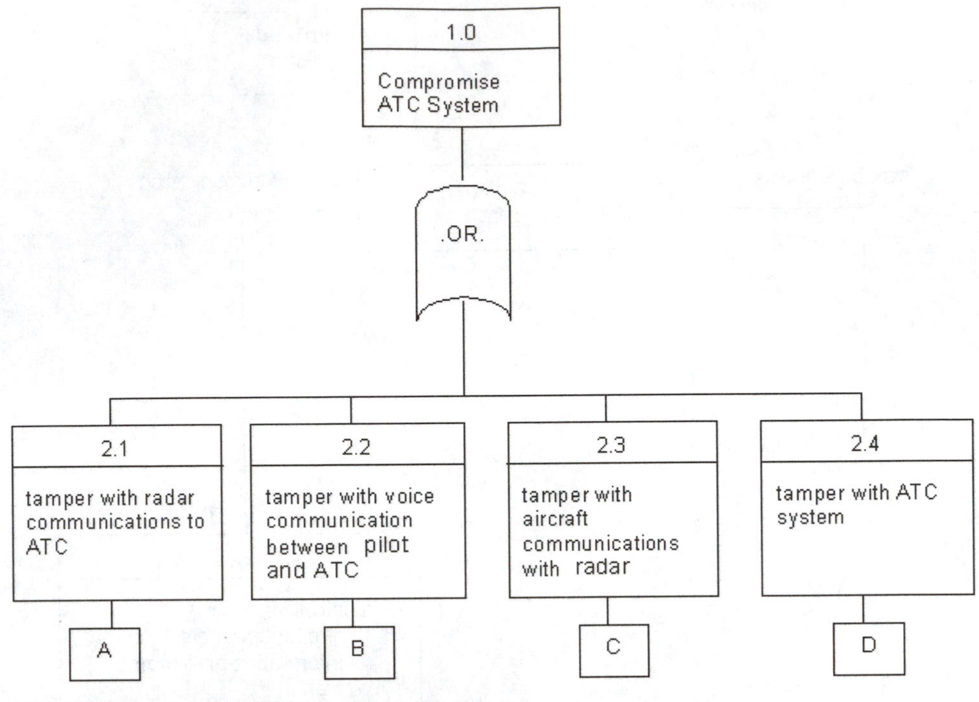

Exhibit 17 Potential Transaction Paths Leading to the Compromise of a Hypothetical ATC System

- Tampering with communication from the aircraft to the radar
- Tampering with the ATC system itself

Continuing with the path, 1.0 ← A, one sees that there are five possible ways to tamper with communication from the radar to the ATC system (Exhibit 18):

- The frequency of the signal sent from the radar could be shifted, so that the ATC does not receive it — it expects a different frequency signal.
- The radar signal could be jammed so that the ATC system cannot receive it.
- The radar signal transmitter could be disabled. (This could be done quite subtly so that it appears that the radar is transmitting normally when in fact it is not.)
- The ATC radar signal receiver could be disabled.
- The signal from the radar could be intercepted and retransmitted.

Note that similar events could lead to the compromise of the ATC system if paths 1.0 ← B or 1.0 ← C were followed (see Exhibits 19 and 20).

Continue down the path 1.0 ← 2.1.5, assuming that the radar signal is intercepted and retransmitted. There are seven ways this could be accomplished (Exhibit 22):

- The signal or message could be erroneously repeated.
- All or part of the signal or message could be deleted.

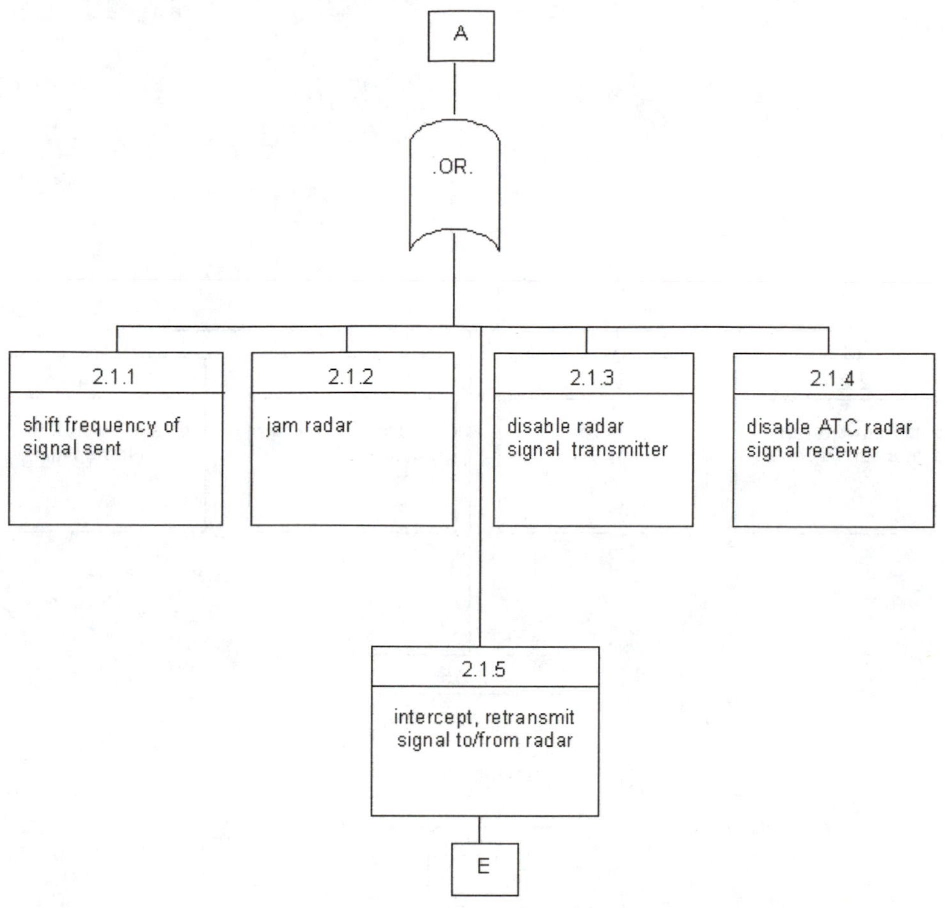

Exhibit 18 Potential Transaction Paths Leading to the Compromise of a Hypothetical ATC System (continued)

- A bogus signal or message could be transmitted.
- Messages or signals could be sent in the wrong order.
- Transmission of the message or signal could be delayed such that the information is no longer real-time.
- The contents or origin of a message could be falsified.
- The message or signal could be made unintelligible.

If instead, the ATC system itself were the target of an attack, there are three ways in which it could be compromised (Exhibit 21):

- The controller terminals could be corrupted.
- The ATC DBMS* could be corrupted.
- Communication between the controller terminals and the ATC DBMS could be corrupted.

* Note that, for the most part, ATC systems only process real-time data; hence, a classical DBMS is not used. The term "DBMS" is used in this example only to refer to a logical grouping of data.

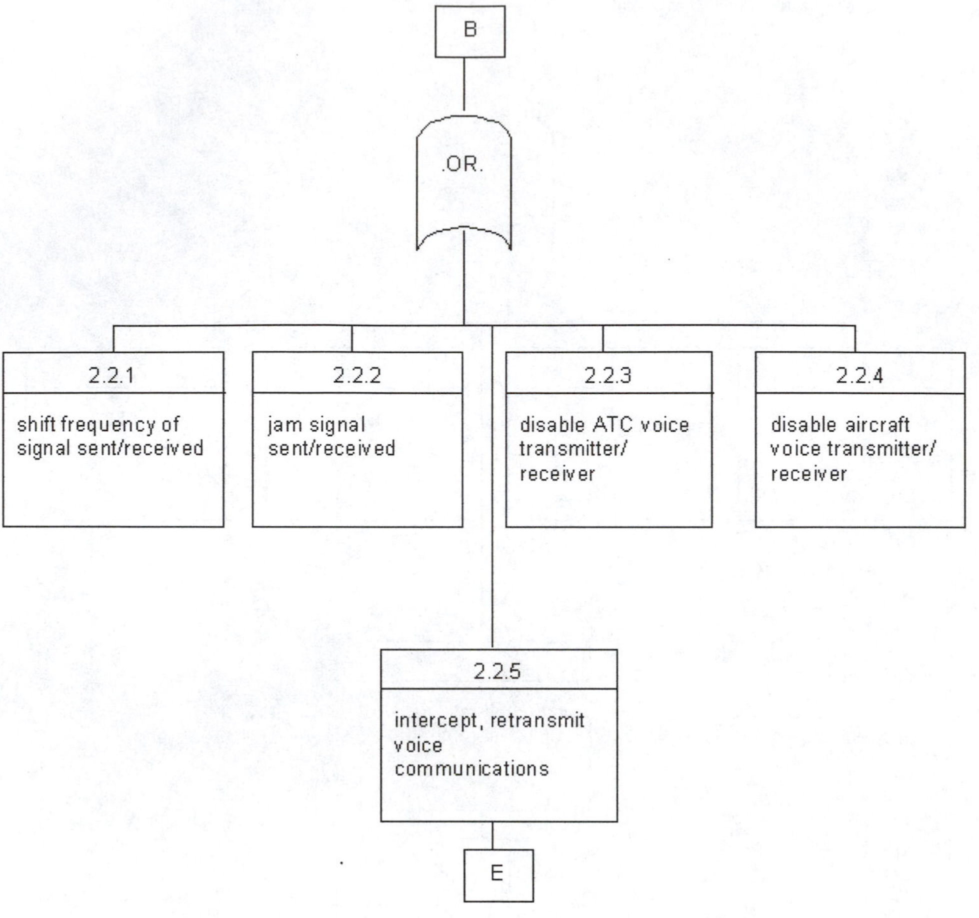

Exhibit 19 Potential Transaction Paths Leading to the Compromise of a Hypothetical ATC System (continued)

The controller terminal could be corrupted by (Exhibit 23):

- Causing the screen to freeze temporarily or permanently
- Displaying duplicate data
- Deleting some data points
- Causing the screen to go blank temporarily or permanently
- Inserting bogus data points
- Delaying the screen refresh showing new data points
- Displaying information for terminal x_1 on terminal x_n, in the case of multiple air traffic controllers
- Crashing the air traffic control terminal

The ATC DBMS could be corrupted by (Exhibit 24):

- Adding bogus data to the DBMS
- Deleting legitimate data from the DBMS
- Modifying legitimate data from the DBMS

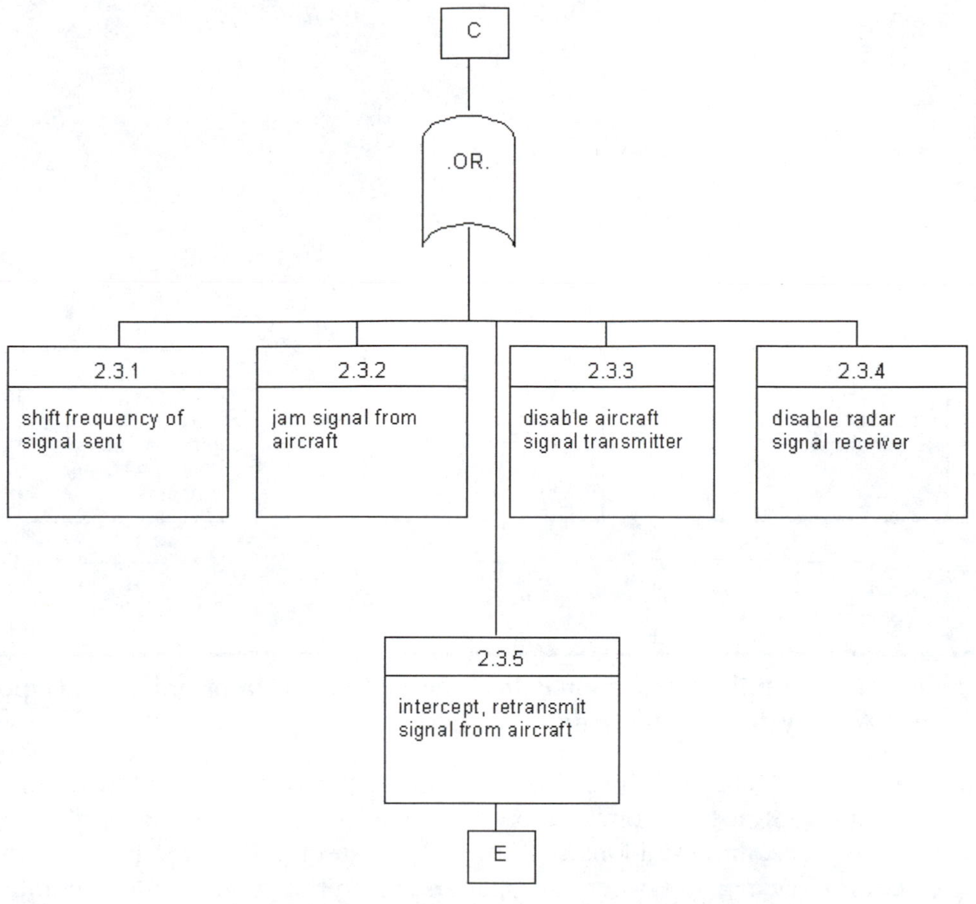

Exhibit 20 Potential Transaction Paths Leading to the Compromise of a Hypothetical ATC System (continued)

- Duplicating data in the DBMS
- Restoring old data so that it overwrites current information
- Scrambling pointers or indices used to access data
- Making the data unintelligible

Communication between the ATC DBMS and terminals could be corrupted by (Exhibit 25):

- Sending wrong information to the ATC terminals
- Sending information to the ATC terminals too early, too late, or in the wrong sequence
- Not sending or withholding information
- Sending information to the wrong terminal(s)
- Crashing the communications links between the DBMS and terminals

There are 61 unique paths in this example; that is, 61 different ways in which the hypothetical ATC system could be compromised. And this is not

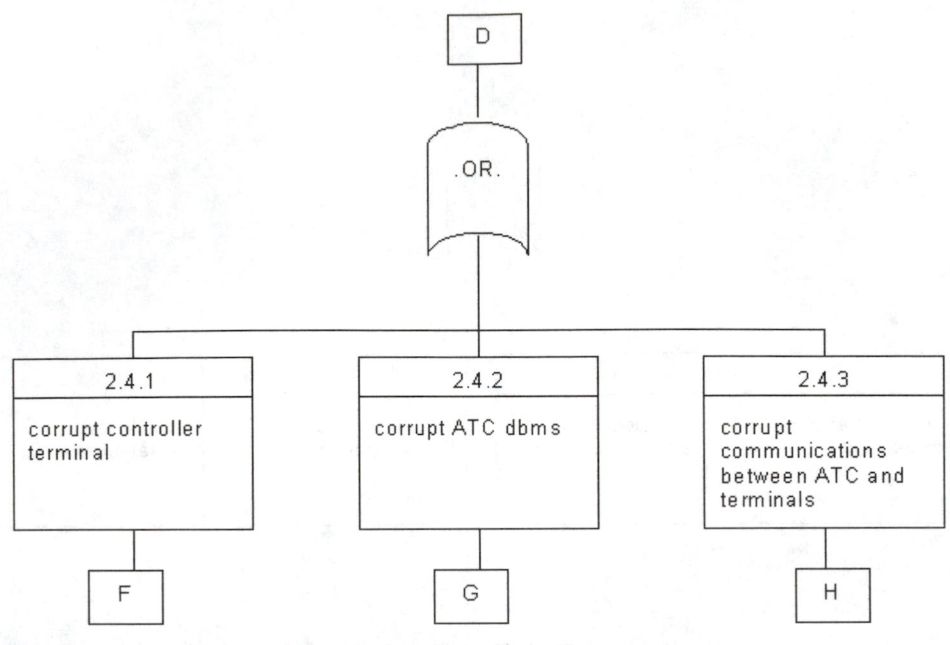

Exhibit 21 Potential Transaction Paths Leading to the Compromise of a Hypothetical ATC System (continued)

an exhaustive example. These 61 are single paths that could lead to a compromise. Suppose a combination of events occurred, such as tampering with the radar communications with the ATC system and tampering with the voice communications between the pilot and air traffic controller. The number of potential compromise paths increases and, most likely, the subtlety of the compromise increases as well.

As shown in this example, a transaction path and compromise may be overt or subtle. The fact that a signal is jammed is quite noticeable, while signal interception, modification, and retransmission may not be. In some cases, the compromise may be so subtle that it goes unnoticed until it is too late.[248] The transaction path chosen will vary, depending on opportunity and intent.[248,391] In this case, the intent could be to disrupt a single flight, an entire airport, or an entire geographical area.

Transaction paths can also be depicted graphically through the use of event trees. Bott of Los Alamos National Laboratories has developed a model that combines event trees and quantitative probabilistic risk assessment (PRA) to analyze potential system compromise paths from insiders and visitors. This approach consists of five steps[220]:

1. Potential compromise paths (discrete event sequences) are identified.
2. Potential compromise paths are grouped.
3. A probability model is developed for each group using historical experience and expert judgment.
4. The probability of occurrence is calculated for each potential compromise path group.

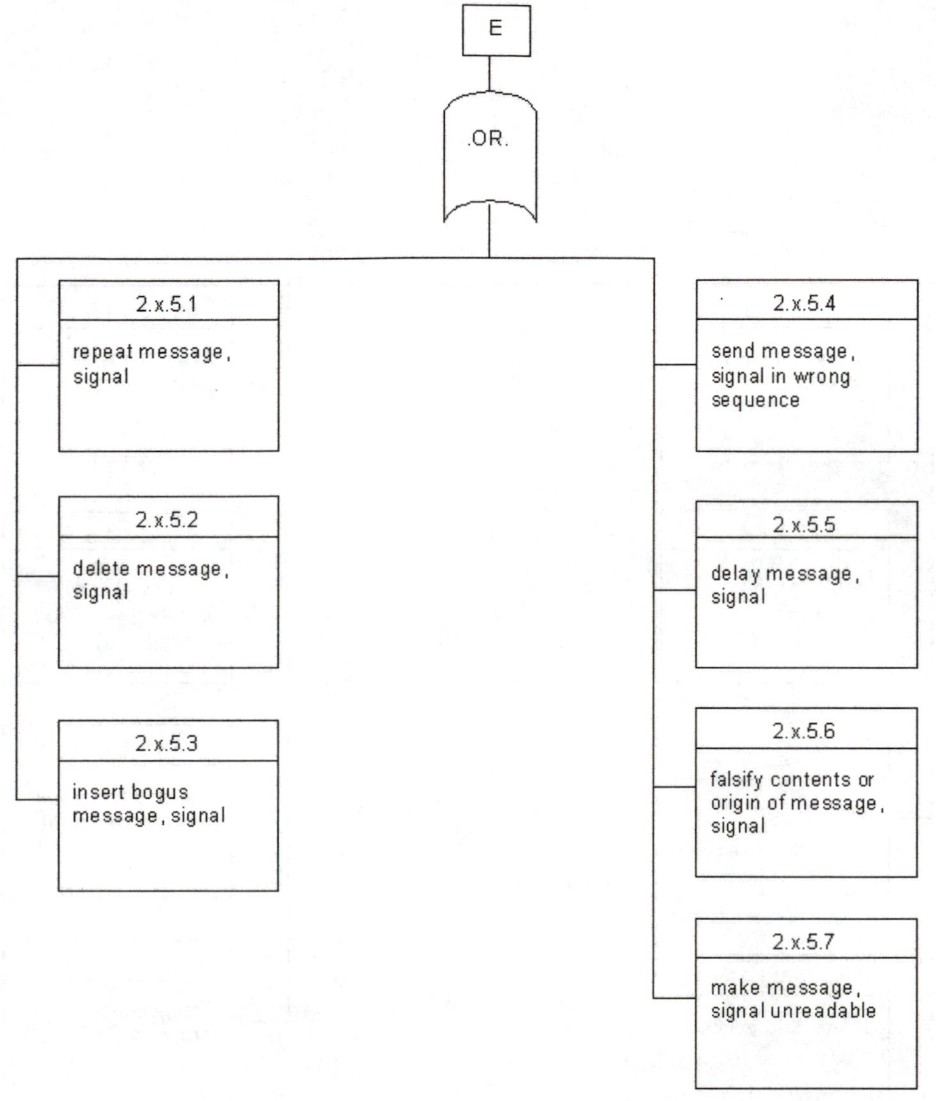

Exhibit 22 Potential Transaction Paths Leading to the Compromise of a Hypothetical ATC System (continued)

5. Compromise path groups are rank ordered according to security resource allocation priority.

Vulnerability and threat analyses are generally performed from the perspective of the system owner. This is a carryover from the days when defense and national security agencies were the only ones concerned about information security. To be complete, vulnerability and threat analyses should be conducted from multiple perspectives, the perspectives of all groups of people who interact with or are affected by a system. Transaction paths help to uncover these different perspectives. Once the different groups of people have been identified, potential system compromise paths are evaluated from each group's vantage

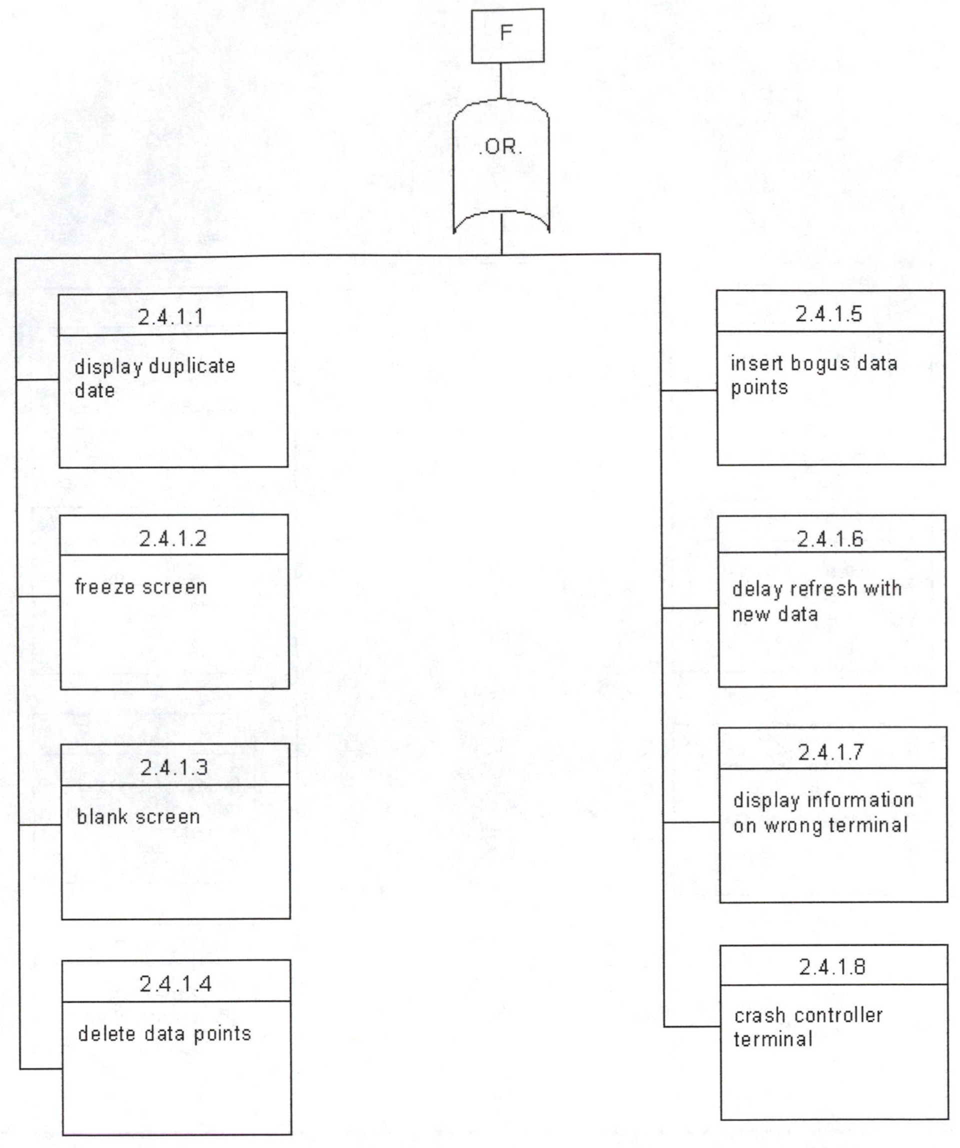

Exhibit 23 Potential Transaction Paths Leading to the Compromise of a Hypothetical ATC System (continued)

point. This analysis helps to uncover new vulnerabilities and new methods of exploitation, as well as refine severity estimates. To illustrate, Exhibit 26 examines the four potential high-level compromises for the hypothetical ATC system from six different threat perspectives.

Threat zones represent a segment of the transaction path that is associated with a specific operational mode/state, operational profile, and time element. Information from the system entity control analysis is factored in when isolating a threat zone. The intent is to zero in on the weakest links in the chain — the events most likely to lead to a system compromise. For example, not all

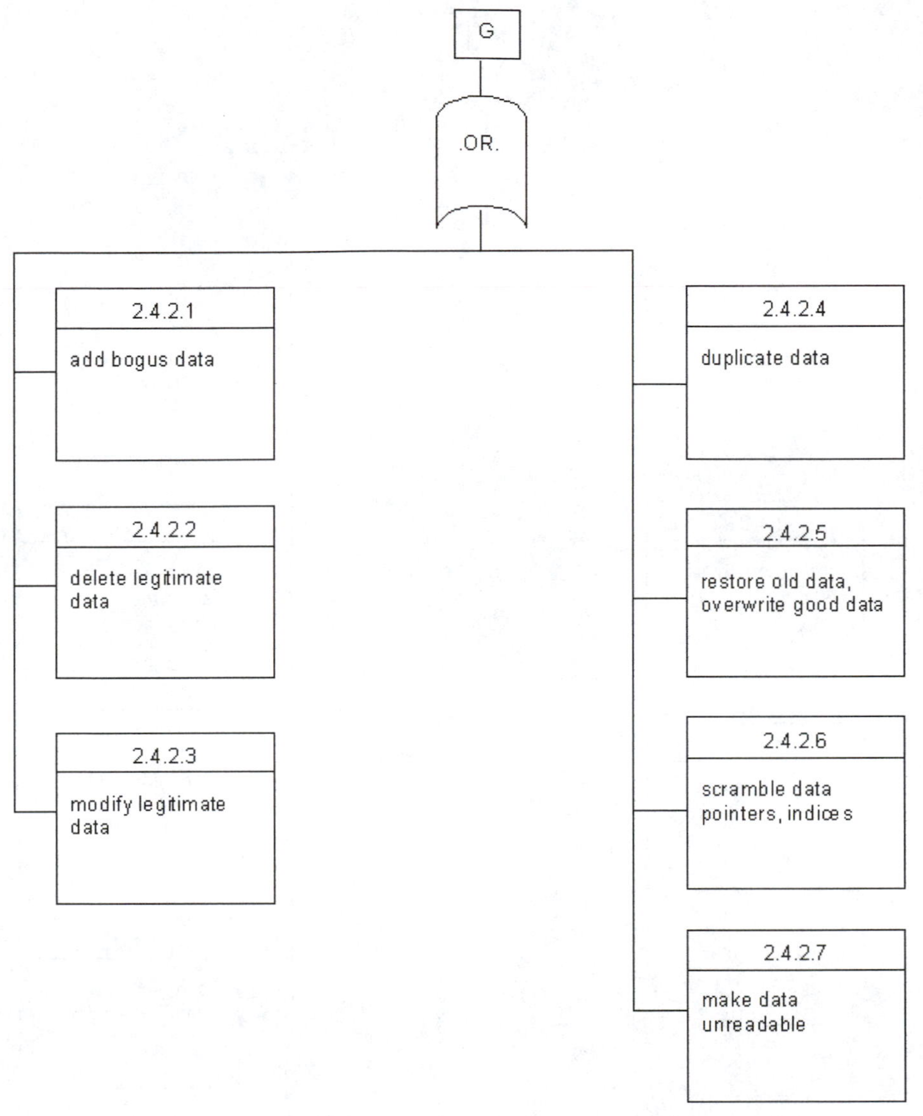

Exhibit 24 Potential Transaction Paths Leading to the Compromise of a Hypothetical ATC System (continued)

61 potential transaction paths that could lead to the compromise of the ATC system example are equally: (1) as likely to occur, or (2) as easy to accomplish, accidentally or intentionally. Rather, for each system, specific combinations of a transaction path segment, operational mode/state, operational profile, time of day/year, etc. are more likely to lead to a compromise. Opportunity, motive, and intent for an attack must also be considered when isolating critical threat zones.[248,391] Once the critical threat zones have been identified and ranked, attack points can be fortified *a priori* and loss prevented.

Overall system risk exposure is derived from several interactive factors, as shown in Exhibit 27:

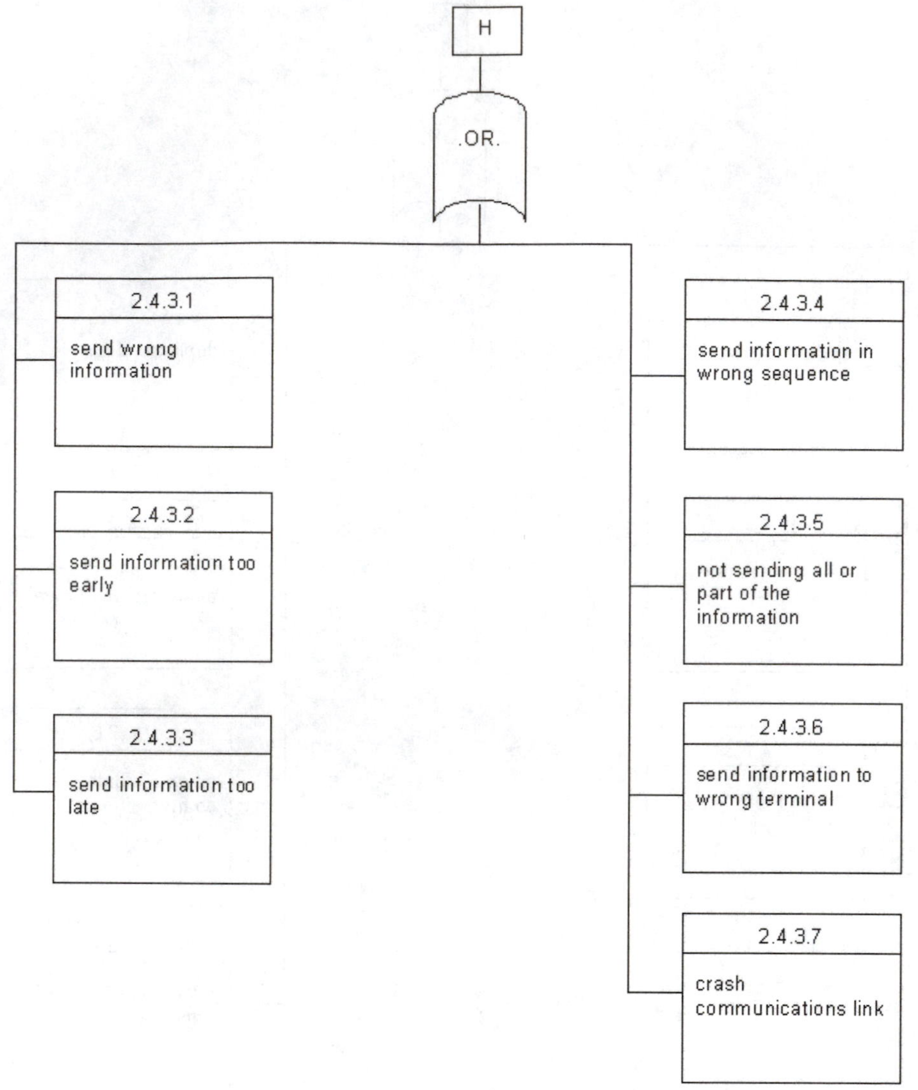

Exhibit 25 Potential Transaction Paths Leading to the Compromise of a Hypothetical ATC System (continued)

- Correlating vulnerability severity and threat likelihood
- Analyzing transaction paths from different threat perspectives
- Isolating critical threat zones

It is essential to remember in all cases — whether evaluating vulnerability severity, threat likelihood, transaction paths, or threat zones — that loss can occur as a result of accidental ***or*** intentional action ***or*** inaction. At the same time, all entities and factors which effect the design, operation, and operational environment of a system should be analyzed. Concerns traditionally associated with OPSEC and physical security should be scrutinized as thoroughly as those associated with INFOSEC. Safety, reliability, and security concerns should be assessed in tandem. In short, the effectiveness of the implementation of threat

Exhibit 26 System Compromises Examined from Different Threat Perspectives

Threat Perspective	*Tamper with Communication between Aircraft and Radar*	*Tamper with Pilot/Air Traffic Controller Voice Communication*	*Tamper with Radar Communication with ATC*	*Tamper with ATC System*
Pilot/crew	Pilots rely on an accurate location signal being sent to the radar. If radar signal and onboard instrumentation disagree, how will pilots know which is correct? In the worst case, pilots may not know signal has been altered.	Pilots assume they are talking with real air traffic controllers. They have no way of knowing otherwise. If information is not received/relayed correctly, severe consequences could result.	Pilots rely on an accurate signal being sent from the radar to the ATC system so that controllers can provide correct landing information.	Pilots are directed by air traffic controllers based on information from the ATC system. If that information has been altered or is incorrect, it could affect the safety of one or more aircraft.
Passengers	Passengers rely on an accurate signal being sent to the radar so that their plane can land safely. They have no way of knowing otherwise.	Passengers rely on the accurate exchange of information between pilot and air traffic controller so that their plane can land safely. They have no way of knowing otherwise.	Passengers rely on accurate information being sent from the radar to the ATC system so that their plane can land safely. They have no way of knowing otherwise.	Passengers rely on the ATC system to provide accurate information to the controller so that their plane can land safely. They have know way of knowing otherwise.
Air traffic controllers	Air traffic controllers assume that information displayed on their screen is correct. They have no way of knowing that is incorrect unless voice communications so indicate. Critical decisions are based on this information, which may affect more than one aircraft.	Air traffic controllers assume that they are talking with real pilots. They have no way of knowing otherwise. If information is not received/relayed correctly, severe consequences could result.	Controller relies on an accurate signal being sent from the radar to the ATC system so that they can provide correct landing information to the pilot.	Air traffic controllers direct pilots and ground crews based on information from the ATC system. Conflicting voice communication is the only way they would know if the ATC information is in error. Erroneous information could lead to severe consequences.

Exhibit 26 System Compromises Examined from Different Threat Perspectives (continued)

Threat Perspective	*Tamper with Communication between Aircraft and Radar*	*Tamper with Pilot/Air Traffic Controller Voice Communication*	*Tamper with Radar Communication with ATC*	*Tamper with ATC System*
ATC system maintenance technicians	—	—	Maintenance technicians only verify that a signal is received. They have no way of knowing if the contents have been altered.	Maintenance technicians only verify that the system functions correctly. They have no way to knowing if the information content is correct.
Radar system maintenance technicians	Maintenance technicians only verify that a signal is received at the correct frequency, timing, etc. They have no way of knowing if the signal content is correct.	—	Maintenance technicians only verify that a signal is sent at the correct frequency, timing, etc. They have no way of knowing if the signal content is correct.	—
Airport ground crews	—	Ground crews are directed to perform certain functions based on information received from the pilot. If that information is incorrect, the consequences could be anything from wasted time to injuries.	Ground crews are directed to perform certain functions based on information received from the radar. If that information is incorrect, the consequences could be anything from wasted time to injuries.	Ground crews are directed to perform certain functions based on information received from the ATC system. If that information is incorrect, the consequences could be anything from wasted time to injuries.

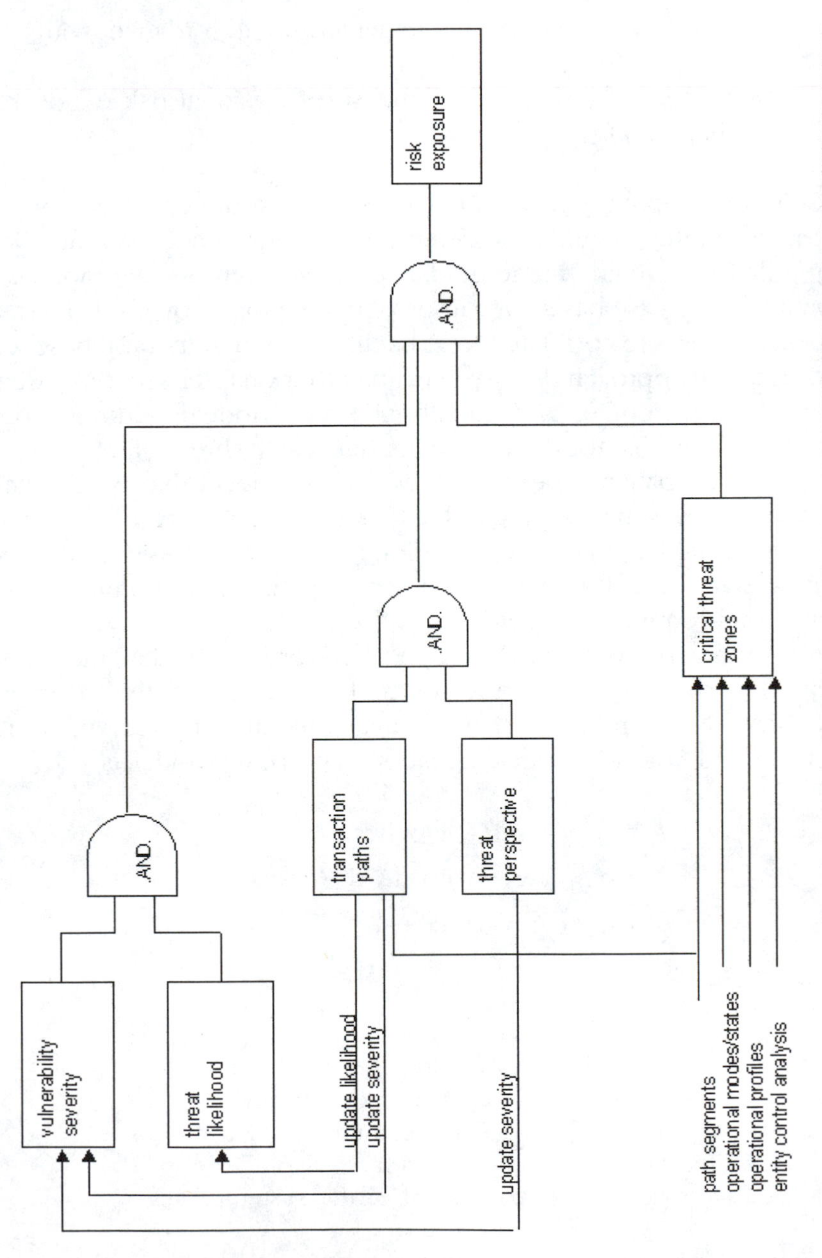

Exhibit 27 Components of Risk Exposure and Their Interaction

control measures is dependent on the thoroughness of the analysis of risk exposure which preceded it.

Risk exposure is determined and reviewed in stages:

1. Initial risk exposure is ascertained to prioritize threat control measures (Chapter 5).
2. Threat control measures are implemented in accordance with these priorities (Chapter 6).
3. The effectiveness of threat control measures (residual risk exposure) is verified (Chapter 7).

The problem remaining is how to decide what constitutes acceptable risk. There are few absolutes to guide the determination of risk acceptability. While laws and regulations provide some guidance, most often the decision has to be made on a case-by-case basis. One approach, developed by the U.K. Health and Safety Executive, is to correlate threat likelihood and vulnerability severity. (This is similar to the approach discussed in an earlier Chapter section ("Identify Threats, Their Type, Source, and Likelihood) for prioritizing threat control measures.) The intent is to discover whether each threat likelihood and vulnerability severity pair has been reduced: (1) to a level that is acceptable, and (2) as low as reasonably practicable (ALARP). A variety of factors can influence the acceptability decision, including the system's mission, availability of alternatives, state of technology, social considerations, economic considerations, contractual requirements, etc.

A second approach has been developed by Nordland[367] that models risk acceptability for rail transportation systems. In addition to the parameters mentioned above, Nordland notes that risk aversion varies by region, country, time in history, and current political situation. The basic model is[367]:

$$\begin{aligned} T &= \text{Risk acceptability} \\ &= b / (C/A * A/J * dA/dt * f(c)) \\ &= b / (C/J * dA/dt * f(c)) \end{aligned}$$

where:

C/A	=	Average number of casualties per accident
A/J	=	Average number of accidents per journey
dA/dt	=	Distribution of accidents over time
f(c)	=	Differential risk aversion factor
b	=	Factor describing the benefit of the system

This model can be used as-is for other transportation systems, such as air traffic control systems, marine navigation systems, and intelligent vehicle systems. This model can also be easily applied to other situations by substituting appropriate factors for journey, such as operational time, and expanding casualty to include items such as financial loss and environmental damage. To illustrate, the model could be adapted as follows for a financial system:

$$T = \text{Risk acceptability}$$
$$= b/\ (C/A * A/J * dA/dt * f(c))$$
$$= b/\ (C/J * dA/dt * f(c))$$

where:

C/A	=	Average number of errors per transaction
A/J	=	Average number of transactions per 24-hour day
dA/dt	=	Distribution of errors over time
f(c)	=	Differential risk aversion factor
b	=	Factor describing the benefit of the system

In addition, the model could be further refined by distinguishing the severity of the errors $C_1 \ldots C_4$ (insignificant … catastrophic). Similar modifications can be made to adapt this model to the telecommunications industry, the nuclear power industry, etc.

Optimally, a combination of both approaches would be used to determine risk acceptability. In the final analysis, risk acceptability should tie back to specified IA goals.

5.6 Summary

The second component of an effective information security/IA program is the vulnerability and threat analyses. Four activities are performed during the vulnerability and threat analyses, as shown in Exhibit 28:

- IA analysis techniques are selected and used.
- Vulnerabilities, their type, source, and severity are identified.
- Threats, their type, source, and likelihood are identified.
- Transaction paths, threats zones, and risk exposure are evaluated.

The terms "vulnerability," "threat," "hazard," and "risk" are often (incorrectly) used interchangeably. These four concepts are related, as shown in Exhibit 1; however, they have distinct meanings. This distinction must be maintained when performing the vulnerability and threat analyses or the results will be confusing and misleading.

Vulnerabilities and threats are identified and characterized so that resources can be applied to the most critical need(s) to prevent loss. The identification and analysis of vulnerabilities and threats considers accidental **and** intentional action **and** inaction. Individual events as well as unusual unplanned combinations and sequences of events that could lead to a failure/compromise are analyzed.

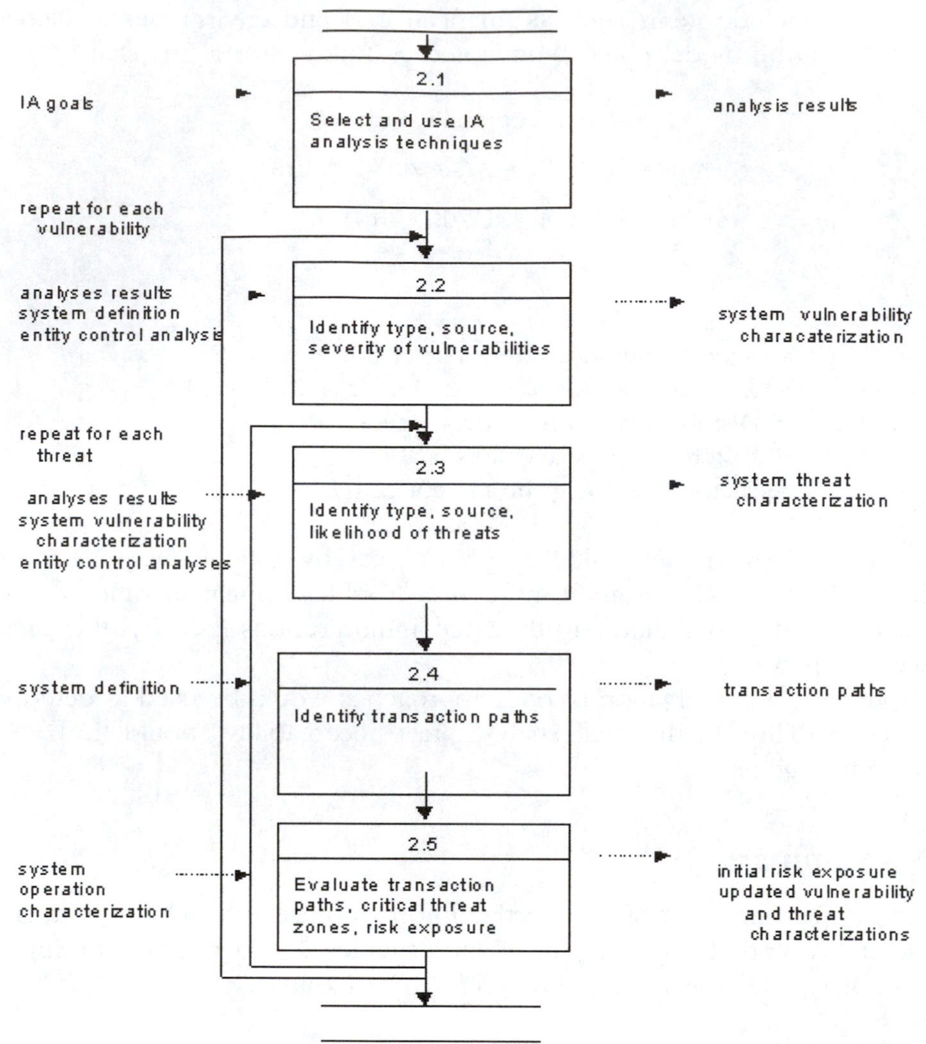

Exhibit 28 Summary of the Activities Involved in Performing Vulnerability and Threat Analyses

Transaction paths are developed to identify all logically possible combinations of discrete activities that could cause a system to be compromised or rendered inoperable. Transaction paths can be developed *a priori* to determine the need for threat control measures, or *a posteriori* as part of an accident/incident investigation. Transaction paths are analyzed from the perspective of multiple stakeholders to refine vulnerability/threat assessments and uncover critical threat zones. Risk exposure is derived from correlating vulnerability severity and threat instantiation likelihood, analyzing transaction paths, and isolating critical threat zones.

Next, Chapter 6 explains how to proactively defend systems and data against loss through IA design techniques and features.

5.7 Discussion Problems

1. When are IA analysis techniques performed? By whom are they performed?
2. For what type of threats are quantitative likelihood estimations most appropriate? For what type of threats are qualitative likelihood estimations most appropriate? Explain your reasoning.
3. What criteria should be used to select IA analysis techniques?
4. Explain the relationship, if any, between: (a) hazards and vulnerabilities, (b) hazards and risk, (c) threats and risk, and (d) vulnerabilities and threats. Give an example of each.
5. What causes vulnerabilities?
6. Identify an example of a potential system failure or compromise for each severity and likelihood level.
7. Which is more important to analyze: (a) an individual event, (b) a sequence of events, or (c) a combination of events? Why?
8. Postulate failure scenarios for the telecommunications backbone, power source, and environmental controls for the online banking example.
9. Would an intentional vulnerability be direct or indirect? Why?
10. Characterize the vulnerabilities associated with routers listed in the chapter section "Identify Vulnerabilities, Their Type, Souce, and Severity."
11. Which is easier to prevent: a vulnerability or a threat? Why?
12. Cite potential examples of a safety vulnerability, a reliability vulnerability, a security vulnerability, and a vulnerability caused by a combination of factors for an air traffic control system.
13. How is the entity control analysis used during the assessment of threat likelihood?
14. What does a transaction path represent? How does it relate to risk exposure?
15. Which threat perspective should be considered when evaluating threat zones? Why?
16. Develop a threat characterization summary for the COTS vulnerabilities listed in Exhibit 10.

Chapter 6

Implement Threat Control Measures

This chapter describes the third component of an effective information security/IA program — implementing threat control measures. Outputs from the previous component, performing vulnerability and threat analyses, are used to prioritize the implementation of threat control measures. The following activities are performed during the implementation of threat control measures:

- The extent of protection needed is determined.
- Controllability, operational procedures, and in-service considerations are evaluated.
- Plans are made for contingencies and disaster recovery.
- The use of perception management is considered.
- IA design features and techniques are selected and implemented.

This book purposely uses the term "threat control measures" rather than "countermeasures." Countermeasures denote reactive responses to attacks. In contrast, threat control measures designate a proactive strategy designed to reduce the incidence of successful attacks and the severity of their consequences.

In 1991, Zebroski[445] identified 11 common precursors to an accident/incident by analyzing several major engineering catastrophes. Recently, Long and Briant[340] developed a corresponding proactive mitigating response to each accident precursor. While Zebroski, Long, and Briant focused on safety, their results are equally applicable to security and reliability. It is interesting to review these recommendations in the context of threat control measures because it demonstrates why the psychology of individuals and organizations — both insiders and outsiders — must be considered in addition to technical issues (see Exhibit 1).

Exhibit 1 Proactive Responses to Common Accident/Incident Precursors

Accident/Incident Precursor[a]	*Proactive Response*[b]
1. Risk management techniques not used	1. Use proven techniques as an aid to technical excellence (see Annex B): ■ IA analysis techniques (Exhibit B.2) ■ IA design techniques and features (Exhibit B.3) ■ IA verification techniques (Exhibit B.4) ■ IA accident/incident investigation techniques (Exhibit B.5)
2. Little preparation for severe events	2. Prepare and practice for emergencies: ■ Involve all stakeholders in contingency planning ■ Keep contingency plans up to date ■ Conduct practice drills regularly
3. Invincible mindset	3. Respect for technology: ■ Awareness of associated hazards ■ Awareness of residual risk exposure ■ Anticipating and preparing for the unexpected
4. Unnecessary acceptance of hazards in system design or operation	4. Maximize safe, secure, and reliable system design and operation: ■ Eliminate avoidable hazards, reduce remaining hazards to ALARP ■ Conduct regular interdisciplinary safety and security reviews ■ Conduct regular independent safety and security reviews
5. Safety, security, reliability matters not recognized or integrated into work of organization	5. Clearly defined responsibilities and authority for safety, security, and reliability matters: ■ Real authority ■ Prominent organizational role ■ Appropriate staffing levels and competency
6. Low priority given to safety, security, and reliability	6. Safety, security, and reliability are paramount: ■ Safety, security, and reliability are an integral part of system design and operation ■ Employees accept responsibility for their actions
7. No systematic processing of experience from elsewhere	7. Learning from others' experiences: ■ Systematic gathering and analysis of lessons learned from other projects: within and outside organization, industrial sector, and country
8. Lessons learned disregarded	8. Learning from ourselves: ■ Encouraging open discussion of what went wrong and why ■ Implementing corrective and preventive action
9. Compliance means safe, secure, reliable enough	9. Striving for excellence: ■ Compliance necessary, but insufficient in itself ■ Continuous process/product improvement
10. Groupthink instead of teamwork	10. Teamwork with robust decision-making: ■ Open sharing of ideas, opinions, concerns ■ Valuing dissenting views

Exhibit 1 Proactive Responses to Common Accident/Incident Precursors (continued)

Accident/Incident Precursor[a]	*Proactive Response*[b]
11. Diffuse responsibilities	11. Accountability and openness: ■ Clearly defined duties and responsibilities ■ Procedures that allow room for professional judgment ■ Open communication channels

[a] Column one summarized/adapted from Zebroski, E., Lessons Learned from Catastrophes, *Risk Management: Expanding Horizons in Nuclear Power and Other Industries,* (Knief, R. et al., Eds.), Hempshire Publishing Corporation, 1991.

[b] Column two summarized/adapted from Long, R. and Briant, V., Vigilance Required: Lessons for Creating a Strong Nuclear Culture, *Journal of System Safety,* Q4, 1999, pp. 31–34.

Exhibit 2 illustrates the chronology of threat control measures. These measures may be proactive or reactive, depending on whether or not they are preceded by proper planning and analyses. It goes without saying that actions which are preplanned will be more successful than those which are not. Initially, threat control efforts focus on preventing faults, failures, vulnerabilities, and attacks that could compromise a system or render it inoperable. Given that this will not be possible in all situations, the ability to detect faults, failures, and attempted attacks is provided.[344] Anomalous behavior is characterized to contain the consequences and formulate an appropriate response. Once the appropriate response is taken, effort is focused on instigating recovery[344] or an emergency shutdown, as the situation warrants, and a return to normal operations. The following chapter sections discuss how these threat control measures are implemented.

6.1 Determine How Much Protection Is Needed

Chapter 4 explained how to determine what needs to be protected and why. Chapter 5 explained how to determine the initial risk exposure. Now it is time to determine the type, level, and extent of protection needed. The type, level, and extent of protection needed is unique to each system. A variety of factors are analyzed and synthesized to determine how much protection a particular system needs, such as (see Exhibit 3):

1. A comparison of the initial risk exposure to the target risk exposure
2. An analysis of system entities and functions that are IA critical or IA related
3. The specification of must work functions (MWFs) and must not work functions (MNWFs)
4. A reassessment of entity control analysis
5. An evaluation of the time element relative to proposed threat control measures
6. A reexamination of privacy issues

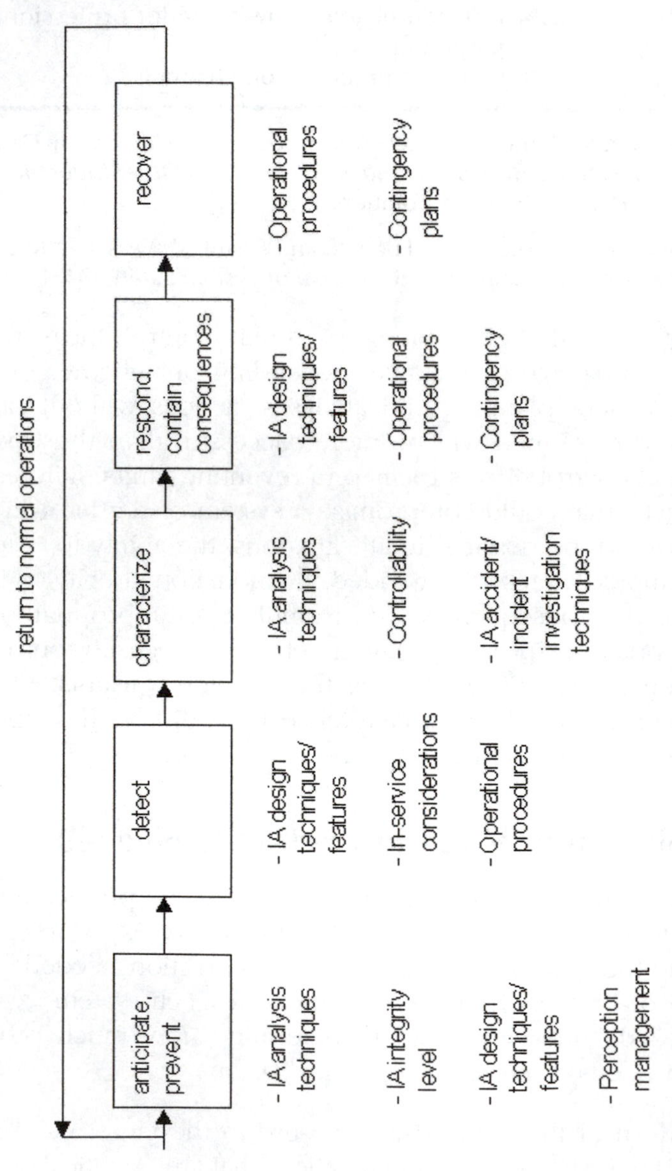

Exhibit 2 Chronology of Threat Control Measures

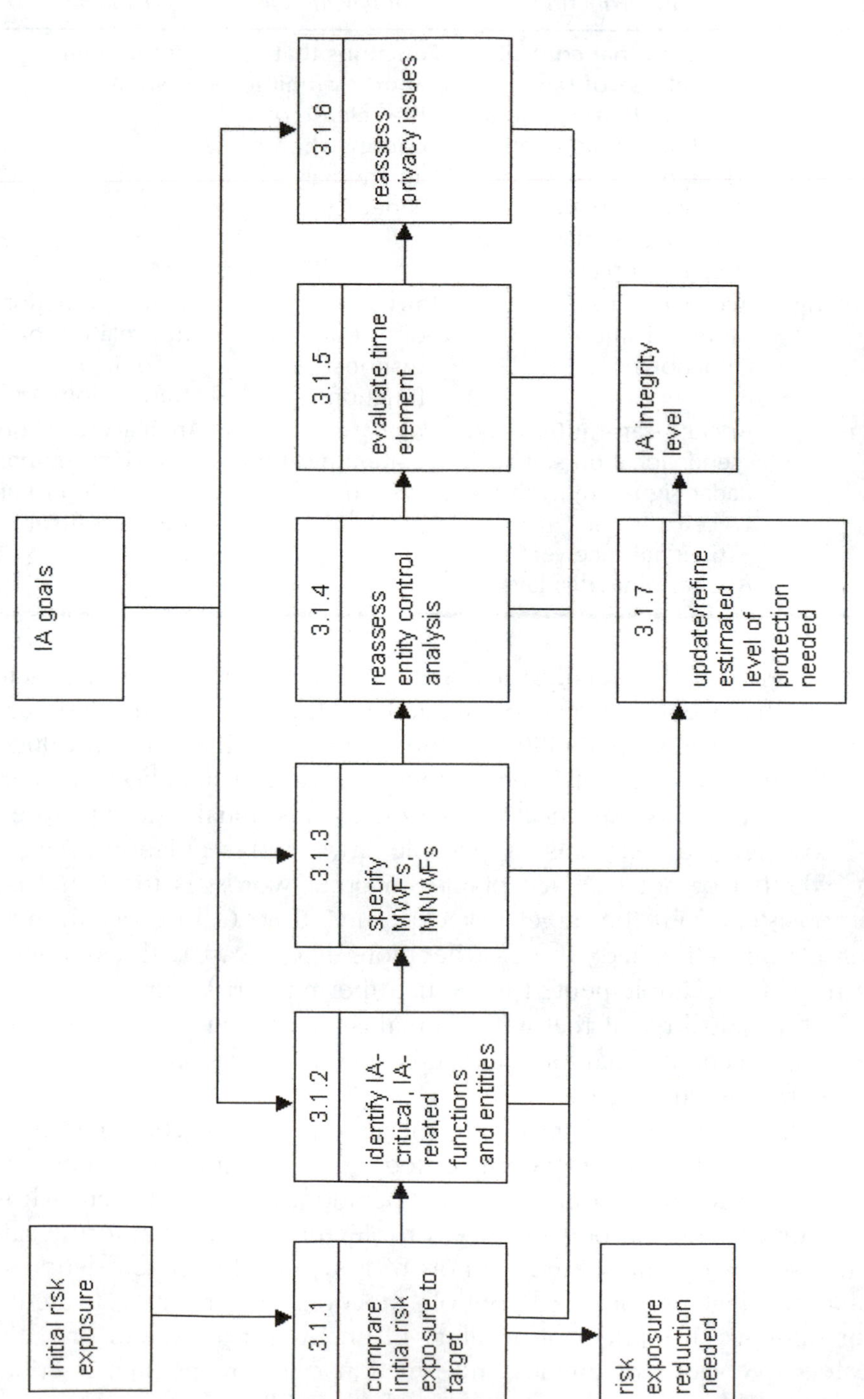

Exhibit 3 Summary of the Activities Involved in Determining the Level of Protection Needed

Exhibit 4 High-Level Identification of Entity Criticality

Example	*IA-Critical Entity/Function*	*IA-Related Entity/Function*	*Not IA-Critical or IA-Related*
Radiation therapy system	Functions that control the release of radiation Functions that verify that the type of radiation, dosage, etc. are within known safe parameters and consistent with the treatment plan	Functions that abort or inhibit the release of energy when an anomaly is detected	Remote billing system
Online banking system	Access control, authentication functions	Intrusion detection and response functions	Ancillary functions not related to account transactions
ATC system	Aircraft transmitter that sends location signal Radar signal transmitter/ receiver ATC signal receiver ATC terminal displays	Voice communication system	Ancillary functions on ATC terminals not related to air traffic control mission

The delta between the initial and target risk exposures is a prime factor in determining the extent of protection needed and the threat control measures to be implemented. The vulnerability and threat analyses (Chapter 5) produced the initial risk exposure, which melded the severity and likelihood of each vulnerability/threat pair with critical threat zones. This initial risk exposure is compared to specified IA goals, applicable laws and regulations, etc. to determine whether or not it is acceptable. In other words, is the initial risk exposure consistent with the target risk exposure? If so (a rare occurrence), no further action is needed. If not (the more likely case), threat control measures need to be implemented to reduce the initial risk exposure to the desired target. Residual risk is that which remains after threat control measures have been implemented. Chapter 7 explains how to assess the effectiveness of threat control measures.

A second factor used in determining the extent of protection needed is the identification of IA-critical and IA-related system entities and functions. IA-critical designates any condition, event, operation, process, or item whose proper recognition, control, performance, or tolerance is essential to the safe, reliable, and secure operation and support of a system. IA-related denotes a system or entity that performs or controls functions which are activated to prevent or minimize the effect of a failure of an IA-critical system or entity. A third category consists of entities and functions that are neither IA-critical nor IA-related. This distinction is illustrated in Exhibit 4 using the three hypothetical systems developed thus far.

The determination of the level of protection needed is tempered by the criticality of the system entity/function. After system entities and functions have been identified as being IA-critical, IA-related, or neither, this information is correlated to the initial risk exposure. In other words, what is the risk exposure for IA-critical and IA-related entities and functions? Is it higher or lower than that for entities and functions that are not IA-critical or IA-related?

Many international standards recommend implementing automatic inhibits to prevent the inadvertent operation of IA-critical functions. The standard formula is that two independent inhibits are required to prevent the inadvertent operation of an IA-critical function that could result in a critical accident/incident, while three independent inhibits are required to prevent the inadvertent operation of an IA-critical function that could result in a catastrophic accident/incident.[18,31,60,64,125,127,130]

A third factor used in determining the extent of protection needed is the specification of must work functions (MWFs) and must not work functions (MNWFs). The concept of and need to specify MWFs and MNWFs originated with NASA. An MWF is software that if not performed or performed incorrectly, inadvertently, or out of sequence could result in a hazard or allow a hazardous condition to exist; for example: (1) software that directly exercises command and control over potentially hazardous functions or hardware, (2) software that monitors critical hardware components, and (3) software that monitors the system for possible critical conditions or states.[126,127] An MNWF is a sequence of events or commands that is prohibited because it would result in a system hazard;[126,127] that is, an illegal state that would have severe consequences. Remember that in the IA domain the consequences of a hazard may or may not be physical.

In most cases, MWFs will be IA-critical. The logic that prevents an MNWF from executing is also IA-critical. The risk exposure of MWFs and MNWFs is evaluated as described above to determine the level of protection needed.

Often, there is a tight coupling between MWFs and MNWFs (see Exhibit 5). For example, in simplest terms, an MWF may specify:

$$\text{if } x \rightarrow \text{then } y$$

A corresponding MNWF may be:

$$\text{if not } x \rightarrow \text{then not } y$$

MNWFs are uncovered through a review of MWFs, particularly an analysis of all possible logic states or truth tables associated with MWFs. A HAZOP study is also a good way to uncover MNWFs because of the inclusion of domain experts in the process. Due to the rigor with which they are developed, formal specifications are also a good source from which to identify MNWFs. Adequate time is usually not taken to specify MNWFs; the emphasis during design and development is on implementing, not inhibiting, functionality. Neglecting to specify MNWFs creates an opportunity for serious vulnerabilities.

While estimating the type, level, and extent of protection a system needs, it is useful to reassess the results of the entity control analysis. A careful review of the entity control analysis should ensure that there is no single point of failure. Entities over which the system owner has partial or no control should

Exhibit 5 High-Level Identification of MWFs and MNWFs

Example	*MWFs*	*MNWFs*
Radiation therapy system	Functions responsible for controlling the accurate release of energy Functions that verify which parameters for a treatment session are within known safe limits and are consistent with the treatment plan	Functions that would allow the erroneous release of radiation Functions that would allow ongoing treatment plans or historical treatment records to be altered or deleted without authorization
Online banking system	Functions responsible for maintaining the confidentiality and integrity of transactions and data	Functions that would allow access to account information without authorization Functions that would allow access control/authentication features to be bypassed
ATC system	Functions responsible for maintaining the integrity and availability of r/t signal location information	Functions that allow r/t location signal information to be altered, deleted, or delayed Functions that would allow two controllers to direct multiple aircraft to the same runway or flight path at the same time

be of particular concern, especially if one of these entities is essential to the correct operation of an IA-critical function or an MWF or the non-operation of an MNWF. In this case, the level of protection needed increases, sometimes dramatically. Contingency planning (see chapter section "Contingency Planning") should be undertaken to plan and prepare for the nonavailability or suboptimal performance of these resources. At the same time, alternative designs that employ redundancy, diversity, and fault tolerance should be evaluated. In the spring of 1998, a major communications satellite and its automatic backup failed for several hours. As reported by Garber,[269] 90 percent of U.S. pagers, or 35 to 40 million customers, some wireless ISPs, television and radio feeds, and credit card verification companies lost service and were caught without a backup strategy. This is a good example of what happens when the results of entity control analysis and contingency planning are ignored.

The time element should not be ignored either when determining the level of protection needed. There are two aspects of the time element to evaluate: (1) the time window during which the protection is needed, and (2) the time interval during which the proposed threat control measures will be effective. In general, different operational modes/states and profiles occur at different times during the day, during the week, on holidays, etc. The level of protection needed may or may not be the same for each. As a result, the type, level, and extent of protection needed for each of these scenarios should be determined. Failing to do so could cause a system to be over- or under-protected in a given situation.

A final factor to consider is privacy. As Morris[357] observes:

> *Secrecy and security are terms usually connoting national and specifically military interests. They have applications, however, far below the national level, ranging from commercial espionage to individual privacy.*

Privacy issues should be reexamined in light of the system design, operation, and operational environment to ensure that corporate or organizational assets, intellectual property rights of the organization and others, and information maintained about employees, customers, vendors, and others are adequately protected. IA goals, business ethics, laws and regulations, and societal norms will each contribute to the determination of what constitutes adequate privacy and the level of protection needed to guarantee it. In one situation, data privacy may be of utmost concern; in another, data integrity may be the driving factor.

In today's technological environment, no industrial sector or application domain is immune from privacy considerations; two of many possible examples follow. Wang, Lee, and Wang[436] have developed a taxonomy of privacy concerns related to e-Commerce, including:

- Improper access to consumer's private computer
- Improper collection of consumer's private information
- Improper monitoring of consumer's Internet activities without notice or authorization
- Improper analysis of consumer's private information
- Improper transfer of consumer's private information to a third party
- Sending unwanted solicitations
- Improper storage of consumer's private information

Rindfleisch[395] has identified privacy concerns related to medical records, to include:

- Insider threats
  - Accidental disclosure
  - Insider curiosity
  - Insider subornation
- Secondary user (quasi-insider) threats
  - Uncontrolled access/usage
- Outsider threats
  - Unauthorized access/usage

Through an analysis and synthesis of these six factors, the risk exposure reduction needed is identified and the estimated level of protection needed is refined. As a result, an IA integrity level is defined for the system or major system entities, as appropriate. IA integrity is a property reflecting the likelihood of a system, entity, or function achieving its required security, safety, and reliability features under all stated conditions within a stated measure of use.[130] An IA integrity level represents the level of IA integrity that must be achieved or demonstrated to maintain the IA risk exposure at or below its acceptable level. Many national and international standards promote the concept of safety integrity levels (SILs) as part of the design, certification, and approval process.[31,38,57,63–65,124,129–130] This book expands that concept to the broader realm of IA. There are five levels of IA integrity, comparable to the five widely used SILs:

4 — Very high
3 — High
2 — Medium
1 — Low
0 — None

IA integrity levels are used to: (1) prioritize the distribution of IA resources so that resources are applied effectively and to the most critical need(s); and (2) to select appropriate threat control measures based on the type, level, and extent of protection needed. Depending on the system architecture, operation, and mission, one system entity may have an IA integrity level of 3 while another entity has an IA integrity of 1. Also, the IA integrity level for security, safety, and reliability functions may vary. For practicality of implementation and assessment, IA integrity levels should not be assigned to too low a level of a component.

While related, IA integrity levels should not be confused with EALs (discussed in Chapter 3). EALs, which do not measure safety or reliability, reflect confidence in security functionality. In contrast, IA integrity levels reflect confidence that a system will achieve and maintain required safety, security, and reliability features under all stated conditions so that the risk exposure is maintained at or below the target; that is, a measure of the robustness and resiliency of a system's IA features and the process(es) used to develop and verify them. This distinction is similar to the distinction between functional safety and safety integrity in IEC 61508[63–69] and other standards.

6.2 Evaluate Controllability, Operational Procedures, and In-Service Considerations

Threat control measures go beyond design features and techniques. Threat control measures encompass any aspect that could enhance the safe, secure, and reliable operation of a system. All entities, including people, are examined for opportunities to reduce risk exposure and improve system integrity. People are often cited as the weakest link in a system because often they: (1) are not aware of safety or security procedures; (2) do not understand the importance of following safety or security procedures, particularly the ramifications of not doing so; and (3) do not execute safety or security features, choosing instead to ignore, bypass, or disable them. At the same time, people have the potential to influence system integrity in a positive manner. As a result, the implementation of threat control measures necessitates an evaluation of additional parameters beyond system design and risk exposure. Specifically, controllability, operational procedures, and in-service considerations are evaluated.

Controllability is a measure of the ability of human action to control the situation following a failure. The concept of controllability originated with the automotive industry, where controllability was defined as "the ability of vehicle occupants to control the situation following a failure."[53] Five controllability categories have been defined by the automotive industry[53]:

Uncontrollable: human action has no effect
Difficult to control: potential for human action
Debilitating: sensible human response
Distracting: operational limitations, normal human response
Nuisance: safety (or security) not an issue

The five categories are mapped directly to the IA integrity levels (4–0). Jesty and Buckley[309] describe the relationship between controllability and integrity levels:

> *The controllability category for each hazard defines an integrity level required for the design of the new (sub)system, which in turn defines the requirements for the process of development.*

Exhibit 6 illustrates this relationship.

Controllability reflects the potential mitigating effect of human action subsequent to vulnerability exploitation and threat instantiation. In other words, can human action be taken to mitigate, contain, or preempt the unfolding consequences of a hazard, physical or cyber? Controllability is derived from both (1) the technical feasibility of taking a mitigating action, and (2) the time interval during which the mitigating action can be taken. Most hazardous situations do not instantly transition from a nonhazardous state to a catastrophic state; rather, there is a chain of events or ripple effect before reaching a catastrophic state. This interval, however small, represents the time when action can be taken to control a hazard or mitigate its consequences. It is important to note that the definition used by the automotive industry refers to the vehicle occupants and not just to the driver. Most likely, the ability to take a controlling action will vary, depending on the threat perspective. Therefore, it is useful to review transaction paths from different threat perspectives to determine controllability.

Most mission-critical systems are designed to be fault tolerant and to either fail safe/secure or fail operational. In both instances, the intent is to keep the system in a known safe/secure state at all times. These proactive design techniques enable a system to respond to one or more failures and hence protect itself. Controllability can be thought of as a human-assisted form of fault tolerance or failing safe/secure. As such, design provisions such as manual override, emergency shutdown, critical bypass, etc. should be implemented to facilitate controllability.

Operational procedures are a major component of threat control measures, although they are often overlooked as such. Operational procedures encompass the totality of IA concerns relative to the safe, secure, and reliable operation of a system in its operational environment. This includes many items

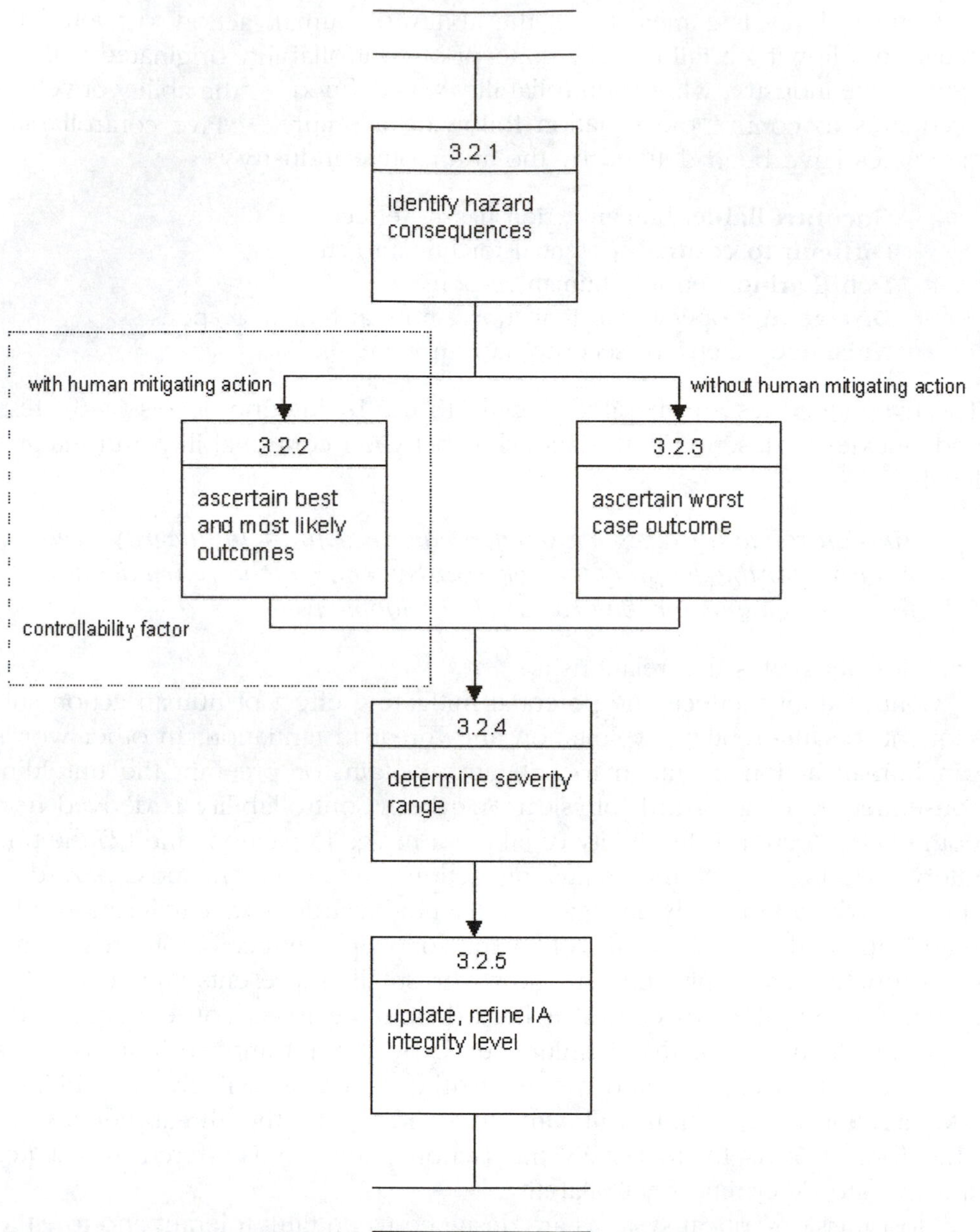

Exhibit 6 Relationship Between Controllability and IA Integrity Levels

traditionally associated with physical security and OPSEC, such as managing cryptographic keys and other security tokens. Safety and security features and procedures that lead to correct operation are described. Procedures are developed for each operational mode/state, including normal operations, abnormal operations, and recovery, and all operational profiles. If developed correctly and followed, operational procedures provide an opportunity to contribute to system integrity; the opposite is equally true.

Operational procedures are reviewed as part of the implementation of threat control measures to determine whether or not they are consistent with and support the IA goals, IA integrity level, and contingency plans; that is, do they treat the broader issues of safety, security, and reliability and not just functionality? Operational procedures are reviewed to ensure that they adequately address all issues related to personnel operations, software/data operations, and administrative operations identified in Chapter 3, Exhibit 10. For each of these issues, the following questions should be pursued:

1. Are the procedures consistent with the IA goals, IA integrity level, and contingency plans? Are all safety and security features and procedures explained?
2. Do the procedures conform to the current as-built system, or is an update needed? Do the procedures define the correct operational environment and any limitations or constraints imposed by it?
3. Are the procedures complete? Do they address all operational modes/states, missions, and profiles? Do they address the decommissioning of sensitive systems and disposal of sensitive information, including expired passwords and keys? Is enough detail provided? Is the information clear, concise, unambiguous, and accessible in a reasonable amount of time?
4. Have staff members been trained in how to follow the procedures?
5. Are the procedures being followed?

The IA challenge hardly disappears once a system is fielded. Consequently, in-service considerations should be evaluated when implementing threat control measures. In-service considerations, as they relate to threat control measures, take two forms: (1) system maintainability, and (2) the system usage profile.

Whetton[439] points out that:

> *... maintainability has an indirect effect on system safety [and security] in that any maintenance action must be done in such a way that it does not introduce new [vulnerabilities or] hazards into the system.*

Maintenance actions, hardware upgrades, software enhancements, new versions of COTS products, etc. can all potentially impact the IA integrity level of a system. As a result, systems — including their threat control measures — should be designed to be maintainable. There are two aspects to this: (1) designing a system so that its functionality, especially IA-critical and IA-related functions, can be maintained; and (2) designing a system so that it is maintainable without disrupting threat control measures. Highlighting requirements that are likely to change and reflecting this in the architecture through information hiding, partitioning, etc. promote the design of systems that are maintainable.[18] A change in operational environment, a change or addition to a system's mission, or extensive maintenance actions should trigger a reassessment/revalidation of the vulnerability and threat analyses.

A second in-service consideration is the system usage profile. A profile should be developed that defines anticipated low, normal, peak, and overload or saturation conditions. System loading may vary by operational mode/state, number of users, time of day, time of week, time of year (holidays), etc. Characteristics for each system load category should be defined and compared against known system constraints/capacity. The integrity of IA-critical functions, IA-related functions, and threat control measures should be verified under low, normal, and peak loading scenarios.

System overload often leads to unpredictable behavior. As a result, systems should be designed to prevent themselves from reaching this state; overload should be defined as an illegal state. Once peak loading has been reached, a monitor should be activated to ensure that the system does not transition from the peak loading threshold to overload. Before a critical situation is reached, protective measures should be invoked to block further user logons, e-mail, database queries, and other transactions, as appropriate. This is a simple technique for blocking denial-of-service attacks. Occasionally, low system loads can cause anomalous system behavior. This situation should also be investigated and remedied, if necessary.

6.3 Contingency Planning and Disaster Recovery

Planning for contingencies is an integral part of risk management in general and implementing threat control measures in particular. Webster's Dictionary defines a contingency as:

> (a) an event, such as an emergency, that is of possible but uncertain occurrence, (b) something liable to happen as an adjunct to something else, (c) something that happens by chance or is caused by circumstances not completely foreseen.

Contingency implies the notion of uncertainty, unforeseen events, and the unknown. Thus, contingency plans identify alternative strategies to be followed or action to be taken to ensure ongoing mission success should unknown, uncertain, or unforeseen events occur. Contingency plans provide planned measured responses to these events, in contrast to an unplanned workaround, the wrong response, or no response at all, in order to return a system to a known safe/secure state.

The activities described thus far in this book have been directed toward preventing, containing, and minimizing the likelihood and severity of system failures/compromises. Given that accidents are not 100 percent preventable, contingency planning provides an opportunity to prepare a measured response beforehand. Contingency planning allows a system owner to be prepared for the loss, unavailability, or anomalous performance of one or more system entities, whether or not the entity is internal (under their control) or external (not under their control). In addition, this planning takes place in an environment in which cool heads and logical thinking prevail, in contrast to panic responses during a crisis situation. The goal is to be prepared for any

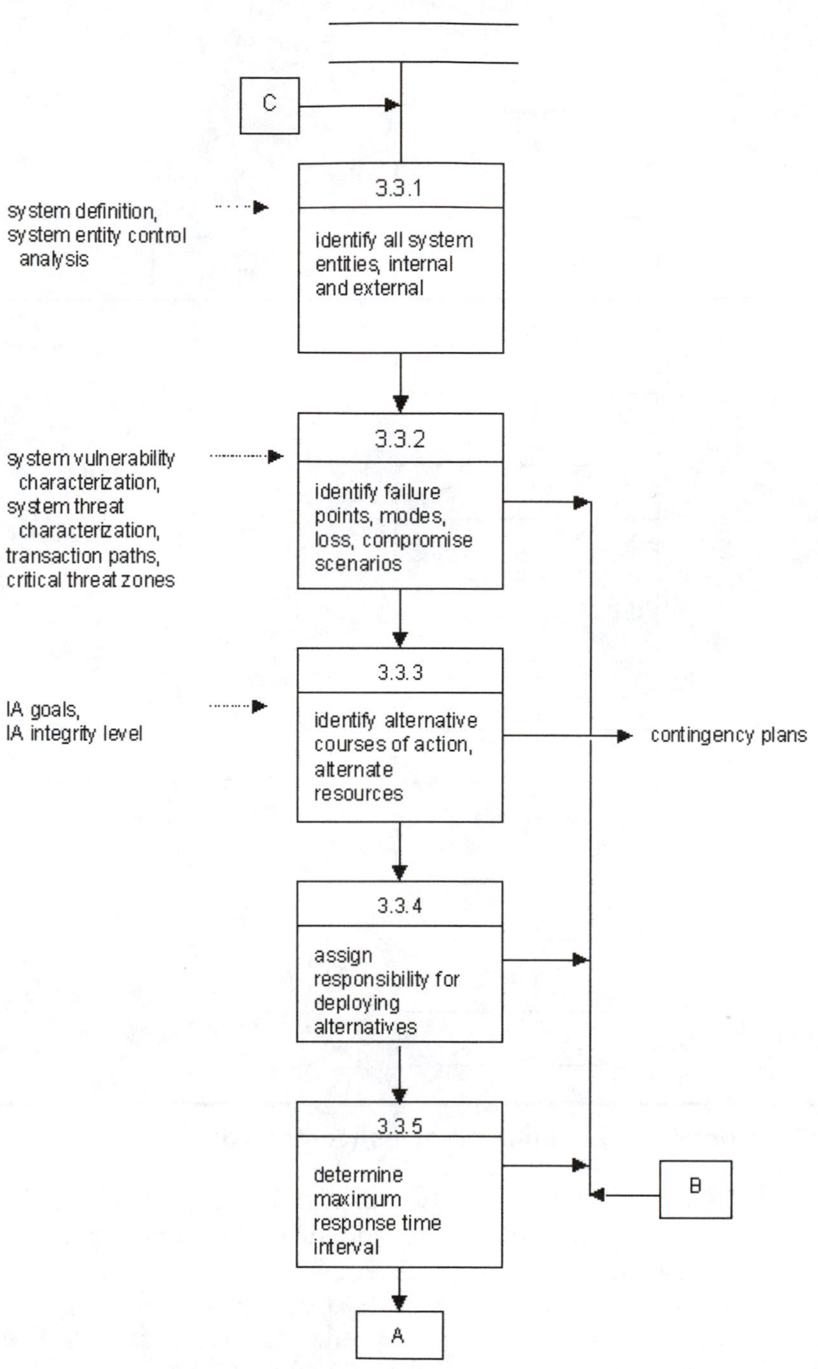

Exhibit 7 Contingency Planning Process

eventuality, and thereby ensure that there is no single point of failure that could lead to an inoperable or compromised system.

Exhibits 7 and 8 illustrate the contingency planning process. The first step is to identify all internal and external system entities and the degree of control the system owner has over each. This information is derived from the system

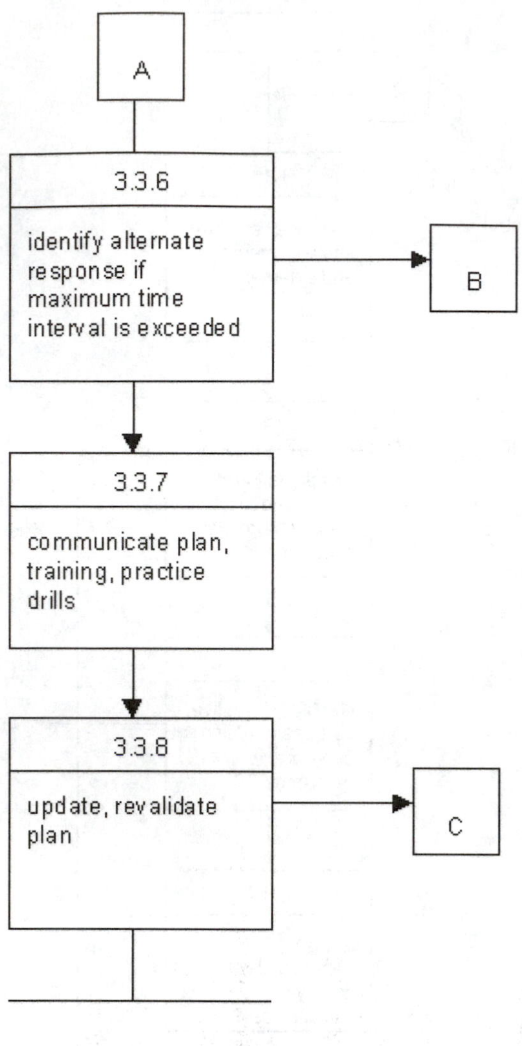

Exhibit 8 Contingency Planning Process (continued)

definition and entity control analysis (Chapter 4). It is important to be thorough when identifying entities and the dependencies between them. Exhibit 9 provides a checklist to review for this step.

The second step is to identify what could go wrong with a system and its entities: the failure points/modes and loss/compromise scenarios. This question is tackled from two angles[47]:

- **Cause and effect**: what could happen and what will ensue (cause consequence analysis)
- **Effects and causes**: what outcomes are to be avoided or encouraged and how each might occur*

* The movie *Frequency*, which was released in May 2000, is a good (fictional) example of this approach; historical events were changed to produce desired outcomes.

Vulnerability/threat characterizations, transaction paths, and critical threat zones (Chapter 5) are analyzed during this process. Particular attention is paid to IA-critical and IA-related entities/functions. Contingency planning assumes worst-case scenarios. For example, consider the ATC system in Chapter 5, Exhibit 16. At a high level, contingency plans should be made for the following scenarios:

- Loss of the radar system (no transmission or reception)
- Loss of voice communication between pilot and air traffic controller
- Loss of ATC DBMS
- Loss of ATC terminals
- Loss of location signal from aircraft (no transmission or reception)
- No air traffic controllers in the control tower

Consider another example closer to home: your neighborhood branch bank. In the last five years, the United States has experienced a wave of bank merger mania. My (what once was a) local bank has merged three times in three years, each time with a larger, more geographically dispersed bank. The merger requires, among other things, that the financial systems of the "old" bank be incorporated into those of the "new" bank and steps be taken to eliminate potential duplicate account numbers. Each time a merger has taken place, the new financial systems have been down two or more days. Given that financial systems are considered critical infrastructure systems, this is unacceptable. Obviously, (1) more robust contingency planning is needed so that transactions do not come to a halt following a merger; (2) an extended period of parallel operations is needed before switching to the new system; and (3) a capability to fall back to the old system is needed, should the new system prove unstable.

Once the various contingencies have been identified, an appropriate response for each is defined, consistent with the IA goals and IA integrity level. This involves formulating alternative courses of action and identifying alternative system resources. Priorities are established for restoring and maintaining critical functionality (degraded mode operations). The availability of alternative sources, services, and resources are specified. This may include redundant or diverse cold spare or hot standby systems/components, switching to a secondary operational site, relying on voice communications instead of data, etc. Exhibit 9 provides a generic list of alternatives to consider.

The fourth step is to assign responsibility for deploying the alternative course of action and resources. Next, the maximum time interval during which the responsive action can be invoked is defined. In almost all situations, there is a fixed time period during which a response is ameliorative; after that interval, the response has no effect or may even make the situation worse. In a crisis situation, it may not always be possible to respond in a timely manner. Hence, secondary courses of action/resources to invoke, if the maximum time interval for the primary response is exceeded, need to be identified.

With any plan, if a contingency plan is to be successful, it must be communicated and staff must be trained. Practice drills should be conducted regularly to both familiarize staff with the plan's provisions and to uncover

Exhibit 9 Contingency Planning Checklist (partial)

Step 1: Identify all system entities, both internal and external.

- Hardware components
- Communications equipment
- System software
- Applications software
- Services
  - Power
  - Environmental
  - Voice communications
  - Data communications
  - Facility concerns
- Archives
  - Electronic
  - Hardcopy
- People
  - Employees
  - Customers
  - System administrators
  - Maintenance technicians
  - Visitors
  - Trainers

Step 3: Formulate alternative courses of action; identify alternate resources.

- Activate cold spare
- Activate hot standby
- Reconfigure system
- Switch to degraded-mode operations, fail operational
- Emergency shutdown, logoff, fail safe/secure
- Restart system
- Restore system/data from local archives
- Restore system/data from offsite archives
- Switch operations to remote location
- Switch to alternate service provider
- Deploy emergency personnel
- Site/application-specific responses, actions, commands

any defects in the plan. Finally, contingency plans should be reviewed, updated, and revalidated at fixed intervals.

6.4 Perception Management

Perception management is a useful tool in many endeavors, including IA. Vendors have a vested interest in managing customers' expectations. Speakers have a vested interest in managing audience expectations. Likewise, system owners have a vested interest in managing the reality users perceive relative to the safe, secure, and reliable operation of a system.

Perception management serves multiple purposes. End users, whether customers of an online business or employees of an organization, gain confidence in a system and the results it produces if the system appears to be robust and provides accurate information quickly while protecting privacy. At the same time, this perception may serve as a deterrent to would-be attackers, both inside and outside the organization; the system is perceived as being extremely difficult to attack. However, one should not go overboard and attempt to give the impression that system safety/security is invincible — that may have the opposite effect by posing a challenge some attackers cannot resist. By the same token, a system should not appear too easy to attack.

Decoys are another perception management device. As Gollmann[277] points out:

> *Sometimes it is not sufficient to hide only the content of objects. Also, their existence may have to be hidden.*

In this case, it may be advisable to deploy decoy servers, decoy screens, decoy files/data, decoy passwords, etc.[248,277,305,375] Decoys can function as a benign security filter, an aggressive security trap that is meant to lure would-be attackers away from critical systems/data and catch them, or some combination thereof. Decoys, which must appear authentic or no one will be fooled, are also an effective method of blocking denial-of-service attacks.

6.5 Select/Implement IA Design Techniques and Features

Threat control measures are primarily implemented through design techniques and features, with operational procedures, contingency plans, and physical security practices being the other main contributing factors. Consequently, design techniques and features should be carefully chosen because of the pivotal role they play in achieving and maintaining IA integrity.

Threat control measures are selected based on the target risk exposure and the level of protection and IA integrity level needed. Controllability, in-service considerations, and perception management are also major determinants. As far back as 1979, DoD 5200.28-M[140] directed that security design techniques and features be chosen based on trade-off studies that evaluated risk analysis, the level of risk that could be tolerated, and cost. Particular threat control measures are chosen in response to specific vulnerabilities, hazards, and threats. Threat control measures represent a solution to a specific defined problem, the intent being to reduce the initial risk exposure to at or below the target. In summary, as Morris[357] notes, threat control measures should be implemented that are efficient, do not degrade system performance, and are appropriate for the level of risk exposure.

Exhibit 10 lists 25 current, proven IA design techniques and features. A description of each technique or feature is provided in Annex B, which describes the purpose, benefits, and limitations of each technique or feature and provides pointers to references for further information.

Exhibit 10 IA Design Techniques and Features

IA Design Techniques and Features	*C/R*	*Type*	*Life-Cycle Phase in which Technique is Used*		
			Concept	*Development*	*Operations*
Access control: Rights Privileges	C2	SA, SE	x	x	x
Account for all possible logic states	C2	SA, SE		x	x
Audit trail, security alarm	C2	SE	x	x	x
Authentication: Biometrics Data origin Digital certificates Kerberos Mutual Peer entity Smartcards Unilateral	C2	SA, SE	x	x	x
Block recovery	C2	All		x	x
Confinement: DTE Least privilege Wrappers	C2	SA, SE		x	x
Defense in depth	C2	All	x	x	x
Defensive programming	C2	All		x	x
Degraded-mode operations, graceful degradation	R2/C2	All		x	x
Digital signatures: Nonrepudiation of origin Nonrepudiation of receipt	C2	SE		x	x
Diversity Hardware Software	C2	SA, SE	x	x	x
Encryption: Asymmetric Symmetric Block Stream Hardware Software	C2	SE	x	x	x
Error detection, correction	C2	ALL		x	x
Fail safe/secure, fail operational	R2/C2	SA, SE		x	x
Fault tolerance	C2	All		x	x
Firewalls, filters	C2	SA, SE		x	x
Formal specifications, animated specifications	C2	SA, SE	x	x	x

Exhibit 10 IA Design Techniques and Features (continued)

IA Design Techniques and Features	*C/R*	*Type*	*Life-Cycle Phase in which Technique is Used*		
			Concept	*Development*	*Operations*
Information hiding	C2	SA, SE		x	x
Intrusion detection, response	C2	SA, SE		x	x
Partitioning: Hardware Software Logical Physical	C2	SA, SE	x	x	x
Plausibility checks	C2	All		x	x
Redundancy	C2	RE	x	x	x
Reliability allocation	C2	RE	x	x	
Secure protocols: IPSec, NLS PEM, PGP, S/MIME SET SSL3, TLS1	C2	All		x	x
Virus scanners	C2	All			x

Source: Adapted from Herrmann, D., *Software Safety and Reliability: Techniques, Approaches and Standards of Key Industrial Sectors*, IEEE Computer Society Press, 1999.

Legend for the codes used in Exhibit 10:

Column	*Code*	*Meaning*
Type	SA	Technique primarily supports safety engineering
	SE	Technique primarily supports security engineering
	RE	Technique primarily supports reliability engineering
	All	Technique supports a combination of safety, security, and reliability engineering
C/R	Cx	Groups of complementary techniques
	Rx	Groups of redundant techniques; only one of the redundant techniques should be used

Design techniques and features are a collection of methods by which a system (or component) is designed and capabilities are added to a system to enhance IA integrity. For custom software/systems, they represent techniques and features to employ when designing and developing a system. For COTS software/systems, they represent techniques and features to specify and evaluate during the product selection/procurement process. In the case of COTS software or systems, the EAL should be specified and verified. The delineation between the two categories (techniques and features) is not exact; hence, they will be considered together.

Exhibit 11 Comparison of ISO OSI Information/Communications and TCP/IP Internet Reference Models

TCP/IP Four-layer Internet Reference Model	*ISO OSI Seven-layer Information/ Communications Reference Model*	*Sample Protocols*	*Functions Performed*	*Sample Primitives*
4: Application layer	7: Application layer	FTP, HTTP, SMTP, SNMP, Telnet, APIs	Execution of distributed applications	End-user data, files, queries, and responses
	6: Presentation layer	Context management, syntax management (ASN)	Conversion of data between systems	Character sets, special characters, file formats
	5: Session layer		Session management, synchronization	
3: Transport layer	4: Transport layer	TCP, TP0-TP4, UDP	Reliable packet assembly, disassembly, sequencing; end-to-end integrity checks	Packets
2: Internet layer	3: Network layer	IP, X.25, ATM	Routing	Packets
1: Network interface layer	2: Data Link layer	IEEE 802.3, LAP-B,D Frame Relay	Transmission, framing, error control	Frames
—	1: Physical layer	V.90, OC-3 SONET, RS-422	Establish physical circuit, electrical or optical	Bits

Exhibit 11 compares the International Organization for Standardization (ISO) Open Systems Interconnection (OSI) seven-layer Information/Communications reference model to the TCP/IP four-layer Internet reference model. Both models present a layered approach to specifying and achieving the reliable exchange and processing of information in distributed environments. The Internet model is more simplistic; it does not address physical connectivity, but it does merge session management, context management, syntax management, and application management into one layer. The table also identifies sample protocols, functions, and primitives associated with each layer.

These models are important in the IA domain because they highlight the need to deploy threat control measures at each layer. This need is often overlooked (by system owners, not necessarily attackers!) and all effort is (mistakenly) focused on protecting the application layer. To help organizations overcome this deficiency, the ISO and International Electrotechnical Commission

(IEC) have jointly published more than 50 security standards[70–123] based on the ISO OSI model. These standards address a variety of topics, applicable to different layers in the model, such as: access control, audit trails, authentication, digital signatures, block ciphers, hashing functions, key management, and security alarms. Readers are encouraged to consult these standards.

The physical layer is the bottom or first layer of the ISO OSI model. The function of this layer is to establish physical connectivity between two or more systems/components that want to communicate. This connection can be established by an electrical connection (V.90), optical connection (OC-3 SONET), a microwave link, a satellite feed, etc. The primitive associated with this layer is a stream of bits. Physical safety and security concerns are dealt with at this layer, along with concerns such as wiretapping, eavesdropping, EMI/RFI, and jamming.

The second layer is the data link layer, which is responsible for transmission, framing, and error control.[403] LANs employ data link layer protocols such as IEEE 802.3. The primitive associated with this layer is data frames. The data link layer shares many of the same safety, security, and reliability concerns as the physical layer.

The network layer is the third layer. This layer is responsible for routing data packets between networks. Protocols commonly used at this layer include IP, X.25, and ATM. In general, the system owner is responsible for the first two layers, while the third layer is part of the critical telecommunications infrastructure system or NII.

The transport layer is the fourth layer. This layer is responsible for ensuring reliable packet assembly, disassembly, and sequencing and performing end-to-end integrity checks. TCP and UDP are common protocols that are employed at this layer. In the TCP/IP model, the transport layer defines port information for layer 4 applications; for example, 21 - FTP, 23 - Telnet, 25 - SMTP, 80 - HTTP. The fifth layer performs session management between two communicating nodes, controlling when each can transmit and receive.

The sixth layer, the presentation layer, performs context management and syntax management, allowing communication between open systems. In the past, for remote systems to communicate, all parties had to use the same operating system, file format, character sets, etc. Today, the ability to send and receive e-mail and execute online applications is near-universal. All of this is made possible by presentation layer protocols.

The seventh or top layer is the application layer. This is the layer that controls and facilitates the distributed execution of applications. End users interact with applications at this layer. End-user data, files, and queries/responses are processed. FTP, SMTP, SNMP, and HTTP are common application layer protocols.

In summary, each layer: (1) serves a different purpose, (2) operates on a different unit of data; and (3) presents different IA challenges. All layers should be reflected in the entity control analysis. Different groups of people (end users, system administrators, software engineers, hardware engineers, communications engineers, …) and organizations (system owner, ISP, telecommunications company, hardware vendor, LAN vendor, …) interact with and are

Exhibit 12 Assignment of Common Vulnerabilities and Threats to ISO OSI and TCP/IP Reference Model Layers

Common Vulnerability/Threat[a]	*ISO OSI Layer(s)*	*TCP/IP Layer(s)*
1. Accidental action, command, response	1–4, 7	1–4
2. Blocking access to system resources	2–4, 7	1–4
3. Browsing	7	4
4. Corruption of resource management information (accidental or intentional)	2–7	1–4
5. Deletion of information or message (accidental or intentional)	3, 4, 6, 7	2–4
6. Denial of service, network flooding, system saturation, lack of capacity planning	2–4	1–3
7. EMI/RFI	2, 3	1, 2
8. Environmental, facility, or power faults or tampering	1	—
9. Illegal operations, transactions, modes/states	2–4, 7	1–4
10. Inference, aggregation	7	4
11. Insertion of bogus data, "man-in-the-middle"	2–4, 7	1–4
12. Jamming	2–4	1–3
13. Lack of contingency planning, backups	1–7	1–4
14. Masquerade, IP spoofing	3, 4, 7	2–4
15. Modification of information (accidental or intentional)	2–4, 7	1–4
16. No fault tolerance, error detection or correction	2–7	1–4
17. Overwriting information (accidental or intentional)	6, 7	4
18. Password guessing, spoofing, compromise	2–4, 7	1–4
19. Replay, reroute, misroute messages	2–4	1–3
20. Repudiation of receipt, origin	2–4, 7	1–4
21. Site/system/application-specific vulnerabilities and threats	1–7	1–4
22. Theft of information, copying, distributing	2–4, 7	1–4
23. Theft of service	2–4, 7	1–4
24. Trojan horse	4, 7	3, 4
25. Unauthorized access to system resources	2–4, 7	1–4
26. Unauthorized use of system resources	2, 3, 7	1, 2, 4
27. Uncontrolled, unprotected portable systems and media, archives, hardcopy	2–4, 7	1–4
28. Unpredictable COTS behavior	2–7	1–4
29. Virus attack	7	4
30. Wiretapping, eavesdropping, leakage	1–4	1–3

[a] *Sources:* Adapted from Denning, D., *Information Warfare amd Security,* Addison-Wesley, 1999; Denning D., *Cryptology and Data Security,* Addison-Wesley, 1982; Gollmann, D., *Computer Security,* John Wiley & Sons, 1999; Morris, D., *Introduction to Communication Command and Control Systems,* Pergamon Press, 1977; Rozenblit, M., *Security for Telecommunications Network Management,* IEEE, 1999.

responsible for the services provided by different layers. Often, these people and organizations are oblivious to layers other than their own. A clear understanding should be established about what needs to be/is/is not protected at each layer. A threat control measure deployed at layer x may provide some protection to the layers above it, but none to the layers below it. Any serious or organized attack will simply attack the weakest layer. Consequently, appropriate threat control measures need to be implemented at each layer.

Exhibit 12 lists 30 common vulnerabilities and threats. Each is assigned to the layer or layers in the ISO OSI and TCP/IP reference models in which it might appear. This knowledge is essential in selecting appropriate IA design techniques and features; it also underscores the need to provide threat control measures at all layers.

Exhibit 13 identifies the IA integrity function provided by each of the 25 IA design techniques and features. In addition, each technique/feature is assigned to the layer or layers in the ISO OSI and TCP/IP reference models in which it can be implemented. Using this knowledge, IA design techniques and features can be selected to eliminate or mitigate specific vulnerabilities/threats at particular layers in the model.

Next, the IA design techniques/features are examined in detail. There is a high degree of interaction and interdependence between the techniques/features; the output of one technique is the input to another technique and the techniques complement or reinforce each other.

Access Control

Access control is a design feature that prevents unauthorized and unwarranted access to systems, applications, data, and other resources. Access control consists of two main components: (1) access control rights that define which people and processes can access which system resources; and (2) access control privileges that define what these people and processes can do with and to the resources accessed.[248] Examples of access control privileges include: read, write, edit, delete, execute, copy, print, move, forward, distribute, etc.

Access controls should be operative at all layers. For example, at the network layer, access control restrains access to one or more networks and the establishment of network sessions. This is similar to blocking outgoing or incoming telephone calls. At the application layer, access control restricts access to, and the execution of, systems, applications, data, and other shared resources. Access may be permanently denied, permanently granted, or granted conditionally based on some variable parameters.

Access control mechanisms are activated immediately after authentication. In simplest terms, an **initiator** (person or process) requests to perform an **operation** on a target **resource**. Access control mechanisms mediate these requests based on predefined access control rules. The initiator/resource combination reflects access control rights, while the initiator/operation combination reflects access control privileges. As noted by Rozenblit,[403] access control rules can be defined three ways:

Exhibit 13 Assignment of IA Techniques and Features to ISO OSI and TCP/IP Reference Model Layers

Technique/Feature	*IA Integrity Function*	*ISO OSI Layer*	*TCP/IP Layer*
Access control: Rights Privileges	Protect IA-critical and IA-related systems, applications, data, and other resources by preventing unauthorized and unwarranted access.	1: Physical 2: Data Link 3: Network 7: Application	1: Network 2: Internet 4: Application
Account for all possible logic states	Prevent system from entering unknown or undefined states that could compromise IA integrity.	7: Application	4: Application
Audit trail, security alarm	Capture information about which people/processes accessed what system resources and when. Capture information about system states and transitions; trigger alarms if necessary. Develop normal system and user profiles for intrusion detection systems. Reconstruct events during accident/incident investigation.	2: Data link 3: Network 4: Transport 7: Application	1: Network 2: Internet 3: Transport 4: Application
Authentication: Biometrics Data origin Digital certificates Kerberos Mutual Peer entity Smartcards Unilateral	Establish or prove the claimed identity of a user, process, or system.	1: Physical 2: Data Link 3: Network 4: Transport 7: Application	1: Network 2: Internet 3: Transport 4: Application
Block recovery	Enhance IA integrity by recovering from an error and transitioning the system to a known safe and secure state.	7: Application	4: Application
Confinement: DTE Least privilege Wrappers	Restrict an untrusted program from accessing system resources and executing system processes.	7: Application	4: Application

Defense in depth	Provide several overlapping subsequent barriers with respect to one safety or security threshold, so that the threshold can only be surpassed if all barriers have failed.[a]	1: Physical 2: Data Link 3: Network 4: Transport 7: Application	1: Network 2: Internet 3: Transport 4: Application
Defensive programming	Prevent system failures and compromises by detecting errors in control flow, data flow, and data during execution and reacting in a predetermined and acceptable manner.[b]	7: Application	4: Application
Degraded-mode operations, graceful degradation	Ensure that critical system functionality is maintained in the presence of one or more failures.[b]	3: Network 4: Transport 5: Session 6: Presentation	2: Internet 3: Transport 4: Application
Digital signatures: Nonrepudiation of origin	Provide reasonable evidence of the true sender of an electronic message or document.	3: Network 7: Application	2: Internet 4: Application
Nonrepudiation of receipt	Provide reasonable evidence that an electronic message or document was received.		
Diversity: Hardware Software	Enhance IA integrity by detecting and preventing systematic failures.	1: Physical 2: Data link 3: Network 7: Application	1: Network 2: Internet 4: Application
Encryption: Asymmetric Symmetric Block Stream Hardware Software	Provide confidentiality for information while it is stored or transmitted.	2: Data Link 3: Network 4: Transport 7: Application	1: Network 2: Internet 3: Transport 4: Application
Error detection, correction	Increase data integrity.	2: Data Link 4: Transport 7: Application	1: Network 3: Transport 4: Application

Exhibit 13 Assignment of IA Techniques and Features to ISO OSI and TCP/IP Reference Model Layers (continued)

Technique/Feature	*IA Integrity Function*	*ISO OSI Layer*	*TCP/IP Layer*
Fail safe/secure, fail operational	Ensure that a system remains in a known safe and secure state following an irrecoverable failure.	3: Network 4: Transport 7: Application	1: Network 2: Internet 3: Transport 4: Application
Fault tolerance	Provide continued correct execution in the presence of a limited number of hardware and/or software faults.[a]	2: Data Link 3: Network 4: Transport 7: Application	1: Network 2: Internet 3: Transport 4: Application
Firewalls, filters	Block unwanted users, processes, and data from entering a network while protecting legitimate users, sensitive data, and processes	3: Network	2: Internet
Formal specifications, animated specifications	Ensure correctness, consistency, completeness, and unambiguousness of the requirements and design for IA-critical and IA-related functions	7: Application	4: Application
Information hiding	Enhance IA integrity by: (1) preventing accidental access to or corruption of critical software and data, (2) minimizing introduction of errors during maintenance and enhancements, (3) reducing the likelihood of CCFs, and (4) minimizing fault propagation.	7: Application	4: Application
Intrusion detection, response	Recognize and respond to a security breach either as it is happening or immediately afterward; initiate appropriate response.	3: Network 4: Transport 7: Application	2: Internet 3: Transport 4: Application
Partitioning: Hardware Software Logical Physical	Enhance IA integrity by preventing IA-critical and IA-related functions/entities from being accidentally or intentionally corrupted by non-IA-related functions/entities.	1: Physical 2: Data Link 3: Network 4: Transport 7: Application	1: Network 2: Internet 3: Transport 4: Application

Plausibility checks	Enhance IA integrity by verifying the validity and legitimacy of critical parameters before acting upon them, detect faults early in the execution cycle and prevent them from progressing into system failures or compromises.	7: Application	4: Application
Redundancy	Enhance hardware reliability and system availability.	1: Physical 2: Data Link 3: Network 4: Transport	1: Network 2: Internet 3: Transport
Reliability allocation	Distribute reliability and maintainability requirements, derived from IA goals, among system entities.	1: Physical 2: Data Link 3: Network 4: Transport 7: Application	1: Network 2: Internet 3: Transport 4: Application
Secure protocols:	Enhance the confidentiality of distributed data communications.		
IPSec, NLS		3: Network	2: Internet
PEM, PGP, S/MIME		7: Application	4: Application
SET		7: Application	4: Application
SSL3, TLS1		4: Transport	3: Transport
Virus scanners	Automatically detect and remove computer viruses before they are activated.	7: Application	4: Application

[a] See IEC 60880 (1986-09), Software for Computers in Safety Systems of Nuclear Power Stations.

[b] See IEC 61508-7 (2000-3) Functional Safety of Electrical/Electronic/Programmable Electronic Safety-Related Systems — Part 7: Overview of Techniques and Measures.

1. Through the use of access control lists that specify the approved initiator(s) for each (group of) target(s)
2. Through the use of access capability lists that specify the target(s) accessible to a (group of) initiator(s)
3. Through the use of security labels, such that each initiator and target is assigned to one or more security label (confidential, secret, top secret, etc.), which in turn defines access control rights and privileges

(See also ISO/IEC 10164-9 and ISO/IEC 10181-3*.)

Exhibit 14 illustrates the three methods for specifying access control rules, using the set of initiators, operations, and resources listed below. Note that initiators can be individuals or user groups.

Often, it is easier to think in terms of the access control list. It is useful to develop the access control list first, and then rotate the matrix to develop the corresponding access capability list. This serves as a crosscheck to ensure that no unintended inferred access control privileges or information flow have been specified. For example, to execute application A, send/receive foreign e-mail, perform Internet searches, or import foreign files access to the organization's LAN/WAN is inferred. Because Henani has access to everything, that is alright. Malachi and Omri only have limited access; hence, design features must be employed to restrict them from other resources connected to the LAN/WAN to which they do not have explicit access control rights. The third option, security labels, is a variation of access control lists. Initiators are groups of people with a certain security clearance who have rights/privileges to access resources having the same or lower classification.

1. Initiators	*2. Operations*	*3. Resources*
a. Malachi	a. Execute desktop office automation functions	a. Desktop PC
b. Omri	b. Send/receive local e-mail	b. Application server
c. Henani	c. Send/receive foreign e-mail	c. E-mail server, LAN/WAN
	d. Remote access	d. Web server, Internet
	e. Perform Internet searches	
	f. Import foreign files	
	g. Execute application A (limited) ■ View some data ■ Print some reports	
	h. Execute application A (full) ■ View all data ■ Enter new data ■ Delete data ■ Edit data ■ Copy files to desktop ■ Print reports	

* ISO/IEC 10164-9(1995-12) Information Technology — Open Systems Interconnection — Systems Management: Objects and Attributes for Access Control.[92]
ISO/IEC 10181-3(1996-09) Information Technology — Open Systems Interconnection — Security Framework for Open Systems: Access Control Framework.[95]

Exhibit 14 Comparison of Methods for Specifying Access Control Rules

	Resources			
Initiators	*Desktop PC, Printer*	*Application Server*	*E-mail Server, LAN/WAN*	*Web Server, Internet*
A. Access Control List				
Malachi	2.a: Execute desktop office automation application	None	2.b: Send/ receive local e-mail	None
Omri	2.a: Execute desktop office automation application	2.g: Execute application A (limited)	2.b: Send/ receive local e-mail	None
Henani	2.a: Execute desktop office automation application	2.h: Execute application A (full)	2.b: Send/ receive local e-mail 2.d: Remote access	2.c: Send/ receive foreign e-mail 2.e: Perform Internet searches 2.f: Import foreign files
B. Access Capability List				
2.a: Execute desktop office automation application	Malachi, Omri, Henani	—	—	—
2.b: Send/receive local e-mail	—	—	Malachi, Omri, Henani	—
2.c: Send/ receive foreign e-mail	—	—	[a]	Henani
2.d: Remote access	—	—	Henani	—
2.e: Perform Internet searches	—	—	[a]	Henani
2.f: Import foreign files	—	—	[a]	Henani
2.g: Execute application A (limited)	—	Omri	[a]	—
2.h: Execute application A (full)	—	Henani	[a]	—

Regardless of which method is used, adequate time must be taken to define access control rights and privileges to the appropriate level of detail. A default of "access denied" should be invoked if the system encounters an unknown or undefined state. Access control rules should be regularly

Exhibit 14 Comparison of Methods for Specifying Access Control Rules (continued)

Initiators	Resources: Desktop PC, Printer	Resources: Application Server	Resources: E-mail Server, LAN/WAN	Resources: Web Server, Internet
C. Security Label				
Confidential	2.a: Execute desktop office automation application	None	2.b: Send/receive local e-mail	None
Secret	2.a: Execute desktop office automation application	2.g: Execute application A (limited)	2.b: Send/receive local e-mail	None
Top secret	2.a: Execute desktop office automation application	2.h: Execute application A (full)	2.b: Send/receive local e-mail, 2.d: Remote access	2.c: Send/receive foreign e-mail, 2.e: Perform Internet searches, 2.f: Import foreign files

[a] Inferred right/privilege.

reviewed, updated, and revalidated. A capability should be implemented to provide emergency revocation of access control rights and privileges. Files defining access control rules must themselves be protected from unauthorized access and modification. An extension to defining access control rules is defining who has the right to update/modify the access control rules, in both normal and abnormal situations.

Specifying access control rights for data files can be complicated. Depending on the application and sensitivity of the information, access control rights can be specified at the field, record, or file level. If access control rights are not specified carefully, a vulnerability is created for aggregation and inference. Also, keep in mind that it is usually easier and less error-prone to (re)design data structures to accommodate a security architecture than to develop complex access control software.

A novel way of expressing access control rights is by time of access. To illustrate:

1. A user/process may be allowed to access certain system resources only at certain times during the day.
2. A user/process may only be allowed to access system resources during a specified time interval after their identity has been authenticated.

3. Time-sensitive information may only be accessed "not before" or "not after" specific dates and times.
4. E-mail, public keys, and other security tokens may have built-in (hidden) self-destruct dates and macros.[277]

This approach is particularly useful for information that is distributed outside the owner's system.

Due to the variety of resources being protected, access control mechanisms are implemented throughout a system. For example, server and network configuration files, username/password, groupname/password, file access privileges, default permissions, server log, server root access, etc. need to be protected as well as data files.[277,405] For some situations, the capabilities of commercial products are employed — using NT™ to define shared directories. In other situations, custom code is written to operate stand-alone or as an enhancement to a commercial capability.

Finally, physical access control issues, such as control of and accountability for portable systems and media, physical access to desktop PCs, servers, cable plant, shared printers, archives, and hardcopy output, should not be overlooked.

Account for All Possible Logic States

One way to prevent a system from entering unknown or undefined states, and thus potentially unstable states, that could compromise IA integrity is to account for all possible logic states. This technique is based on the same concepts and rationale behind specifying MWFs and MNWFs. That is, for each critical decision point or command, all possible logic states that a system could encounter are defined. Truth tables are a straightforward method to uncover logic states. Once the logic states have been identified, an appropriate response (continue normal operations, trigger alarm, request further input/clarification, emergency shutdown, etc.) for each is defined. An extra level of safety and security is provided by implementing an OTHERWISE or default clause to trap exceptions and transient faults. This technique should be applied to all types of software: system software, applications software, firmware, etc. This technique is useful for uncovering missing and incomplete requirements, simple to implement, and of significant benefit in maintaining IA integrity. Exhibit 15 provides an illustration of how to account for and specify responses to all possible logic states. In this example, there are two parameters — temperature and pressure — that can be in any of three states: normal, too high, or too low.

Audit Trail, Security Alarm

An audit trail/security alarm provides several IA integrity functions, including:

1. Capturing information about which people/processes accessed what system resources and when
2. Capturing information about system states and transitions and triggering alarms if necessary

Exhibit 15 How to Account for All Possible Logic States

Step 1: Determine all possible logic states:

Parameter	*Possible Logic States*								
Temperature	0	–	+	0	–	+	0	–	+
Pressure	0	–	+	–	0	0	+	+	–

Step 2: Specify appropriate responses:

```
Do case:
  case temperature = normal .and. pressure = normal
    do continue_normal_operations
  case (temperature = too low .and. pressure = too low) .or.
    (temperature = normal .and. pressure = too low) .or.
    (temperature = too low .and. pressure = normal)
      do trigger_warning
  case (temperature = normal .and. pressure = too high) .or.
    (temperature = too high .and. pressure = too low) .or.
    (temperature = too high .and. pressure = normal)
      do trigger_alert
  case (temperature = too high .and. pressure = too high) .or.
    (temperature = too low .and. pressure = too high)
      do activate_shutdown
```

Step 3: Trap exceptions and transient faults:

```
  Otherwise
    do trigger_alert
Endcase;
```

Note: 0: normal; –: too low; +: too high

3. Developing normal system and user profiles for intrusion detection systems
4. Providing information with which to reconstruct events during accident/incident investigation

Exhibit 16 illustrates the ways in which an audit trail contributes to IA integrity. (See also ISO/IEC 10164-7, ISO/IEC 10164-8, and ISO/IEC 10181-7*.)

An audit trail provides real-time and historical logs of system states, transitions, and resource usage. When a system compromise is expected, a security alarm is triggered. Alarm contents and primary and secondary recipients are defined during implementation. Potential components of a security alarm include[90,99,403]:

---

* ISO/IEC 10164-7(1992-05) Information Technology — Systems Management: Security Alarm Function.[90]

ISO/IEC 10164-8(1993-06) Information Technology — Systems Management: Audit Trail Function.[91]

ISO/IEC 10181-7(1996-08) Information Technology — Security framework for Open Systems: Security Audit and Alarm Framework.[99]

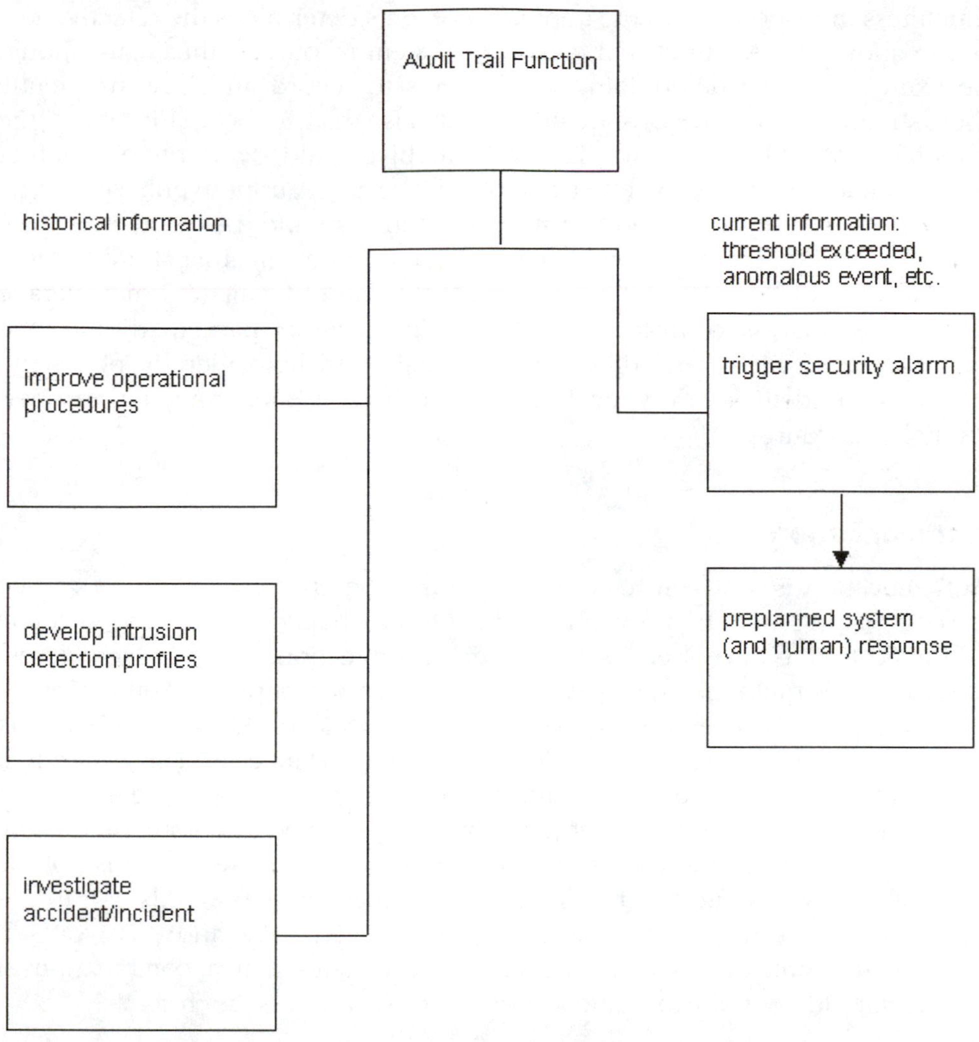

Exhibit 16 Use of Audit Trail Data to Maintain and Improve IA Integrity

- Identity of the resource experiencing the security event
- Date/timestamp of the security event
- Security event type (integrity violation, operational violation, physical violation, security feature violation, etc.)
- Parameters that triggered the alarm
- Security alarm severity (indeterminate, critical, major, minor, warning)
- Source that detected the event
- Service user who requested the service that led to the generation of the alarm
- Service provider that provided the service that led to the generation of the alarm

Audit trails are implemented at several layers in the ISO OSI and TCP/IP reference models. The completeness of the events/states recorded and the timeliness in responding to the anomalous events determines the effectiveness of the audit trail. An audit trail consumes system resources; thus, care should be exercised when determining what events to record and how frequently they should be recorded. A determination also has to be made about the interval at which audit trails should be archived and overwritten. Another implementation issue is whether or not safety and security events should be recorded in a separate audit trail. Audit trails should be protected from unauthorized access to prevent: (1) masking current events that should trigger an alarm, and (2) analysis of historical information to facilitate a masquerade attack. The analysis of historical audit trail information, particularly information collated from several different audit trails, can help identify persistent, previously undetected, low-level attacks and improvements needed in operational procedures.[403]

Authentication

Authentication is a design feature that permits the claimed identity of a user, process, or system to be proven to and confirmed by a second party. Accurate authentication is an essential first layer of protection, upon which access control, audit trail, and intrusion detection functions depend. Authentication may take place at several levels: logging onto an NT™ desktop, e-mail, a bank ATM, a specific application system, etc. In each instance, a user is required to identify him- or herself and prove it through some supporting evidence. A username and supposedly secret password are provided in most cases. There is movement toward the use of more sophisticated parameters because of the vulnerabilities associated with using just usernames and passwords. For example, browsers store previous pages, including usernames and passwords.[277] As several sources conclude, common sense dictates that a combination of factors should be used to authenticate a user or process, such as[260,277,344]:

- individual username/passwords
- User group or category
- Security level, token, PIN
- Time of day
- Terminal ID or location
- Network node, traffic source
- Transaction type
- Biometric information

Fegghi, Fegghi, and Williams[260] point out that, when choosing authentication parameters, consideration should be given to what information is supplied, what information is derived, and what information can be faked.

There are several authentication methods: unilateral, mutual, digital certificates, Kerberos, data origin, peer entity, smartcards, and biometrics. These methods are used for different purposes and at different layers in the ISO OSI and TCP/IP reference models.

Authentication can be unilateral or mutual. When a user logs onto a system, the user is authenticated to the system but the system is not authenticated to the user. In many situations, particularly e-Commerce, it is highly desirable to have mutual authentication in which both parties (users, processes, or systems) are authenticated to each other before any transactions take place. A challenge-response protocol is commonly used to perform mutual authentication. The basic exchange is as follows[403]:

1. x sends an association establishment request, plus a unique string to y.
2. y encrypts the string and sends it back to x along with a new unique string.
3. x decrypts the string, verifies that it is the string sent, then encrypts the second string and sends it to y.
4. y decrypts the message and verifies that it is the string sent.

This protocol makes use of public key encryption and requires a minimum of three message exchanges.[403] The association request can be aborted at any time if a discrepancy is detected.

Digital certificates are used to authenticate the distribution of public keys, software, and other material by binding a public key to a unique identifier. Trusted certificate authorities (CAs) issue digital certificates. The format of digital certificates has been standardized since June 1996 through CCITT X.509 version 3[50,260,403]:

a. X.509 version (1, 2, or 3)
b. Certificate serial number assigned by CA
c. Algorithm used to generate the certificate signature (k)
d. CA name
e. Certificate validity period (start/end dates)
f. Subject name (unique individual or entity)
g. Subject public key information (public key, parameters, algorithm)
h. Optional issuer unique identifiers
i. Optional subject unique identifiers
j. Optional extensions
k. CA digital signature of preceding fields

Certificates can revoked before they expire; hence, it is prudent to check current certificate revocation lists (CRLs) maintained by trusted CAs. Also, digital certificates should be bound to a specific request to prevent replay.[403] It is important to remember that digital certificates guarantee the source; they do not guarantee that software is virus-free or will operate safely, securely, and reliably.[277]

Kerberos, which provides trusted third-party authentication for TCP/IP networks,[409] is an authentication product. It supports unilateral and mutual authentication, primarily user to host, and provides a reasonable degree of confidentiality. Kerberos utilizes tickets as its basic security token. Kerberos is primarily available as a shareware product, although some commercially supported products are beginning to emerge.[433,453,466,478] Kerberos is under consideration to become an Internet standard.[182] At present, NT™ 5.0 uses Kerberos for authentication.[277]

Data origin authentication ensures that messages received are indeed from the claimed sender and not an intruder who hijacked the session.[260,403] Data origin authentication is initiated after an association setup is established and may be applied to all or selective messages.[403]

Peer entity authentication provides mutual application to application authentication. As Rozenblit[403] reports:

> *It provides a (usually successful) second line of defense against intruders who have successfully bypassed connection access control.*

Smartcards are a physical security token that a user presents during the authentication process. They represent an evolution of ATM or credit cards with magnetic strips, in that they contain a limited amount of processing power. Smartcards are currently used to access mobile phone networks, store electronic funds, and perform debit/credit card transactions. In the near future, they may replace employee badges for authentication purposes: entry into secure office spaces, desktop logon, etc.

Chadwick[239] cites the advantages and disadvantages of smartcards:

- **Advantages:**
  - Increased security: private key is unlikely to be copied unless the smartcard is stolen and the thief knows the password and PIN
  - Potential mobility of users; however, mobility is dependent on the availability of smartcard readers
  - Sequential access to one desktop PC or other machine by multiple users

- **Disadvantages:**
  - Cost: which may improve over time
  - Slower performance: 5 to 100 percent slower during message signing and encryption
  - Interoperability problems associated with new technology

As reported by Garber,[271] American Express, Visa, Banksys, and ERG Systems have formed a joint venture called ProtonWorld International to develop an open standard for smartcards, and hence solve the interoperability issues worldwide. Their immediate goal is to define the common electronic purse specifications (CEPS) that will standardize interfaces, electronic cash formats, and security mechanisms, such as public keys. Standardization will also help to minimize smartcard fraud. See www.protonworld.com[486] for the latest information about standardization efforts.

Biometric systems are one of the newest modes of authentication. In simplest terms, a biometric system is a pattern recognition system that establishes the authenticity of a specific physiological or behavioral characteristic possessed by a user.[374] A biometric system has two major components: (1) a high-resolution scanner that acquires and digitizes information, and (2) computer hardware and software that perform the pattern recognition. The two major functions of a biometric system are enrollment and identification. Enrollment, which involves registering biometric information with a known identity, consists of three steps[427]:

1. Capturing a raw biometric data sample from a scanner
2. Processing the raw biometric data to extract the unique details
3. Storing a composite of raw and unique data with an identifier

Identification involves comparing a current biometric sample to known stored samples to verify a claimed identity or to identify a person.[266,427] Identification repeats the capture and processing steps. Then, pattern recognition algorithms are invoked to perform the comparison. Current and planned future applications of biometric identification include access to secure facilities, access to desktop PCs, verification for receipt of welfare payments, verification for home banking privileges, and verification for bank ATM access.

Nine types of biometric systems are currently in use or under development. Each measures a different physical characteristic[266,332]: fingerprints, iris, retina, face, hand, ear, body odor, voice, and signature.

Fingerprint scanning is the oldest technology. Automated fingerprint identification standards began appearing in 1988*. Fingerprint scanning offers 40 degrees of freedom. Lerner[332] reports that the false positive rate, which can be improved if two fingers are scanned, is ~1 percent. Fingerprint scanning may replace passwords in the near future for access to desktop computers.

The algorithm for iris scanning was developed in 1980 by John Daugman of the Cambridge University Computer Science Department. It is only recently, given improvements in computer processing power and cost, that iris scanning technology has become commercially viable. IrisScan, Inc., of New Jersey currently holds the patent for this technology. In simplest terms, iris scanning involves wavelet analysis on a 512-byte pattern, similar to Fourier analysis. As reported by Lerner,[332] iris scanners support 266 degrees of freedom and can perform 100,000 scans per second.

Biometric authentication can also be performed through voice verification. In this case, the enrollment process consists of extracting unique feature vectors from a passphrase that is recorded and stored in a voice print database. Biometric authentication through voice verification is geared toward reducing fraud in three environments: e-Commerce over the Internet, t-Commerce over

---

* ANSI/IAI 1-1988, Forensic Identification — Automated Fingerprint Identification Systems — Benchmark Tests of Relative Performance.[16]
ANSI/IAI 2-1988, Forensic Identification — Automated Fingerprint Identification Systems — Glossary of Terms and Acronyms.[17]
ANSI/NIST-CSL 1-1993, Information Systems — Data Format for the Interchange of Fingerprint Information.[15]

fixed-line telephones, and m-Commerce over mobile/wireless devices. An advantage of voice verification is that it requires "little or no additional infrastructure investment due to the wide availability and low cost of computer microphones and telephones, whether fixed-line or cellular."[282]

Configate's[463] Verimote is a leading voice verification product. As reported by Gordon[282]:

> *... they have developed patent-pending software and adaptive algorithms that use 40 objective voice features and 40 subjective features to confirm the identity of an individual by verifying the unique aspects of his voice.... Subsequent comparisons of the feature vectors have yielded 99.6 percent accuracy.*

Verimote is language independent; unlike some products, it is not tied to English. In addition, the level of security is selectable. For example, a user may be required to repeat randomly selected numbers to further reduce the likelihood of a false positive.

A drop in the cost of biometric systems has expanded their usage. This is turn has given impetus to biometric standardization efforts. As reported by Tilton,[427] the BioAPI consortium, consisting of some 45 companies, is developing a multi-level, platform-independent architecture to support the enrollment and identification functions. The architecture specification is being written in an object-oriented notation. This architecture envisions a biometric service provider (BSP) that will operate between the input device and specific API. A draft standard was released for comment December 1999. At the same time, the biometric data format, common biometric exchange file format (CBEFF), is being defined by the U.S. Biometric consortium and ANSI X.9F4 subcommittee. For the latest information on biometric standards, see www.ibia.org[474] and www.biometrics.org.[459]

The use of biometric identification systems raises performance and privacy issues. While biometric systems are considered more accurate than nonbiometric systems,[266] they still raise concerns about false positives and false negatives given the variability in biometric characteristics.[374] For example, changes in makeup, hair style or color, tinted contact lenses, plastic surgery, a suntan, and presence or absence of a mustache or beard would all change facial characteristics, as would an illness or the normal aging process. Also, what is to prevent a person from placing a photograph or hologram in front of the scanner, or in the case of a voice recognition system, playing a tape recording? The accuracy of biometric systems is, not surprisingly, tied to cost. Some experts think that multi-mode biometric identification may be more accurate than single mode[266]; however this has not yet been proven. The integrity of stored data samples and current data samples is another concern. Biometric data is not immune to misuse and attacks anymore than other types of data.[332] Enrollment fraud is a major concern for the system owners and the individual whose identity has been hijacked.[393] Likewise, the privacy and confidentiality of biometric data must be protected. Until standardization efforts take hold, system integration and interoperability issues will remain. In summary, biometric identification systems are expected to reduce fraud, forgery, and theft[332]; but like other authentication methods, they are not a panacea.

Block Recovery

Block recovery is a design technique that provides correct functional operation in the presence of one or more errors.[69] Block recovery is implemented to increase the integrity of modules that perform critical functions. Exhibit 17 illustrates the basic logic of block recovery.

For each critical module, a primary and a secondary module (employing diversity) are developed. After the primary module executes, but before it performs any critical transactions, an acceptance test is run. This test checks for possible error conditions, such as runtime errors, excessive execution time, or mathematical errors, and performs plausibility checks.[422] If no error is detected, normal execution continues. If an error is detected, control is switched to the corresponding secondary module and another acceptance test is run. If no error is detected, normal execution resumes. However, if an error is detected, the system is reset either to a previous (backward block recovery) or future (forward block recovery) known safe/secure state.

If the system is reset backward, internal states have to be saved at well-defined checkpoints and some compensatory action must be taken to account for events that took place after the state to which the system is being reset.[69,333,422] Forward block recovery is appropriate for real-time systems with fast changing internal states and a small amount of data.[69] After the system has been reset, normal operation continues. Jajodia[305] recommends implementing forward block recovery for anticipated errors and backward block recovery for unanticipated errors.

Confinement

Confinement is a design feature that restricts an untrusted program from accessing system resources and executing system processes. The intent is to prevent an untrusted program from exhibiting unknown and unauthorized behavior, such as:

- Accidentally or intentionally corrupting data
- Accidentally or intentionally triggering the execution of critical sequences
- Initiating a trapdoor or Trojan horse through which executables are misused or corrupted
- Opening a covert channel through which sensitive data is misappropriated

Noninterference is the goal of confinement — preventing interference between independent functions that utilize shared resources and unintended intercomponent communication.[255] Interference can lead to[255]:

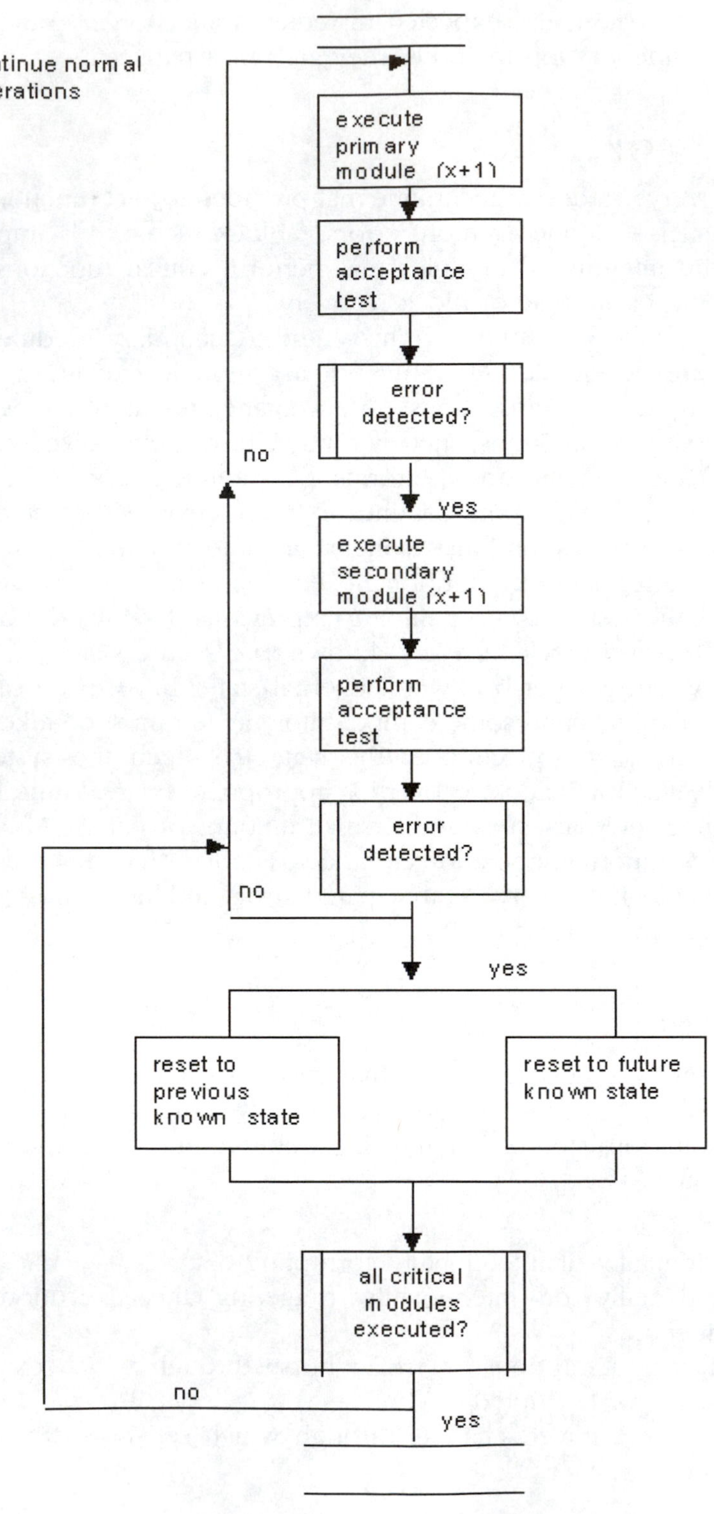

Exhibit 17 Illustration of Block Recovery Logic

- **Data corruption.** Untrusted components overwrite vital information stored in common memory and used by trusted components.
- **Denial of access to critical resources.** Untrusted components can prevent or delay the execution of critical functions by restricting or preventing access to a shared resource. In particular, untrusted components can use too much CPU time or can fail to terminate or crash and hence prevent the trusted components from executing.

Noninterference and separability are used in the information security domain much the same as partitioning and isolation are used in the computer safety domain.

COTS software, mobile code,[405,406] reused software, shareware, and the active content of Web pages are all good candidates for confinement. Confinement can be implemented by:

1. Restricting a process to reading data it has written[277]
2. Limiting executable privileges to the minimum needed to perform its function, referred to as least privilege or sandboxing; for example, child processes do not inherit the privileges of the parent processes[335,405]
3. Mandatory access controls (MAC)
4. Domain and type enforcement (DTE)
5. Language-based confinement of mobile code, per the Java™ security model[335]
6. Wrappers

DTE is a confinement technique in which an attribute called a domain is associated with each subject (user or process), and another attribute called a type is associated with each object (system resource). A matrix is defined that specifies whether or not a particular mode of access to objects of type x is granted to subjects in domain y.[335]

Gollmann[277] gives examples of language-based confinement:

- Applets do not get to access the user's file system
- Applets cannot obtain information about the user's name, e-mail address, machine configuration, etc.
- Applets may make outward connections only back to the server they came from
- Applets can only pop-up windows that are marked "untrusted"
- Applets cannot reconfigure the system, for example by creating a new class loader or a new security manager

Wrappers are a confinement technique that encapsulates datagrams to control invocation and add access control and monitoring functions.[277] They were originally developed for use with secure protocols, such as the encapsulated payload in IPSec or NLS. In the case of IPSec and NLS, the wrapper is used to protect what is encapsulated from the outside world. In the case of confinement, wrappers are used to protect the outside word from what is encapsulated (and untrusted). Since then, their usage has expanded. Fraser, Badger, and Feldman[264] recommend using wrappers to confine COTS software:

> *Using appropriate activation criteria, wrappers can be applied selectively to points of vulnerability, or can be globally applied to all processes on a system. In either case, with respect to a wrapped program, the mediation and additional functionality provided by a wrapper is nonbypassable and protected from tampering. These characteristics, in addition to the fine-grained control that wrappers may provide by potentially processing every system call, give wrappers a great deal of power to add to and enforce security policies.*

Mobile code is also a good candidate for confinement. Sander and Tschudin[406] cite several concerns about mobile code that confinement can help to mitigate:

- Protecting host computers from accidental or intentional errant mobile code
- Protecting mobile agent's code and data from accidental or intentional tampering, corruption, and privacy violations
- Secure routing of mobile code
- Protecting mobile code from I/O analysis

To be effective, all six confinement techniques require thorough upfront analysis to determine how to restrict the untrusted program and to what to restrict it.

Defense in Depth

Defense in depth provides several overlapping subsequent limiting barriers with respect to one safety or security threshold, so that the threshold can only be surpassed if all barriers have failed.[60] The concept of defense in depth, as applied to systems, originated in the nuclear power industry. Defense in depth should be applied to all layers in the ISO OSI and TCP/IP reference models.

Defense in depth is a design technique that reflects common sense. In short, everything feasible is done to prepare for known potential hazards and vulnerabilities. Then, acknowledging that it is impossible to anticipate all hazards and vulnerabilities, especially unusual combinations or sequences of events, extra layers of safety and security features are implemented through multiple complementary design techniques and features. For example, partitioning, information hiding, plausibility checks, and block recovery could be implemented; four layers of protection are better than one. Exhibit 18 illustrates the concept of defense in depth. In this example, each of the six successive defensive layers would have to be surpassed for a compromise to occur. Note that robust access control and authentication are the foundation of this defense strategy.

Defensive Layers

Layer 6 t: intrusion detection r: attempted intrusions are detected, preempted, and contained
Layer 5 t: audit trail, security alarm r: anomalies are detected as they occur
Layer 4. t: secure protocols r: if obtained, data is unintelligible, if altered, data is rejected
Layer 3. t: encryption r: if obtained, data is unintelligible
Layer 2. t: access control r: unknown or unauthorized users, processes cannot access data or systems
Layer 1. t: user, peer entity, and data origin authentication r: only known authorized users and processes are allowed on the system
Layer 0. t: physical security measures r: only known authorized personnel are allowed entry to facilities, equipment rooms, archives, cable plant; portable equipment and media are controlled.

t - IA design technique/feature
r - result

Exhibit 18 Illustration of Defense in Depth

Defensive Programming

Defensive programming prevents system failures or compromises that could affect IA integrity by detecting errors in control flow, data flow, and data during execution and reacting in a predetermined and acceptable manner.[69] Defensive programming is applied to all IA-critical and IA-related functions. Defensive programming is approached from two directions. First, potential software design errors are compensated for; this is accomplished by: (1) performing range, plausibility, and dimension checks at procedure entry and before executing critical commands, and (2) separating read-only and read-write parameters to prevent overwriting. Second, failures in the operational environment are anticipated; this is accomplished by: (1) performing control flow sequence checks to detect anomalous behavior, especially in state transitions; (2) regularly verifying the hardware and software configuration; and (3) conducting plausibility checks on critical input, intermediate, and output variables before acting upon them. In summary, all actions and transitions are verified beforehand as a preventive strategy.

Degraded-Mode Operations, Graceful Degradation

The purpose of degraded-mode operations — or graceful degradation as it is sometimes called — is to ensure that critical system functionality is maintained in the presence of one or more failures.[69] IA-critical and IA-related functions can rarely just cease operation in response to an anomalous event, suspected attack, or compromise. Rather, some minimum level of service must be maintained. Degraded-mode operations allows priorities to be established for maintaining critical functions, while dropping less critical ones, should insufficient resources be available to support them all. The total system (hardware, software, and communications equipment) is considered when planning for degraded-mode operations; often, a system reconfiguration is necessary.[422] Degraded-mode operations is tied directly to and consistent with operational procedures and contingency plans.

The prioritized set of IA-critical and IA-related functions should be specified during the requirements and design phases. Criteria for transitioning to degraded-mode operations is specified. The maximum time interval during which a system is allowed to remain in degraded-mode operations is also defined. Degraded-mode operations should include provisions for the following items, at a minimum[126,127]:

- Notifying operational staff and users that the system has transitioned to degraded-mode operations
- Error handling
- Logging and generation of warning messages
- Reduction of processing load (execute only core functionality)
- Masking nonessential interrupts
- Signals to external resources to slow down inputs
- Trace of system states to facilitate post-event analysis
- Specification of the conditions required to return to normal operations

Degraded-mode operations provides an intermediate state between full operation and system shutdown; hence the name graceful degradation. This allows the minimum priority system functionality to be maintained until corrective action can be taken. Degraded mode operations is another preventive strategy where decisions are made beforehand about how to respond to a potential crisis situation. Without this prior planning and preparation, the ensuing system degradation and compromise will be most ungraceful indeed.

Digital Signatures

Digital signatures provide reasonable evidence of the true sender of an electronic message or document, which is often referred to as nonrepudiation of origin. Digital signatures are created using public key encryption, like RSA. A signature generation algorithm and a signature verification algorithm are involved. The initial digital signature standard (DSS) was issued in May 1994.[165]

A digital signature consists of a fixed-length string of bits that is derived from the original message using public key encryption. This string of bits is attached to the original message before it is sent. In general, a digital signature is generated on the clear text message, the message is encrypted, and then the signature is attached and the message is transmitted.[403] The recipient decrypts the string to verify that the signature reflects the original message. In this way, the recipient knows (1) the message has not been altered, and (2) the real origin of the message. Nonrepudiation of receipt requires the recipient to sign the message and return it to the sender. This provides roundtrip message delivery confirmation.

Digital signatures help to establish the identity of a sender of a document. However, they do not necessarily prove that the sender created the contents of the message.[248] Digital signatures consume additional system resources and require that a reliable key management process be followed.

The use of digital signatures will grow as e-Commerce grows. Legislation passed in the United States during the summer of 2000 will also accelerate this process. As reported by Shuman[413]:

> *At the end of June, U.S. President Bill Clinton signed the Electronic Signature Act. This was no ordinary signature. The President used a smartcard encrypted with his digital signature to "e-sign" the legislation. The new law officially grants electronic digital signatures legal status in court.*

Diversity

Diversity is a design technique employed to enhance IA integrity by detecting and preventing systematic failures. While diversity does not prevent specification errors, it is useful for uncovering specification ambiguities.[422] Diversity can be implemented in hardware and software.

In software diversity, also referred to as n-version programming, more than one algorithm is developed to solve the same problem. The same input is supplied to the n versions, and then the outputs are compared. If they agree, the appropriate action is taken. Depending on the criticality of the application, 100 percent agreement or majority agreement can be implemented[288]; if the results do not agree, error detection and recovery algorithms take control. Diverse software may execute in parallel on different processors or sequentially on the same processor. The first approach increases hardware size, cost, and weight, while the second approach increases processing time.[422] Diversity can be implemented at several stages in the life cycle[129]:

- Development of diverse designs by independent teams
- Development of diverse source code in two or more different languages
- Generation of diverse object code by two or more different compilers
- Implementation of diverse object code using two or more different linking and loading utilities

Hardware diversity employs multiple, different components and modules to perform the same function. This contrasts with hardware redundancy in which multiple units of the same hardware are deployed. To the extent possible, components and modules are chosen that have different rates and types of failures.

The goal of diversity is to decrease the probability of common cause and systematic failures, while increasing the probability of detecting errors.[69] Diversity may complicate supportability issues and synchronization between diverse components operating in parallel.[129] Accordingly, diversity should only be implemented for IA-critical and IA-related functions.

Encryption

Encryption is an IA design feature that provides confidentiality for data while it is stored or transmitted. This is accomplished by manipulating a string of data (clear text) according to a specific algorithm to produce cipher text, which is unintelligible to all but the intended recipients. As shown in Exhibit 19, a series of decisions must be made when implementing encryption.

The first question to answer is: What data needs to be encrypted? This information is derived from the IA goals and may include items such as e-mail, application-specific data, authentication data, private keys, and video teleconference sessions. At the same time, data that does not need to be encrypted is identified; for example, certain fields in a database record may need to be encrypted but not the entire record or file. Because of the time and resources utilized, it is important not to over identify data needing encryption. Conversely, it is equally important not to under identify data needing encryption and in so doing create opportunities for aggregation and inference.

The second question to answer is: Where is the data created, stored, and transmitted? The intent is to uncover all instances of this data so that the most efficient and effective encryption strategy can be employed. The stored and transmitted categories should include printouts, local and organizational hardcopy archives, and electronic archives; there is no point in encrypting active electronic data if printouts and archives are unprotected.

Exhibit 19 Key Decisions to Make when Implementing Encryption

1. What data needs to be encrypted?
   a. E-mail
   b. Text, graphic, video, audio files
   c. Database files
   d. Application data
   e. Telephone conversations and voice mail
   f. Fax transmissions
   g. Video teleconferences
   h. Authentication data files
   i. Private keys
   j. Access control rights and privileges
2. Where is the data:
   a. Created? b. Stored? c. Transmitted?
3. What strength of encryption is needed?
   a. Low b. Medium c. High d. Very high
4. At what level(s) in the ISO OSI or TCP/IP reference models should encryption take place?
   a. Physical b. Data link c. Network d. Transport e. Application
5. Should hardware or software encryption be used?
6. Should block or stream ciphers be used?
7. What cipher mode of operation should be used?
   a. ECB b. CBC c. OFB d. CFB e. Counter
8. Should symmetric or asymmetric keys be used?
9. What key management procedures should be used for:
   a. Key generation
   b. Key distribution
   c. Key verification
   d. Controlling key use
   e. Responding to key compromise
   f. Key change
   g. Key storage
   h. Key recovery, backup
   i. Destroying old keys
10. What encryption algorithm should be used?

Note: Questions 3 through 10 are repeated for each collection of data identified in Questions 1 and 2.

Third, the encryption strength needed is determined; this can vary from low to medium for random office e-mail traffic, to very high for defense or intelligence applications. This information is derived from the IA goals.

Fourth, the level or levels of the ISO OSI and TCP/IP reference models in which to implement encryption are identified. Exhibit 20 depicts potential encryption points in a typical information architecture. As shown, encryption can be implemented at the physical, data link, network, transport, and application layers.

Data link level encryption encrypts all traffic on a single point-to-point link. It is easy to implement because of well-defined hardware interfaces.[409] Data link level encryption is transparent to higher level applications and provides protection against traffic analysis.[241,409] However, data is exposed at network nodes because it must be decrypted to obtain routing information.[241,409]

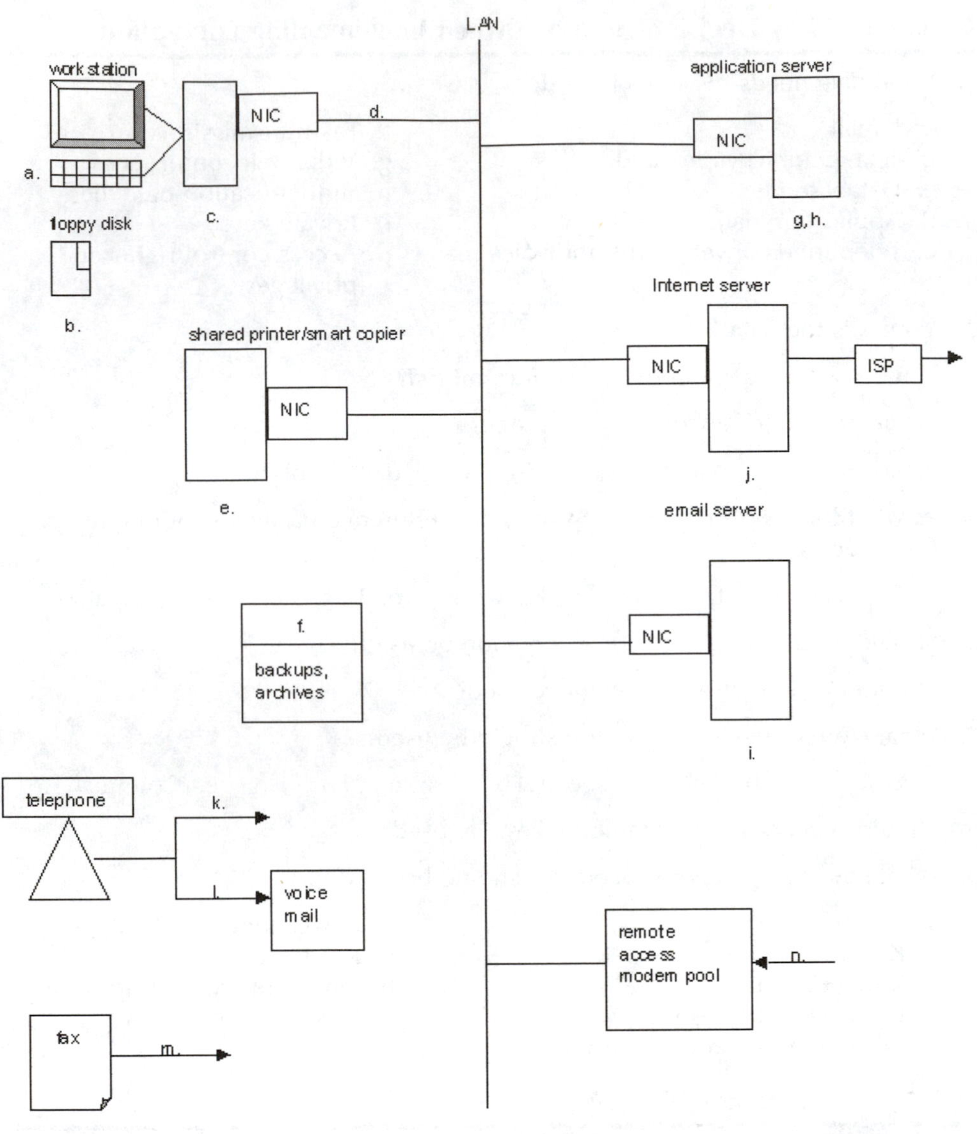

Exhibit 20 Potential Encryption Points in a Typical Information Architecture

Network and transport level encryption utilize a key ID that explains the encryption algorithm, blocksize, integrity check, and validity period. ATM encryption standards are under development.[426] Transport level encryption is implemented using the transport level security (TLS1) protocol, which makes use of TCP virtual circuits. This permits different circuits between the same pair of hosts to be protected with different keys.[241] TLS1 encrypts the TCP header and segment, but not the IP header. Network level encryption is implemented using either IPSec or the network level security (NLS) protocol, which make use of encapsulation. IPSec and NLS encrypt entire packets, including the original IP header, and generate a new IP header. IPSec, NLS, and TLS1 are transparent to higher level applications. IPSec and NLS protect subnets from traffic analysis,[241] while TLS1 does not. Key management is

Legend for Exhibit 20

Encryption Point	*Level of Encryption*	*Type of Encryption*
a. Keyboard to CPU	Data link	Hardware
b. CPU to portable media	Data link	Hardware
c. Local workstation hard drive	Application	Hardware or software
d. Local workstation to LAN	Network	Hardware
e. Local workstation to shared printer/smart copier	Network	Hardware
f. Electronic archives	Application	Software
g. Application server	Application	Software
h. Database management system	Application	Software
i. E-mail server	Transport	Software
j. Internet server	Transport	Hardware
k. Telephone conversations	Data link	Hardware
l. Voice mail storage	Data link	Hardware
m. Fax transmissions	Data link	Hardware
n. Remote access to LAN	Data link	Hardware

more complex than data link level encryption.[409] (See also the discussion of secure protocols.)

Application layer encryption can be implemented in a variety of ways. For example, a custom application can encrypt data stored on a server or in a database. Financial data in spreadsheets can be encrypted on local workstations. Corporate personnel files can be encrypted. Perhaps the best-known instance of application level encryption is e-mail. Several e-mail encryption protocols are available, including PEM, PGP, and S/MIME. In addition to encryption, some of these protocols support digital signatures and digital certificates. A common vulnerability of all application layer security is that the data can be attacked through the operating system before it is encrypted. Another concern is when encryption takes place relative to the browser function, because browsers store previous Web pages.[277] Accordingly, it is beneficial to employ encryption at multiple levels.

To supplement application level encryption, data can also be encrypted while it is stored on a local workstation, on an application server, in backup files, archives, and other portable media. As mentioned, the clear text stores of this information must be controlled as well or the encryption will be to no avail.

The fifth decision is whether hardware or software encryption should be used, inasmuch as encryption algorithms can be implemented in either. Hardware encryption is the primary choice for critical applications and is used almost exclusively by the defense and intelligence communities.[409] This is true for several reasons. Hardware encryption provides algorithm and to some extent key security because the units are designed to: (1) be tamperproof, (2) erase keys if tampering is attempted, and (3) eliminate emanations through shielding.[409] Hardware encryption is considerably faster than software encryption and it offloads intensive calculations from the CPU, thus improving overall system performance. Hardware encryption is implemented in modules, boards, and boxes that are easy to install. Software encryption, while easy to use and upgrade, presents several vulnerabilities not found in hardware encryption. For example, the software encryption task runs the risk of being preempted by a higher priority task or interrupt and being written to disk. This leaves both the key and the data exposed.[409] Likewise, software encryption algorithms are vulnerable to unauthorized and potentially undetected alterations. Key management is also more complex with software encryption.

The sixth decision is whether block or stream ciphers should be used. Block ciphers operate on a fixed number of bits or bytes; if necessary, the last block is padded. Both the cipher text and clear text have the same block size. Block ciphers can be implemented in hardware or software. Stream ciphers operate on asynchronous bit streams, transforming a single bit or byte of data at a time. Stream ciphers are implemented in hardware at the data link level.

The next decision concerns the mode the block or stream cipher will operate in — its mode of operation. Some modes are only applicable to block ciphers, while others work for both block and stream ciphers. The differences between the modes are, for the most part, subtle. A notable difference is the extent to which errors are propagated. The five most common modes are: electronic code book (ECB), cipher block chaining (CBC), output feedback (OFB), cipher feedback (CFB), and counter. ECB mode produces the same results from the same block of data each time. This feature is convenient and simplifies verification, but facilitates cryptoanalysis.[241] In CBC mode, each block of clear text is exclusive OR'd with the previous block of cipher text before encryption. Initialization vectors are supplied for the first block of data. Block ciphers or stream ciphers can operate in OFB mode. In this mode, n-bits of the previous cipher text are exclusive OR'd with the clear text, starting at the right-most bit. This mode has the advantage that errors are not propagated. In CFB mode, the left-most n-bits of the last cipher text block are exclusive OR'd with the first/next n-bits of the clear text. Unfortunately, this mode propagates errors. In counter mode, sequence numbers (rather than previous cipher text) are used as input to the encryption algorithm. The counter is increased by a constant value after each block is encrypted. Block ciphers or stream ciphers can operate in counter mode. Errors are not propagated.

The choice of encryption key type is next. Symmetric or asymmetric keys can be used. When symmetric or secret keys are used, the same key is used for encryption and decryption. The use of symmetric keys is the traditional approach to encryption and was used in the past primarily for defense and intelligence applications. Symmetric keys are appropriate in the following situations:

- The sender and receiver are known to each other and are in the same organization or cooperating organizations.
- The sender and receiver remain constant for a fixed period of time.
- The sending and receiving nodes remain constant for a fixed period of time.

- A long-term relationship between the sender and receiver is anticipated, with a regular need to exchange sensitive information.
- The sender and receiver have the ability to cooperate on key management and other encryption issues.

In contrast, with asymmetric keys, a pair of public and private keys are used. The public key (used for encryption) is shared, while the private key (used for decryption) is not. The two keys are mathematically related but it is not feasible to uncover the private key from the public key. In practice, when A wants to send B a sensitive message, A encrypts the message with B's public key. Then, B decrypts the message with their private key. The first asymmetric key cryptosystems were announced in the late 1970s. Since then, several other systems have been developed. Asymmetric key cryptosystems are considerably slower and use much longer key lengths than symmetric key systems. As Schneier[409] points out, symmetric and asymmetric key systems are designed for different operational profiles:

> *Symmetric cryptography is best for encrypting data. It is orders of magnitude faster and is not susceptible to chosen cipher text attacks. Public key cryptography can do things symmetric cryptography can't; it is best for key management and a myriad of other protocols [digital signatures, key exchange and authentication, digital cash, and so forth].*

Most organizations employ a combination of symmetric and asymmetric key systems. As Lee[330] observes:

> *In practice, the symmetric key and public key systems are not in competition. Most cryptographic schemes on which e-Commerce operations rely use a hybrid of the two systems to exploit the key management flexibility of a public key system and the fast scrambling speeds of symmetric key systems. This hybrid approach is often called key wrapping.*

Key management issues are the next logical decision. Given that most encryption algorithms are publicly available, it is the keys that must be protected. The extent to which a key is protected should be proportional to the sensitivity of the information being encrypted. Several issues must be decided when developing key management plans and procedures; these include:

- Algorithm to use to generate the key
- Process and schedule for changing keys
- How to distribute keys securely
- How to store keys securely, both local and backup copies
- How to verify the authenticity of keys
- Process for recovering "lost" keys

- Process for controlling and revoking keys
- Process for destroying all instances of old keys
- Process for responding to the compromise of a secret or private key

These policies and procedures need to be established by an organization, with the involvement of all stakeholders, prior to implementing encryption. All staff should be thoroughly trained to use the procedures. Periodic audits should be conducted to verify that the procedures are being followed and to look for opportunities to improve them.

The final decision to be made concerns which encryption algorithm to use. Of course, several of the decisions made above will narrow this choice. The strength of an encryption algorithm depends in part on the sophistication of the algorithm and the length of the key.[241,403,409] However, as both Schneier[410] and Ritter[396] point out, longer key lengths by themselves do not necessarily guarantee more security. Rozenblit[403] notes that "the amount of computation it takes, on average, to uncover the secret key increases exponentially with the size of the key." Most sources recommend changing symmetric keys at least once a day[241,403,409]; in fact, in very critical applications, separate keys may be used for each session.[241] Likewise, it is recommended that asymmetric systems employ timestamps to prevent replay.[403]

In addition, there are several implementation details to consider. The processing efficiency of the algorithm, in terms of time and resources used, is a major factor. Efficiency is improved if the encryption blocksize is consistent with the data bus size. Files should be compressed before they are encrypted, while error detection/correction codes should be added after encryption.[409] In situations where confidentiality is particularly important, it may be beneficial to implement multiple or cascade encryption to further inhibit opportunities for cryptoanalysis. In multiple encryption, an algorithm is repeated several times on the same block of data using multiple keys; triple DES is a well-known example of this. In cascade encryption, multiple different algorithms are performed on the same block of data. Finally, while encrypting e-mail increases privacy for the sender and receiver, it potentially decreases system and data integrity for the receiver because, as Garber[272] notes, many commercial anti-virus products have difficulty scanning encrypted e-mail effectively.

Error Detection/Correction

Error detection/correction algorithms are used to increase data integrity during the transmission of data within and among networks and system integrity during the execution of application software. At the network level, error detection/correction algorithms examine data to determine if any data was "accidentally" corrupted or lost, and to discover if any unauthorized changes were "intentionally" made to the data.[357] These errors are compensated for by self-correcting codes at the receiving end or requests for retransmission. At the application software level, error detection/correction algorithms detect anomalous or illegal modes/states, parameters, etc., and initiate the appropriate error handling routines.

Examples of common error detection/correction algorithms used at the network level include longitudal and vertical parity checks, Hamming codes, convolutional codes, recurrent codes, checksums, and cyclical redundancy checks (CRCs).[357] The receiving end performs the error detection and notifies the transmitting end. In response, the transmitting end, in most cases, provides a reason for the error along with an indication of whether the condition is temporary or permanent.[334] If the error condition is expected to be prolonged, the receiving end may request that a new session be established. Morris[357] has identified several factors to consider when selecting which error detection/correction algorithms to implement:

- Type of data to be transmitted
- Degree of accuracy required in received data
- Inherent level of reliability required
- Number (or percent) of incorrect digits or messages that are allowed through
- Delays allowed in the system
- Accepted redundancy of the data allowed (the volume of the data transmitted versus the accuracy required)
- Required throughput in the system (throughput is reduced by redundancy, coding delays, and requests for retransmission)
- Type of links available and the interferences that may be anticipated in the links
- Efficiency of the data transmission or communication links
- Implementation cost and the cost efficiency of the various error control techniques

At the application software level, this technique involves: (1) identifying where possible errors could occur in accessing, manipulating, and relaying information; and (2) defining the appropriate corrective action to be taken in each instance. It is unlikely that error detection/correction will be implemented for all potential error conditions due to program size, response time, schedule, and budget constraints; hence, the focus should be on IA-critical and IA-related functions/entities. Error conditions that might result from accidentally and intentionally induced anomalies, as well as potential transient faults, should be included in the analysis.

Fail Safe/Secure, Fail Operational

Fail safe/secure and fail operational are IA design techniques which ensure that a system remains in a known safe/secure state following an irrecoverable failure. To fail safe/secure means that a component automatically places itself in a known safe/secure mode/state in the event of a failure. In many instances, known safe default values are assumed. Then the system is brought to a known safe/secure mode/state by shutting it down; for example, the shutdown of a nuclear reactor by a monitoring and protection system.[345] To fail operational means that a system or component continues to provide limited critical functionality in the event of a failure. In some instances, a system cannot simply shut down; it must continue to provide some level of service if it is not to be hazardous, such as an aircraft flight control system.[345]

Fail safe/secure and fail operational ensure that a system responds predictably to failures by making proactive design decisions. The first step is to identify all possible failure modes. This is done by developing transaction paths and using IA analysis techniques such as FTA, FMECA, and HAZOP studies. Next, the appropriate response to each failure is specified so that the system will remain in a known safe/secure state. Examples of different types of fail safe/secure or fail operational modes include[288,333,422]:

- Fail operational by transitioning to degraded mode operations
- Fail safe/secure by assuming known safe/secure default values and then activating an emergency shutdown
- Fail operational by transferring to manual or external control
- Fail operational by activating a restart
- Fail safe/secure by activating a hold state, whereby no functionality is provided while action is taken to maintain the system in a safe/secure state and minimize the extent of damage

The correct response to one failure may be to fail safe/secure, while the correct response to another failure in the same system may be to fail operational. Also, the operational mode/state will influence the choice of a failure response.

Fail safe/secure and fail operational designs should be implemented for all IA-critical and IA-related functions/entities at the hardware, software, and system levels. This is essential for maintaining IA integrity. Fault tolerance prevents a limited number of faults from progressing to failures. Those that cannot or are not expected to be handled sufficiently by fault tolerance must be dealt with by fail safe/secure and fail operational designs. Combining fault tolerance and fail safe/secure and fail operational designs is another example of defense in depth.

Fault Tolerance

Fault tolerance increases IA integrity by providing continued correct execution in the presence of a limited number of hardware or software faults.[60,225] As Jajodia[305] notes:

> *Fault tolerance is a natural approach for dealing with information attacks because it is designed to address system loss, compromise, and damage during operation.*

Fault tolerance is a category of IA design techniques that focuses on containing and mitigating the consequences of faults, rather than preventing them. It is important to clarify the terminology used in this regard:

- An **error** is the difference between a computed, observed, or measured value or condition and the true, specified, or theoretically correct value or condition.[44]
- A **fault** is a defect that results in an incorrect step, process, data value, or mode/state.
- A **failure** is failing to or to inability of a system, entity, or component to perform its required function(s), according to specified performance criteria, due to one or more fault conditions.
- A **mistake** is an erroneous human action (accidental or intentional) that produces a fault condition.

Either an error or a mistake can cause a fault, which can lead to a failure:

Error or mistake → Fault → Failure

Fault tolerance attempts to prevent a fault from progressing to a failure, which could compromise a system or render it inoperable. Faults provide an opening for possible attacks, especially if the fault condition can be induced.

There are three types of fault tolerance: hardware, software, and system. As Levi and Agrawala[334] point out, hardware faults are generated by design errors (overload, improper states, etc.) and environmental stresses, which cause physical degradation of materials, while software faults are caused by design errors and runtime errors. However, they note that[334]:

> *One cannot always distinguish hardware from software failures. ...hardware failures can produce identical faulty behavior to that generated by software. Memory failures are equivalent to software failures if they occur during instruction fetch cycles of the processors, generating an erroneous execution of an instruction. A processor whose program counter is inappropriately altered produces an out of order execution of instructions as does a software design error.*

As a result, a combination of hardware, software, and system fault tolerance is needed.

Hardware fault tolerance is usually implemented through redundancy, diversity, power-on tests, BITE, and other monitoring functions. The concept is that if a primary component fails, the secondary component will take over and continue normal operations.

Software fault tolerance is usually implemented through block recovery, diversity, error detection/correction, and other IA design techniques. The basic premise of software fault tolerance is that it is nearly impossible to develop software that is 100 percent defect-free; therefore, IA design techniques should be employed to detect and recover from errors while minimizing their consequences. Software fault tolerance should be implemented in both application and system software. In September 1999, Enea OSE Systems of Sweden announced the first fault tolerant, real-time operating system to be IEC 61508 certified. This product, OSE, offers a "full featured real-time operating system for fault tolerant high-end systems" and supports the "direct message-passing method of interprocess communication, memory protection, and error detection/correction."[415]

System fault tolerance combines hardware and software fault tolerance, with software monitoring the health of both the hardware and the software. System fault tolerance should be employed for IA-critical and IA-related functions. Fault tolerance is an effective method to increase system reliability and availability. It may increase the physical size and weight of a system, which can conflict with specified constraints.

Firewalls, Filters

A firewall is a security gateway between one network and another that uses a variety of techniques to block unwanted users and processes from entering a network while protecting legitimate users, sensitive data, and processes, in accordance with IA goals. Firewalls control access to resources between one network and another. They determine if a particular message or process should be allowed to enter or exit a system[248] by monitoring both incoming and outgoing traffic. Firewalls perform several critical functions, similar to caller-ID and call-blocking on a telephone, which help to maintain IA integrity, including[248,277]:

- Access control based on sender or receiver addresses
- Access control based on the service requested
- Hiding internal network topology, addresses, and traffic from the outside world
- Virus checking incoming files
- Authentication based on traffic source
- Logging Internet activities for future analysis
- Blocking incoming junk e-mail
- Blocking outgoing connections to objectionable Web sites

There are three main types of firewalls: packet filters, application level gateways, and circuit level gateways. Packet filters determine if a packet should be let into a network based on the communication endpoint identifiers.[253] Depending on the source or destination address or port, packets may be purposely dropped. Filtering rules (block or allow) are specified based on source, port, destination, port, and flags. Packets not explicitly allowed by a filter rule are rejected. This, of course, assumes that filtering rules were created with tight specifications. Packet filters can be configured to examine both incoming and outgoing packets. Packet filters are essentially ineffective when UDP is used.[241]

Application level gateways are, in essence, firewalls that are developed to protect specific applications. The most common usage is with e-mail servers. A separate application level gateway is required for each service or application. Usually, all traffic is logged by an application level gateway.

Circuit level gateways, sometimes called proxy firewalls, mediate between two devices attempting to communicate across a firewall[253]; they relay TCP connections. In practice, a caller connects to a port on the outside gateway. If the session is approved, the gateway forwards the information to the destination that is connected to an internal gateway port. Circuit level gateways log the number of bytes sent by TCP address. They are not effective against insider attacks.[241] Because of the different services provided, most organizations use a combination of firewall types.

Several issues arise during the implementation of firewalls. One of the first is how to configure the firewall; the answer, representing a trade-off between security and connectivity, is derived from the IA goals and IA integrity level. Firewalls primarily provide protection at the lower levels of the ISO OSI and TCP/IP reference models. They should be evaluated against known vulnerabilities, specific protection profiles, and content-based attacks.[251] Many commercial firewall products are available. To facilitate the selection process, the Computer Security Institute (CSI)[470] publishes an annual report that compares these products. A persistent concern has been the ability to provide firewall-like protection for home PCs, especially those operating home-based businesses. A remedy for this situation was recently announced. Groner[281] reports that a scaled-down version of CheckPoint's firewall software is being sold on a chip to modem manufacturers for use with home computers.

Formal Specifications, Animated Specifications

Formal methods use mathematical techniques in the specification, design, and verification of computer hardware and software.[422] More precisely, formal methods are[129]:

> *a software specification and production method, based on mathematics that comprises: a collection of mathematical notations addressing the specification, design, and development processes of software production; [the result being] a well-founded logical inference system in which formal verification proofs and proofs of other properties can be formulated [and] a methodological framework within which software may be developed from the specification in a formally verifiable manner.*

In short, formal methods use a formal notation, based on discrete mathematics, to specify and verify system requirements and design. There are a variety of formal notations, or languages, with supporting toolsets available today: B, calculus of communicating systems (CCS), communicating sequential processes (CSP), higher order logic (HOL), language for temporal ordering specification (LOTOS), OBJ, temporal logic, Vienna development method (VDM), and Z. These languages support a combination of computer hardware and software specification and design in concurrent, parallel, sequential, and real-time environments.

A formal specification is a system description written in a formal language. As such, it can be subjected to rigorous mathematical analysis to detect various classes of inconsistencies, incorrectness, and incompleteness.[69,422] The precision required by formal specification languages makes this analysis possible. With some toolsets, the analysis can be performed automatically, similar to a compiler performing syntax checks.[69] Another advantage of formal specifications is that they can be animated to illustrate specified system behavior and, in so doing, either validate requirements or highlight the need for clarifications and corrections. As IEC 61508-7 notes[69]:

> *Animation can give extra confidence that the system meets the* real *requirement as well as the formally specified requirement, because it improves human recognition of the specified behavior.*

Formal specifications were developed to compensate for weaknesses inherent in natural language specifications, in particular the ambiguity and susceptibility to misunderstanding and multiple interpretations.[422] They attempt to bridge the gap between a set of natural language requirements and a design implemented in a computer language. The development of formal languages began in the 1970s. The primary use was in verifying that security kernels correctly implemented a specified security policy and model. The mathematical precision of these languages was well suited to the task. In the 1980s, the safety community adapted and expanded the languages and methods to real-time, safety-critical control systems.[422] The languages, methods, and supporting toolsets continued to evolve and, by the mid-1990s, several national and international standards either mandated or highly recommended their use.[18,24,31,60,69,129]

Formal specifications have many advantages in the IA domain. Incorrect specifications are considered the source of most errors in computer systems[422]; in fact, some consider them to be the source of the most serious errors.[333] A technique that reduces the likelihood of errors being introduced during the specification phase is very beneficial in terms of cost, schedule, and ultimate system performance. Errors, inconsistencies, and ambiguities are resolved before coding begins. Formal specifications help to clarify access control requirements and operational modes/states of IA-critical and IA-related functions. The rigor imposed by the notation forces both positive and negative instances to be specified, similar to specifying MWFs and MNWFs. The process by which formal specifications are verified helps to ensure that stated IA integrity levels will be achieved and can be maintained. Animation permits the feasibility of a system, against specified constraints (memory, I/O, bandwidth, response times, etc.), to be evaluated before full-scale development.[81]

Exhibit 21 illustrates the precision of formal specifications by rewriting Exhibits 14c and 15 in a formal notation.

Information Hiding

Information hiding is an IA design technique that enhances IA integrity by: (1) preventing accidental access to and corruption of critical software and

Exhibit 21 Sample Formal Specifications

A. Exhibit 14C Written as a Formal Specification

SECURITY LABELS

Confidential, Secret, TopSecret, AllModes: F SECURITY LABELS

Confidential ∪ Secret ∪ TopSecret = AllModes
Confidential _ Secret _ TopSecret = 0

DesktopOA ∪ LocalEmail = Confidential
DesktopOA _ LocalEmail = 0

Secret ⊃ Confidential
DesktopOA ∪ LocalEmail ∪ LimitedApplA = Secret
DesktopOA _ LocalEmail _ LimitedApplA = 0

TopSecret ⊃ Secret
DesktopOA ∪ LocalEmail ∪ FullApplA ∪ ForeignEmail ∪ InetSearch ∪
ImportFiles = TopSecret
DesktopOA _ LocalEmail _ FullApplA _ ForeignEmail _ InetSearch _
ImportFiles = 0

B. Exhibit 15 Written as a Formal Specification

OPERATIONAL MODES

NormalOps, TriggerWarning, TriggerAlert, ActivateShutdown, AllModes:
F OPERATIONALMODES

NormalOps ∪ TriggerWarning ∪ TriggerAlert ∪ ActivateShutdown = AllModes
NormalOps _ TriggerWarning _ TriggerAlert _ ActivateShutdown = 0

NormTemp ∪ NormPress = NormalOps
NormTemp _ NormPress = 0

(LowTemp ∪ LowPress) .OR. (NormTemp ∪ LowPress) .OR.
(LowTemp ∪ NormPress) = TriggerWarning
(LowTemp _ LowPress) ∪ (NormTemp _ LowPress) ∪
(LowTemp _ NormPress) = 0

(NormTemp ∪ HighPress) .OR. (HighTemp ∪ LowPress) .OR.
(HighTemp ∪ NormPress) = TriggerAlert
(NormTemp _ HighPress) ∪ (HighTemp _ LowPress) ∪
(HighTemp _ NormPress) = 0

(HighTemp ∪ HighPress) .OR. (LowTemp ∪ HighPress) = ActivateShutdown
(HighTemp _ HighPress) ∪ (LowTemp _ HighPress) = 0

data, (2) minimizing the introduction of errors during maintenance and enhancements, (3) reducing the likelihood of CCFs, and (4) minimizing fault propagation. IEEE Std. 610.12-1990 defines information hiding as:

1. A software development technique in which each module's interfaces reveal as little as possible about the module's innerworkings and other modules are prevented from using information about the module that is not in the module's interface specification;

2. A software development technique that consists of isolating a system function, or set of data and operations on those data, within a module and providing precise specifications for the module.

Information hiding can be applied to data and program logic. Information hiding increases reliability and maintainability by minimizing coupling between modules, while maximizing their cohesion.[81] Data structures and logic are localized and as self-contained as possible. This allows the internal data structures and logic of a module to be changed at a later date without affecting the behavior of other modules or necessitating that they also be changed; hence the four benefits listed above. Accordingly, information hiding is highly recommended by several national and international standards.[18,27,38,69] Object-oriented designs are quite amenable to information hiding.[277]

Intrusion Detection, Response

Intrusion detection and response systems recognize and respond to a security breach, either as it is happening or immediately afterward. Intrusion detection and response systems operate behind a firewall; following the concept of defense in depth, they catch outsider attacks that penetrated a firewall. Insider attacks can also be foiled by intrusion detection and response systems. Lehtinen and Lear[331] quote from a CSI report that "financial losses from network security breaches at 163 businesses surveyed amounted to $123.7 million in 1998." They note that this figure is probably low because many companies under-report information security related losses in order to maintain customer confidence. Regardless, the need for robust intrusion detection and response systems will expand in proportion to the growth of e-Commerce and corporate and government dependence on information infrastructures. It is important to note that the consequences of security breaches are not limited to financial concerns; safety, legal, national security, and other issues can be raised as well. For example, when someone breaks into your house, that is a security breach. What is important, however, is what they do once they are inside.

There are three main types of intrusion detection and response systems[287]: statistical anomaly detection, rules-based detection, and hybrid. Statistical anomaly detection analyzes audit trail data for abnormal user or system behavior that may indicate an impending attack. Current audit trail data is compared against historical audit trail data that is presumed to reflect normal activity. While this approach is straightforward, it has some shortcomings.

First, if the historical data contains an undetected attack, that activity will be built into the normal profile. Second, it is possible for an attacker to learn what normal behavior is and as a result fool the system.[248] Third, if the normal profiles are specified too loosely or too tightly, a wave of false positives or false negatives will be triggered.[248,253,287] Fourth, real-time analysis of audit trail data is resource intensive.[287]

Rules-based detection monitors audit trail data for patterns of activity that match known attack profiles. This approach also has weaknesses. First, only known attack profiles will be detected; new or unforeseen attacks will not be recognized.[248,253,287] Second, the library of known attack profiles must be updated frequently or the system will quickly become obsolete.[248] Third, like statistical anomaly detection, it is resource intensive. Hence, the ideal approach is to deploy a hybrid intrusion detection and response system that combines statistical anomaly and rules-based detection.

There are several details to consider when implementing intrusion detection and response systems. Intrusion detection should be implemented for networks and host computers[331]; the latter is often overlooked. Denning[248] recommends several criteria to evaluate when developing potential attack profiles:

- Unexplained system crashes or restarts
- A series of unsuccessful login attempts
- Creation of accounts with no passwords
- Creation of accounts that grant root access
- Modifications to system programs
- Modifications to Internet configuration parameters
- A reduction in audit trail size (deleting footprints of an attack)
- Hidden files
- Sudden activity on a previously dormant account
- Logging in at strange hours
- Logging in more than once simultaneously
- Unusual activity in guest/visitor accounts

In addition, Cohen[244] makes the astute observation that the first phase of an attack may be to crash the intrusion detection system itself.

Intrusion detection software can be implemented on the network and application servers being monitored, although this is not recommended. As noted above, intrusion detection systems are resource intensive and will affect system performance. Instead, the use of self-contained intrusion detection units is preferred. This practice also helps to isolate the intrusion detection system from an attack.[277] There are several commercial products available that provide this capability. Industry and government are working together to develop standards that will promote vendor interoperability and common product evaluation criteria.[331] A key effort in this direction is the development of the common intrusion specification language (CISL) by the common intrusion detection framework (CIDF) working group.[315] The language will allow multiple vendors to use common parameters and syntax to detect and profile attack modes. As Kenyon reports[315]:

Such communication allows applications to identify and locate assaults more accurately while enabling administrators to deploy advanced response and recovery procedures.

A final implementation detail concerns how to respond to an attack. One option is to have the system automatically respond, with no human intervention. A second option is to trigger an alarm, equivalent to the audit trail security alarm, which requires human action. Primary and secondary recipients of the alarm must be identified along with the time interval during which a response must be taken. A third option is to trigger an alarm. Then, if no human action occurs within a specified time interval, the system automatically responds. It is likely that it will be preferable to use different options in response to the criticality of diverse attack profiles. To preempt a crisis situation, an appropriate response to each attack profile must be (1) specified in the operational procedures for the second and third options, or (2) preprogrammed into the system for the first and third options. The appropriate response is determined by reviewing/revalidating the fail safe/secure and fail operational design provisions.

Partitioning

Partitioning enhances IA integrity by preventing the corruption and compromise of IA-critical and IA-related functions/entities. Partitioning performs two functions: it prevents (1) the non-IA-critical functions/entities of a system from *accidentally* corrupting or interfering with the IA-critical and IA-related functions/entities, and (2) the non-IA-critical functions/entities from being used as a vehicle for *intentionally* corrupting or compromising IA-critical and IA-related functions/entities.

The implementation of partitioning is straightforward. Similar to information hiding, partitioning requires complete interface specifications. Hardware and software partitioning can be implemented. Software partitioning can be logical or physical (such as logically partitioning a hard drive). Ideally, a combination of hardware, software, logical, and physical partitioning should be deployed. IA-critical and IA-related functions/entities are isolated from non-IA-related functions/entities. Both design and functionality are partitioned to prevent accidental and intentional corruption and interference. For example, one approach to protecting desktop workstations and home computers is hardware partitioning. Blackburn[215] reports that Voltaire has developed a security card that physically divides a PC into two different workstations — one public/unsecured and one private/secured. Only one segment can be accessed at a time; however, both segments utilize the same NIC. This product received NSA certification in July 1999.

This technique offers several advantages. First, it reduces the effort required to verify IA-critical and IA-related functions/entities. Second, through the use of partitioning, resources can be focused on the most critical elements in a system. Third, partitioning facilitates fault isolation and minimizes the potential for fault propagation. Partitioning is often referred to as separability in the security community. Several national and international standards either mandate or highly recommend the use of partitioning.[18,24,31,53,126,127,129]

Plausibility Checks

A plausibility check is an IA design technique that enhances IA integrity by verifying the validity and legitimacy of critical parameters before acting upon them. Plausibility checks detect faults early in the execution cycle and prevent them from progressing into failures or system compromises.

The implementation of plausibility checks is straightforward. Checks are performed on parameters that affect IA-critical and IA-related functions/entities before critical operations are performed to verify that the value of the parameters are both plausible and legal. The specific parameters checked will vary by application. Plausibility checks can be used to enhance safety, reliability, and security. Examples of items that can be checked to enhance safety and reliability include[60,129,130]:

- Parameter size (number of bits, bytes, digits, etc., to prevent overflow)
- Array bounds
- Counter values
- Parameters type verification, especially illegal combinations of parameters
- Legitimate called from routine
- Timer values
- Assertions about parameter values, operational mode/state, and pre- and post-conditions
- Range checks of intermediate results

Examples of items that can be checked to enhance security include:

- Is this a normal or feasible time for this user to be logging in (shift/travel/training/leave status)?
- Is this a normal or feasible location for this user to be logging in from (logical and physical network address, terminal ID, etc.)?
- Does this session reflect a normal activity level for this user account in terms of resources accessed and used (connection duration, application usage, files copied, printer usage, etc.)?
- What is the time interval between when this user was authenticated and the present (if too long, should reauthentication be initiated to preempt an imposter)?
- Is this type of request normally initiated by a user or a process?
- Are hard and soft copies being directed to a location normally used by this user?
- Does this account normally receive e-mail from this destination?
- Is it normal for 100 people to receive e-mail from different senders that has the same header? (Prevent distribution of e-mail virus.)

There is a fair degree of synergy between the specification of plausibility checks to be performed by a software application and the definition of normal profiles used by an intrusion detection system.

Redundancy

Redundancy is a fault tolerance design technique employed to increase hardware reliability and system availability.[69,131,368,422] IEEE Std. 610.12-1990 defines redundancy as:

> the presence of auxiliary components in a system to perform the same functions as other elements for the purpose of preventing or recovering from failure.

In this context, identical components are used to perform identical functions. This contrasts with diversity, in which diverse components are used to perform identical functions.

The terms "reliability" and "availability" are often confused. Hence, it is important to clarify them in order to understand the role of redundancy in relation to reliability and availability. Hardware reliability refers to the ability of a system or component to correctly perform its function under certain conditions in a specified operational environment for a stated period of time. Availability is a measurement indicating the rate at which systems, data, and other resources are operational and accessible when needed, despite accidental and intentional subsystem outages and other disruptions. Availability is an outcome of reliability and a reflection of IA integrity. Availability is usually defined as:

$$A = MTBF/(MTBF + MTTR)$$

where: MTBF = Mean time between failures
MTTR = Mean time to repair

This definition is inadequate in the IA domain because it does not take into account failures induced by malicious intentional acts. If, however, the definitions of MTBF and MTTR are expanded such that:

$MTBF_{IA}$ = Mean time between accidental and intentional failures

$MTTR_{IA}$ = Mean time to repair and recover

then the calculation

$$A_{IA} = MTBF_{IA}/(MTBF_{IA} + MTTR_{IA})$$

would be appropriate in the IA domain. One problem remains. While both accidental and intentionally induced failures are random, predicting a failure rate for the latter will be difficult.

Redundancy, and the increased hardware reliability and system availability it provides, are important to IA for several reasons. The historical COMPUSEC model focused on confidentiality, integrity, and availability; without reliability, none of these can be achieved. To be effective, security features must function reliably. To do so, they are dependent on the reliable operation of hardware components, communications equipment, etc. If a hardware or communications component is not reliable, security features can be bypassed and defeated. For example, if firewall hardware is subject to intermittent faults, unauthorized users/processes may slip through. Unreliable hardware and communications equipment can yield incorrect results. Transient memory or CPU faults could lead to data corruption and compromise. Unreliable hardware and communications equipment may cause a critical function, service, or mission not to be performed on time, or at all. This could have security and safety consequences; for example, the loss of a telecommunications backbone or an ATC system. In summary, reliability is essential in achieving security goals and should not be overlooked. As Arbaugh et al.[202] succinctly state:

> *All secure systems assume the integrity of the underlying [hardware and] firmware. They usually cannot tell when that assumption is incorrect. This is a serious security problem.*

In other words, these assumptions need to be backed up by engineering facts.

Hardware redundancy is implemented three ways: active, standby, and monitored. Active redundancy utilizes multiple identical components operating simultaneously to prevent or detect and recover from failures. The redundant components operate in parallel. If a fault is detected in the primary unit, control is switched to the redundant or "hot standby" unit. The transition can be automatic or manual. Standby redundancy also utilizes multiple identical components. However, the redundant or "cold standby" units are not switched on until a fault is detected in the primary unit. Monitored redundancy, often referred to as m-out-of-n redundancy, is a variation of active redundancy. This method monitors the outputs of the parallel components. If discrepancies are found, voting logic is activated (hence the name m-out-of-n) to determine which output is correct and what action should be taken (e.g., switching to a new primary component).[69,422] Monitored redundancy is frequently used in PLCs as triple modular redundancy (TMR).

There are several issues to consider when implementing redundancy. Active redundancy permits a faster transition — the redundant unit is already powered-up and initialized; however, this unit consumes additional power, space, and weight and has been subjected to the same environmental stresses as the primary unit.[362] Standby redundancy provides a slower transition because of the need to power-up and initialize the system.[422] However, the remaining life of this unit is longer than a hot standby because it has not been stressed. Regardless of which method is used, two redundant units are required to trap a single fault, three redundant units are required to trap two faults, etc.[368,422]

Trade-off studies conducted early in the design phase evaluate which option is best for a given application.[131] These studies should ensure that single points of failure are eliminated and that there are no common cause failure modes between redundant units. Redundancy can be implemented anywhere from low-level electronic components to major subsystems. As O'Connor[368] notes:

> *Decisions on when and how to design in redundancy depend upon the criticality of the system or function and must always be balanced against the need to minimize complexity and [development and operational] costs.*

Redundancy is not implemented in software; redundant software simply replicates the same systematic errors.[288,333,422] Instead, diverse software is implemented. Data redundancy is employed, through the use of parity bits and such, with data communication error detection/correction codes. The use of redundancy should be addressed in operational procedures and contingency plans.

Reliability Allocation

Reliability allocation distributes reliability and maintainability requirements among system entities. Reliability is an essential part of IA integrity, as explained above. System reliability requirements are derived from IA goals. Reliability does not just "happen"; rather, like any other requirement, it has to be engineered into a system. The first step in this process is to allocate or apportion reliability and maintainability requirements to the hardware, software, and communications equipment that comprise the system. This step is analogous to the decomposition of functional requirements. Because of the impact of maintainability on operational reliability, these requirements are allocated at the same time.

Reliability allocation serves three main purposes[131]:

1. **Reliability and maintainability targets.** It provides designers, developers, and manufacturers of each part of a system with their target reliability and maintainability requirements. Most large systems today involve multiple organizations and vendors; in this way, each is provided with their reliability and maintainability target.
2. **Monitoring and assessment.** Reliability and maintainability values are available for comparison with assessments made later during the design and development phases. As a result, progress toward achieving reliability and maintainability goals can be monitored. If the evidence indicates that these goals will not be met, corrective action can be taken early in the life cycle.
3. **Trade-off studies.** The process of allocating reliability promotes architectural trade-off studies early in the design phase. Trade-off studies evaluate the technical feasibility and development and operational costs of alternate architectures that meet reliability and maintainability requirements. The extent of fault prevention and fault tolerance needed is also identified.

From its name, reliability allocation sounds simple. In fact, reliability allocation is a sophisticated iterative process that involves four steps.[131] The first step is to assign numerical reliability requirements to system entities and components. It is important to assign reliability requirements at a level (subsystem, component, subcomponent) that is meaningful and verifiable — requirements should not be assigned at a level that is too high or too low. Several factors should be considered when assigning reliability requirements[131,368]: operational mode (continuous or demand), duty cycle, criticality in relation to stated IA integrity level, whether or not the unit is mission repairable, the use of BITE, development risk (especially for new technology), complexity, uncertainty, and historical experience with similar units. The intent is to be realistic when allocating reliability requirements. Acceptable failure rates and the probability of surviving a failure or attack are used to express reliability requirements.

The second step is to determine the maintainability requirements needed to support the reliability requirements. The same conditions listed above are taken into account. Maintainability requirements are generally expressed in terms of an MTTR.

Third, system reliability and maintainability is calculated from the individual components. This is the reverse of the first step. Then system reliability is broken down into values for individual components. Now the values of the individual components are being combined to see if, in fact, if the system reliability and maintainability requirements will be met. In practice, the aggregate system reliability value should be somewhat higher than the stated requirement to compensate for uncertainty.[131,368]

Fourth, component reliability and maintainability requirements are refined through an iterative process of (re)allocation and (re)calculation until the goals are met. Reliability allocations and calculations are generally expressed and analyzed through the use of reliability prediction models, reliability block diagrams,[69,131,132,368] and more recently BBNs.[221,307,361]

Reliability and maintainability requirements are assigned to all system entities (internal, external, hardware, software, and communications equipment) except humans*. Techniques such as FTA, FMECA, and HAZOP studies support the allocation of reliability requirements and are encouraged because they are applicable to both hardware and software. The distinction between random hardware failures and systematic software failures must be maintained when allocating reliability requirements. It is recommended that separate reliability requirements be stated for different types and consequences of failure, taking into account factors such as[132]:

- The severity of the consequences of the failure
- Whether or not recovery from the failure is possible without operator intervention

* Human reliability analysis (HRA) is still subject to academic debate. Reliable, correct, and timely administrator and end-user actions are an important part of mission success. However, at this time, there is no consensus on how this should be estimated or measured.

- Whether or not the failure causes corruption of software or data
- The time required to recover from the failure

Reliability requirements for COTS and reused software should consider historical experience with these products if the previous application is quite similar to the new proposed use.

Secure Protocols

Secure protocols enhance the confidentiality of distributed data communications by providing security services not available through basic communications protocols such as TCP, IP, or X.25. Secure protocols address interoperability issues related to implementing security features, such as placement of a digital signature, algorithms to use to sign and encrypt messages, and key sharing and authentication schemes.[403] Current secure protocols include IPSec, NLS, TLS1, SSL3, SET, PEM, PGP, and S/MIME. While these protocols are used for different purposes, they share a common two-step process. The first step is a digital handshake between the parties that want to communicate. During this step, the parties are authenticated to each other and they negotiate the context of their security association. Encryption algorithms, keys, and other security mechanisms to be used are agreed upon. The second step is the secure exchange of information; sensitive information is exchanged at the level of protection negotiated. If need be, the context of the security association can be updated.

IPSec provides strong one-way authentication for IPv4 and IPv6 packets.[403] Bidirectional communication requires the establishment of two security associations (client → server and server → client) and two sets of encryption keys. IPSec is transparent to users and applications. It attempts to address risks associated with password sniffing, IP spoofing, session hijacking, and denial-of-serve attacks.[372] The IPSec protocol can operate on a router or a firewall. The handshaking process is performed offline. The IPSec authentication header provides data integrity,[372] but not nonrepudiation of origin.[403] A keyed one-way hash function is used to calculate and verify the authentication header data. The second component of IPSec, the encapsulating security payload, can be configured in two modes: transport mode and tunnel mode. Transport mode is used for host-to-host connectivity and provides end-to-end security. In this mode, transport layer frames are encapsulated. In tunnel mode, the entire IP packet is encapsulated and a second IP header is generated for the security gateway. Sequence numbers are assigned to security payloads to prevent replay attacks. Optionally, security payloads can be encrypted before encapsulation, for example, with DES CBC.[277,403] IPv6 mandates the use of IPSec. IPSec is expected to be widely used with virtual private networks (VPNs) and remote connections to corporate intranets.[372] NLS and IPSec perform essentially the same functions.

TLS1, the Transport Layer Security protocol, represents an Internet Engineering Task Force (IETF) standardized version of SSL3. Once it is commercially available, TLS1 is expected to supersede SSL3 in many applications, especially in the ISO OSI environment.[403] TLS1 utilizes TCP virtual circuits. The TCP header and segment are encrypted, but the IP header is not.

SSL3, the Secure Socket Layer protocol, has been promoted by Netscape. It is designed for use in client/server and mobile code environments. The handshake step provides strong peer entity authentication based on X.509v3 digital certificates.[403,405] A separate pair of keys are used for client → server and server → client transactions. The secure transfer step compresses packets and transmits end-user data in encrypted, sequenced blocks.[277,405] Data integrity is ensured through the use of checksums that are produced by a one-way hash function. Currently, SSL3 does not support X.25[405] or provide nonrepudiation.[204]

SET, the Secure Electronic Transactions protocol, supports credit card-based online payment systems. The SET protocol specification, begun in 1996, represents a joint effort by the software industry, VISA, Mastercard, JCB, and American Express. SET is one of the strictest protocols in use today because it must meet the multi-party transactional audit integrity requirements of the financial industry.[260] It provides a secure messaging standard for electronic payments over open and untrusted networks. Internet users are, in effect, linked to credit card payment networks. SET combines X.509 digital certificates and key management framework with extensions to PKCS #7 digital signatures and digital envelopes. Selective multi-party field confidentiality is a key feature of SET; for example, an online merchant cannot see a customer's credit card number, but the financial institution can process the transaction.[260] As e-Commerce expands, so will SET usage. Potential future uses include home banking and online bill payment. The SET protocol is evolving; current information is posted at www.setco.org.[493]

PEM, the Privacy Enhanced Mail protocol, was developed in the late 1980s by the IETF. It was one of the first attempts to provide Internet e-mail privacy. The specification included encryption, digital signatures, and support for symmetric and asymmetric keys. However, because it is incompatible with the Internet mail system, due to seven-bit text messages, it lacks commercial support.

PGP, the Pretty Good Privacy protocol, was the next attempt at providing e-mail privacy. PGP supports digital signatures and encryption but lacks authentication services. It is useful for a small group of casual e-mail users who know each other, but falls short when it comes to scalability and accountability, particularly for large organizations.[260]

The development of S/MIME, the Secure MIME protocol, was a joint effort begun in 1995 by multiple companies under the leadership of RSA Data Security, Inc. The MIME protocol supports the exchange of text, created in diverse languages and character sets, among different computer systems. S/MIME adds PKCS #7 and PKCS #10 security features. Specifically, message origin authentication, message integrity, and nonrepudiation of origin are provided by digital signatures, while message confidentiality is provided by encryption. These features can be optionally selected through human action or set to automatically execute. Originally, S/MIME was used with e-mail; now its use is expanding to secure electronic document interchange (EDI), e-Commerce, and other applications. At present, S/MIME is supported by Netscape Messenger™ and Microsoft Outlook Express™. The IETF is developing S/MIMEv3 as an Internet standard, specifying both message syntax and digital certificate syntax. Current information can be found at www.rsa.com[489] and www.ietf.org.[475]

Virus Scanners

Virus scanners are an IA design feature that automatically detects and removes computer viruses before they are activated. It is important to note that virus scanners detect the presence of viruses — they do not prevent infection. The purpose of virus scanners is to detect and remove viruses before they cause damage, such as deleting, overwriting, prepending, or appending files. The detect/remove process also helps to slow, but not eliminate, the spread of viruses. Virus alerts, real and hoaxes, regularly make the evening news because of the speed with which viruses spread and the extent of damage they are capable of inflicting. The Melissa virus made the rounds in 1999, infecting 1.2 million computers and 53,000 e-mail servers with a damage assessment of $560 million.[272] The Iloveyou virus, in May 2000, was even more destructive. As a result, the need for robust virus scanners is not expected to diminish any time soon.

Viruses are equivalent to cyber termites in that they use the resources of host computers to reproduce and spread, without informed operator action.[245,416] Viruses are spread via floppy disks, CD-ROMs, e-mail attachments, mobile code, and Web browsing.[248] Viruses are classified a variety of different ways[248,277,375]:

- **Boot virus:** Viruses that attack the boot sector of a hard drive or floppy disk and are activated at power-on
- **Macro virus:** viruses that are embedded in word processing documents or spreadsheets as macros and are activated when the macros are executed
- **Program virus:** viruses that attach to and attack *.exe, *.com, *.sys, and *.dll files when executed
- **Transient viruses:** viruses that are active only when the infected program is executing
- **Resident viruses:** viruses that remain in memory and link themselves to the execution of other programs

There are subcategories of viruses: parasitic, stealth, polymorphic, etc. For a complete description of virus types and categories, see Slade*.

Virus scanners are first cousins of intrusion detection systems. They examine code that is on or about to enter a system, looking for known virus profiles.[248] There are four main types of virus scanners[416]: (1) activity monitors, (2) change detection or integrity monitors, (3) pure scanners, and (4) hybrids. Activity monitors are the oldest type of antiviral software. They function similar to intrusion detection systems by looking for suspicious activity patterns that could indicate the presence of virus activity. Change detection or integrity monitors flag system and user files that have been changed and perform integrity checksums. They are apt to generate a lot of false positives unless a method is provided for flagging legitimate changes.[416] Pure scanners examine system and user files, boot sectors, and memory for evidence of infection through comparison with known virus signatures. Some new scanners incorporate heuristic features to detect viruses that have not yet been identified.[416] Most virus scan products on the market today are a hybrid of all three types.

---

* Slade, R., *Guide to Computer Viruses*, Springer-Verlag, 1994.[416]

There are several details to consider when implementing virus scanners. First, the use of virus scanners needs to be complemented with robust antivirus operational procedures. For example[277]:

- All files should be checked before being used.
- Files should only be accepted from known trusted sources.
- Backups should be generated regularly and the integrity of data should be verified before it is backed up.[329]
- The FAT and interrupt tables should be protected.
- The use of default search paths should be minimized.
- Strong file access controls should be implemented.
- E-mail from unknown sources should be deleted.
- Unsolicited e-mail attachments should be considered suspicious and quarantined until they can be verified.
- E-mail chain letters should be blocked at the server.
- A large number of e-mail messages with the same header but different senders should be discarded.

Operational procedures should also specify how frequently virus scan software is executed and updated. It is recommended that both the execution and update process be run automatically and not rely on the actions of end users. Users should be aware that the virus removal process may corrupt original data; this fact reinforces the need for backups. Infected sectors on a hard disk or floppy disk and infected memory locations should be overwritten, more than once, to minimize the likelihood of a virus reappearing. Collaboration between the audit trail function, intrusion detection system, and virus scanner produces the best results. Finally, it should be remembered that the virus scanner itself can be subjected to attack. The latest information on virus alerts and antiviral products is available from http://service.symantec.com,[452] www.cert.org,[460] www.mcaffee.com,[479] and www.symantec.com/avcenter.[495]

In addition to IA design techniques/features, IA integrity depends on common sense, such as having comprehensive and current operational procedures, contingency plans, and physical security practices or protecting Web pages from tampering by storing them on CD-ROMs. As the biblical book of Amos (5:19) says, you do not want to run from a lion only to be caught by a bear.

6.6 Summary

The third component of an effective information security/IA program is the implementation of threat control measures. Five activities are performed during the implementation of threat control measures, as shown in Exhibit 22:

- The type, level, and extent of protection needed are determined.
- Controllability, operational procedures, and in-service considerations are evaluated.

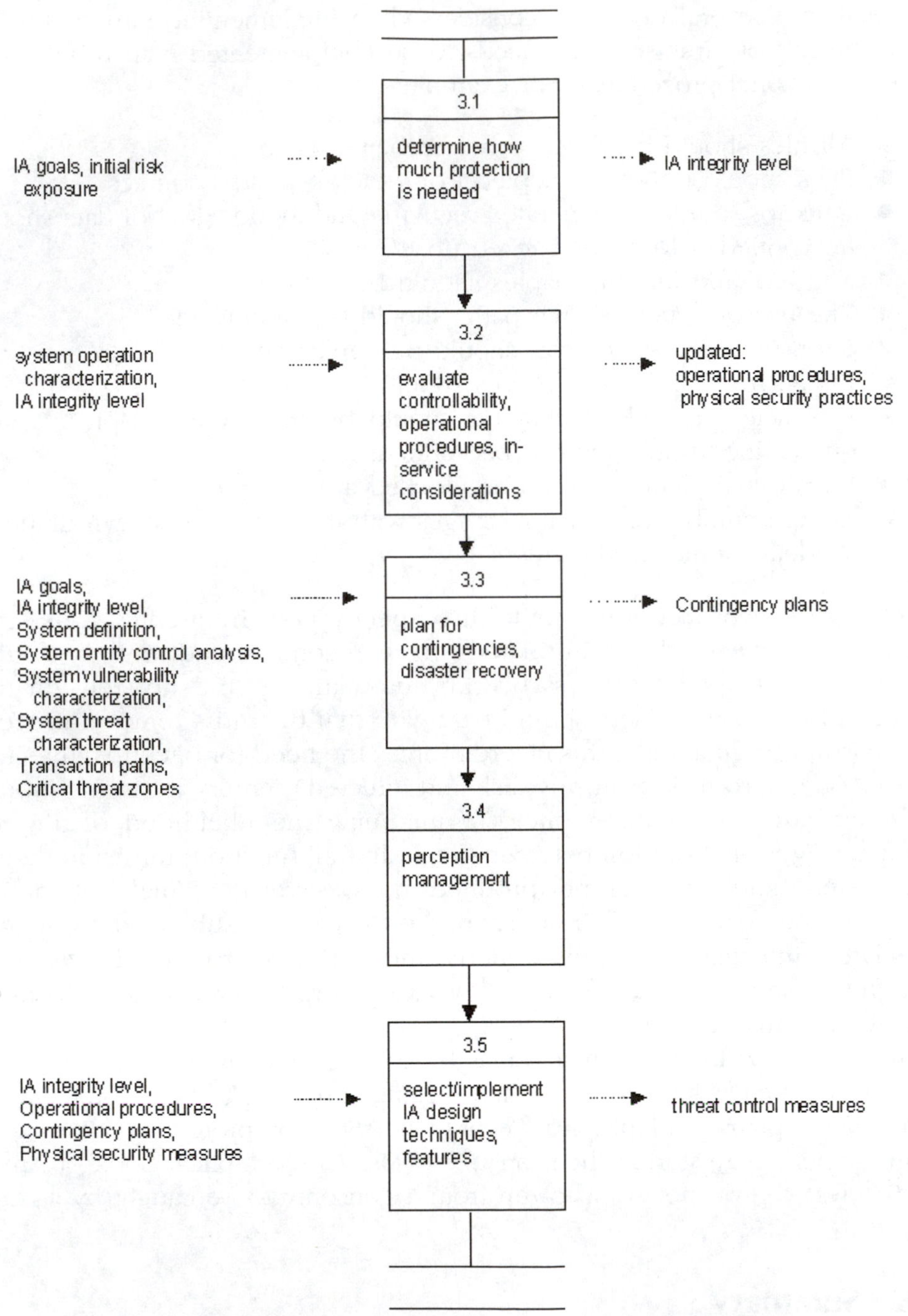

Exhibit 22 Summary of Activities Involved in Implementing Threat Control Measures

- Plans are made for contingencies and disaster recovery.
- The use of perception management is considered.
- IA design techniques and features are selected and implemented.

Exhibit 23 Correlation of IA Design Techniques/Features to the Chronology of Threat Control Measures

Anticipate/Prevent	*Detect/Characterize*	*Respond/Recover*
Access control	Audit trail, security alarm	Audit trail, security alarm
Account for all possible logic states	Block recovery	Block recovery
Authentication	Digital signatures	Degraded-mode operations
Confinement	Diversity	Diversity
Defense in depth	Encryption	Error detection/correction
Defensive programming	Error detection/correction	Fail safe/secure, fail operational
Digital signatures	Intrusion detection	Intrusion detection, response
Encryption	Redundancy	Redundancy
Firewalls, filters	Virus scanner	
Formal specifications, animated specification		
Information hiding		
Partitioning		
Plausibility checks		
Reliability allocation		
Secure protocols		

Threat control measures follow a fixed chronology: anticipate/prevent, detect/characterize, and respond/recover. The first step in implementing threat control measures is to determine the level of protection needed. This is accomplished by comparing the initial risk exposure to the target risk specified in the IA goals to determine the level of risk reduction needed. IA-critical and IA-related functions/entities and MWFs and MNWFs are identified. The entity control analysis and privacy issues are reassessed. Time intervals during which the level of protection is needed and the threat control measures will be effective are examined. From this, the required level of protection needed is updated and refined, leading to the specification of an IA integrity level.

Next, controllability, operational procedures, and in-service considerations are evaluated as opportunities to enhance — not detract from — IA integrity. Contingency plans are made to ensure that IA integrity is maintained in the event that one or more entities or services is inoperable or unavailable. Perception management is employed both to instill confidence in end users and to deter would-be attackers.

Finally, IA design techniques and features are selected and implemented based on (1) where they are effective in the threat control chronology, and (2) the specific vulnerabilities/threats they eliminate or mitigate. Protection is provided at all layers of the ISO OSI and TCP/IP reference models. Exhibit 23 correlates IA design techniques/features to the chronology of threat control measures, and Exhibit 24 correlates IA design techniques/features to common vulnerabilities and threats.

Next, Chapter 7 explains how to determine the effectiveness of threat control measures.

6.7 Discussion Problems

1. How is the need for reducing risk exposure determined?
2. What is the relationship, if any, between threat control measures and time?
3. Is it possible for an entity or function to be both IA-critical and IA-related? Explain your reasoning.
4. Identify MWFs and MNWFs for: (a) a nuclear power generation system, (b) a national security information system, (c) an intelligent transportation system, and (d) an online business.
5. Under what conditions would the IA integrity level be higher for: (a) a system entity than a system, (b) a system than a system entity, (c) security functions/entities than safety functions/entities, and (d) safety functions/entities than security functions/entities?
6. How is the IA integrity level affected by maintainability and operational procedures?
7. Explain the relationship between controllability and: (a) threats, (b) vulnerabilities, and (c) operational procedures.
8. Identify the controllability of the events in transaction path D ← 2.4.3 ← H (Chapter 5, Exhibits 21 and 25) from the six threat perspectives listed in Chapter 5, Exhibit 14. Assume the initial compromise was successful.
9. Who is involved in contingency planning? When are contingency plans developed?
10. How might a tactical defense intelligence system employ decoy entities? How would that differ from the use of decoys by a financial institution?
11. Identify a set of contingencies and responses for the online banking system discussed in Chapter 5.
12. What is the relationship between a system usage profile and threat control measures?
13. What is the relevance, if any, of the ISO OSI and TCP/IP reference models to IA?
14. Which layer in the ISO OSI and TCP/IP reference models is the easiest to attack? Which layer in the ISO OSI and TCP/IP reference models is the most difficult to attack?
15. Explain the differences, similarities, and relationship between: (a) digital certificates and digital signatures, (b) defense in depth and defensive programming, and (c) diversity and redundancy.
16. Which of the IA design techniques and features listed in Exhibit 13 are or are not applicable for: (a) COTS software, (b) custom software, and (c) reused software? Why?
17. Which method of specifying access control rules is best?
18. How many parameters should be used during authentication? How many authentication methods should be used?
19. How can partitioning be used to achieve: (a) security objectives, (b) safety objectives, and (c) reliability objectives?
20. Give examples of IA design techniques/features that complement, interact with, or are dependent on each other.

Exhibit 24 Assignment of IA Design Techniques/Features to Common Vulnerabilities and Threats

Vulnerability/ Threat[a]	*Protective IA Design Techniques/Features*	
Accidental action, command, response	Account for all possible logic states Defense in depth Error detection/correction Fault tolerance Partitioning Reliability allocation	Block recovery Defensive programming Fail safe/secure, fail operational Formal specifications Plausibility checks
Blocking access to system resources	Audit trail, security alarm Firewalls, filters Physical security	Diversity Intrusion detection, response Redundancy
Browsing	Access control Authentication Firewalls, filters	Audit trail, security alarm Encryption Intrusion detection, response
Corruption of resource management information (accidental and intentional)	Access control Authentication Defensive programming Diversity Fault tolerance Information hiding Plausibility checks	Account for all possible logic states Defense in depth Degraded-mode operations Encryption Formal specifications Partitioning Reliability allocation
Deletion of information or message (accidental and intentional)	Access control Authentication	Account for all possible logic states Information hiding
Denial of service, network flooding, system saturation, lack of capacity planning	Access control Audit trail, security alarm Diversity Fault tolerance Formal specifications Redundancy	Account for all possible logic states Degraded mode operations Fail safe/secure, fail operational Firewalls, filters Intrusion detection, response Reliability allocation
EMI/RFI	Error detection/correction	Physical security
Environmental, facility, or power faults or tampering	Degraded mode operations Error detection/correction Fault tolerance Redundancy	Diversity Fail safe/secure, fail operational Physical security Reliability allocation
Illegal operations, transactions, modes/states	Account for all possible logic states Block recovery Defensive programming Fail safe/secure, fail operational Formal specifications Redundancy	Audit trail, security alarm Defense in depth Diversity Fault tolerance Plausibility checks Reliability allocation
Inference, aggregation	Access control Encryption	Authentication Information hiding
Insertion of bogus data, "man-in-the-middle"	Access control Digital signatures Secure protocols	Authentication Encryption

Exhibit 24 Assignment of IA Design Techniques/Features to Common Vulnerabilities and Threats (continued)

Vulnerability/ Threat[a]	*Protective IA Design Techniques/Features*	
Jamming	Degraded-mode operations Physical security	Diversity
Lack of contingency planning, backups	Degraded-mode operations Fail safe/secure, fail operational Operational procedures	Diversity Fault tolerance
Masquerade, IP spoofing	Authentication Error detection/correction Firewalls, filters Secure protocols	Digital signatures Encryption Intrusion detection, response
Modification of information (accidental and intentional)	Access control Authentication Encryption Formal specifications	Account for all possible logic states Digital signatures Error detection/correction Information hiding
No fault tolerance, error detection or correction	Account for all possible logic states Defense in depth Diversity Information hiding Redundancy	Block recovery Defensive programming Fail safe/secure, fail operational Plausibility checks Reliability allocation
Overwriting information (accidental and intentional)	Access control Encryption	Authentication Information hiding
Password guessing, spoofing, compromise	Authentication Secure protocols	Intrusion detection, response
Replay, reroute, misroute messages	Encryption Firewalls, filters Secure protocols	Error detection/correction Intrusion detection, response
Repudiation of receipt, origin	Digital signatures	
Site/system/ application-specific vulnerabilities and threats	Defense in depth Degraded-mode operations Fail safe/secure, fail operational Plausibility checks Redundancy	Defensive programming Diversity Fault tolerance Operational procedures Reliability allocation
Theft of information, copying, distributing	Access control Encryption Operational procedures Secure protocols	Authentication Intrusion detection, response Physical security
Theft of service	Access control Digital signatures Secure protocols	Authentication Intrusion detection, response

Exhibit 24 Assignment of IA Design Techniques/Features to Common Vulnerabilities and Threats (continued)

Vulnerability/ Threat[a]	*Protective IA Design Techniques/Features*	
Trojan horse	Defense in depth Degraded-mode operations Fail safe/secure, fail operational Partitioning	Defensive programming Diversity Fault tolerance
Unauthorized access to system resources	Access control Authentication Digital signatures Firewalls, filters Physical security	Audit trail, security alarm Confinement Encryption Intrusion detection, response Secure protocols
Unauthorized use of system resources	Access control Authentication Physical security	Audit trail, security alarm Intrusion detection, response
Uncontrolled, unprotected portable systems and media, archives, hardcopy	Encryption Physical security	Operational procedures
Unpredictable COTS behavior	Block recovery Defense in depth Diversity Fail safe/secure Information hiding Plausibility checks	Confinement Defensive programming Error detection/correction Fault tolerance Partitioning Reliability allocation
Virus attack	Audit trail, security alarm Diversity Fault tolerance Partitioning Virus scanner	Degraded-mode operations Fail safe/secure, fail operational Intrusion detection, response Physical security
Wiretapping, eavesdropping, leakage	Access control Encryption Physical security	Authentication Intrusion detection, response Secure protocols

Note: There is no one-to-one correspondence between vulnerabilities/threats and IA design techniques/features. Instead, it is the cumulative effect of multiple techniques/features that eliminates or mitigates vulnerabilities/threats. Also, the design techniques/features are effective at different points in the threat control chronology (anticipate/prevent, detect/characterize, respond/recover), as illustrated in Exhibit 23.

Sources: Adapted from Denning, D., *Information Warfare amd Security,* Addison-Wesley, 1999; Denning D., *Cryptology and Data Security,* Addison-Wesley, 1982; Gollmann, D., *Computer Security,* John Wiley & Sons, 1999; Morris, D., *Introduction to Communication Command and Control Systems*, Pergamon Press, 1977; Rozenblit, M., *Security for Telecommunications Network Management*, IEEE, 1999.

Chapter 7

Verify Effectiveness of Threat Control Measures

This chapter describes the fourth component of an effective information security/IA program — verifying the effectiveness of threat control measures. The following activities are performed while verifying the effectiveness of threat control measures:

- IA verification techniques are selected and employed.
- Residual risk exposure is determined and its acceptability evaluated.
- Ongoing vulnerabilities, threats, and survivability are monitored.

Outputs from several previous components serve as inputs to these activities.

The majority of contemporary information security books and standards do not mention the topic of verification at all*. This is rather surprising; why should a user, customer, or system owner have any confidence that a system which has not been verified is secure? Perhaps there is a correlation between this fact and the continual reporting of information security breaches on the evening news. In contrast, computer safety and reliability books and standards include extensive discussions of verification activities.[288]

It is important to understand that the effectiveness of the threat control measures — not generic system functionality — is being verified. This component does not involve general-purpose system validation and verification. As Schneier[411] succinctly states:

> *...[security] flaws cannot be found through normal beta testing. Security has nothing to do with functionality. A cryptography product can function normally and be completely insecure.*

---

* As a historical note, the *Orange Book* specified security testing requirements, by evaluation class, the qualifications of people performing the testing, the duration of the testing, and high-level testing criteria.[135,141]

In Chapter 6, specific threat control measures were implemented in response to particular vulnerabilities and threats. The threat control measures included IA design techniques/features, operational procedures, contingency plans, and physical security practices. This component confirms that these measures do (or do not) in fact eliminate or mitigate the vulnerabilities and threats against which they were deployed. This component also demonstrates whether or not the specified IA integrity level was achieved.

7.1 Select/Employ IA Verification Techniques

A combination of static and dynamic techniques are employed to verify the effectiveness of threat control measures. Exhibit 1 lists 18 proven IA verification techniques. A description of each technique is provided in Annex B, which discusses the purpose, benefits, and limitations of each technique and provides pointers to references for further information.

In addition, several IA analysis and accident/incident investigation techniques can be used to verify the effectiveness of threat control measures, including cause consequence analysis, common cause failure analysis, event tree analysis, HAZOP studies, Petri nets, software and system FMECA, software and system FTA, sneak circuit analysis, barrier analysis, and damage mode effects analysis. Exhibit 2 lists the IA verification role played by each of these techniques.

The effectiveness of threat control measures is verified through a three-step process:

1. Verify that appropriate IA design techniques/features were selected.
2. Verify that IA design techniques/features were implemented correctly.
3. Verify the robustness and resiliency of the threat control measures.

Each step must be successfully completed before continuing to the next step; there is no point in continuing if the preceding step has failed.

The first step is to verify that appropriate IA design techniques/features were selected to eliminate or mitigate specific vulnerabilities/threats. Consult Chapter 6, Exhibit 24 when performing this exercise. Inappropriate techniques/features will be ineffective and may give a false sense of security. Common mistakes include assuming firewalls perform authentication functions or using encryption to enhance data integrity. Mismatches between vulnerabilities/threats and the IA design techniques/features intended to control them are highlighted for correction. The set of IA design techniques/features should be complementary, not redundant; redundant techniques should be highlighted for resolution.

The second step is to verify that the IA design techniques/features were implemented correctly and that the corresponding operational procedures and contingency plans are accurate and complete. Several items are examined, including:

Exhibit 1 IA Verification Techniques

IA Verification Techniques	*C/R*	*Type*	*Life-Cycle Phase in which Technique is Used*		
			Concept	*Development*	*Operations*
Boundary value analysis	C3	All		x	x
Cleanroom	C3	All		x	
Control flow analysis[a]	C3	All		x	x
Data or information flow analysis[a]	C3	All		x	x
Equivalence class partitioning	C3	All		x	x
Formal proofs of correctness	C3	SA, SE	x	x	x
Interface testing	C3	All		x	x
Performance testing	C3	All		x	x
Probabilistic or statistical testing	C3	All		x	x
Regression testing	C3	All		x	x
Reliability estimation modeling	C3	RE		x	x
(IA) requirements traceability	C3	All	x	x	x
Review IA integrity case[a]	C3	All	x	x	x
Root cause analysis[a]	C3	All		x	x
Safety/security audits, reviews, and inspections	C3	SA, SE		x	x
Stress testing	C3	All		x	x
Testability analysis, fault injection, failure assertion	C3	All		x	x
Usability testing	C3	All		x	x

[a] These techniques can also be used during accident/incident investigations.

Source: Adapted from Herrmann, D., *Software Safety and Reliability: Techniques, Approaches and Standards of Key Industrial Sectors,* IEEE Computer Society Press, 1999.

Legend for Exhibit 1

Column	*Code*	*Meaning*
Type	SA	Technique primarily supports safety engineering
	SE	Technique primarily supports security engineering
	RE	Technique primarily supports reliability engineering
	All	Technique supports a combination of safety, security, and reliability engineering
C/R	Cx	Groups of complementary techniques
	Rx	Groups of redundant techniques; only one of the redundant techniques should be used

- Does the threat control measure execute within the correct sequence of events? Is it implemented in the correct execution/attack point in the system?
- Does the threat control measure interact correctly with other IA design techniques/features, especially with regard to defense in depth?
- Have system integration issues been handled correctly; for example, interfaces, parameter initialization and processing, default values and settings, etc.?

Exhibit 2 Verification Role of IA Techniques

Technique	*IA Verification Role*
I. Verification Techniques	
Boundary value analysis	Identify software errors that occur in IA-critical and IA-related functions and entities when processing at or beyond specified parameter limits, whether inputs or outputs.
Cleanroom	Prevent defects from being introduced or remaining undetected in IA-critical and IA-related functions and entities through an evaluation of the completeness, consistency, correctness, and unambiguousness of requirements, design, and implementation.
Control flow analysis	Uncover poor and incorrect program logic structures that could compromise IA integrity.
Data or information flow analysis	Uncover incorrect and unauthorized data transformations and operations that could compromise IA integrity.
Equivalence class partitioning	Identify the minimum set of test cases and test data that will adequately test each input domain.
Formal proofs of correctness	Prove that the requirements, design, and implementation of IA-critical and IA-related functions and entities are correct, complete, unambiguous, and consistent.
Interface testing	Verify that interface requirements are correct and that interfaces have been implemented correctly.
Performance testing	Verify whether or not a system will meet stated performance requirements and that these requirements are correct.
Probabilistic or statistical testing	Provide quantitative assessment of operational IA integrity; verify design integrity against operational profiles.
Regression testing	Verify that changes or enhancements have been implemented correctly and that they do not introduce new errors or affect IA integrity.
Reliability estimation modeling	Estimate software reliability for the present or some future time.
(IA) requirements traceability	Verify that (1) all safety, reliability, and security requirements derived from IA goals are correct; (2) all safety, reliability, and security requirements have been implemented correctly in the end product; and (3) no additional unspecified or unintended capabilities have been introduced.
Review IA integrity case	Determine if the claims made about IA integrity are justified by the supporting arguments and evidence.
Root cause analysis	Identify the underlying cause(s), event(s), conditions, or actions that individually or in combination led to an accident/incident; determine why the defect was not detected earlier.
Safety/security audits, reviews, and inspections	Uncover errors and mistakes throughout the life of the system that could affect IA integrity.
Stress testing	Determine (1) maximum peak loading conditions under which a system will continue to perform as specified and IA integrity will be maintained, and (2) system overload/saturation conditions that could lead to a system compromise or failure.

Exhibit 2 Verification Role of IA Techniques (continued)

Technique	*IA Verification Role*
Testability analysis, fault injection, failure assertion	Verify IA integrity by determining if a system design can be verified and is maintainable, and that it detects and responds correctly to erroneous data, conditions, and states.
Usability testing	Determine if a system performs in the operational environment in a manner acceptable to and understandable by administrators and end users; verify that the design does not contribute to induced or invited errors that could lead to a system compromise or failure.
II. Analysis Techniques	
Cause consequence analysis	Identify inappropriate, ineffective, and missing threat control measures; verify that all accidental and intentional failure modes have a corresponding threat control measure.
Common cause failure analysis	Verify that fault tolerant design components are immune to CCFs.
Event tree analysis	Identify inappropriate, ineffective, and missing threat control measures.
HAZOP study	Verify that all accidental and intentional, physical and cyber, hazards associated with the operation of a system have been eliminated or mitigated.
Petri nets	Verify that deadlock, race, and nondeterministic conditions that could cause a system compromise or failure do not exist.
Software, system FMECA	Examine the effect of accidental and intentional, random and systematic failures on system behavior in general and IA integrity in particular.
Software, system FTA	Identify potential root cause(s) of undesired system events (accidental and intentional) to verify the effectiveness of mitigating design features and operational procedures.
Sneak circuit analysis	Verify that all hidden, unintended, and unauthorized hardware and software logical paths or control sequences that could inhibit desired system functions, initiate undesired system events, or cause incorrect timing and sequencing have been removed.
III. Accident/Incident Investigation Techniques	
Barrier analysis	Ascertain which defensive layers failed or were missing or inadequate during an accident/incident.
Damage mode effects analysis	Postulate which specific threat mechanisms caused an accident/incident from an analysis of the damage modes.

- Is the threat control measure implemented in the correct TCP/IP or ISO OSI layer(s)?
- Have concerns about COTS products been dealt with correctly? Consult Chapter 5, Exhibit 10 when evaluating this.

Verifying that intrusion detection profiles or access control rules have been implemented correctly are examples. Correct implementation in relation to the operational environment, not just the design, is evaluated.[362] Several IA verification techniques can be used during this step, such as boundary value analysis, cleanroom, equivalence class partitioning, formal proofs of correctness, interface testing, performance testing, probabilistic testing, IA requirements traceability, fault injection, and usability testing. Safety/security audits and usability testing and analysis can be used to verify operational procedures and contingency plans.

The first two steps parallel normal verification activities somewhat, although the focus is on safety and security — and not system functionality. The third step, verifying the robustness and resiliency of threat control measures, is when IA verification activities diverge from the norm. Instead of proving that a system functions correctly, the intent is to see how a system's threat control measures can be broken, bypassed, or disabled. This is where the "twisted mindset that can figure out how to get around rules, break systems, and subvert a designer's intentions," described by Schneier,[411] comes into play. A variety of verification techniques can be used to verify the robustness and resiliency of threat control measures: control flow analysis, data flow analysis, interface testing, performance testing, reviewing IA integrity cases, root cause analysis, safety and security audits, stress testing, and fault injection.

From the outside, safety and security testing may appear to be random. In fact, it is quite methodical. An attack, especially an organized attack, follows the same process; however, it is not encumbered or biased by knowledge of the system design and development. Consequently, it is highly recommended that safety and security testing be conducted by an independent team. Most national and international standards require this independence.[18,24,31,38,53,57,60,63–69,124–127,129,130,143]

As mentioned, safety and security testing attempts to discover if and how a system's threat control measures can be defeated, accidentally or intentionally. For example, by:

- Taking advantage of errors in the system design, operational procedures, or physical security practices
- Inducing transient faults, through an unusual combination or sequence of events, that can be exploited for malicious purposes
- Fooling people or processes into doing or permitting something they normally would not
- Co-opting unintended or unauthorized functionality for devious purposes

Design errors, such as timing errors or inconsistencies, not accounting for all possible logic states, incorrect data or control flow, unused or unreachable code, inadequate or inconsistent authentication parameters, and inadequate or conflicting access control rules, can be exploited as easily as loopholes in operational procedures or physical security practices. The design error or operational security loophole may be accidental, but the exploitation is intentional. An attack that takes advantage of design errors is difficult to detect and often remains undetected until it is too late; hence, the importance of this type of verification.

Transient faults are the nemesis of any verification activity. How does one test against an unforeseen temporary state? To illustrate, the first vertical launch of the Space Shuttle in 1980 was delayed two days due to a transient fault. Three computers controlled the main engine in a triple parallel redundant design with 100 percent voting/agreement. Following a transient fault, the three computers did not agree, causing the launch to be halted. It was reported that the transient fault had been experienced once before in the lab, but engineers had been unable to duplicate the condition and as a result verify its resolution.

Safety and security testing verifies system behavior during transient faults; it attempts to uncover all abnormal conditions and events for which the system is not protected. Transient faults can be induced through an unusual unanticipated combination or sequence of events (commands, responses, input, etc.), a sudden change or degradation of the operational environment (power drop or spike, increase in temperature or humidity, temporary saturation of a system entity, etc.), or a temporary loss of synchronization among system entities. Transient faults can be exploited to compromise a system or render it inoperable. As a case in point, during the simulation and testing of nuclear missile software, it was discovered that the targeting coordinates would reset to latitude 0°/longitude 0° if a particular transient fault was introduced at a specific interval during the launch control sequence. Several IA design techniques can be employed to mitigate transient faults, including accounting for all possible logic states, diversity, block recovery, defensive programming, and error detection/correction.

Fooling people into doing or permitting things they normally would not has been around as long as the human race. Remember the biblical story of Sarah pretending to be Abraham's sister so that the Pharaoh would not kill him? Attempting to fool computer processes began with the computer age. Distributed processing, LANs, WANs, and the Internet have made it easier and more widespread. Masquerading, IP-spoofing, "man-in-the-middle," password guessing, and replay attacks are common examples. Some of these attacks require sophistication; others do not. Most systems will be subjected to these generic types of attacks; therefore, all systems should be tested to ascertain their ability to withstand them. At the same time, operational procedures and physical security practices should be evaluated for vulnerabilities to masquerading, spoofing, and replay attacks.

Unintended, unauthorized functionality can serve as a conduit for attacks and intruders. These hidden logic paths, referred to as sneak circuits, permit a user or process to inhibit desired functionality, initiate undesired functionality, and bypass normal safety and security controls. A sneak circuit might give an intruder root access to a server, bypass access control rules, or prevent an audit trail of malicious activity from being recorded. Several companies currently have accounting, timekeeping, and other systems that employees access from a telephone keypad, usually by entering their employee number and password. (For the moment, the inherent insecurity of these systems will be ignored because transactions are conducted over open telephone lines, subject to eavesdropping, replay, masquerading, etc.) Most of these systems have a simplistic user interface, no data integrity or privacy protections, and no immunity from misuse or abuse. One would be surprised how some of these systems respond when a * or # is entered in the middle of a transaction.

Sneak circuits can be designed into a system accidentally or intentionally. Safety and security testing checks for the presence of sneak circuits through a combination of static and dynamic analyses. As Dima, Wack, and Wakid[251] state:

> *Security testing has to do more than just determine if the system conforms to some specification or standard. It must also test the implementation — in other words, it must pinpoint if any of the system's functions are unintended or unauthorized.*

Creative "what-if …" testing is an essential part of verifying the robustness and resiliency of threat control measures. This is the time to explore system behavior in response to "I wonder what would happen if …" test scenarios. The intent is to discover how threat control measures can be broken, bypassed, or disabled. Do not worry about crashing the system; after all, it is preferable to crash the system by finding an ineffective threat control measure rather than to let it remain in the system for an attacker to find. Transaction paths and critical threat zones are analyzed to identify potential attack points and develop "what-if …" test scenarios. Accidental and intentional vulnerabilities, accidental and intentional actions are exercised in "what-if …" test scenarios.

"What-if …" test scenarios are unique to each system and correlate to the required integrity level. Two high-level examples follow. They are intended to (1) illustrate the thrust of safety and security testing, and (2) stimulate ideas about the types of situations and circumstances to test for in "what-if …" test scenarios. Note that these examples are by no means exhaustive. Exhibits 3 through 5 depict "what-if …" test scenarios for the three hypothetical systems discussed in this book: a radiation therapy system, an ATC system, and an online banking system. Exhibit 6 provides a test scenario checklist for three common threat control measures: access control, audit trail/security alarm, and defense in depth.

7.2 Determine Residual Risk Exposure

The initial risk exposure determined the type and extent of threat control measures and IA integrity level required. Now, after the threat control measures have been implemented, an assessment is made of whether or not the residual risk exposure is acceptable and consistent with the target risk exposure. Several questions are pursued in this regard:

1. Did the threat control measures reduce the likelihood and severity of potential hazards as planned?
2. Has the initial risk exposure been reduced to ALARP?

Exhibit 3 Sample High-Level Test Scenarios for Verifying the Effectiveness of Threat Control Measures: The Radiation Therapy System

I. Radiation Therapy System

- How does the system respond to a suboptimal operational environment: (a) heat? (b) humidity? (c) dust? (d) vibration? (e) noise? (f) power faults? (g) EMI/RFI/EMC?

1. Patient records database
   - Can the patient records database be accessed without authorization: (a) from the local clinic LAN? (b) from the remote billing system? (c) from the remote research database? (d) from …?
   - Can information in the patient records database be copied, deleted in whole or in part, modified, or added to without authorization?
   - Does the system record an audit trail of unauthorized access to or use of system resources? Is a security alarm generated?
   - Does the system alert valid operators that unauthorized changes have been made to treatment profiles before a therapy session can begin?
   - How easy is it to fake user authentication parameters?
   - How does one know that: (a) the correct patient's treatment profile is retrieved before a therapy session? (b) the current treatment capture is stored under the correct patient's name? (c) a query against past treatments retrieves the correct patient's records?
   - Can patient records be overwritten accidentally or intentionally?
   - Can the patient records database be accidentally or intentionally saturated, from internal or external sources, so that no records can be retrieved?
2. Treatment planning system
   - Can information about the tumor characteristics, treatment algorithm, or treatment plan be accessed without authorization: (a) from the local clinic LAN? (b) from the remote billing system? (c) from the remote research database? (d) from …?
   - Can the tumor characteristics information, treatment algorithm, or treatment plan be copied, deleted in whole or in part, modified, or added to without authorization?
   - Does the system record an audit trail of unauthorized access to or use of system resources? Is a security alarm generated?
   - Does the system alert valid operators that unauthorized changes have been made to the treatment plan, tumor characteristics, or treatment algorithm before a therapy session can begin?
   - How easy is it to fake user authentication parameters?
   - Does the system automatically check for illegal combinations of beam type, duration, dosage, number of targets (if fractionated therapy), etc.?
   - Can the software that performs these checks be surreptitiously altered? Does the system detect and alert valid operators of these unauthorized modifications?
   - How does one know that a treatment plan is stored under the correct patient's name?
   - Can a treatment plan be overwritten accidentally or intentionally?
   - Can the treatment planning system be accidentally or intentionally saturated, from internal or external sources, so that no plans can be retrieved?
3. Radiation delivery unit
   - Does the radiation unit in fact deliver the correct dosage to targets specified in the treatment profile?

Exhibit 3 Sample High-Level Test Scenarios for Verifying the Effectiveness of Threat Control Measures: The Radiation Therapy System (continued)

- Does the radiation unit deliver radiation: (a) other than as specified: different beam type, dosage, etc.? (b) when not specified? Can it be surreptitiously be made to do (a) or (b)?
- Can the firmware controlling the radiation unit be surreptitiously modified? Does the system alert valid operators of unauthorized changes before beginning a therapy session?
- Can the electrical, electronic, or mechanical components be induced to fail: (a) at certain times? (b) in certain modes? Does the system detect and alert valid system operators of these failures? Are the events that lead to these failures detectable? Preventable?
- What is the minimum safe interval between therapy sessions so that treatment profiles for one patient are not accidentally carried forward to the next?
- What ensures that default or uninitialized treatment parameters are not used?

4. People
   - Are the operators, calibration, and maintenance staff cognoscente of system safety and security features and procedures?
   - Are they proficient at using these features and procedures?
   - Are safety and security procedures followed?
   - Do operators, trainers, calibration and maintenance staff know how to report and respond to: a) an anomalous situation? b) a suspected safety or security compromise? c) warnings and alarms?
   - Have they been trained about how and when to invoke contingency plans?

---

3. Is the residual risk exposure acceptable within known operational constraints?
4. Has the specified IA integrity level been demonstrated?
5. Are there opportunities to improve or optimize IA design techniques/features, operational procedures, contingency plans, or physical security practices?

Residual risk exposure is evaluated for all applicable scenarios:

- Different operational modes/states, profiles, environments, and missions
- Normal and abnormal conditions and events
- Independent, dependent, and simultaneous hazards
- Random and systematic failures
- Accidental and malicious intentional failures
- Physical and cyber hazards

At the same time, the analysis verifies that the threat control measures did not introduce any new hazards. It is highly recommended that an internal assessment be supplemented by an independent assessment of the adequacy, appropriateness, and effectiveness of threat control measures.

Using the results from the static and dynamic analyses, threat control measures are mapped to vulnerabilities/threats to develop a threat control

Exhibit 4 Sample High-Level Test Scenarios for Verifying the Effectiveness of Threat Control Measures: The ATC System

II. ATC System

1. Pilot, aircraft flight control/navigation system
   - Can pilots be fooled into thinking that they are talking with real air traffic controllers when, in fact, they are not?
   - Can instrumentation readings be accidentally or intentionally altered or corrupted? Is an alarm generated or any evidence provided to alert the pilot of this situation?
   - Can flight control software be accidentally or intentionally altered or corrupted? Is an alarm generated or any evidence provided to alert the pilot or maintenance crew of this situation?
   - Can the aircraft location signal, sent to the ATC radar, be: (a) frequency modulated without authorization? (b) jammed? (c) intercepted? (d) retransmitted, such that the signal is erroneously repeated at a later time, deleted and replaced by a bogus signal, transmitted in the wrong sequence, delayed, modified, or corrupted?
   - Can the aircraft location signal transmitter be disabled accidentally or intentionally, such that it is not transmitting but the controls indicate that it is functioning normally?
2. Radar
   - Can the radar be fooled into "thinking" that a bogus signal is in fact coming from a real aircraft?
   - Can the radar receiver be disabled accidentally or intentionally, such that it is not receiving aircraft location signals but the controls indicate it is functioning normally?
   - Can the radar transmitter be disabled accidentally or intentionally, such that it is not transmitting information to the ATC system but the controls indicate it is functioning normally?
   - Can the signal from the radar to the ATC system be: (a) frequency modulated without authorization? (b) jammed? (c) intercepted? (d) retransmitted, such that the signal is erroneously repeated at a later time, deleted and replaced by a bogus signal, transmitted in the wrong sequence, delayed, modified, or corrupted?
   - Can radar system software be accidentally or intentionally altered or corrupted? Is an alarm generated or any evidence provided to alert the operators or maintenance crew of this situation?
3. ATC system
   - Can air traffic controllers be fooled into thinking they are talking to real pilots when, in fact, they are not?
   - Can the air traffic control system be fooled into "thinking" that a bogus signal is in fact coming from a real radar system?
   - Can the ATC system receiver be disabled accidentally or intentionally, such that it is not receiving signals from the radar but the controls indicate it is functioning normally?
   - Can the ATC system receiver detect whether or not signals from the radar have been repeated, resequenced, delayed, modified, or corrupted?
   - Can the air traffic controller terminal be accidentally or intentionally corrupted, so that the screen freezes temporarily or permanently, duplicate data is displayed, some data points are deleted, the screen goes blank temporarily, bogus data points can be inserted, screen refreshes with new data points are delayed, information is displayed on the wrong air traffic controller's terminal, or the terminal becomes inoperable?

Exhibit 4 Sample High-Level Test Scenarios for Verifying the Effectiveness of Threat Control Measures: The ATC System (continued)

- Can the ATC DBMS be accidentally or intentionally corrupted, so that bogus data can be added to the database, legitimate data can be deleted from the database, data can be modified or duplicated, old data can overwrite current data, pointers or indices used to access the data are scrambled, or the data is unintelligible or unavailable?
- Can communication between the ATC DBMS and air traffic controller terminals be accidentally or intentionally corrupted, so that information is sent to the wrong controller's terminal, information is sent to controllers' terminals too early, too late, or in the wrong sequence, information is withheld or not sent to the controllers' terminals, wrong information is sent to a controller's terminal, or the communication link between the ATC DBMS and controllers' terminals is inoperable?
- How does the system respond to a suboptimal operational environment: (a) heat? (b) humidity? (c) dust? (d) vibration? (e) noise? (f) power faults? (g) EMI/RFI/EMC?

effectiveness assessment, as shown in Exhibit 7. First, the specific vulnerability/threat is identified, along with the severity, likelihood, and TCP/IP or ISO OSI layers in which it occurs. Next, the IA design techniques and features deployed to control this specific vulnerability/threat are identified. The TCP/IP or ISO OSI layer(s) in which the techniques are effective is (are) listed. The phase(s) in the threat control chronology in which the techniques are effective is (are) indicated: anticipate/prevent, detect/characterize, and respond/recover. The EAL and the demonstrated integrity level of the system are cited.

Given this information, the threat control effectiveness assessment seeks to uncover any mismatches or gaps in controlling this vulnerability/threat. Seven key factors are investigated as part of this assessment:

1. The appropriateness of this set of techniques for eliminating or mitigating this vulnerability/threat (Chapter 6, Exhibit 24 is reviewed)
2. The effectiveness of this set of techniques against all operational modes/states and profiles in which this vulnerability/threat occurs (the system operation characterization is reviewed)
3. Whether or not this set of techniques covers all layers in the TCP/IP or ISO OSI reference model in which the vulnerability/threat occurs (Chapter 6, Exhibits 12 and 13 are reviewed)
4. Whether or not this set of techniques covers all phases of the threat control chronology (Chapter 6, Exhibit 23 is reviewed)
5. Whether or not the EAL is appropriate and the static and dynamic analyses results positive
6. Whether or not the demonstrated IA integrity level corresponds to the required IA integrity level
7. Whether or not this set of techniques provides adequate defense in depth

Exhibit 5 Sample High-Level Test Scenarios for Verifying the Effectiveness of Threat Control Measures: The Online Banking System

III. Online Banking System

1. Home PC/user
   - Can a home PC user fake authentication parameters to the online banking system?
   - Can a home PC user bypass access control rules when acting as a legitimate user or masquerading as another user?
   - Can a home PC user intentionally saturate the online banking system so that it becomes unstable and exhibits unpredictable behavior?
   - Can a home PC user accidentally or intentionally provide erroneous input that could lead to a system compromise or failure?
   - Can account transactions be accidentally or intentionally erased, inhibited, modified, or initiated without authorization?
   - Can the transaction audit trail be accidentally or intentionally altered, corrupted, or erased?
   - Can data files be accessed without executing the appropriate application software?
   - Are data files containing authentication parameters protected?
   - Can account data be accessed without authorization: (a) from other financial institutions? (b) from other internal bank systems? (c) from …?
   - How does the system respond to a suboptimal operational environment: (a) heat? (b) humidity? (c) dust? (d) vibration? (e) noise? (f) power faults? (g) EMI/RFI/EMC?
   - Can account transactions be initiated without authorization: (a) from other financial institutions? (b) from other internal bank systems? (c) from …?
2. Online banking system
   - Can account data be accidentally or intentionally overwritten, modified, deleted, copied, read, printed, or added to without authorization?
   - Can the online banking system be fooled into "thinking" it is interacting with a legitimate user or other financial system when, in fact, it is not?
   - Can hidden accounts exist in the system?
   - Can funds be surreptitiously moved from account to account but appear to be in the correct account for audit purposes?
   - Can transaction records be accidentally or intentionally linked to the wrong account number?
   - Can transient fault conditions be induced so that access controls are bypassed and transactions are not recorded?
   - How does the system respond to a suboptimal operational environment: (a) heat? (b) humidity? (c) dust? (d) vibration? (e) noise? (f) power faults? (g) EMI/RFI/EMC?
3. Communications link between home PC user and online banking system
   - How secure are the communications protocols?
   - Can sessions be hijacked or listened to?
   - Can authentication parameters or transaction data be intercepted?
   - Can this information be used to initiate a fake session later?
   - Can a home PC user be prevented from accessing the online banking system?
   - Can transaction data be modified between the home PC user and the online banking system?
   - Can an intruder listen to online banking transactions to learn about a person's financial status and habits?

Exhibit 6 Checklist for Verifying the Effectiveness of Three Threat Control Measures

1. Access control
   - Have all access control rules been validated?
   - Have all access control rules been implemented correctly?
   - Are there any unintended data or control flows?
   - Are all inferred access control rules acceptable?
   - Are the access control rules consistent and complete?
   - Are the access control features implemented in the correct TCP/IP or ISO OSI layers? In the correct execution sequence?
   - What happens when an access control feature is saturated?
   - What happens when the process invoked immediately *preceding* access control is disabled or fails?
   - What happens when the process invoked immediately *after* access control is disabled or fails?
   - What happens if a transient fault is introduced during access control mediation?
   - What happens if the authentication function fails, is bypassed, or disabled?
   - What happens if the authentication parameters passed to the access control function are corrupted?
   - Can the table defining access control rights and privileges be accidentally or intentionally overwritten, copied, modified, deleted in whole or in part, or added to without authorization?
2. Audit trail, security alarm
   - Does the audit trail record all necessary activity? Are the activities recorded at meaningful intervals?
   - Does the audit trail record unnecessary events?
   - Can the audit trail be accidentally or intentionally overwritten, modified, deleted in whole or in part, copied, or added to without authorization?
   - Can the audit trail function be intentionally bypassed, disabled, or induced to fail?
   - What happens if the audit trail function becomes saturated?
   - Can events recorded in the audit trail be faked to cover malicious activity and prevent an alarm from being triggered?
   - Are alarms triggered in a timely manner?
   - Are the alarm false-positive and false-negative rates acceptable?
   - Can the parameters for triggering an alarm be accidentally or intentionally overwritten, modified, copied, deleted in whole or in part, or added to without authorization?
   - What happens if there is no human-initiated response to an alarm?
   - What happens if there is no computer-initiated response to an alarm?
   - Is it possible to block events from being recorded in the audit trail?
   - Is it possible to intercept an alarm before it is distributed?
3. Defense in depth
   - Are the defensive layers complementary or redundant?
   - Do the techniques cover all phases of the threat control chronology?
   - Do the techniques cover all applicable layers in the TCP/IP or ISO OSI reference models?
   - Are the defensive layers subject to CCFs?
   - Are there dependencies between the techniques, for example, the input to one technique is dependent on the output of another technique?
   - If the technique(s) responsible for anticipate/prevent fails is bypassed or disabled, will the detect/characterize and respond/recover techniques function correctly?

Exhibit 6 Checklist for Verifying the Effectiveness of Three Threat Control Measures (continued)

- If the detect/characterize technique(s) fails is bypassed or disabled, will the respond/recover technique(s) function correctly?
- Are there any unnecessary time delays after the failure of one defensive layer and before the next defensive layer becomes effective or is activated?
- Does the failure of one defensive layer reveal any information or create additional vulnerabilities for the other defensive layers?
- Can all the defensive layers be simultaneously saturated or attacked?
- Do the defensive layers include operational procedure provisions, contingency plan provisions, and physical security practices?

Answers to these inquiries highlight missing, inappropriate, and ineffective threat control measures for individual vulnerabilities/threats. Information about individual vulnerabilities/threats is combined to produce a threat control effectiveness summary, as shown in Exhibit 8. Responses to the seven key inquiries are summarized by vulnerability/threat severity. The resulting one-page digest quantitatively illustrates the acceptability of the residual risk or, conversely, the need for further risk reduction activities.

The information needed to evaluate these seven factors is found in the IA integrity case. An IA integrity case is a systematic means of gathering, organizing, analyzing, and reporting the data needed by internal, contractual, regulatory, and certification authorities to confirm that a system has met the specified IA goals and integrity level and is fit for use in the intended operational environment. Many national and international standards require a system safety or system reliability case as part of the certification and approval process.[31,38,57,63–65,124,129,130] This book expands that concept to the broader realm of IA.

Presenting information in a logical, complete, and concise manner is the hallmark of a well-founded IA integrity case. Exhibit 9 depicts the structure of an IA integrity case. Section 1 states the IA goals for the system, the justification for those goals, and the required IA integrity level. This information was developed in activities 1.1 (Chapter 4) and 3.1 (Chapter 6). Section 2 states assumptions that have been made about the development environment, operational environment, operational profiles, and operational mission of the system. Claims are made about the relevance of previous experience with similar systems or technology and the design, development, and verification techniques and processes used. Relevant evaluations of COTS products by independent laboratories are cited, such as an EAL.

Section 3 (Exhibit 9) contains the evidence needed to substantiate the conclusions and recommendations in Section 5. This evidence represents the results of all the analyses conducted to date. To be credible, the evidence must be complete and current — several of these analyses are updated frequently. Additional backup or supporting information can be included in Annex A. The evidence incorporates the following:

Exhibit 7 Threat Control Effectiveness Assessment

System/Entity:

Date:

I. Vulnerability/Threat Identification[1]

No.	Description	Severity	Likelihood	*Present in layer(s)*	
				TCP/IP	*ISO OSI*
1					

II. Threat Control Measures[2]

IA Design Technique/ Feature	*Effective in Layer(s)*		*Threat Control Chronology Effectiveness*			*EAL*	*IA Integrity Level*
	TCP/IP	*ISO OSI*	*A/P*	*D/C*	*R/R*		
1a							
1b							
1c							

Key: A/P - anticipate/prevent; D/C - detect/characterize; R/R - respond/recover.

II. Assessment[3]

a. Is this set of techniques appropriate for eliminating or mitigating this vulnerability/threat?
b. Is this set of techniques effective against all operational modes/states and profiles in which this vulnerability/threat occurs?
c. Does this set of techniques cover all layers in which the vulnerability/threat occurs?
d. Does this set of techniques cover all phases of the threat control chronology?
e. For each technique/feature: (a) is the EAL appropriate? (b) are the static and dynamic analysis results positive?
f. Is the demonstrated IA integrity level of this set of techniques consistent with the required IA integrity level?
g. Does this set of techniques provide adequate defense in depth?
h. Are there any mismatches or gaps in controlling this vulnerability/threat?

[1] A separate template is prepared for each vulnerability/threat pair. The information in Part I comes from the system vulnerability and threat characterizations.

[2] All threat control measures that eliminate or mitigate the vulnerability/threat cited in Part I are listed.

[3] Except for h, all answers should be an unequivocal yes or no; if no, a rationale should be provided.

- System vulnerability characterization
- System threat characterization
- Critical threat zones
- IA design techniques/features implemented
- Demonstrated IA integrity level
- Threat control effectiveness assessment
- Residual risk exposure

Exhibit 8 Threat Control Effectiveness Summary

	Vulnerability/Threat Severity							
	Catastrophic		*Critical*		*Marginal*		*Insignificant*	
Assessment Criteria	#	%	#	%	#	%	#	%
1. TCP or ISO OSI layers:								
a. Covered								
b. Not covered								
2. Operational modes/states, operational profiles:								
a. Covered								
b. Not covered								
3. Phases of threat control chronology:								
a. Covered								
b. Not covered								
4. EAL, static and dynamic analysis results:								
a. Appropriate								
b. Inappropriate								
5. Demonstrated IA integrity level:								
a. Appropriate								
b. Inappropriate								
6. Defense in depth:								
a. Adequate								
b. Inadequate								
7. Threat control gaps or mismatches:								
a. None remaining								
b. Some remaining								
Total vulnerabilities/threats		100%		100%		100%		100%

This information was developed in activities 2.2, 2.3, and 2.5 (Chapter 5), 3.5 (Chapter 6), and 4.1 and 4.2 (Chapter 7).

A chronological list of issues and their resolution is kept in Section 4. Section 5 contains the conclusions and recommendations from various stakeholders that the assumptions, claims, and evidence presented prove (or do not prove) that the IA goals and integrity level have been (or will be) achieved and maintained. A Certification Authority may concur, nonconcur, or request more information. Section 6 contains a chronology of reviews/approvals for the system.

An IA integrity case is a living document.[289] The case commences as soon as the IA goals are defined. Assumptions, claims, and evidence are added to the case throughout the system's development and operational phases. The IA integrity case is reviewed at regular milestones to verify that a system is on track for attaining or maintaining its IA goals and integrity level. An IA integrity case should be reviewed/revalidated whenever any of the claims,

Exhibit 9 Structure of an IA Integrity Case

System:________________

as of:__________

last review/approval:__________

1. IA goals
   a. IA goals for this system
   b. Justification for the IA goals
   c. IA integrity level required for this system
2. Assumptions and claims
   a. Assumptions about development environment, operational environment, operational profiles, operational mission
   b. Claims about previous experience with similar systems and technology
   c. Claims about design, development, and verification techniques and processes used
   d. Evaluations of COTS products by independent laboratories, such as an EAL
3. (Current) evidence
   a. System vulnerability characterization
   b. System threat characterization
   c. Critical threat zones
   d. IA design techniques/features implemented
   e. Demonstrated IA integrity level
   f. Threat control effectiveness assessment and summary
   g. Residual risk exposure
4. Outstanding issues
5. Conclusions and recommendations
   a. System developer
   b. System owner
   c. Regulatory authority (if applicable)
   d. Certification Authority
6. Approval, certification history

Annex A Backup, supporting information
   a. System definition
   b. System operational characterization
   c. System entity control analysis
   d. Transaction paths
   e. Operational procedures
   f. Contingency plans
   g. Static and dynamic analysis results
   h. Real-world experience with end users

assumptions, or evidence has changed, or following a system enhancement, correction, modification, reconfiguration, failure, or compromise. An IA integrity case should be reviewed as part of an accident/incident investigation to ascertain which claim(s), assumption(s), or evidence was (were) false.

7.3 Monitor Ongoing Risk Exposure, Responses, and Survivability

Verification of the effectiveness of threat control measures does not end once a system is fielded. In fact, some would argue, with merit, that is when the real verification of threat control effectiveness takes place. The ability to maintain a specified integrity level in the real-world operational environment, despite accidental and malicious intentional actions, is what information security/IA is all about.

The effectiveness of threat control measures during the in-service phase of a system is often appraised as a function of survivability. Survivability is defined as the capability of a system to fulfill its mission, in a timely manner, in the presence of attacks, failures, or accidents.[336] As Linger[336] observes:

> *Survivability depends on three key capabilities: resistance, recognition, and recovery. Resistance is the capability of a system to repel attacks. Recognition is the capability to detect attacks as they occur and to evaluate the extent of damage and compromise. Recovery, the hallmark of survivability, is the ability to maintain essential services and assets during an attack, limit the extent of damage, and restore full services following an attack.*

Accordingly, a survivability assessment covers the full threat control chronology: anticipate/prevent, detect/characterize, respond/recover. This reinforces the need for defense in depth — a threat control measure designed to anticipate/prevent an attack may be disabled or bypassed, leaving the detect/characterize and respond/recover threat control measures to protect the system. Fault tolerance, fault containment, maintainability, and the ability to efficiently transition to degraded mode operations, a fail safe/secure or fail operational state when needed are characteristics of robust survivability. Contingency plans and operational procedures are also evaluated in regard to their contribution to survivability. Wylie et al.[444] point out that data as well as systems must be designed to be survivable. The importance of maintainability in relation to survivability is often overlooked. However, as Jackson[304] notes:

> *Maintainability is the systematic assessment of the effectiveness of maintenance strategies and can have considerable influence on system safety [and security].*

The resilience of all IA design techniques/features must be continually assessed. As McSteen and Pesante[350] point out:

> *... the security of an organization's online information and information systems will depend on, among other things, that organization's ability to stay current on ever-changing attack methods and the [inherent] security vulnerabilities in the technology they are using.*

Survivability should be reassessed at regular intervals. Changes or additions to the operational mission, profile, or environment and/or system enhancements, modifications, or reconfiguration should trigger an update to the system vulnerability/threat characterizations and a reevaluation of the threat control effectiveness assessment. It is highly recommended that internal survivability assessments be supplemented by those performed by independent teams.

Human and organizational factors are also considered when assessing survivability. One way to do this is to see how an organization's practices compare to the common accident/incident precursors and the proactive responses cited in Chapter 6, Exhibit 1. To ensure objectivity, an independent assessment is recommended. In addition, contingency plans and operational procedures should be examined in light of human-factor engineering concerns, especially proclivities toward induced or invited errors. Accidental induced or invited errors can lead to a system failure or create an opening for a malicious intentional act that leads to a system compromise. Real-world feedback from system administrators and end users about problems they have experienced, features they do not like, and recommendations they have for improving the plans and procedures must be incorporated.

7.4 Summary

The fourth component of an effective information security/IA program is verifying the effectiveness of threat control measures. Three activities are performed when verifying the effectiveness of threat control measures (as shown in Exhibit 10):

- IA verification techniques are selected and employed.
- Residual risk exposure is determined and its acceptability is evaluated.
- Ongoing vulnerabilities, threats, and survivability are monitored.

After threat control measures have been implemented, it is essential to verify that they do in fact eliminate or mitigate the vulnerabilities and threats against which they were deployed. Likewise, the IA integrity level achieved must be demonstrated. Without actual verification, there is no factual basis upon which to claim that a system is safe, secure, or reliable. To ensure objectivity, internal verification activities should be supplemented by those performed by independent teams.

A combination of static and dynamic analysis techniques are used to verify the effectiveness of threat control measures throughout the life of a system. A three-step process is followed:

1. Verify that appropriate IA design techniques/features were selected.
2. Verify that IA design techniques/features were implemented correctly.
3. Verify the robustness and resiliency of the threat control measures.

The third step is critical. It attempts to discover how threat control measures can accidentally or intentionally be broken, bypassed, or disabled. Creative

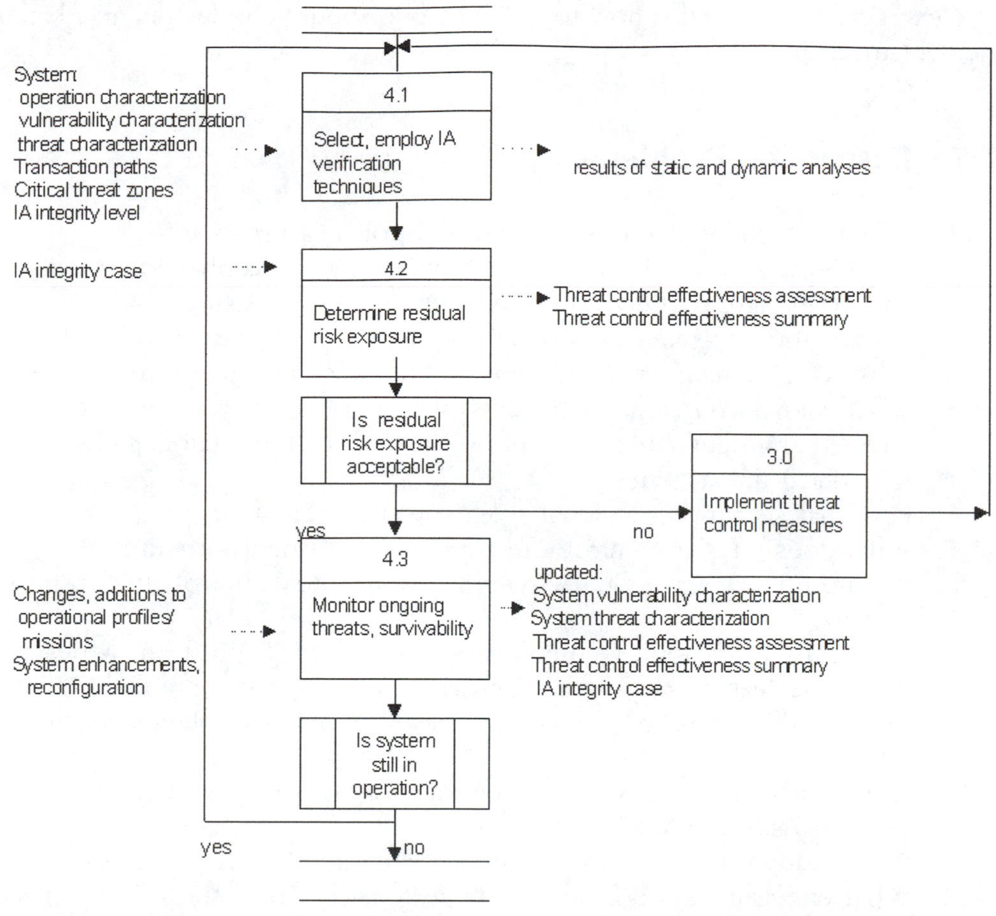

Exhibit 10 Summary of Activities Involved in Verifying the Effectiveness of Threat Control Measures

"what-if …" test scenarios are developed from an analysis of transaction paths and critical threat zones. Particular attention is paid to transient faults and sneak circuits.

Results of the static and dynamic analyses are mapped to vulnerabilities/ threats to develop a threat control effectiveness assessment. Missing, inappropriate, ineffective, and redundant threat control measures are identified, along with gaps in covering all phases of the threat control chronology and applicable layers in the TCP/IP or ISO OSI reference models. Residual risk exposure is compared to the target to determine acceptability or the need for further risk reduction. An IA integrity case is a systematic means of collecting, organizing, analyzing, and reporting the information needed to evaluate residual risk.

Accidental and intentional vulnerabilities and threats are monitored throughout the life of a system. The effectiveness of threat control measures during the in-service phase is often assessed as a function of survivability. Human and organizational factors, such as opportunities for induced or invited errors, are evaluated as part of a survivability assessment.

Next, Chapter 8 explains how to and why one should conduct an accident/incident investigation.

7.5 Discussion Problems

1. When is the effectiveness of threat control measures verified?
2. What is the same, what is different between generic verification activities and verifying the effectiveness of threat control measures?
3. How is the effectiveness of COTS threat control products verified?
4. Why is the robustness and resiliency of threat control measures verified?
5. What role do the following items play in IA verification activities, if any: (a) transient faults, (b) sneak circuits, (c) transaction paths, and (d) critical threat zones?
6. For what scenario is residual risk exposure evaluated?
7. What does a threat control effectiveness assessment measure?
8. What can you learn about IA integrity from a threat control effectiveness summary?
9. Should IA verification techniques be selected to: (a) test an IA design technique/feature, or (b) test a known or suspected vulnerability/threat?
10. What is the purpose of including assumptions and claims in an IA integrity case?
11. How is residual risk exposure determined? How is the acceptability of residual risk evaluated?
12. What is involved in assessing survivability, and when is it assessed?
13. What effect, if any, do the following items have on the effectiveness of threat control measures: (a) human factors, (b) operational procedures, (c) contingency plans, (d) physical security practices, and (e) temperature?
14. How could a risk acceptability model, based on that discussed in Chapter 5.5, be used to determine the acceptability of a threat control effectiveness summary?
15. Develop some "what-if ..." test scenarios for an intelligent transportation system. Identify which IA verification techniques would be used in each instance.

Chapter 8

Conduct Accident/Incident Investigations

This chapter describes the fifth component of an effective information security/IA program — conducting an accident/incident investigation. The process of how to conduct and accident/incident investigation is explained, as well as the reasons why one should conduct an investigation. The following activities are performed while conducting an accident/incident investigation:

- The cause, extent, and consequences of the failure/compromise are analyzed.
- Recovery mechanisms are initiated.
- The accident/incident is reported.
- Remedial measures are deployed.
- Legal issues are evaluated.

There is extensive interaction between this component and the preceding four components, as the following chapter sections demonstrate.

Before proceeding, it is important to clarify terminology. The terms "accident" and "incident," "failure" and "compromise" are used to mean different things in diverse publications. Occasionally, these terms are even used interchangeably. This book, taking into account both the technical and legal usage of the terms, defines them as follows:

> **accident:** (1) technical — any unplanned or unintended event, sequence, or combination of events that results in death, injury, or illness to personnel or damage to or loss of equipment or property (including data, intellectual property, etc.), or damage to the environment[127,422,425]; (2) legal — any unpleasant or unfortunate occurrence that causes injury, loss, suffering, or death; an event that takes place without one's foresight or expectation.[214]

incident: any unplanned or unintended event, sequence, or combination of events that does not result in death, injury, or illness to personnel or damage to or loss of equipment, property (including data, intellectual property, etc.), or damage to the environment, but has the potential to do so.

In short, an accident results in unexpected loss, physical or cyber. The person or entity incurring the loss may or may not be the responsible party; often a second or third party is involved. An accident can result from accidental or intentional action or inaction. Case law distinguishes between avoidable and unavoidable accidents, a point that is particularly relevant when investigating technology-related accidents/incidents. (*Note:* Some standards refer to accidents as mishaps.)

In contrast, an incident is a near-miss that could have resulted in an accident but did not. Incidents often precede accidents as an early warning of a more serious underlying problem; hence, the need to investigate them as well.

Failure: failing to or inability of a system, entity, or component to perform its required function(s), according to specified performance criteria, due to one or more fault conditions.

Compromise: an unwarranted and uninvited offensive incursion, infringement, or encroachment of a system, usually by stealth, that defeats safety and security mechanisms to violate and usurp resources and data in a hostile and injurious manner.

A failure implies that a system, entity, or component did not or could not perform its prescribed function(s). Fault tolerance attempts to prevent component and entity failures from becoming system failures. Three categories of failures are commonly recognized: (1) incipient failures are failures that are about to occur; (2) hard failures are failures that result in a complete system shutdown; and (3) soft failures are failures that result in a transition to degraded mode operations or a fail operational status.[44] A failure, particularly of an IA-critical or IA-related function/entity, directly impacts IA integrity.

A compromise represents the digital equivalent of trespassing, infringement, wrongful breaking, entering, and appropriation of data and resources. A system may or may not be rendered inoperable by a compromise; however, sensitive information and/or resources are misappropriated (stolen), usurped, or exposed.

An accident, incident, or compromise is preceded by the failure of one or more safety and security mechanisms (IA design technique/feature, operational procedures, physical security practices, etc.). If one extends the fault tolerance paradigm:

```
                                                    → Incident
                                                    |
Accidental or intentional  → Fault(s) → Failure(s) → → Accident
  error or mistake                                  |
                                                    → Compromise
```

The legal and engineering professions differ on how they define and categorize causes. It is important to be aware of these differences when conducting an accident/incident investigation. The standard engineering definition is[31]:

> **Cause:** the action or condition by which a hazardous event (physical or cyber) is initiated — an initiating event. The cause may arise as the result of failure, accidental or intentional human error, design inadequacy, induced or natural operational environment, system configuration, or operational mode(s)/state(s).

The standard legal definition is[214]:

> **Cause:** each separate antecedent of an event. Something that precedes and brings about an effect or result. A reason for an accident or condition.

In legal matters, causation is used to assess negligence. Exhibit 1 compares legal and engineering cause categories.

8.1 Analyze Cause, Extent, and Consequences of Accident/Incident

Known or suspected accident/incidents should be investigated whenever they occur, whether during the development or operational phases. Accidents/incidents during the development phase are indicative of underlying design deficiencies, misunderstandings about the operation or mission of a system, and incompatible components. Accidents/incidents during the operational phase may result from any of the above causes, as well as deficiencies in the operational environment, operational procedures, physical security practices, and system survivability characteristics.

There are several compelling reasons to investigate accidents/incidents, regardless of their severity, including:

1. To determine in fact what did and did not happen, how it happened, and why it happened or was allowed to happen
2. To ascertain the extent of the consequences and the corresponding need for (immediate) recovery mechanisms, and (long-term) remedial measures
3. To gather the information necessary to file an accurate report of the accident/incident
4. To evaluate legal issues

If an accident/incident is not investigated, useful information is thrown away. The end result is that there are no facts upon which to base immediate recovery mechanisms — recovery efforts will be ineffective or haphazard at best. There are no facts upon which to base long-term remedial measures to ensure that the accident/incident or a similar one does not occur in the future.

Exhibit 1 Comparison of Legal and Engineering Cause Categories

Legal Category	*Engineering Category*	*Definition*
Concurrent cause	No exact engineering equivalent. Concurrent causes might be considered dependent parallel root causes.	Causes acting contemporaneously and together, causing injury that would not have happened in the absence of either. Two distinct causes operating at the same time to produce a given result.[214]
Contributing cause	No exact engineering equivalent. Contributing causes might be considered intermediate causes.	Any factor that contributes to a result, although its causal nexus may not be immediate.[214]
Intervening cause	No exact engineering equivalent. A positive intervening cause may result from an effective threat control measure, defensive layer, or emergency response. A negative intervening cause may result from erroneous human action in response to an accident precursor.	An independent cause that intervenes between the original event and the accident/ incident, negates the natural course of events, and produces a different result, positive or negative.
Direct, proximate, or legal cause	Basic, underlying, or root cause	Underlying cause(s), event(s), conditions, or actions that individually or in combination led to the accident/incident; primary precursor event(s) that has (have) the potential for being corrected.
Probable or reasonable cause	No engineering equivalent.	A reasonable ground for belief in certain alleged facts. A set of probabilities grounded in the factual and practical considerations that govern the decisions of reasonable and prudent persons and is more than mere suspicion but less than the quantum of evidence required for conviction.[214]
Remote cause	No engineering equivalent.	A cause which would not according to experience of mankind lead to the event which happened.[214]
No exact legal equivalent	Intermediate cause	An event between the underlying cause and the accident/incident that occurs within the direct chain of events; an epiphenomenon.

Other insights gained from an accident/incident investigation are lost, such as previously unknown latent vulnerabilities/threats. Evidence necessary to pursue legal action is discarded. In summary, the short- and long-term returns on investment from conducting an accident/incident investigation are manifold.

Conducting an accident/incident investigation is a branch of forensic engineering. There is a common misperception that forensic engineering is a mysterious, magical, and occasionally devious endeavor. Not at all. According to Webster's Dictionary, forensic simply means "belonging to, used in, or suitable to courts of justice." Black's Law Dictionary[214] defines forensic engineering as:

> *The application of the principles and practice of engineering to the elucidation of questions before courts of law. Practice by legally qualified professional engineers who are experts in their field, by both education and experience, and who have experience in the courts and an understanding of jurisprudence. A forensic engineering engagement may require investigations, studies, evaluations, advice to counsels, reports, advisory opinions, depositions, and/or testimony (expert witness) to assist in the resolution of disputes relating to life or property in cases before courts or other lawful tribunals.*

Accident/incident investigations may be conducted solely for internal purposes, as part of a regulatory process, to share information within or among industrial sectors, or pursuant to legal action. A forensic accident/incident investigation adds the notion that evidence is collected, organized, analyzed, and presented in a manner that is appropriate for a court of law. A regulatory accident/incident investigation is more formal that one conducted solely for internal purposes. Likewise, a forensic accident/incident investigation is more formal than a regulatory one. However, the techniques and methods used in all three are the same.

Petroski[380] explains that conducting a forensic accident/incident investigation is equivalent to performing failure analysis, something with which safety and reliability engineers have extensive experience. Essentially, one determines *what* happened, *how* it happened, *why* it happened or was allowed to happen, and the resultant consequences. The process is similar to performing a digital autopsy; however, in this case, it is necessary to look beyond the "patient" to locate all the contributing factors and sources of accidental and intentional errors, mistakes, faults, and failures that led to the accident/incident. An investigation involves synthesizing scenarios that describe "how could" an accident/incident occur with scenarios that depict "how did" an accident/incident occur through inductive and deductive reasoning. The credibility of an investigation rests on the ability to remain objective, eliminate bias or prejudice, separate fact, opinion, assumptions and theory, and distinguish "symptoms" from the "disease" — all while being thorough and accurate. As Petroski[380] states:

> *Although some of the acute interest in accident postmortems no doubt stems from legal and insurance claims, there is considerable engineering experience to be gained in understanding exactly what caused a failure. ...they are necessary and necessarily drawn out because they can involve a painstaking sifting and analysis of clues as subtle as Sherlock Holmes ever had to deal with.*

Today, is it unlikely that during the life of a system an accident/incident will not be experienced. Prior preparation facilitates effective and efficient accident/incident investigations, whether internal, independent, regulatory, or forensic. Poe[385] recommends planning, coordination, and training to address the following issues:

- The speed, accuracy, and completeness of information collection
- Reporting channels and responsibilities, inside and outside the team
- Standardized report forms (draft and final)
- Designated participant lists, per accident scenario, to ensure an interdisciplinary team
- A generic checklist of questions to ask, per accident scenario, to stimulate avenues of investigation
- A fixed chain of custody for evidence, given the fleeting nature of digital evidence
- Procedures for obtaining consent of witnesses prior to conducting critical incident interviews

There are plenty of open sources to examine when collecting evidence for an accident/incident investigation. There is no need to resort to clandestine methods. Analyses of early evidence point to other sources of primary, secondary, and tertiary evidence, in what becomes an iterative process. Digital evidence is supplemented by critical incident interviews. As the evidence accumulates, it is sifted (relevant/irrelevant evidence), validated, and organized (direct/indirect evidence, time sequence, etc.) until a clear picture begins to emerge of what exactly happened. Inductive and deductive reasoning are applied to the evidence to explain how and why the accident/incident occurred. Evidence sources include those that are unique to an accident/incident and those that are common to all accidents/incidents. A sample list of generic evidence sources is given in Exhibit 2. This list is illustrative, not exhaustive. An examination of generic evidence sources often uncovers unique evidence sources; as a result, most investigations begin with generic sources.

Ladkin[321] describes the main tasks of an accident/incident investigation, a process he refers to as "why — because analysis", as:

1. A general formal definition of causal influence
2. Precise specifications of system and entity behavior
3. Evidence collection and analysis
4. A method of tracing more evidence from the evidence in hand
5. A method of validating the causal reasoning

Exhibit 2 Generic Accident/Incident Evidence Sources

1. Background information
   - System definition
   - System operation characterization
   - System entity control analysis
   - Vulnerability and threat characterizations
   - Transaction paths, critical threat zones
   - IA design techniques/features
   - Threat control effectiveness assessment and summary
   - System design and verification data
   - IA integrity case (assumptions, claims, evidence)
   - Operational procedures, contingency plans, physical security practices
   - System software inventory and configuration (workstation and server); identify what is COTS, custom, authorized, not authorized to be installed
   - Serial numbers of commercial products
   - Authentication parameter file and implementation logic, current and archived
   - Access control rules, definition, and implementation logic, current and archived
2. Previous experiences and observations
   - Prior incident/anomalous activity reports
   - Log of recent preventive, adaptive, and corrective maintenance actions, including system reconfiguration, enhancements, and upgrades
   - History of SPRs, STRs, ECRs, and help desk calls
   - Recent backups
3. Accident/incident characteristics
   - System failure mode, state, and characteristics
   - Chronology of system modes/states and conditions leading up to and including the accident/incident and its aftermath
   - Operational profile, mission, and environment up to and including the accident/incident and its aftermath
   - Names/IDs of all active users and processes
   - System and entity loading characteristics
   - Printouts of anomalous events
   - Message, process, and file header IDs and tags
   - Logical and physical addresses of network nodes, system resources, users, message traffic
   - Message traffic logs, routing tables, e-mail directories, address books
   - Memory, OS, register, buffer, hard disk dumps (server and workstation)
   - System audit trails
   - Keystroke logs
   - Browser screens
   - Printouts of screen freezes (system administrator and end user)
   - Physical security logs, video and audio surveillance tapes
   - Critical incident interviews

The causal explanation, evidence, and reasoning must be correct and sufficient; all three must undergo competent validation "so that other people can tell they are correct."[321] Adequate attention must be paid to the operational environment, operational procedures, and the physical and digital characteristics of the accident. Ladkin and Philley both caution against searching for a single underlying cause of an accident, especially early in an investigation. As Ladkin[321] states:

> *In distinction to a common supposition, most complex system accidents are dependent on many factors, not just a single causal chain.*

Philley[381] adds that:

> *Isolating one cause as "the" root cause may leave other potential hazards in an uncorrected condition. The investigator should continue to identify, examine, and evaluate all underlying causes.*

Philley notes that identification of a single root cause may cause an investigation to be stopped prematurely and result in over simplistic and incomplete reasoning about the evidence. Similar to Poe,[385] Philley[381] recommends having an interdisciplinary team conduct and validate an investigation.

Intermediate and root causes are extrapolated from the available evidence. This extrapolation, in turn, points to gaps in the evidence and the need for further investigation. The identification of causes should explore all potential initiating and intermediate events, including:

- Random or time-dependent hardware failures[31]
- Systematic or time-dependent software failures
- Latent vulnerabilities/threats
- Accidental or intentional operator error
- Natural and induced environmental effects[31]
- Deficiencies in operational procedures, contingency plans, and physical security practices
- Accidental or intentional design inadequacies:
  - Ineffective defensive layers and threat control measures
  - Inadequate safety and security margins
  - Unintended operating modes caused by sneak circuits[31]
  - Material inadequacies and incompatibilities[31]
  - Erroneous hardware/software interaction[31]
- Natural or induced transient faults
- Inadvertent operation of IA-critical function
- Accidental or intentional modification of interrupt table[277]
- Accidental or intentional redirection of pointers[277]

A combination of techniques is used to investigate accidents/incidents. Exhibit 3 lists eight proven IA accident/incident investigation techniques. A description of each technique is provided in Annex B, which discusses the purpose, benefits, and limitations of each technique and provides pointers to references for further information.

In addition, several IA analysis and verification techniques can be used during an accident/incident investigation, including BBNs, cause consequence analysis, event tree analysis, HAZOP studies, Petri nets, FMECA, FTA, sneak circuit analysis, and root cause analysis. These techniques are useful for identifying and distinguishing "how did" accident scenarios and "how could" accident scenarios. The IA integrity case is reviewed to determine which assumptions, claims, and evidence were false. Exhibit 4 lists the accident/incident investigation role played by each of these techniques.

Exhibit 3 IA Accident/Incident Investigation Techniques

IA Accident/Incident Investigation Techniques	*C/R*	*Type*	*Life-Cycle Phase in which Technique is Used*		
			Concept	*Development*	*Operations*
Barrier analysis[a]	C4	SA, SE		x	x
Critical incident interviews	C4	SA, SE		x	x
Damage mode effects analysis[a]	C4	SA, SE		x	x
Event and causal factor charting	R4/C4	SA, SE		x	x
Scenario analysis	C4	SA, SE		x	x
Sequentially timed event plot (STEP) investigation system	R4/C4	SA, SE		x	x
Time/loss analysis (TLA) for emergency response evaluation	C4	SA, SE			x
Warning time analysis	C4	SA, SE			x

[a] These techniques can also be used during verification.

Legend for Exhibit 3

Column	*Code*	*Meaning*
Type	SA	Technique primarily supports safety engineering
	SE	Technique primarily supports security engineering
	RE	Technique primarily supports reliability engineering
	All	Technique supports a combination of safety, security, and reliability engineering
C/R	Cx	Groups of complementary techniques
	Rx	Groups of redundant techniques; only one of the redundant techniques should be used

Next, the accident/incident investigation techniques are discussed in detail. There is a high degree of interaction and interdependence between the techniques: the output of one technique is used as the input to another technique and the techniques complement or reinforce each other.

Barrier Analysis

Barrier analysis is used during an investigation to ascertain which defensive layers failed or were missing or inadequate. Barrier analysis helps to determine accident/incident causation by examining each defense in depth layer (or barrier) for accidental or intentional unwanted control, data, or information flow, as illustrated in Exhibit 5. Hazardous control and information flows to/from people and processes are uncovered and how they penetrated or bypassed existing defensive layers is determined. Defensive layers that failed or were missing or inadequate are identified, as well as those that did not fail. As a result, the need for new or modified defensive layers is highlighted. In practice, IA design techniques/features are referred to as "hard barriers,"

Exhibit 4 Accident/Incident Investigation Role of IA Techniques

Technique	*Accident/Incident Investigation Role*
I. Investigation Techniques	
Barrier analysis	Determine which defensive layers failed or were missing or inadequate during an accident/incident.
Critical incident interviews	Collect evidence about an accident/incident and previous related mistakes, anomalies, and near-misses from operational personnel.
Damage mode effects analysis	Postulate which specific threat mechanisms caused an accident/incident from an analysis of the damage modes.
Event and causal factor charting	Graphically reconstruct the events, immediate, intermediate, and root cause(s) of an accident/incident.
Scenario analysis	Develop avenues to investigate from causation theories and hypothetical event chains.
Sequentially timed event plot (STEP) investigation system	Expound a diagram of linked, sequentially timed events and their causal relationships that demonstrates how an accident/incident occurred.
Time/loss analysis (TLA) for emergency response evaluation	Evaluate the: (1) effect of human intervention following an accident/incident, (2) controllability of an accident/incident, and (3) effectiveness of mitigating threat control measures over time.
Warning time analysis	Investigate the delta between the available and actual response times (human and automatic) to an accident/incident and the contributing factors, such as erroneous, unforeseen, or unnecessary delays.
II. Analysis Techniques	
Bayesian Belief networks (BBNs)	Provide a methodology for reasoning about uncertainty as part of an accident/incident investigation.
Cause consequence analysis	Identify inappropriate, ineffective, and missing threat control measures; verify that all accidental and intentional failure modes had a corresponding threat control measure.
Event tree analysis	Identify inappropriate, ineffective, and missing threat control measures.
HAZOP study	Verify that all accidental and intentional, physical and cyber, hazards associated with the operation of a system had been eliminated or mitigated.
Petri nets	Verify that deadlock, race, and nondeterministic conditions that could cause a system compromise or failure did not exist.
Software, system FMECA	Examine the effect of accidental and intentional, random and systematic failures on system behavior in general and IA integrity in particular.
Software, system FTA	Identify potential root cause(s) of undesired system events (accidental and intentional) to verify the effectiveness of mitigating design features and operational procedures.
Sneak circuit analysis	Verify that all hidden, unintended, and unauthorized hardware and software logical paths or control sequences that could inhibit desired system functions, initiate undesired system events, or cause incorrect timing and sequencing had been removed.

Exhibit 4 Accident/Incident Investigation Role of IA Techniques (continued)

Technique	*Accident/Incident Investigation Role*
III. Verification Techniques	
Control flow analysis	Uncover poor and incorrect program logic structures that could have compromised IA integrity.
Data or information flow analysis	Uncover incorrect and unauthorized data transformations and operations that could have compromised IA integrity.
Review IA integrity case	Determine if the claims made about IA integrity were justified by the supporting arguments and evidence.
Root cause analysis	Identify the underlying cause(s), event(s), conditions, or actions that individually or in combination led to an accident/incident; determine why the defect was not detected earlier.

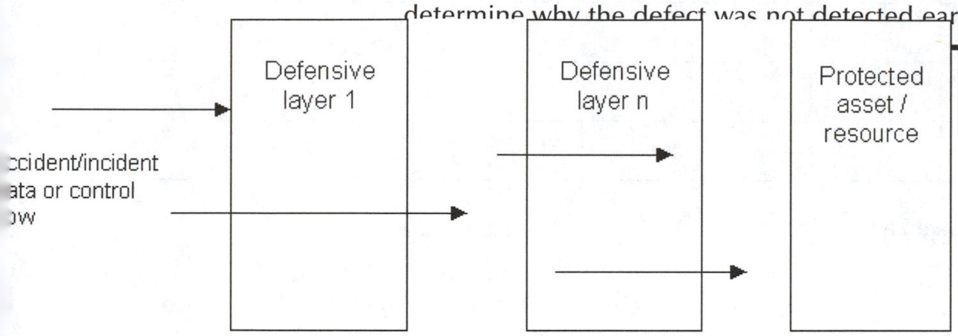

Defensive layer 1

Defensive layer n

Protected asset / resource

Exhibit 5 Barrier Analysis Concept

while operational procedures and physical security measures are referred to as "soft barriers." Barrier analysis does not evaluate an entire system, only the defensive layers.

Observations and recommendations are recorded in a barrier analysis report, as shown in Exhibit 6. Existing threat control measures are listed in Part I, along with their intended defensive function. The location of each threat control measure (the TCP/IP or ISO OSI layer and execution point) and its type (anticipate/prevent, detect/characterize, respond/recover) is cited. Next, the accident/incident status is recorded, indicating whether the layer was effective, partially effective, or failed. Part II of the report identifies new defensive layers that are needed. Each recommended new threat control measure is listed, along with the defensive function it will serve, the implementation location, and type. An explanation of the defensive layer this new measure is replacing or reinforcing is provided, with a supporting rationale.

Critical Incident Interviews

Critical incident interviews are conducted to collect evidence from operational personnel about an accident/incident and previous related mistakes, anomalies,

Exhibit 6 Barrier Analysis Report

Barrier Analysis Report for:______________________

as of date:____________________

I. Existing Defensive Layers

Threat Control Measure	*Function*	*Location*[a]	*Type*[b]	*Accident/Incident Status*			*Remarks*
				Effective	*Partially Effective*	*Failed*	

II. New Defensive Layers Needed

Threat Control Measure	*Function*	*Location*[a]	*Type*[b]	*Defensive Layer Being Replaced or Reinforced*	*Rationale*

[a] TCP/IP or ISO OSI layer and execution point.

[b] Anticipate/prevent, detect/characterize, or respond/recover.

and near-misses. Key personnel with first-hand experience in developing, using, administering, and maintaining the system that failed or was compromised are interviewed. The interview focuses on experience with or observations about the system immediately before and during the accident/incident and mistakes, anomalies, and near-misses experienced or observed in the past. Operator actions, system modes/states, conditions, functions, malfunctions, etc. are discussed. Printouts, server and workstation OS and memory dumps, audit trails, test results, network and system configuration reports, and such are collected to support verbal accounts. This information is analyzed to expose potential immediate, intermediate, and chronic accident/incident precursors.

People closest to and with the most experience using a system have invaluable insights that other people do not and that may not be readily apparent from technical evidence alone. They also help ensure accurate interpretations of events.

Interviewers need to be careful to separate fact from opinion, subjective from objective data. Interviews must be conducted in an open, positive environment so that witnesses do not feel threatened, intimidated, coerced, or fearful of employment-related retaliation.

Damage Mode Effects Analysis

Damage mode effects analysis is a deductive technique that provides an early assessment of survivability and the effect of an accident/incident on a system's mission/operation. Damage mode effects analysis is an extension of an FMECA. It examines the damage mode for each IA-critical and IA-related function, entity, component, and subcomponent, specifically[425]:

- The type of damage experienced
- Primary, secondary, and cascading damage effects on this and other functions, entities, and systems
- Variation in the damage mode by operational mode/state, profile, and mission
- The local, next higher level, and end effect(s) of the damage

The damage modes are analyzed to postulate which specific threat mechanisms caused an accident/incident. The survivability assessment provides essential input to recovery efforts and often exposes latent vulnerabilities. The effectiveness of this technique is proportional to the ability to analyze damage modes immediately during or after an accident/incident. If legal action is pursued as the result of an accident/incident, a damage mode effects analysis must be performed.

Event and Causal Factor Charting

Event and causal factor charts depict a detailed sequence of facts and activities that led to an accident/incident. The right-most block on the chart is the primary event — the accident/incident. The immediate cause is shown in the next block, on the left parallel to the first block. Reasons that permitted or contributed to the immediate causes are listed underneath. This process is continued backward to the underlying root cause(s)/event(s). Unknown events are shown as gaps (?) in the diagram and highlight areas needing further investigation. Causes are categorized as human or system actions. Cascading and lateral events are recorded as well so that all pertinent avenues of investigation are explored.

Event and causal factor charts summarize what is known and unknown about an accident/incident in a format that is easily understood by all stakeholders. The sequential nature of the charts facilitates an unfolding investigation. Arrows connecting cause and event blocks represent potential primary and secondary prevention points; this information can be used to reinforce defensive layers. Event and causal factor charts do not capture the exact timing of events. As a reminder[425]:

> *... care must be taken not to limit analysis to merely addressing the symptoms of a problem. The symptoms are sometimes causes in themselves; however, they are often only indications that other factors must be pursued to find the underlying causes.*

Exhibit 7 depicts an event and causal factor chart. The accident/incident in this example is a patient dying after a radiation therapy session. This example was chosen because it (1) illustrates the interaction between safety and security engineering, and (2) highlights the need for security engineering beyond the commercial, defense, and intelligence domains. The same accident/incident scenario is used in Exhibits 9 through 11 to demonstrate the similarities and differences between event and causal factor charts and STEP diagrams.

Scenario Analysis

Scenario analysis is conducted to develop avenues to investigate from causation theories and hypothetical event chains. During scenario analysis, all system entities, components, operational profiles, modes/states, environment, and missions and operator actions are examined by an interdisciplinary team. This team, under the guidance of a neutral facilitator, attempts to surmise all possible, credible, and logical scenarios that could have caused or contributed to an accident/incident. The starting point for the team is the fact that the accident/incident occurred. They do not examine evidence; rather, they develop causation theories and hypothetical event chains, based on experience and inductive reasoning, that become avenues to investigate. Scenario analysis, because it is not dependent on extensive evidence, is particularly well suited for investigating novel accidents/incidents for which little or no historical data exists.[425] Successful scenario analysis is dependent on an accurate understanding of the system that failed or was compromised, without letting that knowledge constrain visualization of potential threat scenarios[425]:

> *An unfettered mind and an active imagination lead to mastery [of this technique]. ... It can be argued that over-familiarity with the system under analysis restricts the freedom of thought processes necessary to successful application.*

(*Note:* Do not confuse this technique with formal scenario analysis discussed in Section B.2 and Chapter 6.)

Sequentially Timed Event Plot (STEP) Investigation System

The purpose of the sequentially timed event plot (STEP) investigation system is to expound a diagram of linked, sequentially timed events and their causal relationships, which demonstrates how an accident/incident occurred. The STEP investigation system is an analytical methodology that develops accident process descriptions. A diagram of sequentially timed, multi-linear events depicts acci-

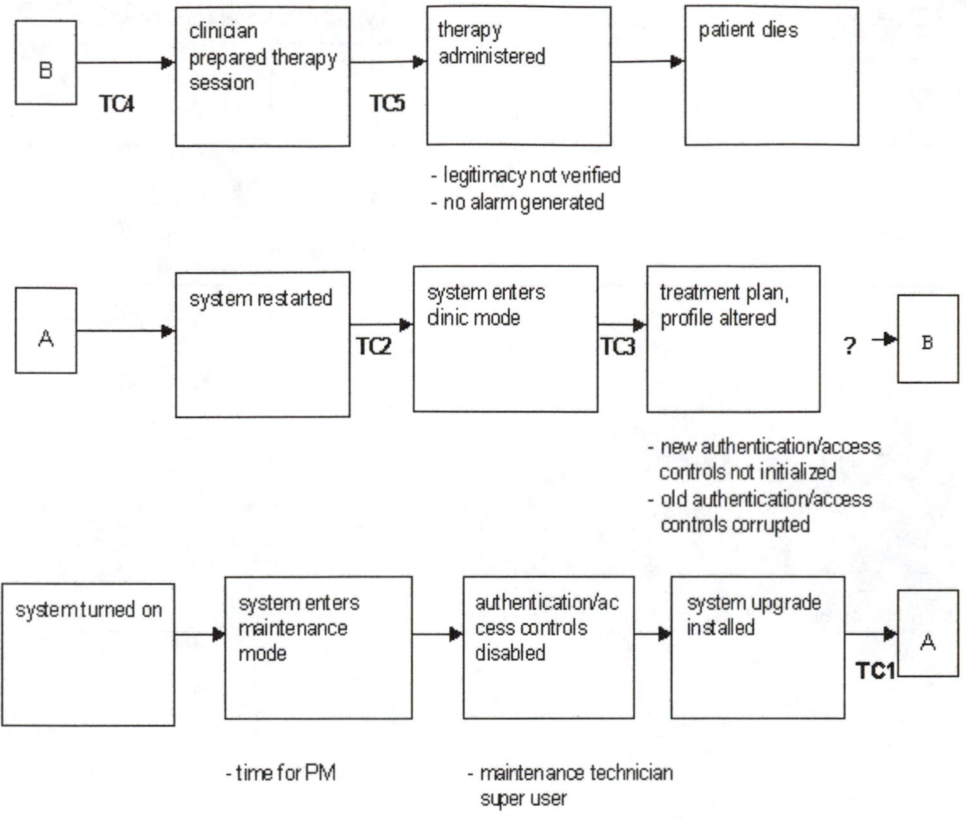

Threat control barriers	
TC1	System is restarted with upgrade. Maintenance technician should have verified that all safety and security features worked correctly, including authentication and access controls.
TC2, TC3	System should have generated an alarm indicating that the new authentication and access controls had not been initialized and that the old authentication and access controls were corrupted. Alarm status should have prohibited access to patient records database and treatment planning system.
TC4	Clinician fails to notice or report that system does not perform authentication.
TC5	Clinician should have verified (manually) legitimacy of treatment profile before initiating therapy. System should have automatically verified legitimacy of treatment profile before initiating therapy. Alarm status should have prohibited therapy session.

Exhibit 7 Event and Causal Factor Chart

dent/incident causal relationships. Direct, converging, and diverging relationships of immediate, intermediate, and underlying events are illustrated. STEP diagrams visually display the sequence and timing aspects of accident/incident precursors. The event chain necessary to produce the accident/incident outcome is linked together; accident data is transformed into event building blocks.[425] Uncertainties or gaps in the event chain are highlighted for further

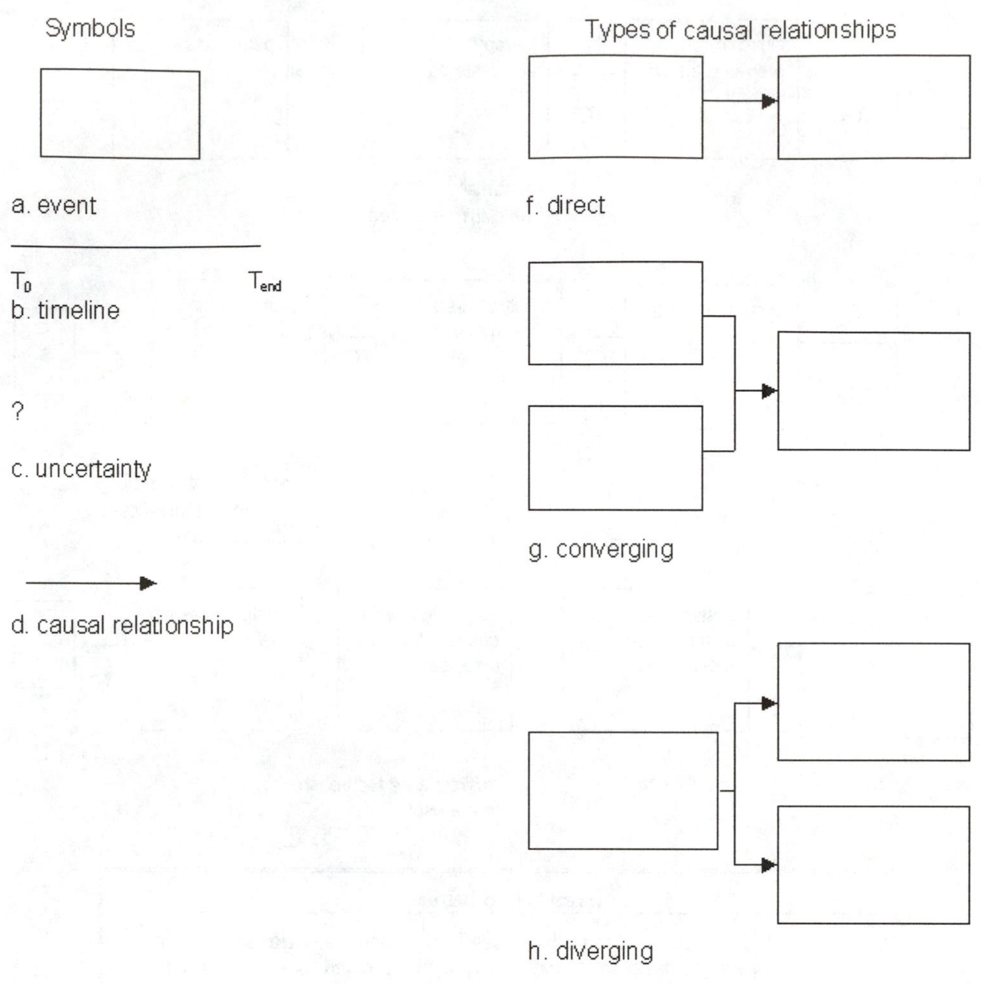

Exhibit 8 Standard STEP Investigation System Symbols and Notation

investigation. Standard symbols and notation are used to develop a STEP diagram, as shown in Exhibit 8.

The STEP investigation system supports an in-depth, thorough, and focused analysis of an accident/incident. STEP diagrams are easy to understand; consequently, they can be reviewed and verified by multiple stakeholders. An unlimited number of logical possibilities (accidental/intentional, human/computer action) can be investigated.[425] STEP diagrams expose misunderstandings about how a system "should" versus "does" operate and deficiencies in operational procedures, contingency plans, and physical security practices. A skilled facilitator is needed to keep the analysis proceeding at a level that is meaningful and relevant to the investigation. The analysis should not be at too high or too low a level.

Exhibits 9 through 11 are a STEP diagram of the radiation therapy session accident/incident introduced in Exhibit 7. Note that a STEP diagram captures more detail than an event and causal factor chart. Events are associated with actors and timestamps. Relationships between actors and events are recorded.

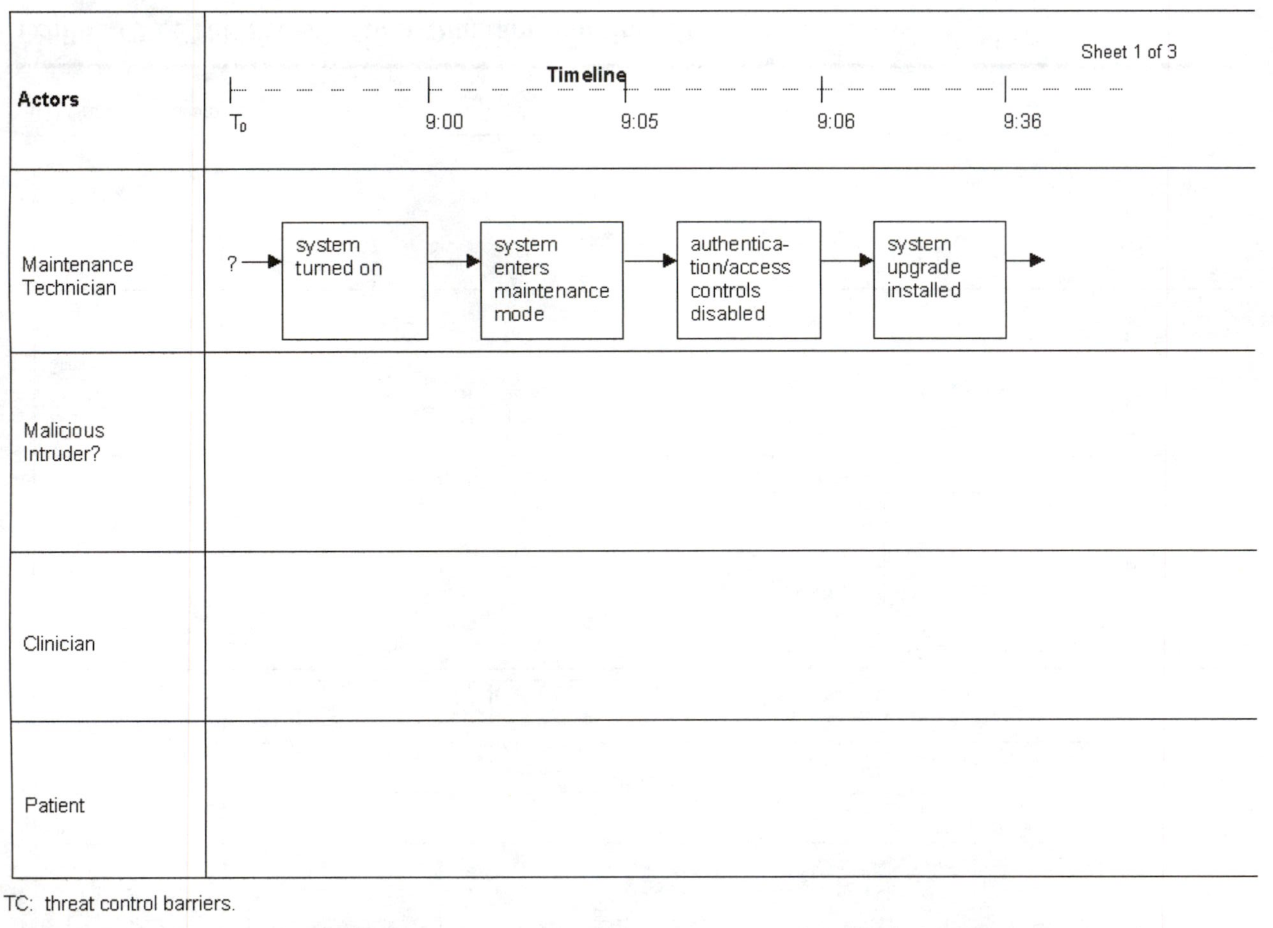

Exhibit 9 STEP Investigation Diagram

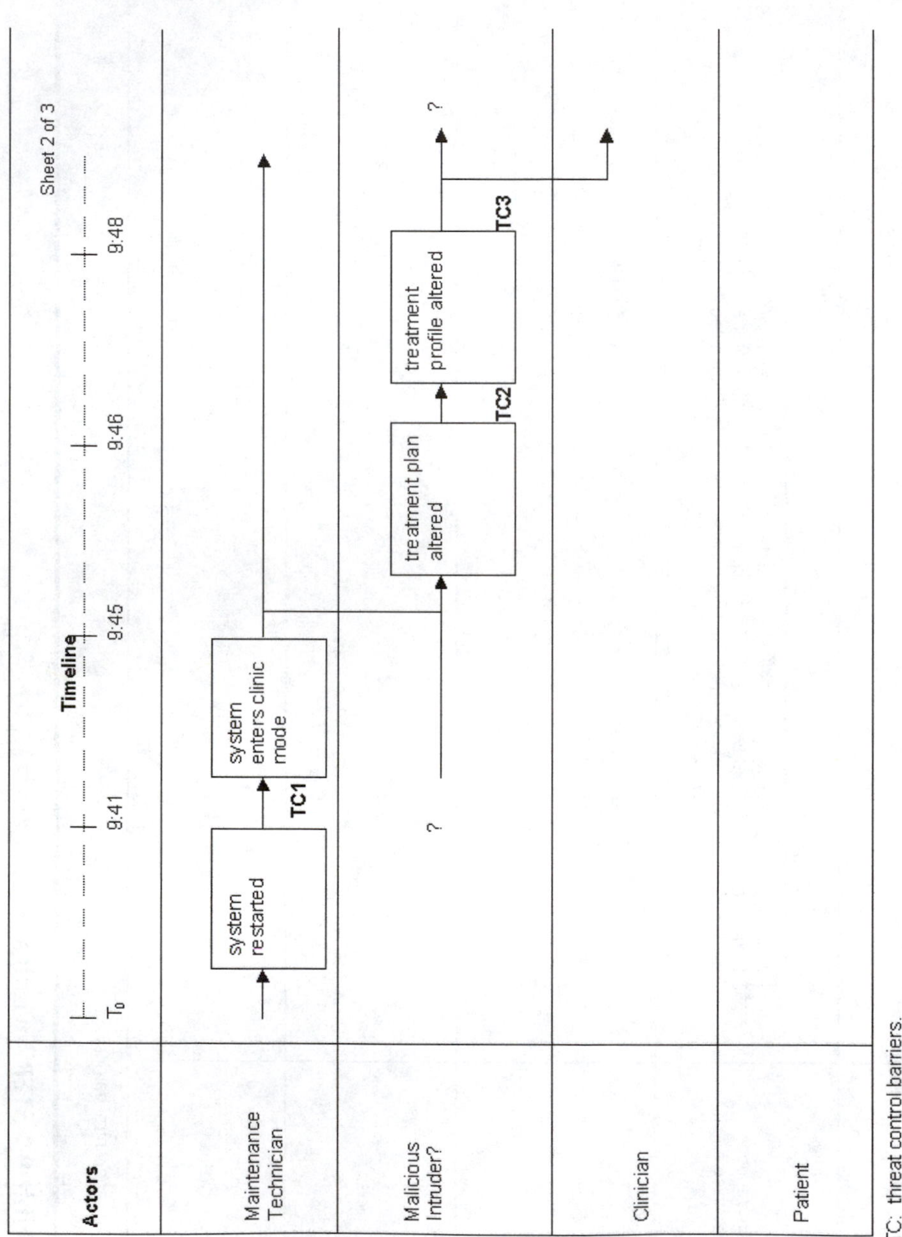

TC: threat control barriers.

Exhibit 10 STEP Investigation Diagram (continued)

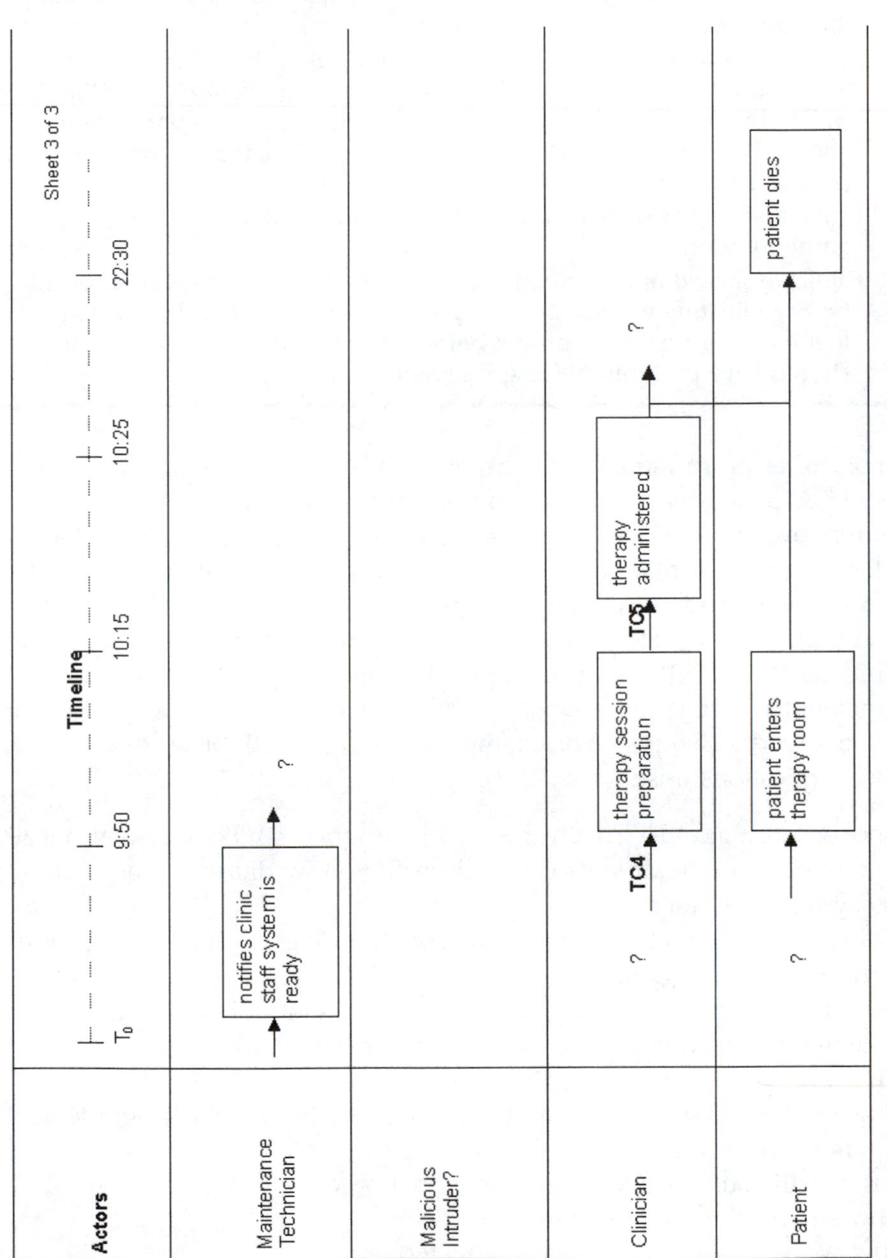

TC: threat control barriers.

Exhibit 11 STEP Investigation Diagram (continued)

Legend for Exhibits 9 through 11

Threat Control Barriers	
TC1	System is restarted with upgrade. Maintenance technician should have verified that all safety and security features worked correctly, including authentication and access controls.
TC2, TC3	System should have generated an alarm indicating that the new authentication and access controls had not been initialized and that the old authentication and access controls were corrupted. Alarm status should have prohibited access to patient records database and treatment planning system.
TC4	Clinician fails to notice or report that system does not perform authentication.
TC5	Clinician should have verified (manually) legitimacy of treatment profile before initiating therapy. System should have automatically verified legitimacy of treatment profile before initiating therapy. Alarm status should have prohibited therapy session.

Barrier analysis is performed to determine why defensive layers failed and the accident/incident was allowed to progress. Scenario analysis and critical incident interviews are conducted to resolve gaps in the STEP diagram. Pieces of the STEP diagram are filled in as an investigation unfolds. It is often useful to develop an event and causal factor chart as draft input to a STEP diagram.

An event and causal factor chart illustrates what happened during an accident/incident. A STEP diagram explains what happened and how. An accident/incident investigation must also answer the question of why did it or why was it allowed to happen. For example, looking at Exhibits 9 through 11, the following questions arise:

1. Who ordered and approved the system upgrade? Who knew about it?
2. Who altered the treatment plan and profile? How did they know about the system upgrade?
3. Was the maintenance technician collaborating with the malicious intruder or just negligent?
4. Was the clinician collaborating with the malicious intruder or just negligent?
5. Is negligence always accidental or can it be intentional?
6. What do physical security logs show?
7. Why was the system audit trail not archived before the upgrade and restarted afterward?
8. Is the malicious intruder a person or a process?
9. Who should the patient's family sue?
10. How many other patients were affected?

Time/Loss Analysis (TLA) for Emergency Response Evaluation

TLA "defines and organizes data needed to assess the objectives, progress, and outcome of an emergency response" to an accident/incident.[425] TLA serves several purposes. It evaluates the (1) effect of human intervention following an accident/incident, (2) controllability of an accident/incident, and (3) effectiveness of mitigating threat control measures over time. The results of TLA are recorded in TLA graphs.

TLA graphs measure and compare actual versus natural loss following an accident/incident. Intervention data is recorded at vertical points on the *x*-axis time line. Loss units (number of fatalities or injuries, property damage, financial loss, loss of productivity, environmental damage, etc.) are recorded on the *y*-axis. T_0 is when the accident/incident commences. T_{end} correlates to the time of the last directly related loss. The natural loss curve is estimated over time given no human intervention. The actual loss curve plots the sequential effect of each intervening action T_n. The slope between T_0 and T_1 is the same for both curves and represents the effectiveness of automatic mitigating (detect/characterize, respond/recover) threat control measures over time. The delta between the actual and natural loss curves from T_1 on is a function of the controllability of the accident/incident and the value of human intervention. The general shape of the curves is more important than precise data points.[425] TLA graphs can also be used to analyze alternative hypothetical intervention strategies[425] and contingency plans. Criteria for measuring loss units must be standardized and objective. TLA must be performed, or at least begun, promptly after an accident/incident because the evidence tends to dissipate.

Exhibit 12 present TLA graphs for four different accident/incident emergency response scenarios. The first graph (Exhibit 12a) illustrates the TLA for a single system in which human intervention was effective and lowered the total loss experienced. Exhibit 12b illustrates the TLA for a single system in which human intervention was ineffective and actually increased the total loss experienced. There are several possible explanations for this, including:

1. The situation was misdiagnosed and the wrong corrective action was applied.
2. The operational procedures or contingency plans were in error in describing how to respond to this situation.
3. A critical step was omitted or performed in the wrong sequence during the emergency response.
4. The emergency response was applied after the interval during which it could have been effective.
5. The operational procedures or contingency plans were deficient; they did not cover this situation and operational personnel guessed how to respond.
6. The operational procedures and contingency plans were correct, but operational personnel had no training or familiarity with them.

The reason for counterproductive human emergency response will be significant if legal action is taken subsequent to an accident/incident.

Exhibit 12c illustrates the TLA across multiple parallel systems in which human intervention was effective and lowered the actual loss experienced by all three systems. This example depicts the results of accident/incident propagation across

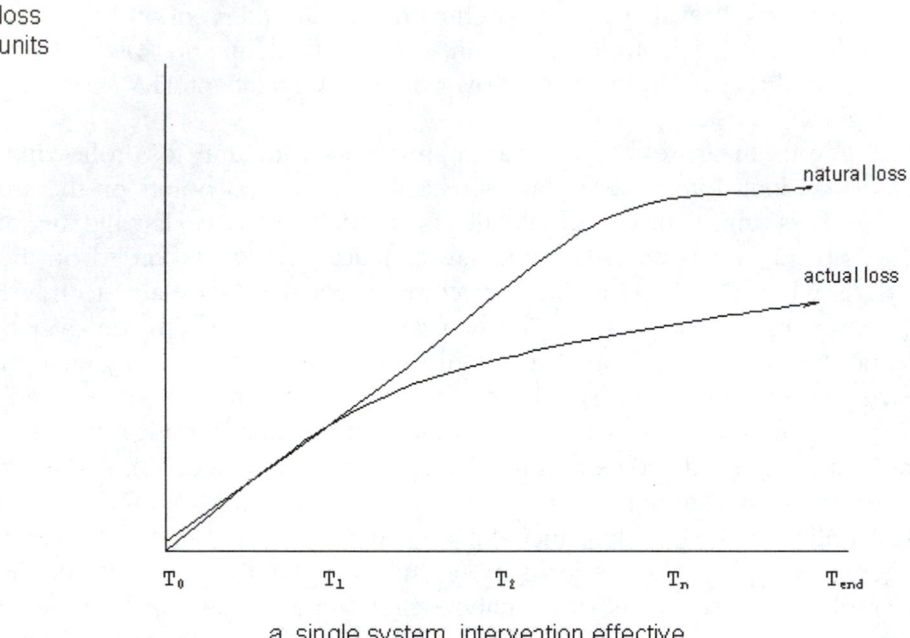

a. single system, intervention effective

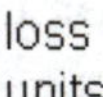

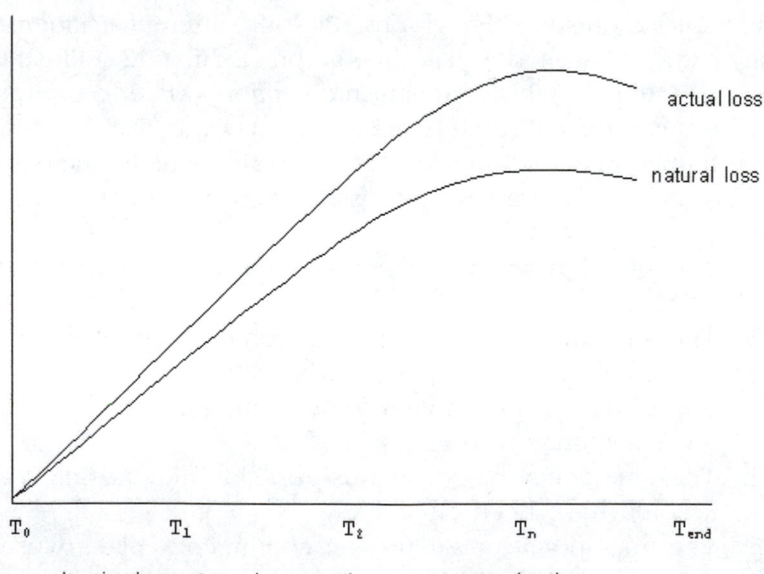

b. single system, intervention counterproductive

Exhibit 12 TLA Graphs

parallel systems, usually within one organization. The time taken to respond to the second, third, and n^{th} system is longer, due to notification/response logistics, but the actual loss is still less than the natural loss.

Exhibit 12d illustrates the TLA across multiple cascading systems in which human intervention was effective and lowered the actual loss experienced by all three systems. This example depicts the results of accident/incident

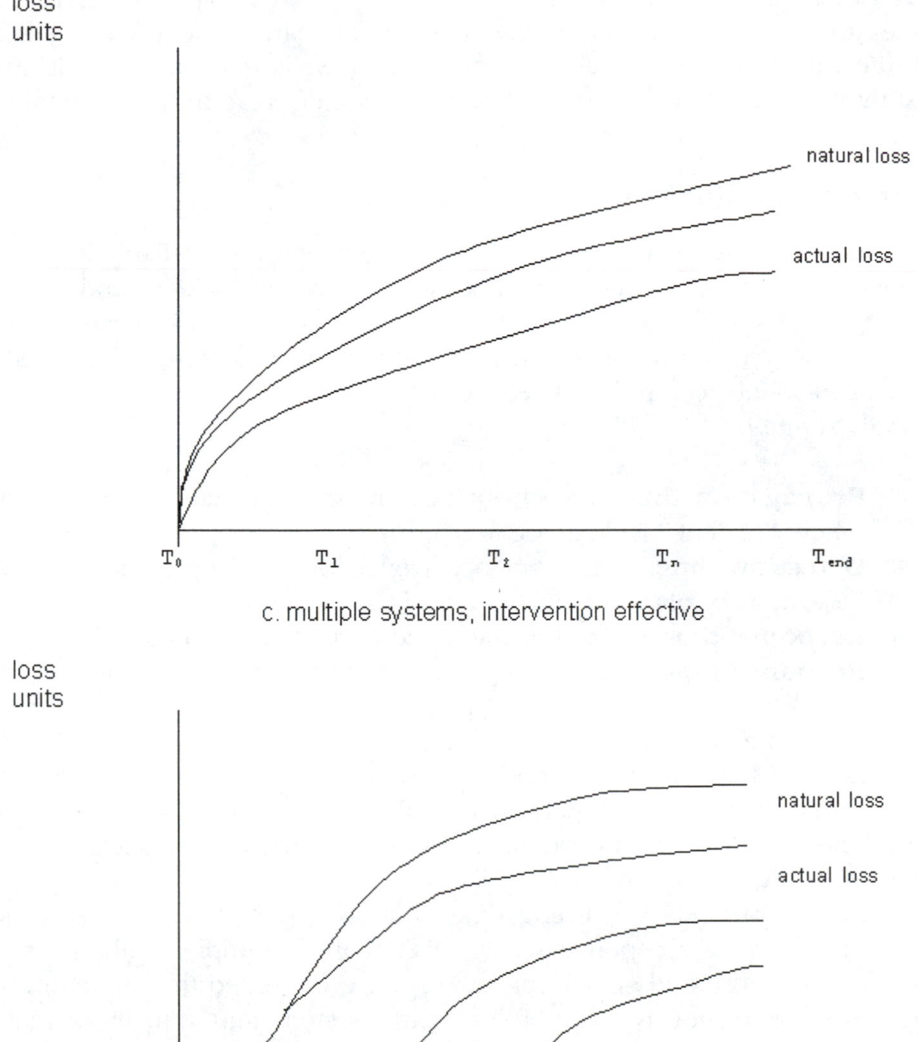

Exhibit 12 TLA Graphs (continued)

propagation across cascading systems belonging to multiple organizations, analogous to accidents/incidents that propagate via the Internet. If accident/incident data is shared and reported quickly (see chapter section "Report Accident/Incident"), the time taken to respond to the second, third, and n^{th} system is less, lowering the actual loss.

Another interesting avenue to investigate is the T_0 to T_1 curve. If TLA and barrier analysis are combined, points on the curve can be identified to indicate the interval during which each defensive layer was effective before it failed. In summary, TLA can be used to evaluate a variety of different scenarios.

Warning Time Analysis

Warning time analysis investigates the delta between the available and actual response times (human and automatic) to an accident/incident and the contributing factors, such as erroneous, unforeseen, or unnecessary delays. Warning time analysis examines various intervals along the time line from when an accident/incident occurred and recovery mechanisms were initiated. Specific intervals scrutinized include[31]:

- **Propagation time:** time from occurrence of initiating event to time when accident/incident occurred
- **Detection time:** time from occurrence of initiating event to earliest indication or alarm
- **Response $time_A$:** time for automatic corrective action
- **Response $time_H$:** time for human-initiated corrective action

Warning time analysis evaluates the effectiveness of anomaly detection, the time available for a response, and the adequacy of emergency operational procedures and contingency plans, especially when system reconfiguration or redundant switchover was needed. A comparison between the available and actual response times is made.

Exhibit 13 presents a warning time analysis report. Several observations can be made from a report such as this. In this example, both the actual automatic response and actual human response exceeded the minimum time available. The responsiveness of automatic system and human actions in preventing an accident/incident can be measured as a function of the delta between the minimum and actual response times. Deltas between minimum and actual response times, both automatic system and human, need to be explained as part of an accident/incident investigation; that is, (1) what caused the delays, (2) were the delays accidental or intentional, (3) were the delays avoidable or unavoidable, and (4) what can be done to eliminate or reduce delays in the future.

Exhibit 14 summarizes the interaction between the different accident/incident investigation techniques. The figure is not meant to show a chronology in which to use the techniques, but rather the information flow among the techniques. Some techniques are used to develop "how did" accident scenarios; others are used to develop "how could" accident scenarios. Some techniques are usually only performed once, while others are repeated as evidence accumulates and unknowns or uncertainties are resolved.

Barrier analysis reports have multiple uses beyond their original scope. When combined with TLA graphs, they measure the effective interval of each

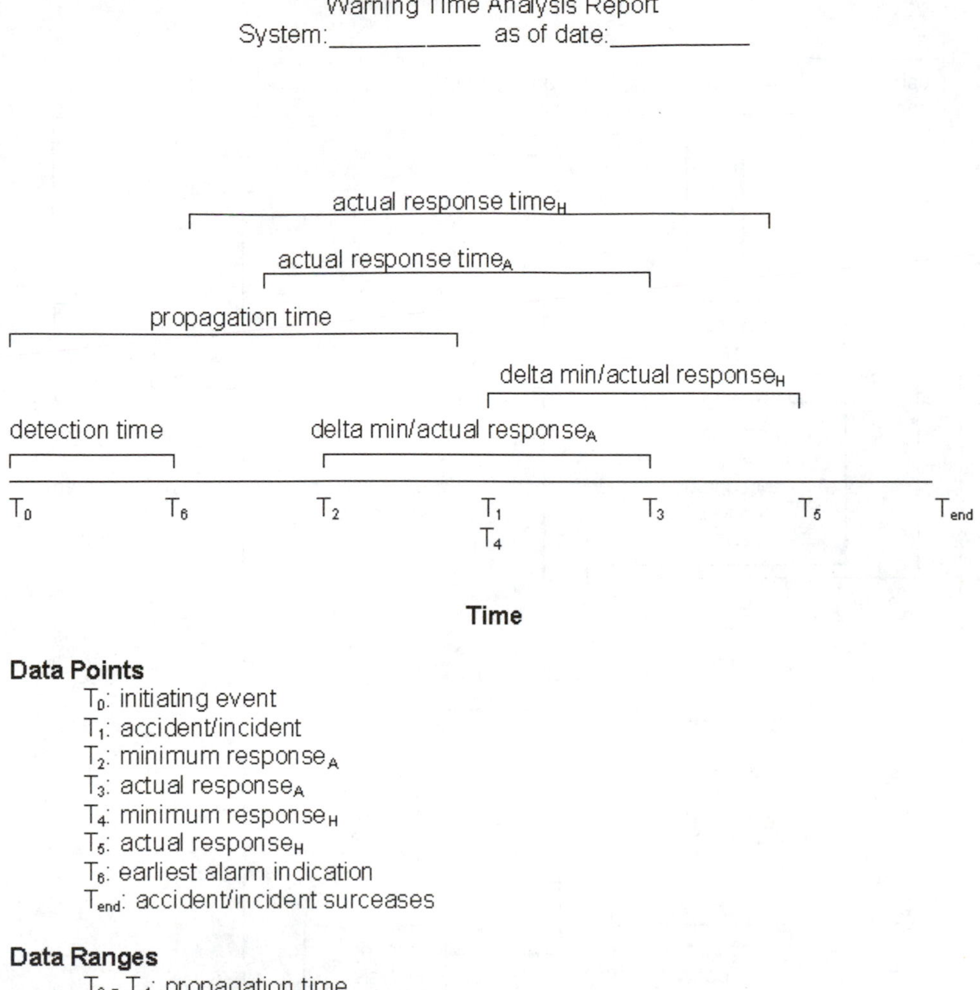

Data Ranges

- T_0 - T_4: propagation time
- T_0 - T_6: detection time
- T_0 - T_3: actual response time$_A$
- T_0 - T_5: actual response time$_H$
- T_2 - T_3: delta minimum/actual response time$_A$
- T_4 - T_5: delta minimum/actual response time$_H$

Exhibit 13 Warning Time Analysis Report

defensive layer prior to failure. The failure of defensive layers is captured on event and causal factor charts and STEP diagrams. Failed defensive layers are analyzed when performing damage mode effects analysis.

Information collected during critical incident interviews provides useful input to damage mode effects analysis, event and causal factor charts, and scenarios analysis. As mentioned earlier, event and causal factor charts can be developed as draft input to a STEP diagram. TLA graphs capture timing specifics about intervention actions that are recorded on STEP diagrams. Scenario analysis supports reasoning about unknowns, unce[illegible]inties, and gaps in STEP diagrams; it also identifies new avenues to inv[illegible]

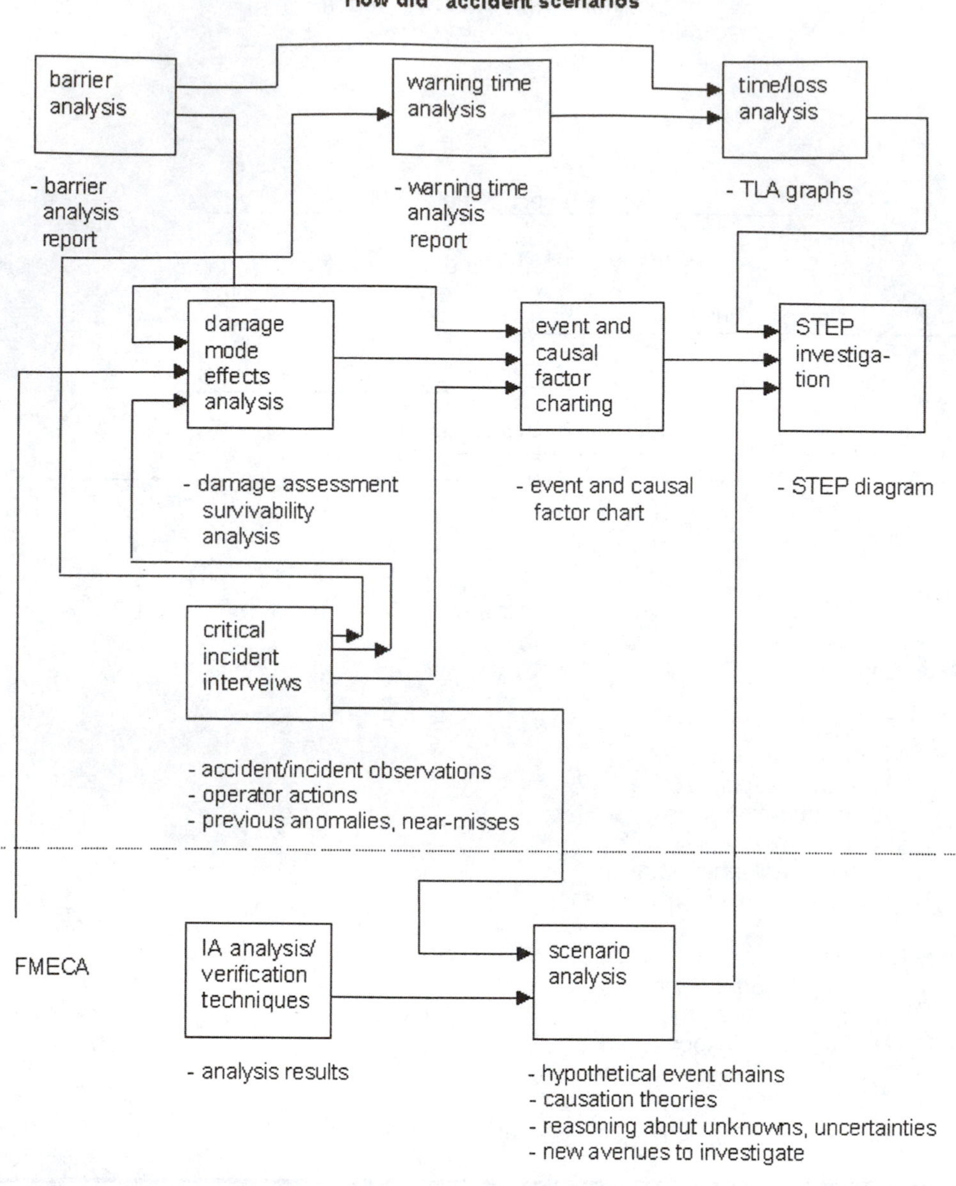

Exhibit 14 Interaction Between Accident/Incident Investigation Techniques

8.2 Initiate Short-Term Recovery Mechanisms

After an accident/incident occurs, the cause, extent, and consequences are investigated. The initial report of the accident/incident triggers immediate short-term recovery mechanisms. This process is discussed below. Complete follow-up accident/incident reports stimulate long-term remedial measures. That process is discussed in the chapter section "Deploy Remedial Measures." Initiating recovery mechanisms and reporting an accident (chapter section

Exhibit 15 Accident/Incident Recovery Steps

1. Review preliminary investigation results about cause(s), extent, and consequences of the accident/incident.
2. Determine what can and cannot be recovered in the short term:
   a. Systems
   b. Communication equipment
   c. Hardware
   d. System software
   e. Application software, services
   f. Data
3. Ascertain when each system, entity, and component can and should be restored:
   a. Technical considerations
   b. Operational priorities
   c. Safety and security priorities
4. Decide how each system, entity, and component can and should be restored:
   a. Level of service to be restored
   b. Actions, commands necessary to effect recovery
   c. Verifying effectiveness of recovery efforts
5. Notify customers, end users, system administrators, maintenance staff, etc.
   a. Problem experienced
   b. Emergency precautions
   c. Estimated recovery time

"Report Accident/Incident") are parallel activities. Exhibit 15 summarizes the five steps involved in initiating recovery mechanisms.

The preliminary accident/incident investigation results drive the emergency recovery response. In many cases, there is a one-to-one if this cause/consequences, then take this recovery action. Pre-accident modes/states and conditions, dependencies and interactions among systems and entities, and automatic system and human-initiated corrective action already taken (whether or not it was correct or effective) are taken into account before initiating recovery mechanisms.

The second step is to determine what systems and entities can and cannot be recovered in the short term. In particular, which internal and external systems, entities, hardware, communications equipment, system software, applications software/services, and data can or cannot be restored. The extent of the damage, whether or not the entities are under your control, and other logistical matters will factor into this determination.

The third step is to ascertain when each system and entity can and should be restored. This step can be complex. Technical requirements and priorities are interleaved with operational requirements and priorities. Several factors are meshed together:

1. When is it technically feasible to restore each entity and component?
2. What is the optimum sequence in which entities and components should be restored, from a technical perspective, taking into account dependencies and logistical considerations?
3. What are the operational priorities for restoring various systems and services?
4. What are the safety and security priorities for restoring various threat control measures?

In short, an entire system and all of its entities cannot be restored all at once after an accident/incident; instead, recovery is effected gradually.

Prior to initiating recovery mechanisms, one must verify that the accident/incident has been contained and mitigated, that it is in effect "over" and not likely to recur or take new unanticipated twists and turns. Premature recovery efforts may interfere with automatic system and human-initiated action taken to contain and mitigate an accident/incident. In the worst-case scenario, this can result in a prolonged cycle of an accident/incident, failed automatic and human responses, failed recovery efforts, and accident/incident propagation and recurrence.

The fourth step is to decide how each system, entity, and component can and should be restored. This step involves several decisions, such as what level of service should be restored, what actions and commands are necessary to effect recovery, and how to verify the effectiveness of recovery efforts.

The level of service to be restored in the short term will depend on the extent and consequences of the accident/incident and operational priorities. Some sessions and processes may need to be terminated immediately to reduce system load and the possibility of further failure or compromise. Critical transactions may be "frozen" or checkpointed to prevent loss of critical data. A limited number of IA-critical services may be restored immediately while further recovery is pending. The number and location of users who can access the limited services may also be restricted initially.

Operational procedures and contingency plans should spell out the step-by-step actions and commands necessary to effect recovery. They should also identify who to contact for further help. Transaction paths and critical threat zones should be consulted to locate attack points and the corresponding recovery points. Recovery actions and commands can involve any of the following:

- Activating cold spare or hot standby redundant hardware
- Reconfiguring a system or network
- Restarting, reloading, reinitializing a system or data from local or offsite archives
- Switching operations to a remote location
- Switching to an alternate service provider
- Restoring and restarting access control rules, authentication parameters and processing, security audit trail/alarm, and other threat control measures

Before the restored services can be turned over to users, the effectiveness of the recovery efforts must be verified. This involves verifying the robustness of the restored services and the robustness of the restored threat control measures. In particular, the ability of the restored threat control measures to withstand a new or repeat accident/incident needs to be verified; a survivability assessment is paramount.

The first four steps are more or less sequential. The fifth step, notification, is an ongoing activity that occurs in parallel with the other four steps. A critical component of recovery is notifying customers, end users, system administrators, maintenance staff, etc. that an accident/incident has occurred. Initially, they should be informed about the type of problem experienced; the description should be concise and not overly technical. Concurrently or immediately afterward, they should be advised of any emergency precautions to take. The third piece of information to convey is the estimated time required for a limited recovery and for a full recovery. It is important to keep all stakeholders informed during recovery efforts; without accurate and timely information, they might accidentally sabotage or further complicate recovery efforts.

In summary, the effectiveness and timeliness of recovery efforts are entirely dependent on prior planning, preparation, coordination, and training. All the information needed to perform steps 2 through 5 should be recorded in the operational procedures and contingency plans. The thoroughness of the operational procedures and contingency plans and the familiarity of operational personnel with them are key ingredients for a quick and successful recovery. The other option, or course, is panicked guessing.

8.3 Report Accident/Incident

Reporting an accident/incident is an essential part of investigating, responding to, and recovering from it. An initial report should be filed as soon as an accident/incident is known or suspected. The initial report describes the characteristics of the accident/incident, the time it was first detected, suspected cause and source (if this information is available at the time), the consequences to date, and estimated recovery time and actions needed. Later, as more is known about the accident/incident, follow-up reports are filed. Facts and objective observations replace earlier theories and suppositions.

Organizations need to have clearly defined accident/incident reporting channels and responsibilities, inside and outside the organization. Employees, end users, and customers should be encouraged to report known or suspected accidents/incidents; this is not the responsibility of a system administrator alone. People who report an accident/incident may or may not participate in the subsequent investigation; most likely, they will participate in critical incident interviews.

There are several reasons to report an accident/incident, inside and outside an organization, and benefits to be derived from doing so. As Bond[218] observes:

> *…an accident is the invasion of the unaware by the unknown. To reduce accidents, we must make the person aware of the hazards unknown by him but known too well by others.… A wise man learns from his own experience, but a wiser man learns from the experiences of others.*

First, an accident/incident must be reported before the situation can be corrected. If the accident/incident is reported in a timely manner, the damage/loss experienced by this and other systems can be minimized, as shown in the TLA graphs (Exhibit 12). Second, reporting the results of an accident/incident investigation and what was learned from it reduces the likelihood of recurrence, within and among organizations.[218] Third, customers and employees will have more confidence in an organization that reports accidents/incidents; they gain the impression that the organization is being open and is on top of the situation. This is another example of perception management. Fourth, an organization may have a legal responsibility to report accidents/incidents to stockholders, customers, the public, or a regulatory agency, depending on the nature of the organization and the legal jurisdiction in which it resides.[248] Fifth, an accident/incident must have been reported if subsequent legal action is to be taken. Finally, as Rathmell[391] points out:

> *...national information assurance can only be achieved if threat assessments and early warnings are distributed widely across industry and to the public.*

There are a variety of potential sources to notify of known or suspected accidents/incidents outside an immediate organization. The computer emergency response team coordination center (CERT/CC) was established November 1988 at Carnegie Mellon University Software Engineering Institute (SEI). CERT/CC provides a 24-hour central point of contact and clearinghouse for identifying vulnerabilities and responses. CERT/CC maintains a knowledge base of computer network and system vulnerabilities and best practices.[350] The center also studies Internet security vulnerabilities, provides incident response services, publishes security alerts, and researches security and survivability issues in wide-area computing. During the first ten years in operation, CERT/CC responded to 14,000 incidents, published 180 advisories, replied to 200,000 e-mail messages, and answered 15,000 hotline calls.[379] The time to get acquainted with CERT/CC is before one experiences an accident/incident. They can be contacted at www.cert.org.[460]

CERT/CC resources are available to the public. U.S. government agencies have the option of subscribing to the federal computer incident response center (FedCIRC), managed by the General Services Administration (GSA). FedCIRC was established October 1998 and provides 24-hour hotline, e-mail, and help desk support, as well as security alerts and advisories. FedCIRC can be contacted at: www.fedcirc.gov.[469]

The U.S. National Infrastructure Protection Center (NIPC) is managed by the FBI.[326] Established in 1998, the NIPC's mission is to "detect, deter, warn, and respond to attacks on the nation's critical infrastructures," both physical and cyber, and "to serve as the government's information clearinghouse for both security and responses to attacks by individuals and foreign governments."[196] Among other things, the NIPC is developing a multi-source database of known threats and actual intrusions, successful and unsuccessful responses, prevention strategies, and computer crime trends. Indispensable to NIPC's success is the cooperation and exchange of information between public and private organizations. Accordingly, the formation of the public-private Partnership for Critical Infrastructure Security was announced January 2000.[355]

Initial members of the Partnership included: RSA Security, Cisco Systems, Network Associates, Microsoft, and CERT/CC.[355] Information about NIPC and the Partnership can be found at www.fbi.gov/nipc/index.htm.[468]

Readers may also want to contact local and national law enforcement agencies. In the United States, the damage threshold for computer crime to be prosecuted is very low — only a few thousand dollars. Lost productivity most certainly should be included in the damage estimate. A good organization to contact in this regard is the High Tech Crime Network at www.htcn.org.[472]

The news media should also be contacted if one needs to alert customers quickly, for example, to not use ATMs, to not access online banking systems, or that credit card information has been compromised.

Software vendors are also beginning to post information about security features, vulnerabilities, alerts, and patches; see, for example, Microsoft's security site at www.microsoft.com/security.[480]

A major challenge facing the NIPC and CERT/CC is the need for standardized reporting of accidents/incidents. Without standardized reporting elements, notation, and criteria, the data accumulated and shared has little value. Vulnerabilities, threats, responses, consequences, etc. need to be reported and categorized uniformly. In this way, keyword searches, queries about how to respond to an emergency situation or prevention strategies for a particular threat, and statistical reports showing the prevalence of certain types of malicious activity can be generated quickly with a reasonable degree of accuracy and shared across multiple organizations.[226] A main premise of the Partnership for Critical Infrastructure Security and NIPC is that the privacy of individuals and corporations will be protected when collecting, reporting, storing, and aggregating this information; without demonstrated privacy protections, it is unlikely that many organizations will participate.

This is not a new challenge. The U.S. Department of Energy (DoE), Federal Aviation Administration (FAA), Food and Drug Administration (FDA), Occupational Safety and Health Administration (OSHA), and National Safety Transportation Board (NSTB) have had accident/incident reporting systems for years. The degree of success these agencies have had in collecting and reporting standardized data varies. One of the more successful efforts has been the DoE Computerized Accident/Incident Reporting System (CAIRS); the need for standardized data elements and codes was recognized early. Between 1981 and 1993, 50,000 accident/incident investigation reports were entered into CAIRS.[226] What is unique about the NIPC and CERT/CC challenge is that the data is voluntarily reported; unlike the other systems, there is no legal mandate to report the information.

It was previously mentioned that safety and reliability engineers have considerable forensic engineering experience, although they do not refer to it as such. They also have considerable experience in developing and using standardized failure reporting and analysis systems, usually referred to as a data reporting and corrective action system (DRACAS) or failure reporting and corrective action system (FRACAS). A DRACAS or FRACAS is a good model to follow when reporting or collecting accident/incident information.

All in-service anomalies are recorded in a DRACAS or FRACAS. This information is used to determine the safety and security significance of the anomaly, whether the anomaly is a symptom of a more serious underlying problem, and the immediate precautions to be taken.[130] Anomaly reporting often results in the identification of a new vulnerability/hazard or reclassification of known vulnerabilities/hazards.[130,131] In addition, anomaly reporting supports change impact analysis as part of initiating recovery mechanisms. It is important that accident/incident reports be submitted promptly[131]:

> *All reported faults/failures need to be considered for possible action as quickly as possible. If action is not taken quickly it is likely that the affected items will be returned for repair and valuable data which could have been obtained by a detailed investigation will be lost.*

A DRACAS or FRACAS accurately and consistently categorizes accidents/incidents according to their cause, significance, and frequency.[131] The cause establishes the exact root and intermediate causes of the accident/incident. Care must be taken not to draw premature or unsubstantiated conclusions. As an analogy, the fact that a light is on or a car is parked in front of a house **only** means that the light is on and the car is parked in front of a house; it does not mean that someone is home. The significance of an accident/incident rates its effect on the ability to perform essential mission capabilities. A quantitative measurement of the frequency and duration of the accident/incident is captured for trend analysis purposes. The remaining useful life of the system is also assessed after an accident/incident.

Exhibits 16 and 17 present a standardized accident/incident report template. Confidential information, such as individual name, organization name, address, and contact information has been removed. The report is in two parts. The first part (Exhibit 16) contains the accident/incident description. Information about the anomaly, its severity, and the conditions under which it was experienced is captured through a combination of category codes and free text fields. This information is necessary to classify the accident/incident so that (1) the information can be accurately shared with other organizations via alerts, and (2) the appropriate emergency response can be determined. As much of this information is provided as possible in the initial report, without unduly delaying it. Additional detail and corrections are provided in follow-up reports. An important section (11) is the identification of other systems/entities inside and outside the organization that may also be impacted by the accident/incident.

The second part of the report (Exhibit 17) is the accident/incident assessment. This part of the report records the causes and consequences of the accident/incident, including estimated damages. Two important sections are the recommendations for short-term recovery mechanisms (11) and the lessons learned to be applied to long-term remedial measures (12).

8.4 Deploy Long-Term Remedial Measures

An accident/incident investigation is undertaken to discover what exactly happened, how it happened, and why it happened or was allowed to happen.

Exhibit 16 Accident/Incident Report: Part I-Description

I. Accident/Incident Description

Report Field	*Initial Report*	*Follow-up Report*
1. Report reference number	x	x
2. Anomaly classification (see Chapter 6, Exhibit 12)	x	x
3. Description of failure/compromise	x	x
4. Severity: a. Catastrophic c. Critical b. Marginal d. Insignificant	x	x
5. Date/time first detected or experienced	x	x
6. Frequency experienced	x	x
7. Duration	x	x
8. Mission significance: a. Failure of IA-critical functions/entities (cite) b. Failure of IA-related functions/entities (cite) c. Failure of MWFs (cite) d. Failure of MNWFs (cite) e. No option but to fail safe/secure f. No option but to fail operational g. Total loss of system h. Loss of critical/sensitive data i. Number of personnel affected	x	x
9. Primary systems/entities affected: a. Entity/system ID and origin b. System/entity type c. Number of systems/entities affected	x	x
10. Time in operation prior to accident/incident	x	x
11. Other systems/entities inside and outside organization that may be impacted	x	x
12. System configuration, version numbers, etc.	x	x
13. Network configuration, version numbers, etc.	x	x
14. Assumptions	x	x

The results of an accident/incident investigation drive emergency short-term recovery mechanisms; form the basis of reports submitted to CERT/CC, FedCIRC, NIPC, HTCN, and other internal and external organizations; and may precipitate legal action. Equally important, accident/incident investigation results stimulate long-term remedial measures.

Accident/incident investigation reports are analyzed to learn from the what, how, and why of an accident/incident. The most obvious reason is to determine what remedial measures are necessary to prevent the same or similar accidents from recurring. As Petroski[380] succinctly states:

> *No matter how tragic a failure might be, it is obviously more tragic if it could have been anticipated and prevented.*

Exhibit 17 Accident/Incident Report: Part II-Assessment

II. Accident/Incident Assessment

Report Field	*Initial Report*	*Follow-up Report*
1. Conditions that produced accident/incident	?	x
2. Critical event sequence		x
3. Related near-misses		x
4. Consequences		
a. Likely	x	
b. Actual		x
5. Corrective action taken		
a. Automatic system	x	x
b. Human initiated	x	x
6. Investigation techniques used		x
a. Barrier analysis		
b. Critical incident interviews		
c. Damage mode effects analysis		
d. Event and causal factor charting		
e. Scenario analysis		
f. STEP investigation system		
g. TLA for emergency response		
h. Warning time analysis		
i. Other		
7. Investigation results: include reports, diagrams, graphs, etc.		x
8. Intermediate and root causes		x
a. Design error		
b. Implementation error		
c. Operational procedures error		
d. Contingency plan error		
e. Physical security practices error		
f. Accidental human action		
g. Malicious intentional human action		
h. Inadvertent operation		
i. Failure or unavailability of key infrastructure system		
j. Other		
9. Remaining useful life of system		x
10. Estimated loss/damages		x
11. Recommendations for short-term recovery	?	x
12. Observations/lessons learned for long-term remedial measures		x

Not preventing avoidable accidents may have legal consequences (see chapter section "Evaluate Legal Issues").

Second, during the course of an accident/incident investigation, latent vulnerabilities and threats are often uncovered. An analysis of the investigation results presents an opportunity to employ remedial measures to eliminate or mitigate the latent vulnerabilities and threats before they cause damage or loss.

Third, because an accident/incident investigation is not limited to technical issues, needed improvements in operational procedures, contingency plans, physical security measures, training, logistical matters, etc. are exposed as well.[31,320,381] Again, an analysis of accident/incident investigation results presents an opportunity to employ remedial measures to eliminate these deficiencies before they cause damage or loss.

In general, catastrophic accidents are investigated more thoroughly than less-serious accidents/incidents because of their severity and less frequent occurrence.[320] It is debatable whether this is a wise approach. Accident/incident investigations should be conducted for the purpose of organizational learning and feedback, not just for the purpose of collecting actuarial or other legal data.[320] As mentioned, incidents are often precursors to or early warnings of impending accidents. There is much to be learned about the need for remedial measures from analyzing them. A thorough incident investigation, if acted upon, may forestall an accident. Conversely, failing to thoroughly investigate an incident that subsequently leads to an accident may have legal consequences. Reporting and analysis of known and suspected near-misses should be encouraged. Many organizations mistakenly discourage the reporting and analysis of incidents, leading to "surprise" when a serious accident occurs. Under-reporting and under-analysis of incidents can have solemn technical, financial, and legal consequences.

The analysis of accident/incident results reinforces the need for standardized reporting of accident/incident data. To be meaningful, uniform data elements, categories, and evaluation criteria must be used. Exhibit 18 illustrates the information flow between accident/incident investigations, reports, and remedial measures.

The DRACAS/FRACAS functions as the central accident/incident information storage and retrieval system. Information is collected about the accident/incident, how and why it occurred, and what corrective action was needed to respond to and recover from it so that individuals and organizations can learn from their mistakes and those of others. Accident/incident information is collected, reported, and analyzed throughout the life of a system. All malfunctions, accidents, anomalies, near-misses, deviations, and waivers should be analyzed.[31] Lessons learned are derived from analyzing accident/incident reports, which can then be deployed as remedial measures. Lessons learned can take many forms, including the[31,320]:

- Discovery of new prevention strategies, tools, and techniques
- Identification of new vulnerabilities and threats
- Demonstrated effectiveness of threat control measures
- Demonstrated effectiveness of verification activities
- Improved operational procedures, contingency plans, and physical security practices
- The need for design changes

In summary, the lessons learned from an accident/incident make clear what worked, what did not work, and what needs to be changed. To ensure

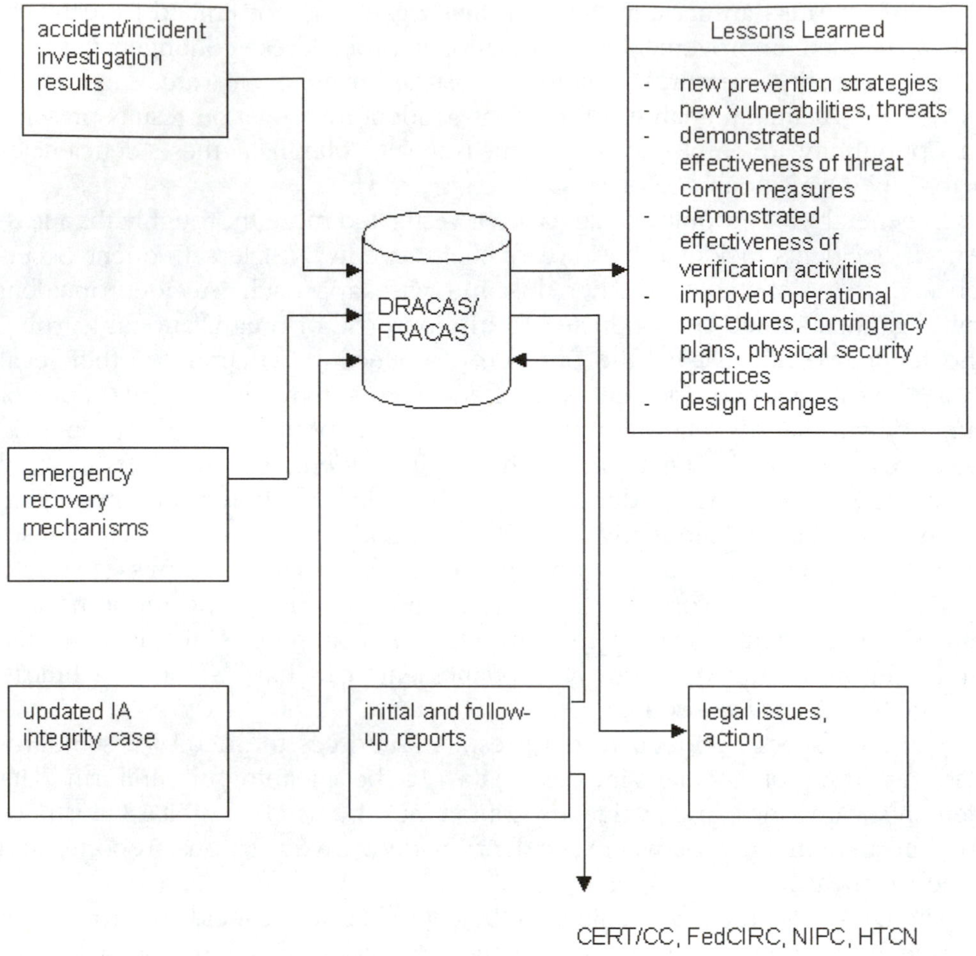

Exhibit 18 Information Flow Between Accident/Incident Investigations, Reports, and Remedial Measures

that the correct lesson is learned from an accident/incident, it is essential that an investigation be thorough, accurate, unbiased, and that fact, opinion, theory, and assumptions are clearly delineated. The IA integrity case is updated to reflect the accident/incident investigation results, particularly the lessons learned.

8.5 Evaluate Legal Issues

This chapter section is not part of a legal textbook, nor is it offering legal advice. Rather, the purpose of this chapter section is to make the reader aware of the legal issues involved in information security/IA and the need to seek appropriate legal counsel.

Several legal terms are used outside their precise legal meaning in everyday speech. Hence, it is important to clarify the legal definition and usage of these terms before discussing the related issues. The following definitions are from Black's *Law Dictionary*[214]:

> **Defect:** deficiency; imperfection; insufficiency; the absence of something necessary for completeness or perfection; a deficiency in something essential to the proper use for the purpose for which a thing is to be used; a manufacturing flaw, a design defect, or inadequate warnings. A design defect exists whenever the design itself poses unreasonable dangers to consumers.
> **Damage:** loss, injury, or deterioration, caused by the negligence, design, or accident of one person to another, in respect of the latter's person or property; the harm, detriment, or loss sustained by reason of injury.
> **Injury:** any wrong or damage done to another, either his person, rights, reputation, or property; the invasion of any legally protected interest of another.
> **Negligence:** failure to use such care as a reasonably prudent and careful person would use under similar circumstances; the doing of some act which a person of ordinary prudence would not have done under similar circumstances or failure to do what a person of ordinary prudence would have done under similar circumstances; conduct which falls below the norm for the protection of others against unreasonable risk of harm. It is characterized by inadvertence, thoughtlessness, inattention, recklessness, …
> **Liability:** condition of being or potentially subject to an obligation; condition of being responsible for a possible or actual loss, penalty, evil, expense, or burden; condition that creates a duty to perform an act immediately or in the future; including almost every character of hazard or responsibility, absolute, contingent, or likely.
> **Assumption of risk:** a plaintiff may not recover for an injury to which he assents, that is, that a person may not recover for an injury received when he voluntarily exposes himself to a known and appreciated danger. The requirements for the defense … are that: (1) the plaintiff has knowledge of facts constituting a dangerous condition, (2) he knows that the condition is dangerous, (3) he appreciates the nature or extent of the danger, and (4) he voluntarily exposes himself to the danger. Secondary assumption of risk occurs when an individual voluntarily encounters known, appreciated risk without an intended manifestation by that individual that he consents to relieve another of his duty.

At the beginning of this chapter, an accident was defined to involve death, injury, loss or damage. Consequently, an accident may involve multiple legal issues, regardless of whether the accident is the result of accidental or malicious intentional action. Defects include design defects, such as inadequate or ineffective threat control measures, and inadequate warnings to customers and end users. Injuries and loss may be to a person, his reputation, or property, physical or cyber. For example, if sensitive personnel, financial, medical, or other information is compromised, a person's reputation could be damaged; identity theft and employment discrimination are two of many possible scenarios. Negligence incorporates errors of commission and errors of omission that did not prevent the accident from occurring. Legal liability determines who was responsible for preventing the accident and thus paying damages to the injured party. Assumption of risk is equivalent to the concept of informed consent prior to authorizing risky medical procedures. Depending on what risk was knowingly assumed, damages paid by the liable party or parties may be reduced. In summary:

$$\text{Negligence} \rightarrow \text{Defect} \rightarrow \text{Injury} \rightarrow \text{Damage} \rightarrow \begin{array}{c}\text{Liability to pay} \\ \text{Damages for injury}\end{array}$$

In the realm of information security/IA, legal issues and responsibilities can arise from many different perspectives, including system owner, end user, system administrator, victim, customer, stockholder, and test/certification lab. Legal issues, responsibilities, and liability can be distributed among individuals and organizations. Falla[259] points out that:

> *Liability can fall on the manufacturer, supplier, distributor, or certifier of products. ... Suppliers of components can also be liable. In cases where the component is used in products which are exposed to the general public, the extent of such liability can be enormous.*

Little case law exists in the field to date, it is still evolving. As Wood[442] observes:

> *...the risks of cyberspace go far beyond the military and raise complex and unprecedented ethical and legal issues that current policies, organizations, laws, and procedures cannot readily answer.*

Given this situation, most sources recommend a proactive legal risk management approach.[230,248,259] The first step is to define appropriate boundaries of authority and responsibility for technical and legal decisions and oversight. Liability issues should be reviewed throughout the development and operation of a system and at predefined milestones. The connection between technical and legal risk should be examined regularly.[230] As Falla[259] notes:

> *...attaching a particular legal step or procedure to each event in the life cycle ... helps legal precautions to be taken at appropriate times and often also preempts the escalation of legal problems.*

Given that technology itself is continuously evolving, it is sometimes possible to use the legal defense that current industry best practices were followed. To do so, (1) best practices, like those described in this book, actually have to have been followed, and (2) all stakeholders have to be aware of and live up to these legal responsibilities. Burnett[230] summarizes these responsibilities as follows:

> **Designer:** the system designer/developer is responsible for ensuring that the system will fail safe/secure or fail operational, as appropriate, in all situations so that no damage or loss is incurred.

Technical experts: technical experts, whether employees or consultants, are responsible for maintaining complete, in-depth, and current competence in their field, such that this competence is above average, but not necessarily at the genius level.

Component suppliers: component suppliers, such as COTS vendors, are responsible for accurately representing component capabilities, limitations, claims, labelling, and instructions for use.

Testing and certification labs: testing and certification labs are responsible for accurately explaining what was and was not tested or evaluated, providing accurate test results, an accurate description of test coverage, and defensible reliability, safety, and security claims. Test and certification labs are responsible for employing competent people to perform the tests/evaluation and verifying that facts, opinions, and assumptions are separated.

Product liability stems from the concept that products must be fit for all purposes for which goods of that kind are commonly used. This concept, often referred to as "fitness for use" or "fitness for purpose," implies that products are free from defects, safe, reliable, and secure. If a technical failure results in loss or damage, liability for damages may be incurred. Liability can be limited by two types of remedies: (1) replacement/repair and (2) limiting damages to a particular amount. Liability cannot be restricted when negligence is a factor and death or serious injury (physical or cyber) results.

Liability may be civil or criminal, depending on the nature of the accident, and falls under the due-care or strict liability criteria. Without going into too much legalese, the plaintiff must establish that[230,259]:

- The manufacturer and/or supplier owed the plaintiff a duty of care.
- There has been a breach of this duty that caused the damage/loss; for example, failing to adequately verify the safety or security of a system or component.
- The kind of damage sustained was reasonably foreseeable as a consequence of that breach.
- Damage/loss has, in fact, occurred.

The concept of strict liability in tort eliminates the due-care criteria; the plaintiff only has to demonstrate the last two items.[420]

A product may be considered defective if it exhibits safety, reliability, or security behavior that is less than that to which people are generally entitled to expect.[230] Damage may result in personal injury, material damage, economic loss, environmental corruption, administrative chaos, and privacy violations.

A related legal issue to consider is warranties. The U.S. Uniform Commercial Code (UCC S2-315) equates fitness for purpose to implied warranties. In the past, the concept of express and implied warranties has been applied to commercial products, such as COTS software. In the future, as information security/IA case law evolves, it is not inconceivable that the concept of implied warranties could be applied to online banking systems and other IT services.

Another legal issue concerns the assumption of risk, primary and secondary. If the plaintiff knew about the risk, understood the potential consequences, appreciated the nature and extent of the risk, and voluntarily accepted this risk, liability for damages may be limited.[214,420] If, however, these four criteria are not met, the risk is considered to be unassumed. Accident/incident investigations clarify risk assumed and unassumed by all stakeholders.

System owners may be liable for the theft or fraudulent use of information or resources, whether these crimes are committed by insiders or outsiders. It is even conceivable that stockholders could sue a corporation for negligence if such a crime occurred.[248] A proactive legal risk management approach is the best defense in this situation. This approach should include what is referred to as a good-faith effort to prevent such crimes, for example[248]:

> *...written policies and procedures against crime, security awareness programs, disciplinary standards, monitoring and auditing systems that represent applicable industry practice, reporting detected crimes to law enforcement agencies, and cooperating with investigations.*

As an analogy, if there are locks on the doors and windows of one's house and an electronic burglar alarm, one is more likely to collect on an insurance policy after a burglary than if one leaves the doors and windows open.

This discussion has been presented from the perspective of current U.S. law to enlighten the reader on the legal issues involved in information security/IA and the need to seek legal counsel. The laws pertaining to computer crime, civil and criminal liability, and mandatory privacy protections vary from country to country. Often, computer crime laws are not enacted until after a major offense has been committed. Campen[236] observes that:

> *Information security is an international issue, involving diverse cultures that do not hold a common view of personal privacy in cyberspace or how it should be secured.*

8.6 Summary

The fifth component of an effective information security/IA program is conducting an accident/incident investigation. Five activities are performed while conducting an accident/incident investigation, as shown in Exhibits 19 and 20.

- The cause, extent, and consequences of the failure/compromise are analyzed.
- Recovery mechanisms are initiated.
- The accident/incident is reported.
- Remedial measures are deployed.
- Legal issues are evaluated.

Accident/incident investigations are conducted for legal and engineering reasons. As a result, it is important to understand and distinguish between the

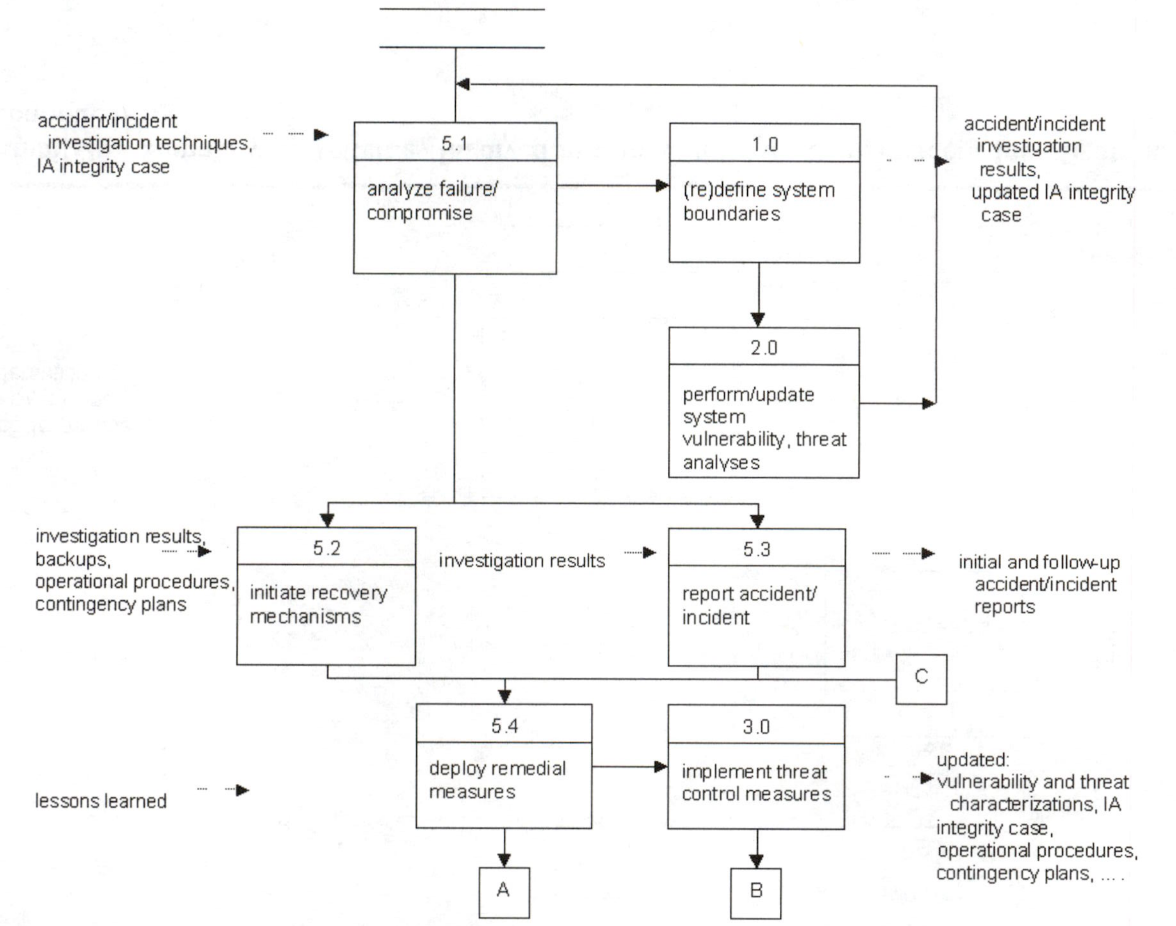

Exhibit 19 Summary of Activities Involved in Conducting Accident/Incident Investigations

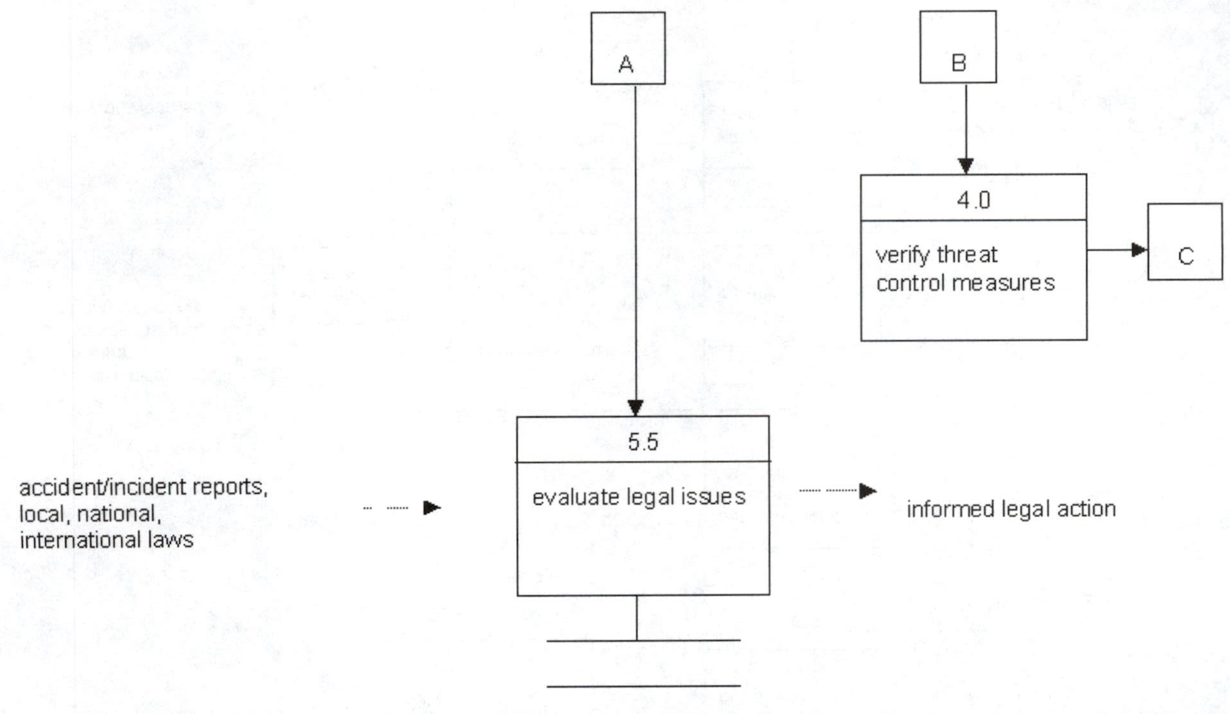

Exhibit 20 Summary of Activities Involved in Conducting Accident/Incident Investigations (continued)

legal and engineering usage of terms, such as accident, incident, failure, compromise, and cause.

Accident/incident investigations are conducted to determine, in fact, what did and did not happen, how it happened, and why it happened or was allowed to happen. There are plenty of open sources to examine when collecting evidence for an accident/incident investigation. Analyses of early evidence point to other sources of evidence in what becomes an iterative process. Inductive and deductive reasoning is applied to the evidence to explain how and why an accident/incident occurred. A combination of techniques is used to investigate an accident/incident by developing "how could" and "how did" accident scenarios. The same techniques are used to conduct an internal, independent, regulatory, or forensic investigation. The credibility of an accident/incident investigation rests on the ability to remain objective; eliminate bias or prejudice; separate fact, opinion, assumptions, and theory; and distinguish "symptoms" from the "disease" — all while being thorough and accurate.

Initial accident/incident reports trigger short-term recovery mechanisms. Preliminary investigation results about the cause(s), extent, and consequences of the accident/incident are reviewed. A determination is made about what can and cannot be recovered in the short term. When and how each system, entity, and component can and should be restored are ascertained. Customers, end users, system administrators, maintenance staff, etc. are notified about the accident/incident and the status of recovery efforts. The effectiveness and timeliness of recovery efforts are entirely dependent on prior planning, coordination, and training as well as complete operational procedures and contingency plans.

Reporting an accident/incident is an essential part of investigating, responding to, and recovering from it. There are several reasons to report an accident/incident, inside and outside an organization, and benefits to be derived from doing so:

1. An accident/incident must be reported before the situation can be corrected.
2. Reporting the results of an accident/incident and what was learned from it reduces the likelihood of recurrence, within and among organizations.
3. Customers and employees will have more confidence in an organization that reports accidents/incidents.
4. An organization may have a legal responsibility to report an accident/incident.
5. An accident/incident must have been reported if subsequent legal action is to be taken.

Standardized initial and follow-up reports should be filed to internal and external organizations such as CERT/CC, FedCIRC, NIPC, and HTCN.

Follow-up accident/incident reports stimulate long-term remedial measures. The results of accident/incident investigations are analyzed to derive lessons learned, such as[31,320]:

- Identification of new vulnerabilities and threats
- Demonstrated effectiveness of threat control measures
- Demonstrated effectiveness of verification activities
- Improved operational procedures, contingency plans, and physical security practices
- The need for design changes

There are several legal issues involved in information security/IA. Legal issues and responsibilities may arise from many different perspectives, including system owner, end user, system administrator, victim, customer, stockholder, test/certification lab, etc. Engineers need to be aware of these issues, seek appropriate legal counsel, and pursue a proactive legal risk management strategy.

8.7 Discussion Problems

1. Explain the relationship, if any, between a compromise and: (a) an accident, (b) a vulnerability, (c) a threat control measure, (d) a failure, and (e) intentional malicious action.
2. When are accidents/incidents investigated? Why?
3. Why would an organization want or not want to conduct: (a) an internal accident/incident investigation, (b) an independent investigation, and (c) a forensic investigation?
4. What is determined during an accident/incident investigation?
5. How are sources of evidence located? Give some examples.
6. How are IA analysis and verification techniques used during an investigation?
7. Describe the similarities and differences between event and causal factor charting and the STEP investigation system.
8. Describe the similarities and differences between warning time analysis and time/loss analysis.
9. Why should accident/incident reports be filed?
10. When are accident/incident reports filed? Who are they submitted to?
11. Create an accident/incident report for the most recent serious anomaly or near-miss experienced by your organization. Include a warning time analysis report and a TLA graph.
12. Why is it important to delineate fact, opinion, theory, and assumptions during an accident/incident investigation?
13. What is the first priority during accident/incident recovery?
14. What is the key to a quick and successful recovery effort?
15. Which accidents/incidents are avoidable?

16. Is the return on investment from investigating incidents worthwhile?
17. Who has the legal responsibility and liability for ensuring that the following are safe, secure, and reliable: (a) a system, (b) a component, (c) an external entity, (d) COTS products, and (e) a service?
18. Explain the connection, if any, between fitness for purpose and assumption of risk.

Annex A

Glossary of Acronyms and Terms

The discipline of computer security/IA is replete with acronyms and terminology. This annex defines these acronyms and terms as they are used in this book. Standardized definitions have been used wherever possible. When more than one standardized definition exists, multiple definitions are provided. When the legal and technical definitions of a term differ, both are provided. More complete definitions of IA analysis, design, verification, and accident/incident investigation techniques are given in Annex B: Glossary of Techniques.

Access control: Design feature(s) that protect IA-critical and IA-related systems, applications, and data by preventing unauthorized and unwarranted access to these resources.

Access control check: The security function that decides whether a subject's request to perform an action on a protected resource should be granted or denied.[216]

Accident: (1) Technical — any unplanned or unintended event, sequence, or combination of events that results in death, injury, or illness to personnel or damage to or loss of equipment or property (including data, intellectual property, etc.), or damage to the environment.[127,422,425] (2) Legal — any unpleasant or unfortunate occurrence that causes injury, loss, suffering, or death; an event that takes place without one's foresight or expectation.[214]

ACL: Access control list.

Activity monitor: Antiviral software that checks for signs of suspicious activity, such as attempts to rewrite program files, format disks, etc.[416]

AES: Advanced Encryption Standard, a new encryption standard, whose development and selection was sponsored by NIST, that will support key lengths of 128, 192, and 256 bits (see Reference 175).

AH: Authentication header.

ALARP: As low as reasonably practical; a method of correlating the likelihood of a hazard and the severity of its consequences to determine risk exposure acceptability or the need for further risk reduction.

Application proxy: A type of firewall that controls external access by operating at the application layer.[349] Application firewalls often readdress outgoing traffic so that it appears to have originated from the firewall rather than the internal host.[154]

AS: Authentication server; part of Kerberos KDC.

Assumption of risk: A plaintiff may not recover for an injury to which he assents; that is, that a person may not recover for an injury received when he voluntarily exposes himself to a known and appreciated danger. The requirements for the defense … are that: (1) the plaintiff has knowledge of facts constituting a dangerous condition, (2) he knows that the condition is dangerous, (3) he appreciates the nature or extent of the danger, and (4) he voluntarily exposes himself to the danger. Secondary assumption of risk occurs when an individual voluntarily encounters known, appreciated risk without an intended manifestation by that individual that he consents to relieve another of his duty.[214]

Audit trail: A set of records that collectively provides documentary evidence of system resources accessed by a user or process to aid in tracing from original transactions forward and backward to their component source transactions.

Authentication: To establish, verify, or prove the validity of a claimed identity of a user, process, or system.

Authentication header: An IPSec protocol that provides data origin authentication, packet integrity, and limited protection from replay attacks.

Authorization: Permission granted to access or use specific system resources or processes; access control privileges.

Availability: A measurement indicating the rate at which systems, data, and other resources are operational and accessible when needed, despite accidental and malicious intentional subsystem outages and environmental disruptions. Availability is usually defined as: MTBF/(MTBF + MTTR). However, this definition fails to take into account malicious intentional failures. (See expanded definition provided in Chapter 6.)

Backdoor: A function built into a program or system that allows unusually high or even full access to the system, either with or without an account in a normally restricted account environment. The backdoor sometimes remains in a fully developed system either by design or accident.[416] (*See also* trap door.)

Bayesian Belief network: Graphical networks that represent probabilistic relationships among variables. The nodes represent uncertain variables and the arcs represent the causal/relevance relationships between the variables. The probability tables for each node provide the probabilities of each state of the variable for that node, conditional on each combination of values of the parent node.[431]

BBN: Bayesian Belief network.

Biometric system: A pattern recognition system that establishes the authenticity of a specific physiological or behavioral characteristic possessed by a user.[374]

BIT: Built-in test.

Block ciphers: Encryption algorithms that operate on a fixed number of bits of data at a time, known as the blocksize. For example, DES operates on 64-bit (8-byte) blocks of data. Contrast with stream ciphers.

Brute-force attack: A form of cryptoanalysis where the attacker uses all possible keys or passwords in an attempt to crack an encryption scheme or login system.[349]

BSP: Biometric service provider.

Built-in test: A design feature that provides information on the ability of the item to perform its intended functions. BIT is implemented in software or firmware and may use or control BIT equipment (BITE).[127]

C&A: Certification and accreditation; a comprehensive evaluation of the technical and nontechnical security features of a system to determine if it meets specified requirements and should receive approval to operate.

CA: Certificate authority.

Cause: (1) Technical — the action or condition by which a hazardous event (physical or cyber) is initiated — an initiating event. The cause may arise as the result of failure, accidental or intentional human error, design inadequacy, induced or natural environment, system configuration, or operational modes/states.[31] (2) Legal — each separate antecedent of an event. Something that precedes and brings about an effect or result. A reason for an accident or condition.[214]

CBEFF: Common biometric exchange file format; being defined by U.S. biometric consortium and ANSI X9F4 subcommittee.

CBC: Cipher block chaining.

CC: Common Criteria; *see* ISO/IEC 15408.

CCF: Common cause failure.

CEPS: Common electronic purse specifications; a standard used with smartcards.

CERT/CC: Computer emergency response team coordination center, a service of CMU/SEI.

Certificate authority: A trusted third party that associates a public key with proof of identity by producing a digitally signed certificate.[349]

CGI: Common gateway interface.

CHAP: Challenge handshake authentication protocol.

Challenge handshake authentication protocol: A secure login procedure for dial-in access that avoids sending in a password in the clear by using cryptographic hashing.

CIDF: Common intrusion detection framework model.

Cipher text: A message that has been encrypted using a specific algorithm and key. (Contrast with plain text.)

CISL: Common Intrusion Specification Language.

CMF: Common mode failure.

Cohesion: The manner and degree to which the tasks performed by a single software module are related to another. Types of cohesion include coincidental, communication, functional, logical, procedural, sequential, and temporal.[44,127]

Common cause failure: Failure of multiple independent system components occurring from a single cause that is common to all of them.[31]

Common mode failure: Failure of multiple independent system components that fail in the identical mode.[31]

Communications security: A collection of engineering activities that are undertaken to protect the confidentiality, integrity, and availability of sensitive data while it is being transmitted between systems and networks.

Compromise: An unwarranted and uninvited offensive incursion, infringement, or encroachment of a system, usually by stealth, that defeats safety and security mechanisms to violate and usurp resources and data in a hostile and injurious manner.

COMPUSEC: Computer security.

Computer security: Preventing, detecting, and minimizing the consequences of unauthorized actions by users (authorized and unauthorized) of a computer system.

COMSEC: Communications security.

Confidentiality: The characteristic of information being disclosed by or made available only to authorized entities at authorized times and in the approved manner.[189] Confidentiality does not guarantee integrity.[433]

Confinement: (1) Confining an untrusted program so that it can do everything it needs to do to meet the user's expectation, but nothing else.[335] (2) Restricting an untrusted program from accessing system resources and executing system processes. Common confinement techniques include DTE, least privilege, and wrappers.

Contingency plan: Providing a planned measured response to the sudden loss, unavailability, or anomalous performance of one or more system entities, whether internal or external, in order to quickly return the system to a known safe and secure state.

Continuous-mode operation: Systems that are operational continuously, 24 hours a day, 7 days a week.

Controllability: The ability to control the situation following a failure. (Note that controllability has a different meaning when used in the context of testability analysis.)

Controlled security mode: A system is operating in the controlled security mode when at least some users with access to the system have neither a security clearance nor a need-to-know for all classified material contained in the system. However, the separation and control of users and classified material on the basis, respectively, of security clearance and security classification are not essentially under operating system control as in the multilevel security mode.[140]

CORBAsecurity: The Object Management Group standard that describes how to secure CORBA environments.

Coupling: The manner and degree of interdependence between software modules. Types include common environment coupling, content coupling, control coupling, data coupling, hybrid coupling, and pathological coupling.[44,127]

Countermeasure: *See* threat control measure.

Covert channel: (1) A communications channel that allows a process to transfer information in a manner that violates the system's security policy.[140] (2) An information flow that is not controlled by a security mechanism.[120–122]

Covert storage channel: A covert channel that involves the direct or indirect writing of a storage location by one process and the direct or indirect reading of the storage location by another process. Covert storage channels typically involve a finite resource that is shared by two subjects at different security levels.[140]

Covert timing channel: A covert channel in which one process signals information to another by modulating its own use of system resources in such a way that this manipulation affects the real response time observed by the second process.[140]

Critical software: A defined set of software components that have been evaluated and whose continuous operation has been determined essential for safe, reliable, and secure operation of the system. Critical software is composed of three elements: (1) safety-critical and safety-related software, (2) reliability-critical software, and (3) security-critical software.[32]

CRL: Certificate revocation list.

Cross certificate: A certificate issued by a certificate authority in one domain whose subject resides in another domain, the purpose of which is to enable different domains to convey trust in each other so that they can interoperate.

Cryptography: The science of transforming messages for the purpose of making the message unintelligible to all but the intended receiver.[249]

CSI: Computer Security Institute.

DAC: Discretionary access controls.

Damage: Loss, injury, or deterioration caused by the negligence, design, or accident of one person to another, in respect of the latter's person or property; the harm, detriment, or loss sustained by reason of an injury.[214]

DASS: Distributed authentication security service.

Data integrity: The state that exists when computerized data is the same as that in the source information and has not been exposed to accidental or malicious addition, alteration, or destruction.

Data safety: Ensuring that: (1) the intended data has been correctly accessed, (2) the data has not been manipulated or corrupted intentionally or accidentally, and (3) the data is legitimate.[288]

Deadlock: A situation in which computer processing is suspended because two or more devices or processes are each awaiting resources assigned to the other.[127]

Dedicated security mode: A system is operating in the dedicated security mode when the system and all of its local and remote peripherals are exclusively used and controlled by specific users or groups of users who have a security clearance and need-to-know for the processing of a particular category and type of classified material.[140]

Defect: Deficiency; imperfection; insufficiency; the absence of something necessary for completeness or perfection; a deficiency in something essential to the proper use for the purpose for which a thing is to be used; a manufacturing flaw, a design defect, or inadequate warning.[214]

Defense in depth: Provision of several overlapping subsequent limiting barriers with respect to one safety or security threshold, so that the threshold can only be surpassed if all barriers have failed.[60]

Defensive programming: Designing software that detects anomalous control flow, data flow, or data values during execution and reacts in a predetermined and acceptable manner. The intent is to develop software that correctly accommodates design or operational shortcomings; for example, verifying a parameter or command through two diverse sources before acting upon it.[68]

Degraded-mode operation: Maintaining the availability of the more critical system functions, despite failures, by dropping the less critical functions. Also referred to as graceful degradation.[68]

Demand-mode operation: Systems that are used periodically on-demand; for example, a computer-controlled braking system in a car.

Denial of service: (1) Prevention of authorized access to resources or the delaying of time-critical operations.[120–122] (2) Sending a series of e-mail, connection requests, etc. to the target system with the intent of inducing saturation.

Dependability: That property of a computer system such that reliance can be justifiably placed on the service it delivers. The service delivered by a system is its behavior as it is perceived by its user(s); a user is another system or human that interacts with the former.[390]

DES: Data encryption standard; *see* FIPS PUB 46-3.[155]

DIAP: Defense-wide IA program (U.S. DoD).

Digital certificate: A document containing public-key material combined with fields identifying the owner and issuer of the certificate. The CA digitally signs the document to ensure validity of the contents.[349]

Digital signature: (1) A string of characters that can be generated only by an agent that knows some secret and hence provides evidence that such an agent must have generated it.[362] (2) A block of data attached to a message or document that binds the data to a particular individual or entity so that it can be verified by the receiver or an independent third party.[248]

DII: Defense information infrastructure.

Discretionary access controls: A non-policy-based means of restricting access to objects based on the identity of subjects or groups to which they belong. The controls are discretionary in the sense that a subject with a certain access permission is capable of passing that permission (perhaps indirectly) on to any other subject.

DITSCAP: U.S. DoD IT Security Certification and Accreditation Process.

Diversity: Using multiple different means to perform a required function or solve the same problem. Diversity can be implemented in software and hardware.

Domain: The set of objects that a subject (user or process) has the ability to access.

Domain and type enforcement: A confinement technique in which an attribute called a domain is associated with each subject and another attribute called a type is associated with each object. A matrix specifies whether a particular mode of access to objects of a type is granted or denied to subjects in a domain.[335]

DSS: Digital signature standard; *see* FIPS PUB 186.[165]

DSSA: Distributed system security architecture; developed by Digital Equipment Corporation.

DTE: Domain and type enforcement.

Dynamic analysis: Exercising the system being assessed through actual execution; includes exercising the system functionally (traditional testing) and logically through techniques such as failure assertion, structural testing, and statistical-based testing. Major system components have to have been built before dynamic analysis can be performed.

EAL: Evaluation assurance level.

EAP: Extensible Authentication Protocol.

EMC: Electromagnetic conductance.

EMI: Electromagnetic interference.

Encapsulated Security Payload: An IPSec protocol that provides confidentiality, data origin authentication, data integrity services, tunneling, and protection from replay attacks.

Encapsulation: *See* wrappers.

Encryption: (1) Symmetric — a systematic method of scrambling information to provide confidentiality using secret keys for encryption and decryption. (2) Asymmetric — a systematic method of scrambling information to provide confidentiality using one key to encrypt messages and one key to decrypt messages. The two keys, referred to as public and private keys, only work in designated pairs. Encryption can be implemented in hardware or software with block or stream ciphers.

Error: The difference between a computed, observed, or measured value or condition and the true, specified, or theoretically correct value or condition.[44]

Error of commission: An error that results from making a mistake or doing something wrong.

Error of omission: An error that results from something that was not done.

ESP: Encapsulated Security Payload protocol.

Evaluation assurance level: One of seven levels defined by the Common Criteria[52,120–122] that represent the degree of confidence that specified functional security requirements have been met by a commercial product.

Extensible Authentication Protocol: An IETF standard means of extending authentication protocols, such as CHAP and PAP, to include additional authentication data; for example, biometric data.[349]

Fail operational: The system must continue to provide some degree of service if it is not to be hazardous; it cannot simply shut down — for example, an aircraft flight control system.[345] (*See* degraded-mode operation.)

Fail safe/secure: (1) A design wherein the component/system, should it fail, will fail to a safe/secure condition.[425] (2) The system can be brought to a safe/secure condition or state by shutting it down; for example, the shutdown of a nuclear reactor by a monitoring and protection system.[345]

Failure: Failing to or inability of a system, entity, or component to perform its required function(s), according to specified performance criteria, due to one or more fault conditions. Three categories of failure are commonly recognized: (1) incipient failures are failures that are about to occur; (2) hard failures are failures that result in a complete shutdown of a system; and (3) soft failures are failures that result in a transition to degraded-mode operations or a fail operational status.[44]

Failure minimization: Actions designed or programmed to reduce failure possibilities to the lowest rates possible.[425]

Fault: A defect that results in an incorrect step, process, data value, or mode/state.

Fault tolerance: Built-in capability of a system to provide continued correct execution in the presence of a limited number of hardware or software faults.[60]

FedCIRC: The U.S. federal government Computer Incident Response Center; managed by the General Services Administration (GSA).

Firewall: A security gateway between two networks that uses a variety of techniques, such as proxy filters, packet filters, application level gateways, and circuit level gateways, to block unwanted users, processes, and data while protecting legitimate users and sensitive data and processes.

Flooded transmission: A transmission in which data is sent over every link in the network.

FMECA: Failure mode effects criticality analysis; an IA analysis technique that systematically reviews all components and materials in a system or product to determine cause(s) of their failures, the downstream results of such failures, and the criticality of such failures as accident precursors. FMECA can be performed on individual components (hardware, software, and communications equipment) and integrated at the system level. *See* IEC 60812(1985).

Formal design: The part of a software design written using a formal notation.[129]

Formal method: (1) A software specification and production method, based on discrete mathematics, that comprises: a collection of mathematical notations addressing the specification, design, and development processes of software production, resulting in a well-founded logical inference system in which formal verification proofs and proofs of other properties can be formulated, and a methodological framework within which software can be developed from the specification in a formally verifiable manner.[129] (2) The use of mathematical techniques in the specification, design, and analysis of computer hardware and software.[422]

Formal notation: The mathematical notation of a formal method.[129]

Formal proof: The discharge of a proof obligation by the construction of a complete mathematical proof.[129]

Formal specification: The part of the software specification written using a formal notation.[129]

FTA: Fault tree analysis; an IA analysis technique by which possibilities of occurrence of specific adverse events are investigated. All factors, conditions, events, and relationships that could contribute to that event are analyzed.[425] FTA can be performed on individual components (hardware, software, and communications equipment) and integrated at the system level. *See* IEC 61025(1990).

FTP: File Transfer Protocol; an application layer protocol.

Functional safety: The ability of a safety-related system to carry out the actions necessary to achieve or maintain a safe state for the equipment under control.[65]

GII: Global information infrastructure.

GPKI: Global public key infrastructure.

Graceful degradation: *See* degraded-mode operation.

Guard: A component that mediates the flow of information or control between different systems or networks.[362]

HAG: High assurance guard.

Hardware reliability: The ability of an item to correctly perform a required function under certain conditions in a specified operational environment for a stated period of time.

Hardware safety integrity: The overall failure rate for continuous-mode operations and the probability to operate on demand for demand-mode operations relative to random hardware failures in a dangerous mode of failure.[69]

Hazard: A source of potential harm or a situation with potential to harm.[56] Note that the consequences of a hazard can be physical or cyber.

Hazard likelihood: The qualitative or quantitative likelihood that a potential hazard will occur. Most international standards define six levels of hazard likelihood (lowest to highest): incredible, improbable, remote, occasional, probable, and frequent.

Hazard severity: The severity of the worst-case consequences should a potential hazard occur. Most international standards define four levels of hazard severity (lowest to highest): insignificant, marginal, critical, and catastrophic.

HAZOP: Hazard and operability study; a method of determining hazards in a proposed or existing system, their possible causes and consequences, and recommending solutions to minimize the likelihood of occurrence. Design and operational aspects of the system are analyzed by an interdisciplinary team.[69]

HTTP: Hypertext Transfer Protocol; an application layer protocol.

I&A: Identification and authentication.

IA: Information assurance.

IA-critical: A term applied to any condition, event, operation, process, or item whose proper recognition, control, performance, or tolerance is essential to the safe, reliable, and secure operation and support of a system.

IA integrity: The likelihood of a system, entity, or function achieving its required security, safety, and reliability features under all stated conditions within a stated measure of use.[130]

IA integrity case: A systematic means of gathering, organizing, analyzing, and reporting the data needed by internal, contractual, regulatory, or Certification Authorities to confirm that a system has met the specified IA goals and IA integrity level and is fit for use in the intended operational environment. An IA integrity case includes assumptions, claims, and evidence.

IA integrity level: The level of IA integrity that must be achieved or demonstrated to maintain the IA risk exposure at or below its acceptable level.

IA-related: A system or entity that performs or controls functions which are activated to prevent or minimize the effect of a failure of an IA-critical system or entity.

ICSA: Internet Computer Security Association.

IDS: Intrusion detection system.

IETF: Internet Engineering Task Force; a public consortium that develops standards for the Internet.

IKE: Internet Key Exchange protocol.

Incident: Any unplanned or unintended event, sequence, or combination of events that does not result in death, injury, or illness to personnel or damage to or loss of equipment or property (including data, intellectual property, etc.) or damage to the environment, but has the potential to do so; a near-miss.

Information assurance: (1) An engineering discipline that provides a comprehensive and systematic approach to ensuring that individual automated systems and dynamic combinations of automated systems interact and provide their intended functionality, no more and no less, safely, reliably, and securely in the intended operational environment(s). (2) Information operations that protect and defend information and information systems by ensuring their availability, integrity, authentication, confidentiality, and nonrepudiation; including providing for restoration of information systems by incorporating protection, detection, and reaction capabilities (DoD Directive 5-3600.1).

Information hiding: (1) A software development technique in which each module's interfaces reveal as little as possible about the module's inner workings and other modules are prevented from using information about the module that is not in the module's interface specification.[18] (2) A software development technique that consists of isolating a system function, or set of data and operations on those data, within a module and providing precise specifications for the module.[69]

INFOSEC: (1) The combination of COMSEC and COMPUSEC — the protection of information against unauthorized disclosure, transfer, modification, or destruction, whether accidental or intentional. (2) Protection of information systems against unauthorized access to or modification of information, whether in storage, processing, or transit, and against denial of service to authorized users, including those measures necessary to detect, document, and counter such threats.[154]

Infrastructure system: A network of independent, mostly privately owned, automated systems and processes that function collaboratively and synergistically to produce and distribute a continuous flow of essential goods and services.[176,178] The eight critical infrastructure systems defined by PDD-63 are: telecommunications, banking and finance, power generation and distribution, oil and gas distribution and storage, water processing and supply, transportation, emergency services, and government services.[178]

Inhibit: A design feature that provides a physical interruption between an energy source and a function actuator. Two inhibits are independent if no single failure can eliminate them both.[28,127]

Injury: Any wrong or damage done to another, either his person, rights, reputation, or property; the invasion of any legally protected interest of another.[214]

Integrity level: (1) A range of values of an item necessary to maintain system risks within acceptable limits. For items that perform IA-related mitigating functions, the property is the reliability with which the item must perform the mitigating function. For IA-critical items whose failure can lead to threat instantiation, the property is the limit on the frequency of that failure.[58] (2) A range of values of a property of an item necessary to maintain risk exposure at or below its acceptability threshold.[48]

Intelligent transportation systems: A subset or specific application of the NII that provides real-time information and services to the transportation sector. Specific examples include: travel and transportation management systems, travel demand management systems, public transportation operation systems, electronic payment systems, commercial vehicle operation systems, emergency management systems, and advanced vehicle control and safety systems.[224]

Internetwork: A group of networks connected by routers so that computers on different networks can communicate; the Internet.

Intrusion detection: Recognition of a security breach, either as it is happening or immediately afterward.[433]

IO: Information operations.

IP: Internet Protocol.

IPC: Inter-process communication.

IPSec: The security architecture for IP; developed by the IETF to support reliable and secure datagram exchange at the IP layer. The IPSec architecture specifies AH, ESP, Internet Key Exchange (IKE), and Internet Security Association Key Management Protocol (ISAKMP), among other things.

IP spoofing: An intruder fakes his IP address to masquerade as a trusted host during address-based authentication.[372]

ISAKMP: Internet Security Association Key Management Protocol.

ISSA: Information Systems Security Association.

ITS: Intelligent transportation systems.

IW: Information warfare.

KDC: Key distribution center.

Kerberos: A network authentication product that also provides a confidentiality service.

KMI: Key management infrastructure.

Least privilege: Confinement technique in which each process is given only the minimum privileges it needs to function; also referred to as sandboxing. (*See also* need-to-know.)

Letter bomb: A Trojan horse that will trigger when an e-mail message is read.

Liability: Condition of being or potentially subject to an obligation; condition of being responsible for a possible or actual loss, penalty, evil, expense, or burden. Condition that creates a duty to perform an act immediately or in the future, including almost every character of hazard or responsibility, absolute, contingent, or likely.[214]

Logic bomb: A Trojan horse that will trigger when a specific logical event or action occurs.

LRA: Local registration authority (for digital certificates).

MAC: (1) Mandatory access controls. (2) Message authentication codes. (3) Media access control.

Mandatory access controls: A policy-based means of restricting access to objects based on the sensitivity (as represented by a label) of the information contained in the objects and the formal authorization (access control privileges) of subjects to access information of such sensitivity.

Man-in-the-middle attack: Scenarios in which a malicious user can intercept messages and insert other messages that compromise the otherwise secure exchange of information between two parties.[349]

Mediation: Action by an arbiter that decides whether or not a subject or process is permitted to perform a given operation on a specified object.

Message authentication codes: A value computed from the message and a secret cryptographic key to provide assurance about the source and integrity of a message; also referred to as keyed hash functions.

Mishap risk: An expression of the possibility and impact of an unplanned event or series of events resulting in death, injury, occupational illness, damage to or loss of equipment or property (physical or cyber), or damage to the environment in terms of potential severity of consequences and likelihood of occurrence.[143] (*See also* risk.)

MISPC: Minimum interoperability specification of PKI components; a standard that specifies a minimal set of features, transactions, and data formats for the various certification management components that make up a PKI.

Mistake: An erroneous human action (accidental or intentional) that produces a fault condition.

MLS: Multi-level secure.

MNWF: Must not work function.

Multi-level secure: A class of systems containing information with different sensitivities that simultaneously permits access by users with different security clearances and needs-to-know, but prevents users from obtaining access to information for which they lack authorization.

Must not work function: Sequences of events or commands that are prohibited because they would result in a system hazard.[126,127]

Must work function: Software that if not performed or performed incorrectly, inadvertently, or out of sequence could result in a hazard or allow a hazardous condition to exist. This includes (1) software that directly exercises command and control over potentially hazardous functions or hardware; (2) software that monitors critical hardware components; and (3) software that monitors the system for possible critical conditions or states.[126,127]

MWF: Must work function.

National information infrastructure: The total interconnected national telecommunications network of a country, which is made up of the private lines of major carriers, numerous carriers and interconnection companies, and thousands of local exchanges that connect private telephone lines to the national network and the world.[279]

NCSA: National Computer Security Association; superseded by ICSA.

NCSC: National Computer Security Center; part of the U.S. Department of Defense.

Need-to-know: A method of isolating information resources based on a user's need to have access to that resource in order to perform their job but no more; for example, a personnel officer needs access to sensitive personnel records and a marketing manager needs access to sensitive marketing information but not vice versa. The terms "need-to-know" and "least privilege" express the same idea. Need-to-know is generally applied to people, while least privilege is generally applied to processes.

Negligence: Failure to use such care as a reasonably prudent and careful person would use under similar circumstances; the doing of some act which a person of ordinary prudence would not have done under similar circumstances or failure to do what a person of ordinary prudence would have done under similar circumstances; conduct that falls below the norm for the protection of others against unreasonable risk of harm. It is characterized by inadvertence, thoughtlessness, inattention, recklessness, etc.[214]

Network sink: A router that drops or misroutes packets, accidentally or on purpose. Intelligent network sinks can cooperate to conceal evidence of packet dropping.

NIAP: Joint industry/government (U.S.) National IA Partnership.

NII: National information infrastructure of a specific country.

NIPC: U.S. National Infrastructure Protection Center.

NLS: Network Layer Security Protocol.

Noninterference: The property that actions performed by user or process A of a system have no effect on what user or process B can observe; there is no information flow from A to B.[255]

Nonrepudiation: A security service by which evidence is maintained so that the sender and recipient of data cannot deny having participated in the communication.[154] Referred to individually as nonrepeduation of origin and nonrepudiation of receipt.

Operational error: An error that results from the incorrect use of a product, component, or system.

Operational profile: The set of operations that the software can execute along with the probability with which they will occur.[343]

Operations security: The implementation of standardized operational security procedures that define the nature and frequency of the interaction between users, systems, and system resources, the purpose of which is to (1) maintain a system in a known secure state at all times, and (2) prevent accidental or intentional theft, destruction, alteration, or sabotage of system resources.

OPSEC: Operations security.

OSI: Open Systems Interconnection; a seven-layer model from the ISO that defines and standardizes protocols for communicating between systems, networks and devices. (*See* the standards listed in Section C.1 of Annex C.)

PAP: Password Authentication Protocol.

Partitioning: Isolating IA-critical, IA-related, and non-IA-related functions and entities to prevent accidental or intentional interference, compromise, and corruption. Partitioning can be implemented in hardware or software. Software partitioning can be logical or physical. Partitioning is often referred to as separability in the security community.

Password: A private character string that is used to authenticate an identity.

Password sniffing: Eavesdropping on a communications line to capture passwords that are being transmitted unencrypted.[372]

PDU: Protocol data unit.

PEM: Privacy Enhanced Mail; an e-mail encryption protocol.

Pest program: Collective term for programs with deleterious and generally unanticipated side effects; for example, Trojan horses, logic bombs, letter bombs, viruses, and malicious worms.[362]

PGP: Pretty Good Privacy; an e-mail and file encryption protocol.

Physical security: Protection of hardware, software, and data against physical threats, to reduce or prevent disruptions to operations and services and loss of assets.

PKI: Public key infrastructure.

Plain text: A message before it has been encrypted or after it has been decrypted using a specific algorithm and key; also referred to as clear text. (Contrast with cipher text.)

PP: Protection profile.

Privacy: The rights of individuals and organizations to determine for themselves when, how, and to what extent information about them is to be transmitted to others.[344] Privacy concerns transcend the boundaries of automated systems.

Private key: In a public-key asymmetric cryptosystem, the private key counterpart of a public key; the key that is private to the owner and does not need to be shared.[362]

Public key: In a public-key asymmetric cryptosystem, the public key counterpart of a private key; the key that is public and does not need to be protected.[362]

Public key cryptosystem: An asymmetric cryptosystem that uses a public key and a corresponding private key.[362]

Public key infrastructure: A network of services that includes certificate authorities, certificate repositories, and directory services for storing and finding public key certificates, and certificate revocation lists for managing keys that expire or are revoked.[248]

Qualitative: Inductive analytical approaches that are oriented toward relative, nonmeasurable, and subjective values, such as expert judgment.[425]

Quantitative: Deductive analytical approaches that are oriented toward the use of numbers or symbols to express a measurable quantity, such as MTTR.[425]

RADIUS: Remote Authentication Dial-In User Service.

Random failure: Failures that result from physical degradation over time and variability introduced during the manufacturing process.

Recognition: Capability to detect attacks as they occur and to evaluate the extent of damage and compromise.[336]

Recovery: The ability to maintain essential services and assets during an attack, limit the extent of damage, and restore full services following an attack.[336]

Redundancy: Controlling failure by providing several identical functional units, monitoring the behavior of each to detect faults, and initiating a transition to a safe/secure condition if a discrepancy is detected.[69]

Reference monitor: (1) An access control concept that refers to an abstract machine that mediates all accesses to objects by subjects.[135,141] (2) A system component that mediates usage of all objects by all subjects, enforcing the intended access controls.[362]

Reliability critical: A term applied to any condition, event, process, or item whose recognition, control, performance or tolerance is essential to reliable system operation or support.

Remote Authentication Dial-In User Service: An IETF standard protocol that supports authentication, management, and accounting for remote and dial-in users.[349]

Residual risk: The risk that remains after threat control measures have been employed. Before a system can be certified, a determination must be made about the acceptability of residual risk.

Residue: Accessible vestiges of de-allocated resources, such as memory.

Resistance: Capability of a system to repel attacks.[336]

RFI: Radio frequency interference.

Risk: A combination of the likelihood of a hazard occurring and the severity of the consequences should it occur. (*See also* mishap risk.)

Risk analysis: A series of analyses conducted to identify and determine the cause(s), consequences, likelihood, and severity of hazards. Note that a single hazard may have multiple causes.

Risk control: Techniques that are employed to eliminate, reduce, or mitigate risk, such as inherent safe and secure (re)design techniques/features, alerts, warnings, operational procedures, instructions for use, training, and contingency plans.

Risk dimension: *See* threat perspective.

Risk exposure: The exposure to loss presented to an organization or individual by a risk; the product of the likelihood that the risk will occur and the magnitude of the consequences of its occurrence.[48]

Risk management: Systematic application of risk analysis and risk control management policies, procedures, and practices.

Root cause: Underlying cause(s), event(s), conditions, or actions that individually or in combination led to the accident/incident; primary precursor event(s) that have the potential for being corrected.

RSA: Rivest-Shamir-Adelman public key encryption algorithm; *see* PKCS #1.[179]

S/MIME: Secure Multipurpose Internet Mail Extensions; an e-mail and file encryption protocol.

Safety-critical: A term applied to any condition, event, operation, process, or item whose proper recognition, control, performance, or tolerance is essential to safe system operation and support (such as a safety-critical function, safety-critical path, or safety-critical component.[143]

Safety-critical software: Software that performs or controls functions which, if executed erroneously or if they failed to execute properly, could directly inflict serious injury to people, property, or the environment or cause loss of life.[288]

Safety integrity: (1) The likelihood of a safety-related system, function, or component achieving its required safety features under all stated conditions within a stated measure of use.[130] (2) The probability of a safety-related system satisfactorily performing the required safety functions under all stated conditions within a stated period of time.[65]

Safety integrity level: An indicator of the required level of safety integrity; the level of safety integrity that must be achieved and demonstrated.

Safety kernel: An independent computer program that monitors the state of the system to determine when potentially unsafe system states may occur or when transitions to potentially unsafe system states may occur. A safety kernel is designed to prevent a system from entering an unsafe state and retaining or returning it to a known safe state.[126,127,435]

Safety-related software: Software that performs or controls functions that are activated to prevent or minimize the effect of a failure of a safety-critical system.[288]

Sanitization: (1) Removing the classified content of an otherwise unclassified resource. (2) Removing any information that could identify the source from which the information came.

Secure Electronic Transactions protocol: Used in conjunction with SSL3 and TLS1 to encrypt credit card information so that only the customer and their bank see it, but not the merchant.

Secure Socket Layer: Internet protocol used to protect credit card numbers and other sensitive data between a Web browser and a Web server; developed by Netscape Communications. (*See also* TLS1.)

Security: (1) Freedom from undesirable events, such as malicious and accidental misuse; how well a system resists penetrations by outsiders and misuse by insiders.[362] (2) The protection of system resources from accidental or malicious access, use, modification, destruction, or disclosure.[58] (3) The protection of resources from damage and the protection of data against accidental or intentional disclosure to unauthorized persons or unauthorized modifications or destruction.[344] Security concerns transcend the boundaries of an automated system.

Security association: The keying material and set of mechanisms (cryptographic algorithms, hashing functions, etc.) agreed upon by two entities that will be used to protect and authenticate communications.

Security-critical: A term applied to any condition, event, process, or item whose recognition, control, performance, or tolerance is essential to secure system operation or support.

Security kernel: The hardware, firmware, and software elements of a trusted computing base that implement the reference monitor concept. It must mediate all accesses, be protected from modification, and be verifiable as correct.[135,141]

Sensitivity label: A hierarchical classification and a set of nonhierarchical components that are used by mandatory access controls to define a process's resource access rights.

Session hijacking: An intruder takes over a connection after the original source has been authenticated.

SET: Secure Electronic Transactions protocol.

SHA: Secure hash algorithm; *see* FIPS PUB 180.[162]

SIGINT: A broad range of operations that involve the interception and analysis of signals across the electromagnetic spectrum.

SIL: Safety integrity level.

Smartcard: A small computer the size of a credit card that is used to perform functions such as identification and authentication.

SML: Strength of mechanism; a rating used by the IA Technical Framework to rate the strength or robustness required for a security mechanism. Currently, three ratings are defined: SML1 — low, SML2 — medium, and SML3 — high. The SML is derived as a function of the value of the information being protected and the perceived threat to it.[152] Compare with SOF.

SMTP: Simple Mail Transfer Protocol.

SNA: Survivable network analysis method; developed by the CERT/CC.

SNMP: Simple Network Management Protocol.

SOF: Strength of function; a rating used by the Common Criteria (ISO/IEC 15408) to rate the strength or robustness required for a security mechanism. Currently, three ratings are defined: basic, medium, and high. The SOF is derived as a function of the value of the information being protected and the perceived threat to it.[120–122] Compare with SML.

Software integrity level: The integrity level of a software item.[58]

Software reliability: A measure of confidence that the software produces accurate and consistent results that are repeatable, under low, normal, and peak loads, in the intended operational environment.[288]

Software reliability case: A systematic means of gathering, organizing, analyzing, and reporting the data needed by internal, contractual, regulatory, and Certification Authorities to confirm that a system has met specified reliability requirements and is fit for use in the intended operational environment; includes assumptions, claims, evidence, and arguments. A software reliability case is a component in a system reliability case.[289]

Software safety: Design features and operational procedures which ensure that a product performs predictably under normal and abnormal conditions, and the likelihood of an unplanned event occurring is minimized and its consequences controlled and contained; thereby preventing accidental injury or death, environmental or property damage, whether intentional or accidental.[288]

Software safety case: A systematic means of gathering, organizing, analyzing, and reporting the data needed by internal, contractual, regulatory and Certification Authorities to confirm that a system has met specified safety requirements and is safe for use in the intended operational environment; includes assumptions, claims, evidence, and arguments. A software safety case is a component in a system safety case.[289]

SPI: Security parameter index; part of IPSec.

Spoofing: Taking on the characteristics of another user, system, or process for the purposes of deception.[362]

SSL3: Secure Socket Layer protocol; *see also* TLS1.

ST: Security target.

Static analysis: Analytical techniques used to assess the safety, reliability, security, and performance of a system without executing it. Static analysis techniques generally fall into seven categories[130]:

1. **Subset analysis** — evaluate whether or not source code complies with the specified safe subset of a language.

2. **Metrics analysis** — evaluate software safety, security, and reliability metrics exhibited by the requirements, design, and source code against the goals specified for these values, such as complexity.
3. **Control flow analysis** — evaluate the structure of the code to determine if the sequence of events is correct under normal and abnormal situations and the presence of sneak circuits, unused, or unreachable code.
4. **Data use analysis** — evaluate whether or not data elements are used as specified.
5. **Information flow analysis** — evaluate that dependencies between inputs and outputs only occur as specified.
6. **Semantic/path analysis** — evaluate the correctness of the translation from formal specification, to design logic, and subsequently code.
7. **Safety, reliability, and security properties analysis** — analyze worst-case conditions for system performance, timing accuracy, capacity loading, etc. against specified safety, reliability, and security requirements.

An advantage of static analysis is that it can be performed throughout the life of a system. Exhibits B.2, B.4, and B.5 (Annex B) cite static analysis techniques.

Steganography: Hiding a message so that it is undetectable by all except those who know of its presence; for example, embedding a message in a document, image, audio, or video recording.

Stream cipher: Encryption algorithms that operate on a single bit or byte of data at a time. Contrast with block ciphers.

Survivability: The capability of a system to fulfill its mission, in a timely manner, in the presence of attacks, failures, or accidents.[336] A survivability assessment covers the full threat control chronology.

System high: A system is operating at system high security mode when the system and all of its local and remote peripherals are protected in accordance with the requirements for the highest classification category and types of material contained in the system. All users having access to the system have a security clearance, but not necessarily a need-to-know for all material contained in the system. In this mode, the design and operation of the system must provide for the control of concurrently available classified material in the system on the basis of need-to-know.[140]

System integrity level: The integrity level of a system.[58]

System reliability: The composite of hardware and software reliability for a specified operational environment. System reliability measurements combine qualitative and quantitative assessments.[337]

System safety: The application of engineering and management principles, criteria, and techniques to achieve acceptable mishap risk, within the constraints of operational effectiveness, time, and cost, throughout the life of a system.[143]

System safety engineering: An engineering discipline that employs specialized professional knowledge and skills in applying scientific and engineering principles, criteria, and techniques to identify and eliminate hazards, in order to reduce the associated mishap risk.[143]

System survivability: The ability to continue to make resources available, despite adverse circumstances including hardware malfunctions, accidental software errors, accidental and malicious intentional user activities, and environmental hazards such as EMC/EMI/RFI.

Systematic failure: Failures that result from an error of omission, error of commission, or operational error during a life-cycle activity.[69]

Systematic safety integrity: A qualitative measure or estimate of the failure rate due to systematic failures in a dangerous mode of failure.[69]

Tampering: An intentionally caused event that results in modification of a system, its intended behavior, or data.[362]

TCB: Trusted computing base.

TCP: Transport Control Protocol.

TCSEC: U.S. Department of Defense Trusted Computer System Evaluation Criteria; *see* CSC-STD-001-83.[135,141]

Telnet: An application layer protocol.

Threat: The potential danger that a vulnerability may be exploited intentionally, triggered accidentally, or otherwise exercised.[362]

Threat analysis: A series of analyses conducted to identify threats and determine their type, source, and severity.

Threat control measure: (1) A proactive design or operational procedure, action, or device used to reduce the risk caused by a threat. (2) A proactive design technique, device, or method designed to eliminate or mitigate hazards, and unsafe and unsecure conditions, modes and states.

Threat perspective: The perspective from which vulnerability/threat analyses are conducted (system owner, administrator, certifier, customer, etc.); also referred to as risk dimension.

Time bomb: A Trojan horse that will trigger when a particular time and/or date is reached.

TLS1: Transport Layer Security protocol.

TNI: Trusted network interpretation of TCSEC; *see* NCSC-TG-011.[145,146]

TOCTTU: Time of check to time of use; the time interval between when a user is authenticated and when they access specific system resources.

TOE: Target of evaluation.

Transport Layer Security protocol: The public version of SSL3, being specified by the IETF.

Transaction path: One of many possible combinations of a series of discrete activities that cause an event to take place. All discrete activities in a transaction path are logically possible. Qualitative or quantitative probability measures can be assigned to a transaction path and its individual activities.

Transport mode: An IPSec protocol used with ESP or Alt in which the ESP or Alt header is inserted between the IP header and the upper-layer protocol of an IP packet.[252]

Trap door: A hidden software or hardware mechanism that permits system protection mechanisms to be circumvented. It is activated in some non-apparent manner; for example, a special "random" key sequence at a terminal.[135,141]

Trojan horse: (1) A program with hidden side effects that are not specified in the program documentation and are not intended by the user executing the program.[277] (2) A computer program with an apparent useful function that contains additional (hidden) functions that surreptitiously exploit the legitimate authorizations of the invoking process to the detriment of security. For example, making a "blind copy" of a sensitive file for the creator of the Trojan horse.[135,141]

Trusted computer system: A system that employs sufficient hardware and software integrity measures to allow its use for simultaneously processing a range of sensitive or classified information.

Trusted computing base: The totality of protection mechanisms within a computer system, including hardware, software, and communications equipment, the combination of which is responsible for enforcing a security policy. A TCB consists of one or more components that together enforce a unified security policy over a product or system. The ability of a trusted computing base to correctly enforce a security policy depends solely on the mechanisms within the TCB and on the correct input by system administrative personnel of parameters (such as a user's clearance) related to the security policy.[135,141]

Trusted guard: A computer system that is trusted to enforce a particular guard policy, such as ensuring the flow of only unclassified data from a classified system or ensuring no reverse flow of pest programs from an untrusted system to a trusted system.[362]

Tunnel mode: A IPSec protocol used with ESP in which the header and contents of an IP packet are encrypted and encapsulated prior to transmission, and a new IP header is added.[252]

UDP: User Datagram Protocol.

URL: Uniform resource locator.

Virtual private network: A logical network that connects the geographically dispersed resources of an enterprise over a public network, providing secure global communications across the enterprise without the need for private leased lines.

Virus: An entity that uses the resources of a host computer to reproduce itself and spread, without informed operator action.[416]

VPN: Virtual private network.

Vulnerability: A weakness in a system that can be exploited to violate the system's intended behavior relative to safety, security, reliability, availability, integrity, etc.[362]

Worm: A program that distributes itself in multiple copies within a system or across a distributed system; a worm can be beneficial or harmful.[362]

Worm attack: A harmful exploitation of a worm that can act beyond normally expected behavior, perhaps exploiting security vulnerabilities or causing denials of service.[362]

Wrapper: Encapsulating data or programs to add access controls and monitoring capabilities. Wrappers are used with IPSec and as a confinement technique.

Annex B

Glossary of Techniques

Current proven techniques that can be used to achieve and assess different aspects of information assurance throughout the life of a system are listed in Exhibits 2 through 5:

Exhibit 2 lists IA analysis techniques
Exhibit 3 lists IA design techniques and features
Exhibit 4 lists IA verification techniques
Exhibit 5 lists IA accident/incident investigation techniques

The exhibits identify (1) which techniques and groups of techniques are complementary or redundant; (2) the primary focus of each technique: safety, security, or reliability; and (3) the generic life-cycle phases in which the techniques can be used. Each project team should choose a complementary set of analysis, design, and verification techniques that are appropriate for the size, complexity, criticality, cost, and duration of their specific project/system. The results obtained from using these techniques is included as part of the evidence in the IA integrity case.

Many techniques used during the concept and development phases can also be used during the operational phase to (1) verify that the required IA integrity level is being maintained, (2) investigate an accident/incident, and (3) determine why a system did not achieve its stated IA goals. Likewise, many techniques serve multiple purposes. For example, some IA analysis techniques can also be used during verification and accident/incident investigation. Techniques that serve multiple purposes are noted in the exhibits.

Following each exhibit, a description of the technique* is provided in the following format:

---

* Annex B of *Software Safety and Reliability: Techniques, Approaches, and Standards of Key Industrial Sectors*, by Debra S. Herrmann, IEEE Computer Society Press, 1999, lists tools that are commercially available tools to automate many of these techniques.

Exhibit 1 Legend for Exhibits 2 through 5

Column	*Code*	*Meaning*
Type	SA	Technique primarily supports safety engineering
	SE	Technique primarily supports security engineering
	RE	Technique primarily supports reliability engineering
	All	Technique supports a combination of safety, security, and reliability engineering
C/R	Cx	Groups of complementary techniques
	Rx	Groups of redundant techniques; only one of the redundant techniques should be used.

- **Purpose:** summary of what is achieved using the technique; why the technique should be used.
- **Description:** summary of the main features of the technique and how to implement it.
- **Benefits:** how the technique enhances IA integrity or facilitates assessment; any cost benefits derived from using the technique.
- **Limitations:** factors that may limit the use of the technique, affect the interpretation of the results obtained, or impact the cost-effectiveness of the technique.
- **References:** sources for more information about the technique.

Exhibit 1 explains the codes used in Exhibits 2 through 5.

B.1 IA Analysis Techniques

B.1.1 Bayesian Belief Networks (BBNs)

Purpose: To provide a methodology for reasoning about uncertainty as part of risk analysis and assessment.

Description: Bayesian belief networks (BBNs) are graphical networks that represent probabilistic relationships among variables (events or propositions). The nodes represent uncertain variables and the arcs represent the cause/relevance relationships among the variables. The probability tables for each node provide the probabilities of each state of the variable for that node, conditional on each combination of values of the parent node.[5] As new knowledge or uncertainties are discovered, this information can be propagated through the BBN.

Benefits: BBNs provide the ability to combine logical inferences, objective evidence, and subjective expert judgment in one complete model. The graphical nature of BBNs improves communication among different stakeholders, developers, and assessment teams.

Limitations: The use of an automated tool, such as Hugin's BBN tool, is required to develop the models in a reasonable amount of time.

Exhibit 2 Information Assurance Analysis Techniques

IA Analysis Techniques	*C/R*	*Type*	*Life-cycle Phase in which Technique is Used*		
			Concept	*Development*	*Operations*
Bayesian belief networks (BBNs)[a]	C1	All	x	x	x
Cause consequence analysis[a,b]	R1/C1	SA, SE	x	x	x
Change impact analysis	C1	All		x	x
Common cause failure analysis[b]	C1	All	x	x	x
Develop operational profiles, formal scenario analysis	C1	All	x	x	x
Develop IA integrity cases	C1	All	x	x	x
Event tree analysis[a,b]	R1/C1	All	x	x	x
Functional analysis	C1	SA, SE	x	x	x
Hazard analysis	C1	SA, SE	x	x	x
HAZOP studies[a,b]	C1	SA, SE	x	x	x
Highlighting requirements likely to change	C1	All	x		
Petri nets[a,b]	C1	SA, SE		x	x
Reliability block diagrams	C1	RE	x	x	x
Reliability prediction modeling	C1	RE	x	x	
Response time, memory, constraint analysis	C1	All		x	x
Software, system FMECA[a,b]	C1	All	x	x	x
Software, system FTA[a,b]	R1/C1	SA, SE	x	x	x
Sneak circuit analysis[a,b]	C1	SA, SE		x	x
Usability analysis	C1	SA, SE	x	x	x

[a] These techniques can also be used during verification.

[b] These techniques can also be used during accident/incident investigation.

Source: Adapted from Herrmann, D., *Software Safety and Reliability: Techniques, Approaches and Standards of Key Industrial Sectors*, IEEE Computer Society Press, 1999.

References:

1. Bouissou, M., Martin, F., and Ourghanlian, A., Assessment of a safety-critical system including software: A Bayes-belief network for evidence sources, *Proceedings of the Annual Reliability and Maintainability Symposium (RAMS'99)*, IEEE, 1999, 142–150.
2. Jensen, F., *An Introduction to Bayesian Belief Networks*, Springer-Verlag, 1996.
3. Neil, M. and Fenton, N., Applying BBNs to critical systems assessment, *Safety Systems*, 8(3), 10–13, 1999.

4. Neil, M., Littlewood, B., and Fenton, N., Applying BBNs to system dependability assessment, *Safety-Critical Systems: The Convergence of High Tech and Human Factors*, Springer-Verlag, 1996, 71–94.
5. www.agena.co.uk; BBN articles and tutorials.

B.1.2 Cause Consequence Analysis

Purpose: To enhance IA integrity by identifying possible sequences of events that can lead to a system compromise or failure.

Description: Cause consequence analysis is a hybrid technique that combines fault tree analysis and event tree analysis. Beginning with a critical event, a cause consequence diagram is developed backward and forward from that event. The backward portion of the diagram is equivalent to a fault tree. The forward portion of the diagram is equivalent to an event tree in which possible consequences of the sequence of events are identified. Standard symbols have been defined for cause consequence diagrams so that propagation conditions, timing information, and probability of occurrence can be recorded and analyzed.

Benefits: Cause consequence diagrams are particularly well suited to studying start-up, shutdown, and other sequential control problems.[2] They facilitate analysis of combinations of events and alternative consequence paths.[2]

Limitations: Separate diagrams are required for each initiating event.[2]

References:

1. IEC 61508-7, Functional Safety of Electrical/Electronic/Programmable Electronic Safety-Related Systems, Part 7: Overview of Techniques and Measures.
2. Leveson, N., *Safeware: System Safety and Computers*, Addison-Wesley, 1995.
3. Nielsen, B., The Cause Consequence Diagram Method as a Basis for Quantitative Accident Analysis, RISO-M-1374, 1971.
4. System Safety Society, *System Safety Analysis Handbook*, 2nd ed., July 1997.

B.1.3 Change Impact Analysis

Purpose: To analyze *a priori* the potential local and global effects of changing requirements, design, implementation, data structures, and/or interfaces on system performance, safety, reliability, and security; prevent errors from being introduced during enhancements or maintenance.

Description: Changing or introducing new requirements or design features may have a ripple effect on a current or proposed system. A change or fix can be applied to one part of a system with detrimental or unforeseen consequences to another part. Change impact analysis evaluates the extent and impact of proposed changes by examining which requirements and design components are interdependent. The analysis evaluates whether or not the proposed change could invoke a vulnerability/threat, affect a threat control measure, increase the likelihood or severity of a vulnerability/threat, adversely affect IA-critical or IA-related software, or change the criticality of a software component.[5] Change impact analysis should be conducted when[2]:

- The operational environment has changed
- System components are being modified or replaced
- The system is to be used for a new or different application than it was originally designed
- Changes are proposed to the requirements, design, implementation
- Preventive, corrective, or adaptive maintenance is being performed

Change impact analysis can also be used to support analysis of alternatives, by highlighting which alternative can be implemented most efficiently, and to identify the extent of reverification and revalidation needed. (*See also* Regression Testing.)

Benefits: The potential for uncovering latent defects or introducing new errors when implementing changes or enhancements is minimized.

Limitations: The scope of the analysis determines its effectiveness.

References:

1. Arnold, R. and Bohner, S., *Software Change Impact Analysis*, IEEE Computer Society Press, 1996.
2. DEF STAN 00-55, Requirements for Safety-Related Software in Defence Equipment, Part 1: Requirements, U.K. Ministry of Defence (MoD), August 1, 1997.
3. DEF STAN 00-55, Requirements for Safety-Related Software in Defence Equipment, Part 2: Guidance, U.K. Ministry of Defence (MoD), August 1, 1997.
4. IEC 61508-7, Functional Safety of Electrical/Electronic/Programmable Electronic Safety-Related Systems, Part 7: Overview of Techniques and Measures.
5. NASA GB-1740.13.96, *Guidebook for Safety-Critical Software — Analysis and Development*, NASA Glenn Research Center, Office of System Safety and Mission Assurance, 1996.
6. System Safety Society, *System Safety Analysis Handbook*, 2nd ed., July 1997.

B.1.4 Common Cause Failure (CCF) Analysis

Purpose: To enhance IA integrity by identifying scenarios in which two or more failures or compromises could occur as the result of a common design defect.

Description: Common cause failure (CCF) analysis seeks to identify intermediate and root causes of potential failure modes. The results of CCF analysis are often documented graphically by event trees. This information is analyzed to determine failures that could result from common design defects, hardware failures, or operational anomalies and to propose the requisite mitigating actions, such as the need for diversity. CCF analysis includes hardware, software, and communications equipment. It is essential that fault-tolerant designs be verified through CCF analysis. (*See also* Diversity, Redundancy, and Root Cause Analysis.)

Benefits: Common cause failure analysis results in a more robust system architecture.

Limitations: The extent to which the analysis is carried out (e.g., how far back intermediate and root causes are identified) determines its effectiveness.

References:

1. IEC 61508-7, Functional Safety of Electrical/Electronic/Programmable Electronic Safety-Related Systems, Part 7: Overview of Techniques and Measures.
2. Space Product Assurance: Safety, European Space Agency, ECSS-Q-40A, April 19, 1996.
3. System Safety Society, *System Safety Analysis Handbook*, 2nd ed., July 1997.

B.1.5 Develop Operational Profiles and Formal Scenario Analysis

Purpose: To identify operational profiles; capture domain knowledge about MWFs and MNWFs; understand human factors safety, reliability, and security concerns.

Description: A scenario-based test model is developed from the analysis of operational profiles, user views, and events. Operational profiles are an ordered sequence of events that accomplishes a functional requirement specified by an end user.[1] User views are a set of system conditions specific to a class of users.[1] Events are particular stimuli that change a system state or trigger another event.[3] Operational profiles are recorded in a formalized tree notation, similar to that used for finite state machines. Probabilities are assigned to each potential set of operations.[1,2]

Benefits: The development of operational profiles and formal scenario analysis helps to identify deadlock, nondeterministic conditions, incorrect sequences, incorrect initial and terminating states, and errors caused by an incomplete understanding of the domain knowledge. (*See also* Usability Testing.)

Limitations: The development of operational profiles and formal scenario analysis is somewhat labor intensive; both developers and end users are involved.

References:

1. Herrmann, D., *Software Safety and Reliability: Techniques, Approaches and Standards of Key Industrial Sectors*, IEEE Computer Society Press, 1999.
2. Hsia, P., *Testing the Therac-25: A Formal Scenario Approach, Safety and Reliability for Medical Device Software*, Herrmann, D. (Ed.), Health Industries Manufacturers Association (HIMA) Report No. 95-8, 1995, tab 6.
3. Lyu, M. (Ed.), *Handbook of Software Reliability Engineering*, IEEE Computer Society Press, 1996.
4. Pant, H., Franklin, P., and Everett, W., A structured approach to improving software-reliability using operational profiles, *Proceedings of the Annual Reliability and Maintainability Symposium*, IEEE, 1994, 142–146.

B.1.6 Develop IA Integrity Case

Purpose: To collect, organize, analyze, and report information to prove that IA integrity requirements have been (or will be) achieved and maintained.

Description: An IA integrity case is a living document throughout the life of a system, from initial concept through decommissioning. An IA integrity case consists of seven components (see Chapter 7, Exhibit 9):

- IA goals
- Assumptions and claims
- (Current) evidence

- Conclusions and recommendations
- Outstanding issues
- Approval, certification records
- Backup, supporting information

The preliminary IA integrity case provides a justification that the recommended architecture and threat control measures will achieve specified IA goals. It can be prepared during the proposal or BAFO stage. The interim IA integrity case collects ongoing evidence that indicates a project is on track for meeting specified IA requirements. It is prepared during the development and assessment stage. The operational IA integrity case is a complete set of evidence that the specified IA integrity requirements were met and are being maintained. (*See also* Review IA Integrity Case.)

Benefits: The structure imposed by developing an IA integrity case helps system designers and developers to be more thorough when addressing IA integrity issues. Organized and complete IA integrity cases help certifying authorities to perform a more effective and thorough assessment.

Limitations: None.

References:

1. DEF STAN 00-42, Reliability and Maintainability Assurance Guides, Part 2: Software, U.K. Ministry of Defence (MoD), September 1, 1997.
2. DEF STAN 00-55, Requirements for Safety-Related Software in Defence Equipment, Part 1: Requirements, U.K. Ministry of Defence (MoD), August 1, 1997.
3. DEF STAN 00-55, Requirements for Safety-Related Software in Defence Equipment, Part 2: Guidance, U.K. Ministry of Defence (MoD), August 1, 1997.
4. Herrmann, D., *Software Safety and Reliability: Techniques, Approaches and Standards of Key Industrial Sectors*, IEEE Computer Society Press, 1999.
5. Herrmann, D. and Peercy, D., Software Reliability Cases: The bridge between hardware, software and system safety and reliability, *Proceedings of the Annual Reliability and Maintainability Symposium (RAMS'99)*, IEEE, 1999, 396–402.
6. JA 1002, Software Reliability Program Standard, Society of Automotive Engineers (SAE), 1998.
7. Storey, N., *Safety-Critical Computer Systems*, Addison-Wesley, 1996.

B.1.7 Event Tree Analysis

Purpose: To enhance IA integrity by preventing defects through analysis of sequences of system events and operator actions that could lead to failures, compromises, or unstable states.

Description: Event trees organize, characterize, and quantify potential system failures in a methodical manner.[5] An event tree is developed in a graphical notation following a six-step process:

1. Identify all possible events (accidental and intentional) that could initiate a system compromise or failure.
2. Identify the system response.
3. Identify the mitigating threat control measure(s).
4. Group initiating events with their corresponding responses.

5. Identify initiating event/response branches that will lead to a system compromise or failure.
6. Assign probabilities to each branch in the event tree.

This process is repeated until all initiating events and threat control measures have been evaluated. Note that it is possible for some responses to act as new initiating events.

Benefits: Event tree analysis is considered to be one of the more exhaustive analysis techniques and particularly well suited for high-risk systems.[5]

Limitations: The effectiveness of this technique is proportional to the ability to anticipate all unwanted events and all of the potential causes of these events.[3] Use of an automated tool is necessary. Event tree analysis can be very time-consuming if not focused correctly.

References:

1. Bott, T., Evaluating the risk of industrial espionage, *Proceedings of the Annual Reliability and Maintainability Symposium (RAMS'99)*, IEEE, 1999, 230–237.
2. IEC 61508-7, Functional Safety of Electrical/Electronic/Programmable Electronic Safety-Related Systems, Part 7: Overview of Techniques and Measures.
3. Leveson, N., *Safeware: System Safety and Computers*, Addison-Wesley, 1995.
4. Storey, N., *Safety-Critical Computer Systems*, Addison-Wesley, 1996.
5. System Safety Society, *System Safety Analysis Handbook*, 2nd ed., July 1997.

B.1.8 Functional Analysis

Purpose: To identify safety and security hazards associated with normal operations, degraded mode operations, incorrect usage, inadvertent operation, absence of function(s), and accidental and intentional human error.

Description: Functional analysis is conducted to identify potential hazards that could result from correct or incorrect functioning and use of the system. Functional analysis is conducted throughout the life cycle, from concept definition, requirements specification and design, to implementation and operation. The first step is to diagram relationships between components and their functions, including lower level functions; for example[2]:

- Principal functions
- Subsidiary functions
- Warning functions
- Operator indication and control functions
- Protection functions
- Human operator initiated functions
- Failure mitigation functions

Accidental and intentional, random and systematic failures are examined. All functional modes are evaluated, including:

- Normal operation
- Abnormal operation
- Degraded mode operations

- Incorrect operation
- Inadvertent operation
- Absence of functionality
- Human error that causes functions to be operated too fast, too slow, or in the wrong sequence

Benefits: Functional analysis is a comprehensive technique. It highlights the contribution of low-level functions to hazards and complements FTA, FMECA, and HAZOP studies.

Limitations: To employ this technique effectively, all stakeholders must be involved in the analysis, and the analysis must be carried out to the lowest-level functions.

References:

1. DEF STAN 00-56, Safety Management Requirements for Defense Systems Containing Programmable Electronics, Part 1: Requirements, U.K. Ministry of Defence (MoD), December 13, 1996.
2. DEF STAN 00-56, Safety Management Requirements for Defense Systems Containing Programmable Electronics, Part 2: General Application Guidance, U.K. Ministry of Defence (MoD), December 13, 1996.

B.1.9 Hazard Analysis

Purpose: To enhance IA integrity by identifying potential hazards associated with using a system so that appropriate mitigation features can be incorporated into the design and operational procedures.

Description: Hazard analysis is a category of techniques used to identify hazards so that they can be eliminated or mitigated. FTA, event tree analysis, sneak circuit analysis, and Petri nets are all examples of hazard analysis techniques.

Hazard analyses are performed throughout the life cycle to explore safety, reliability, and security concerns. A preliminary hazard analysis is performed based on the requirements specification and concept of operations. Subsequent hazard analyses are performed on the design, source code, operational profiles, and the operational system. All anomalies and recommended corrective action are noted as part of the hazard analyses and tracked to closure. Examples of items to evaluate during a hazard analysis include:[2,3,4]

- Cause(s) of a hazard or vulnerability, whether accidental or intentional
- Severity of the consequences of a hazard
- Likelihood of a threat triggering a hazard
- Alternative threat control strategies
- Effective exception handling
- Effective handling of errors
- Efficient transitioning to degraded mode operations, fail safe/secure, or fail operational when needed
- Conditions that could cause a system to enter an unknown or unsafe/unsecure state, such as transient faults, excessive interrupts, and saturation

Benefits: Potential hazards are identified early during the life cycle, when it is easier and cheaper to eliminate or mitigate them. The hazard analysis process, by identifying the severity and likelihood of hazards, facilitates the efficient assignment of resources to the most critical hazards.

Limitations: The comprehensiveness of the hazard analyses determines their utility.

References:

1. CE-1001-STD Rev. 1, Standard for Software Engineering of Safety-Critical Software, CANDU Computer Systems Engineering Centre for Excellence, January 1995.
2. Leveson, N., *Safeware: System Safety and Computers*, Addison-Wesley, 1995.
3. Storey, N., *Safety-Critical Computer Systems*, Addison-Wesley, 1996.
4. System Safety Society, *System Safety Analysis Handbook*, 2nd ed., July 1997.

B.1.10 HAZOP Studies

Purpose: To prevent potential hazards (accidental and intentional, physical and cyber) by capturing domain knowledge about operational environment, parameters, modes/states, etc. so that this information can be incorporated in the requirements, design, and operational procedures.

Description: A hazard and operability (HAZOP) study is a method of discovering hazards in a proposed or existing system, their possible causes and consequences, and recommending solutions to minimize the likelihood of occurrence.[1] The hazards can be physical or cyber, and result from accidental or malicious intentional action. Design and operational aspects of the system are analyzed by an interdisciplinary team. A neutral facilitator guides the group through a discussion of how a system is or should be used. Particular attention is paid to usability issues, operator actions (correct and incorrect, under normal and abnormal conditions), and capturing domain knowledge. A series of guide words are used to determine correct design values for system components, interconnections and dependencies between components, and the attributes of the components.

Benefits: This is one of the few techniques to focus on (1) hazards arising from the operational environment and usability issues and (2) capturing domain knowledge from multiple stakeholders.

Limitations: The facilitator must be adequately trained in the methodology for the sessions to be effective.

References:

1. DEF STAN 00-58, HAZOP Studies on Systems Containing Programmable Electronics, Part 1: Requirements, U.K. Ministry of Defence (MoD), interim, July 25, 1996.
2. DEF STAN 00-58, HAZOP Studies on Systems Containing Programmable Electronics, Part 2: General Application Guidance, U.K. Ministry of Defence (MoD), interim, July 25, 1996.
3. IEC 61508-7, Functional Safety of Electrical/Electronic/Programmable Electronic Safety-Related Systems, Part 7: Overview of Techniques and Measures.
4. Leveson, N., *Safeware: System Safety and Computers*, Addison-Wesley, 1995.
5. Redmill, F., Chudleigh, M., and Catmur, J. *System Safety: HAZOP and Software HAZOP*, John Wiley & Sons, 1999.
6. Storey, N., *Safety-Critical Computer Systems*, Addison-Wesley, 1996.
7. System Safety Society, *System Safety Analysis Handbook*, 2nd ed., July 1997.

B.1.11 Highlighting Requirements Likely to Change

Purpose: To enhance the maintainability of threat control measures and IA integrity.

Description: During concept definition and requirements specification, time is taken to identify requirements that are likely to change in future system releases, due to anticipated enhancements, upgrades, and changes or additions to the operational mission. Attention is focused on IA-critical and IA-related functions/entities. This information is then fed into the design process. Components that are likely to change are partitioned from those that are more stable.

Benefits: Future maintainability and supportability is simplified. The cost of implementing and planning for new system releases is reduced. The likelihood of disrupting a threat control measure when performing adaptive maintenance is reduced.

Limitations: None.

References:

1. CE-1001-STD Rev. 1, Standard for Software Engineering of Safety Critical Software, CANDU Computer Systems Engineering Centre for Excellence, January 1995.
2. DEF STAN 00-41/Issue 3, Reliability and Maintainability, MoD Guide to Practices and Procedures, U.K. Ministry of Defence (MoD), June 25, 1993.

B.1.12 Petri Nets

Purpose: To identify potential deadlock, race, and nondeterministic conditions that could lead to a system compromise or failure.

Description: Petri nets are used to model relevant aspects of system behavior at a wide range of abstract levels.[2] Petri nets are a class of graph theory models that represent information and control flow in systems that exhibit concurrency and asynchronous behavior.[2,3,6] A Petri net is a network of states and transitions. The states may be marked or unmarked; a transition is enabled when all the input places to it are marked.[2,3,6] When enabled, it is permitted but not obliged to fire. If it fires, the input marks are removed and each output place from the transition is marked instead.[2,3,6] These models can be defined in purely mathematical terms, which facilitates automated analysis, such as producing reachability graphs.[2]

Benefits: Petri nets can be used to model an entire system, subsystems, or subcomponents at conceptual, top-level design, and implementation levels.[2] They are useful for identifying deadlock, race, and nondeterministic conditions that could lead to a system compromise or failure.

Limitations: The production of Petri nets can be time-consuming without the use of an automated tool.

References:

1. Buy, U. and Sloan, R., Analysis of real-time programs with simple time Petri nets, *Proceedings of the International Symposium on Software Testing and Analysis (ISSTA)*, ACM Press, 1994, 228–239.
2. Herrmann, D., *Software Safety and Reliability: Techniques, Approaches and Standards of Key Industrial Sectors*, IEEE Computer Society Press, 1999.
3. Jensen, K., *Coloured Petri Nets: Basic Concepts, Analysis Methods and Practical Use*, Springer-Verlag, Vol. 1, 1996; Vol. 2, 1995.

4. Lindemann, C., *Performance Modelling with Deterministic and Stochastic Petri Nets*, John Wiley & Sons, 1998.
5. NASA GB-1740.13.96, *Guidebook for Safety-Critical Software — Analysis and Development*, NASA Glenn Research Center, Office of System Safety and Mission Assurance, 1996.
6. Peterson, J., *Petri-Net Theory and the Modeling of Systems*, Prentice-Hall, 1981.
7. System Safety Society, *System Safety Analysis Handbook*, 2nd ed., July 1997.

B.1.13 Reliability Block Diagrams

Purpose: To enhance IA integrity by diagrammatically identifying the set of events that must take place and the conditions that must be fulfilled for a system or task to execute correctly[1,2]; support initial reliability allocation, reliability estimates, and design optimization.

Description: Reliability block diagrams illustrate the relationship between system components with respect to the effect of component failures on overall system reliability. These relationships generally fall into four categories:

- A serial system
- A dual redundant system
- M out of n redundant systems
- A standby redundant system

Reliability block diagrams are annotated to show[1]:

- The reliability and maintainability values assigned to each block, such as MTBF and MTTR
- Assumptions about each component
- Operational profiles
- Item criticality
- Dependencies between blocks that are not apparent from the diagram
- Development risk

Benefits: Reliability block diagrams are useful for analyzing systems that are composed of multiple diverse components, such as hardware, software, and communications equipment.

Limitations: A reliability block diagram does not necessarily represent the system's operational logic or functional partitioning.[4]

References:

1. DEF STAN 00-41/Issue 3, Reliability and Maintainability, MoD Guide to Practices and Procedures, U.K. Ministry of Defence (MoD), June 25, 1993.
2. IEC 61508-7, Functional Safety of Electrical/Electronic/Programmable Electronic Safety-Related Systems, Part 7: Overview of Techniques and Measures.
3. IEC 61078(1991), Analysis Techniques for Dependability — Reliability Block Diagram Method.
4. O'Connor, P., *Practical Reliability Engineering*, 3rd ed., John Wiley & Sons, 1991.
5. Storey, N., *Safety-Critical Computer Systems*, Addison-Wesley, 1996.

B.1.14 Reliability Prediction Modeling

Purpose: To predict the future reliability of a software system.

Description: The failure probability of a new program, usually one that is under development, is predicted in part by comparing it to the known failure probability of an existing operational program. The criteria for determining the degree of similarity include: design similarity, similarity of service use profile, procurement and project similarity, and proof of reliability achievement. The generic reliability prediction process also involves estimating the fault density per KSLOC. This value is then used to predict the number of errors remaining in the software and the time it will take to find them.

Benefits: This model can be executed at any time during the life cycle.

Limitations: The validity of the prediction depends on the similarity between the program, its operational environment and operational profile(s), and that to which it is compared. None of the current reliability prediction models incorporate data from qualitative assessments or static analysis techniques.

References:

1. ANSI/AIAA R-0133-1992, Recommended Practice for Software Reliability.
2. BS5760, Part 8: Guide to the Assessment of Reliability of Systems Containing Software, British Standards Institution (BSI), October 1998.
3. DEF STAN 00-42, Reliability and Maintainability Assurance Guide, Part 2: Software, U.K. Ministry of Defence, 1998.
4. IEEE Std. 982.1-1988, IEEE Standard Dictionary of Measures to Produce Reliable Software.*
5. IEEE Std. 982.2-1988, IEEE Guide for the Use of the Standard Dictionary of Measures to Produce Reliable Software.
6. Lyu, M. (Ed.), *Handbook of Software Reliability Engineering*, IEEE Computer Society Press, 1996.
7. Musa, J., *Software Reliability Engineering*, McGraw-Hill, 1999.
8. Peters, W., *Software Engineering: An Engineering Approach*, John Wiley & Sons, 1999.
9. Storey, N., *Safety-Critical Computer Systems*, Addison-Wesley, 1996.

B.1.15 Response Time, Memory, Constraint Analysis

Purpose: To ensure that the operational system will meet all stated response time, memory, and other specified constraints under low, normal, and peak loading conditions.[3]

Description: Constraint analysis evaluates restrictions imposed by requirements, the real world, and environmental limitations, as well as the design solution.[2] Engineering analyses are conducted by an integrated product team to evaluate the system architecture and detailed design. The allocation of response time budgets between hardware, system software, application software, and communications equipment are examined to determine if they are realistic and comply with stated requirements. An assessment is made to determine if the available memory is sufficient for the system and application software. Minimum

* Note that this standard began an update cycle in late 1999.

and maximum system throughput capacity under low, normal, peak, and overload conditions is estimated. Timing and sizing analysis for IA-critical and IA-related functions/entities are evaluated against maximum execution time and memory allocation, particularly under worst-case scenarios. Items to consider when quantifying timing/resource requirements include[2,4]:

- Memory usage versus availability
- I/O channel usage (load) versus capacity and availability
- Execution time versus CPU load and availability
- Sampling rates versus rates of change of physical parameters
- Sensor/actuator accuracy and calibration
- Physical time constraints and response times
- Minimum time required to transition between modes/states
- Minimum time required for human response/action
- Off-nominal environments

Benefits: Design deficiencies, which could cause safety and security vulnerabilities are uncovered before full-scale development.

Limitations: This static analysis technique should be supplemented by performance and stress testing.

References:

1. Briand, L. and Roy, D., *Meeting Deadlines in Hard Real-Time Systems: The Rate Monotonic Approach*, IEEE Computer Society Press, 1999.
2. IEC 61508-7, Functional Safety of Electrical/Electronic/Programmable Electronic Safety-Related Systems, Part 7: Overview of Techniques and Measures.
3. Leveson, N., *Safeware: System Safety and Computers*, Addison-Wesley, 1995.
4. NASA GB-1740.13.96, *Guidebook for Safety-Critical Software — Analysis and Development*, NASA Glenn Research Center, Office of System Safety and Mission Assurance, 1996.
5. Storey, N., *Safety-Critical Computer Systems*, Addison-Wesley, 1996.

B.1.16 Software, System FMECA

Purpose: To examine the effect of accidental and intentional, random and systematic failures on system behavior in general and IA integrity in particular.

Description: A failure mode effects criticality analysis (FMECA) identifies the ways in which a system could fail accidentally or be made to fail intentionally, and thus impact IA integrity. All stakeholders are involved in an FMECA to ensure that all aspects of a failure are adequately evaluated. FMECAs are conducted and refined iteratively throughout the life of a system. There are three types of FMECA: functional FMECA, design FMECA, and interface FMECA.[7] FMECA can and should be conducted at the system entity level (hardware, software, communications equipment, human factors) and at the system level. FMECAs (1) help to optimize designs, operational procedures, and fault tolerance strategies, (2) uncover operational constraints imposed by a design, and (3) verify the robustness of IA design techniques/features or the need for corrective action.[1]

The procedure for conducting a software FMECA is straightforward.[1–3,6,7,9] The software is broken into logical components, such as functions or tasks. Potential worst-case failure modes are predicted for each component. The cause(s) of these failure modes and their effect on system behavior is (are) postulated. Finally, the severity and likelihood of each failure mode are determined. In general, quantitative likelihoods are used to estimate random failures, while qualitative likelihoods are used to estimate systematic failures. Reliability block diagrams and the system operation characterization are used as inputs to an FMECA. Type failure modes examined include[1]:

- Premature operation
- Failure to operate at a prescribed time
- Intermittent operation
- Failure to cease operation at a prescribed time
- No output, wrong output, partial output
- Failure during operation

The effect of each failure mode is evaluated at several levels, such as[1]:

- Local effect
- Effect at the next higher level of assembly or function
- Effect on the system and its operational mission

The effect of failures is examined at different levels to (1) optimize fault containment strategies and (2) identify whether or not a failure at this level creates the conditions or opportunity for a parallel attack, compromise, or failure. The principle data elements collected, analyzed, and reported for each failure mode are:

- System, entity, and function
- Operational mission, profile, and environment
- Assumptions and accuracy concerns
- The failure mode
- Cause(s) of the failure
- Likelihood of the failure occurring
- Severity of the consequences of the failure
- Responsible component, event, or action
- Current compensating provisions: anticipate/prevent, detect/characterize, and respond/recover
- Recommended additional mitigation

Benefits: The results of an FMECA can be used to prioritize and verify threat control measures and as input to an FTA.

Limitations: An FMECA only captures known potential failure modes; it does not accommodate reasoning about uncertain or unknown failure modes.[4,5] The development of a software FMECA can be labor intensive unless an automated tool is used.[1]

References:

1. DEF STAN 00-41/Issue 3, Reliability and Maintainability, *MoD Guide to Practices and Procedures*, U.K. Ministry of Defence (MoD), June 25, 1993.
2. IEC 60812(1985), Analysis Techniques for System Reliability — Procedure for Failure Modes Effects Analysis (FMEA).
3. IEC 61508-7, Functional Safety of Electrical/Electronic/Programmable Electronic Safety-Related Systems, Part 7: Overview of Techniques and Measures.
4. Leveson, N., *Safeware: System Safety and Computers*, Addison-Wesley, 1995.
5. NASA GB-1740.13.96, *Guidebook for Safety-Critical Software — Analysis and Development*, NASA Glenn Research Center, Office of System Safety and Mission Assurance, 1996.
6. Raheja, D., *Assurance Technologies: Principles and Practices*, McGraw-Hill, 1991.
7. SAE Recommended Best Practices for FMECA, (draft) March 1999.
8. Storey, N., *Safety-Critical Computer Systems*, Addison-Wesley, 1996.
9. System Safety Society, *System Safety Analysis Handbook*, 2nd ed., July 1997.

B.1.17 Software, System FTA

Purpose: To identify potential root cause(s) of undesired system events (accidental and intentional) so that mitigating features can be incorporated into the design and operational procedures.

Description: FTA (fault tree analysis) aids in the analysis of events, or combinations of events, that will lead to a physical or cyber hazard.[2] Starting at an event that would be the immediate cause of a hazard, the analysis is carried out backward along a path.[3,4] Combinations of events are described with logical operators (AND, OR, IOR, EOR).[3,4] Intermediate causes are analyzed in the same manner back to the root cause.[3,4] A software FTA follows the same procedure as a hardware or system FTA to identify the root cause(s) of a major undesired event.[2] An FTA should be developed iteratively throughout the life cycle and in conjunction with an FMECA.[2]

Benefits: A software FTA can be merged with a hardware or system-level FTA. FTA complements FMECA.[1] The effects of nontechnical failures can be analyzed, such as human error, weather, etc.[1] All possible component failure combinations are identified.[1]

Limitations: A fault tree only captures known potential faults; it does not accommodate reasoning about uncertain or unknown faults.[4,5] The development of a software FTA can be labor intensive unless an automated tool is used.[1,4]

References:

1. DEF STAN 00-41/Issue 3, Reliability and Maintainability, *MoD Guide to Practices and Procedures*, U.K. Ministry of Defence (MoD), June 25, 1993.
2. Herrmann, D., *Software Safety and Reliability: Techniques, Approaches and Standards of Key Industrial Sectors*, IEEE Computer Society Press, 1999.
3. IEC 61025(1990), Fault Tree Analysis.
4. IEC 61508-7, Functional Safety of Electrical/Electronic/Programmable Electronic Safety-Related Systems, Part 7: Overview of Techniques and Measures.
5. Leveson, N., *Safeware: System Safety and Computers*, Addison-Wesley, 1995.

6. NASA GB-1740.13.96, *Guidebook for Safety-Critical Software — Analysis and Development,* NASA Glenn Research Center, Office of System Safety and Mission Assurance, 1996.
7. Raheja, D., *Assurance Technologies: Principles and Practices*, McGraw-Hill, 1991.
8. Storey, N., *Safety-Critical Computer Systems*, Addison-Wesley, 1996.
9. System Safety Society, *System Safety Analysis Handbook*, 2nd ed., July 1997.

B.1.18 Sneak Circuit Analysis

Purpose: To identify hidden unintended or unexpected hardware or software logic paths or control sequences that could inhibit desired system functions, initiate undesired system events, or cause incorrect timing and sequencing, leading to a system compromise or failure.[3]

Description: Sneak circuits are latent conditions that are intentionally or accidentally designed into a system, which may cause it to perform contrary to specifications and affect safety, reliability, and security.[2,5,6] Maintenance assist modes are examples of intentional benign sneak circuits; however, if these techniques are not implemented correctly, they can have unintended negative consequences.[7] Trap doors and Trojan horses are examples of malicious intentional sneak circuits.

The first step in sneak circuit analysis is to convert the design into a topological network tree, identifying each node of the network.[1–3] The use and interrelationships of instructions are examined to identify potential sneak circuits.[2] All possible paths through a software component or circuit are examined because sneak circuits can result from a combination of hardware, software, and operator actions. Categories of sneak circuits that are searched for include[1]:

- **Sneak paths,** which cause current, energy, data, or logical sequence to flow along an unexpected path or in an unintended direction
- **Sneak timing,** in which events occur in an unexpected or conflicting sequence
- **Sneak indications,** which cause an ambiguous or false display of system operating conditions and thus can result in an undesired action by an operator or process
- **Sneak labels,** which incorrectly or imprecisely label system functions or events, such as system inputs, controls, displays, buses, etc. and thus may mislead an operator into applying an incorrect stimulus to the system

Hardware sneak circuits include[3] sneak paths, sneak opens, sneak timing, sneak indications, and sneak labels. Software sneak circuits include[3] sneak outputs, sneak inhibits, sneak timing, and sneak messages.

The final step is to recommend appropriate corrective action to resolve anomalies discovered by the analysis.[5]

Benefits: Unintended, unauthorized logic paths and control sequences are identified and removed prior to a system being fielded. These defects are not normally found by other testing and analysis methods.[1]

Limitations: Sneak circuit analysis is somewhat labor intensive and should only be applied to IA-critical and IA-related functions/entities. Use of an automated tool is required.[1]

References:

1. DEF STAN 00-41/Issue 3, Reliability and Maintainability, *MoD Guide to Practices and Procedures*, U.K. Ministry of Defence (MoD), June 25, 1993.
2. Herrmann, D., *Software Safety and Reliability: Techniques, Approaches and Standards of Key Industrial Sectors*, IEEE Computer Society Press, 1999.
3. IEC 61508-7, Functional Safety of Electrical/Electronic/Programmable Electronic Safety-Related Systems, Part 7: Overview of Techniques and Measures.
4. Raheja, D., *Assurance Technologies: Principles and Practices*, McGraw-Hill, 1991.
5. Storey, N., *Safety-Critical Computer Systems*, Addison-Wesley, 1996.
6. System Safety Society, *System Safety Analysis Handbook*, 2nd ed., July 1997.
7. Whetton, C., Maintainability and its influence on system safety, *Technology and Assessment of Safety-Critical Systems*, Springer-Verlag, 1994, 31–54.

B.1.19 Usability Analysis

Purpose: To enhance operational IA integrity by ensuring that software is easy to use so that effort by human users to obtain the required service is minimal[1]; prevent accidental induced or invited errors that could lead to a system failure or compromise.

Description: Human error is a principal cause of accidental serious system failures and compromises. The likelihood of such errors can be influenced by IA design features/techniques.[2] Usability analysis is a method of analyzing a system design to identify ways to eliminate or reduce the likelihood of accidental induced or invited errors. This method consists of three steps[2]: hierarchical task analysis, human error identification, and error reduction. During hierarchical task analysis, all human tasks, activities, and steps are identified for administrators, end users, and maintenance staff. This information is analyzed and recorded in a tabular format:

- **Stimulus** human received to take some action
- **Action** human takes in response to the stimulus
- **Feedback** human receives from taking the action

Next, each stimulus/action/feedback scenario is examined for opportunities or factors that could contribute to human error. Specific items examined include[2]:

- **Information presentation;** for example, the distinctiveness of different types of parameters and commands when they are displayed and entered, and the clarity of units of measure
- **Distractions** in the operational environment; for example, lighting, noise, motion, or vibration
- **Human factors;** for example, skill level, mental and physical fatigue, boredom, overload, and stress, ease of learning how to use the system, adequacy of warnings, alarms, and operator feedback

Finally, action is taken to eliminate or mitigate errors that have the highest likelihood and severity, by[2]:

- Implementing defense in depth
- Improved ergonomics
- Improved operational procedures and contingency plans
- Improved training

Many of the attributes evaluated relate to human factor engineering issues. Attributes should be evaluated under all operational modes/states and profiles. Usability analysis should be conducted on the requirements, design, and implementation of IA-critical and IA-related functions/entities. All stakeholders should be involved.

Benefits: Usability analysis is one of the few techniques to consider the operational environment and as such helps to reduce the likelihood of accidental induced or invited errors.

Limitations: Participation by the end users and human factor engineers is critical.

References:

1. CE-1001-STD Rev. 1, Standard for Software Engineering of Safety Critical Software, CANDU Computer Systems Engineering Centre for Excellence, January 1995.
2. DEF STAN 00-41/Issue 3, Reliability and Maintainability, *MoD Guide to Practices and Procedures*, U.K. Ministry of Defence (MoD), June 25, 1993.
3. Hackos, J. and Redish, J., *User and Task Analysis for Interface Design*, John Wiley & Sons, 1998.
4. Hix, D. and Hartson, H., *Developing User Interfaces: Ensuring Usability Through Product and Process*, John Wiley & Sons, 1993.
5. Nielsen, J. and Mack, R., *Usability Inspection Methods*, John Wiley & Sons, 1994.

B.2 IA Design Techniques/Features

B.2.1 Access Control

Purpose: To protect IA-critical and IA-related systems, applications, and data by preventing unauthorized and unwarranted access to these resources.

Description: Access control is a set of design features that is implemented to control access to system resources, such as networks, computer systems, individual software applications, data, utilities, and peripherals such as printers. Access control consists of two main components: (1) access rights that define which people and processes can access which system resources, and (2) access privileges that define what these people and processes can do with or to the resources accessed.[2] Examples of access privileges are read, write, edit, delete, execute, copy, print, move, forward, distribute, etc. Access control rights and privileges can be defined on a need-to-know basis or by a security classification scheme. Access control rights and privileges are generally defined in a matrix format by user name, user roles, and local or global user groups. Access control is usually implemented through a combination of commercial operating system utilities and custom code. Two important aspects of implementing access control are

Exhibit 3 Information Assurance Design Techniques and Features

IA Design Techniques and Features	*C/R*	*Type*	*Life-cycle Phase in which Technique is Used*		
			Concept	*Development*	*Operations*
Access control	C2	SA, SE	x	x	x
Rights					
Privileges					
Account for all possible logic states	C2	SA, SE		x	x
Audit trail, security alarm	C2	SE	x	x	x
Authentication	C2	SA, SE	x	x	x
Biometrics					
Data origin					
Digital certificates					
Kerberos					
Mutual					
Peer entity					
Smartcards					
Unilateral					
Block recovery	C2	All		x	x
Confinement	C2	SA, SE		x	x
DTE					
Least privilege					
Wrappers					
Defense in depth	C2	All	x	x	x
Defensive programming	C2	All		x	x
Degraded-mode operations, graceful degradation	R2/ C2	All		x	x
Digital signatures	C2	SE		x	x
Nonrepudiation of origin					
Nonrepudiation of receipt					
Diversity	C2	SA, SE	x	x	x
Hardware					
Software					
Encryption	C2	SE	x	x	x
Asymmetric					
Symmetric					
Block					
Stream					
Hardware					
Software					
Error detection, correction	C2	All		x	x
Fail safe/secure, fail operational	R2/ C2	SA, SE		x	x
Fault tolerance	C2	All		x	x
Firewalls, filters	C2	SA, SE		x	x
Formal specifications, animated specifications	C2	SA, SE	x	x	x
Information hiding	C2	SA, SE		x	x

Exhibit 3 Information Assurance Design Techniques and Features (continued)

IA Design Techniques and Features	*C/R*	*Type*	*Life-cycle Phase in which Technique is Used*		
			Concept	*Development*	*Operations*
Intrusion detection, response	C2	SA, SE		x	x
Partitioning	C2	SA, SE	x	x	x
Hardware					
Software					
Logical					
Physical					
Plausibility checks	C2	All		x	x
Redundancy	C2	RE	x	x	x
Reliability allocation	C2	RE	x	x	
Secure protocols	C2	All		x	x
IPSec, NLS					
PEM, PGP, S/MIME					
SET					
SSL3, TLS1					
Virus scanners	C2	All			x

Source: Adapted from Herrmann, D., *Software Safety and Reliability: Techniques, Approaches and Standards of Key Industrial Sectors*, IEEE Computer Society Press, 1999.

(1) determining who has permission to define/change access control rights and privileges and (2) protecting the table that defines the access control rights and privileges from unauthorized manipulation and corruption (see Chapter 6, Exhibit 14).

Benefits: Access control provides a first layer of defense in protecting critical system resources.

Limitations: Effective implementation of access control depends on (1) taking the time to define a comprehensive set of access control rights and privileges, including permissions to create/change these definitions; (2) protecting the table containing these definitions from unauthorized manipulation and corruption; and (3) a robust authentication capability.[2]

References:

1. Blakley, B., *CORBA Security: An Introduction to Safe Computing with Objects*, Addison-Wesley, 1999.
2. Denning, D., *Information Warfare and Security*, Addison-Wesley, 1999.
3. Gollmann, D., *Computer Security*, John Wiley & Sons, 1999.
4. Gong, L., *Inside Java™ 2 Platform Security: Architecture, API Design and Implementation*, Addison-Wesley, 1999.
5. ISO/IEC 10164-9(1995-12), Information Technology, Open Systems Interconnection — Systems Management: Objects and Attributes for Access Control.
6. ISO/IEC 10181-3(1996-09), Information Technology, Open Systems Interconnection — Security Framework for Open Systems: Access Control Framework.
7. Rozenblit, M., *Security for Telecommunications Network Management*, IEEE, 1999.

B.2.2 Account for All Possible Logic States

Purpose: To prevent a system from entering unknown or undefined states, and thus potentially unstable states, which could compromise IA integrity.

Description: Mission-critical systems act upon and respond to a variety of inputs and commands that come from operators, sensors, actuators, and processes. Any given parameter can be in a finite number of states. The same holds true for a combination of parameters. These states can be specified in a truth table. For example, if two parameters are monitored together and they both can only be "on" or "off," there are four possible logic states that could be encountered. Hence, the software monitoring these two parameters should be designed to respond to each of the four logic states, no matter how unlikely they are to occur. This is easily accomplished through the use of a CASE statement. An extra layer of safety and security is provided by including an OTHERWISE clause to trap exceptions (see Chapter 6, Exhibit 15).

Benefits: This technique helps to ensure accurate and predictable system responses to all possible conditions and states, thereby lowering the likelihood of anomalous behavior. This technique is also useful for uncovering missing or incomplete requirements specifications and trapping transient faults.

Limitations: Some additional system resources are used by including the logic to handle all possible logic states. However, the cost is trivial when compared to the consequences of the potential hazards thus prevented.

References:

1. Herrmann, D., *Software Safety and Reliability: Techniques, Approaches and Standards of Key Industrial Sectors*, IEEE Computer Society Press, 1999.

B.2.3 Audit Trail, Security Alarm

Purpose: To capture evidence of the system resources accessed by a user or process to aid in tracing from original transactions forward or backward to their component transactions.

Description: An audit trail is a design feature that provides an ongoing system monitoring and logging function. An audit trail serves four purposes. First, it captures information about which people and processes accessed what system resources and when they did so. Second, it captures information about system states and transitions, the availability and loading of system resources, and the general "health" of the system. When abnormal events are logged, they trigger warnings and alarms so that action can be taken to prevent or minimize the effects of hazardous events. For example, an alarm may trigger the shutdown of an unstable nuclear power plant or the blocking of an intrusion attempt. The alarms may trigger a combination of automatic processes and operator alerts. Third, audit trail data is used to develop normal system and user profiles as well as attack profiles for intrusion detection systems. Fourth, audit trails are also used to reconstruct events during accident/incident investigation (see Chapter 6, Exhibit 16).

Benefits: An audit trail provides real-time and historical logs of system states, transitions, and resource usage. It is essential for safe, secure, and reliable system operation and for performing trend analysis and pattern recognition of anomalous events.

Limitations: The completeness of the events/states recorded and the timeliness in responding to anomalous events determine the effectiveness of the audit trail. An audit trail consumes system resources; thus, care should be exercised when determining what events to record and how frequently they should be recorded. A determination also has to be made about the interval at which audit trails should be archived and overwritten.

References:

1. Gollmann, D., *Computer Security*, John Wiley & Sons, 1999.
2. Rozenblit, M., *Security for Telecommunications Management*, IEEE, 1999.

B.2.4 Authentication

Purpose: To establish or prove the validity of a claimed identity of a user, process, or system.

Description: Authentication is a design feature that permits the claimed identity of a user, process, or system to be proven to and confirmed by a second party. Authentication is invoked prior to access control rights and privileges. A combination of parameters can be used to establish an identity, such as user name, password, biometric information, location, and traffic source. There are weaknesses associated with each of these parameters; thus, it is best to use a combination of parameters and not rely on any one alone. To protect the user and the system, authentication should be bidirectional; that is, the user should be authenticated to a system and a system should be authenticated to a user. The latter is an important step in preventing site switching and other security compromises while connected to the Internet.

Benefits: A strong authentication strategy is essential for implementing effective access control rights and privileges.

Limitations: The effectiveness of an authentication strategy is determined by (1) the selection of parameters to be verified, and (2) how stringent the verification process is. The goal is to minimize the number of false positives and false negatives.

References:

1. Blakley, B., *CORBA Security: An Introduction to Safe Computing with Objects*, Addison-Wesley, 1999.
2. Gollmann, D., *Computer Security*, John Wiley & Sons, 1999.
3. ISO/IEC 9594-8(1995-09), Information Technology — Open Systems Interconnection — The Directory: Authentication Framework, 2nd ed.
4. ISO/IEC 9798-1(1991-09), Information Technology — Security Techniques — Entity Authentication Mechanism, Part 1: General Model.
5. ISO/IEC 10181-2(1996-05), Information Technology — Open Systems Interconnection — Security Framework for Open Systems: Authentication Framework.
6. Oppliger, R., *Authentication Systems for Secure Networks*, Artech House, 1996.
7. Rozenblit, M., *Security for Telecommunications Management*, IEEE, 1999.
8. Tung, B., *Kerberos: A Network Authentication System*, Addison-Wesley, 1999.

B.2.5 Block Recovery

Purpose: To enhance IA integrity by recovering from an error and transitioning the system to a known safe and secure state.

Description: Block recovery is a design technique that provides correct functional operation in the presence of one or more errors.[2] For each critical module, a primary and secondary module (employing diversity) are developed. After the primary module executes, but before it performs any critical transactions, an acceptance test is run. This test checks for possible error conditions, such as runtime errors, excessive execution time, or mathematical errors, and performs plausibility checks.[4] If no error is detected, normal execution continues. If an error is detected, control is switched to the corresponding secondary module and another acceptance test is run. If no error is detected, normal execution resumes. However, if an error is detected, the system is reset either to a previous (backward block recovery) or future (forward block recovery) known safe and secure state.

In backward block recovery, if an error is detected, the system is reset to an earlier known safe state. This method implies that internal states are saved frequently at well-defined checkpoints. Global internal states can be saved or only those for critical functions. In forward block recovery, if an error is detected, the current state of the system is manipulated or forced into a future known safe state. This method is useful for real-time systems with small amounts of data and fast-changing internal states[2] (see Chapter 6, Exhibit 17).

Benefits: A system is quickly transitioned to a known safe state and the consequences of a failure are contained.[3]

Limitations: Potential vulnerability to common cause failures must be clearly understood in order to transition the system forward or backward far enough[4] (see also common cause failure analysis).

References:

1. Herrmann, D., *Software Safety and Reliability: Techniques, Approaches and Standards of Key Industrial Sectors*, IEEE Computer Society Press, 1999.
2. IEC 61508-7, Functional Safety of Electrical/Electronic/Programmable Electronic Safety-Related Systems, Part 7: Overview of Techniques and Measures.
3. Leveson, N., *Safeware: System Safety and Computers*, Addison-Wesley, 1995.
4. Storey, N., *Safety-Critical Computer Systems*, Addison-Wesley, 1996.

B.2.6 Confinement

Purpose: To restrict an untrusted program from accessing system resources and executing system processes.

Description: Confinement refers to a set of design features that purposely limit what an untrusted program can access and do. The intent is to prevent an untrusted program from exhibiting unknown and unauthorized behavior, such as:

- Accidentally or intentionally corrupting data
- Accidentally or intentionally triggering the execution of critical sequences

- Initiating a trapdoor or Trojan horse through which executables are misused or corrupted
- Opening a covert channel through which sensitive data is misappropriated

This is accomplished by giving the untrusted program access to the minimum set of system resources it needs to perform its function and no more.[4] Default settings and optional features are disabled. Confinement is particularly useful when COTS products are employed, given the prevalence of undocumented features.

Least privilege, domain and type enforcement (DTE), and wrappers are examples of confinement. In least privilege, child processes do not inherit the privileges of the parent processes. DTE is a confinement technique in which an attribute (called a domain) is associated with each subject (user or process) and another attribute (called a type) is associated with each object (system resource). A matrix is defined that specifies whether or not a particular mode of access to objects of type x is granted to subjects in domain y.[2] Wrappers encapsulate untrusted software to control invocation and add access control and monitoring functions.[3]

Benefits: Potential hazards resulting from the use of untrusted programs are minimized.

Limitations: Thorough analysis is needed to determine how to restrict the untrusted program and what to restrict it to. The effectiveness of confinement is dependent on this up-front analysis.

References:

1. Badger, L., Sterne, D., Sherman, D., and Walker, M., A domain and type enforcement UNIX prototype, *Usenix Computing Systems*, Vol. 9, 1996.
2. Fraser, T. and Badger, L., Ensuring continuity during dynamic security policy reconfiguration in DTE, *IEEE Symposium on Security and Privacy*, 1998, 15–26.
3. Fraser, T., Badger, L., and Feldman, M., Hardening COTS software with generic software wrappers, *IEEE Symposium on Security and Privacy*, 1999.
4. Lindquist, U. and Jonsson, E., A Map of Security Risks Associated with Using COTS, *Computer* (IEEE Computer Society), 31(6), 60–66, 1998.

B.2.7 Defense in Depth

Purpose: To provide several overlapping subsequent limiting barriers with respect to one safety or security threshold, so that the threshold can only be surpassed if all barriers have failed.[3]

Description: Defense in depth is a design technique that reflects common sense. In short, everything feasible is done to prepare for known potential hazards. Then, acknowledging that it is impossible to anticipate all hazards, especially unusual combinations or sequences of events, extra layers of safety and security are implemented through multiple complementary design techniques and features such as those cited in Exhibit 3. For example, partitioning, information hiding, plausibility checks, and block recovery could be implemented in a system; four layers of protection are better than one (see Chapter 6, Exhibit 18).

Benefits: Defense in depth is one of the few techniques that targets potential unknown and unforeseen hazards.

Limitations: There are some additional resources used when implementing defense in depth. However, the cost is trivial when compared to the consequences of the potential hazards thus prevented.

References:

1. CE-1001-STD Rev. 1, Standard for Software Engineering of Safety Critical Software, CANDU Computer Systems Engineering Centre for Excellence, January 1995.
2. Herrmann, D., *Software Safety and Reliability: Techniques, Approaches and Standards of Key Industrial Sectors*, IEEE Computer Society Press, 1999.
3. IEC 60880(1986-09), Software for Computers in Safety Systems of Nuclear Power Stations.

B.2.8 Defensive Programming

Purpose: To prevent system failures or compromises by detecting errors in control flow, data flow, and data during execution and reacting in a predetermined and acceptable manner.[1]

Description: Defensive programming is a set of design techniques in which critical system parameters and requests to transition system states are verified before acting upon them. The intent is to develop software that correctly accommodates design or operational shortcomings. This involves incorporating a degree of fault/failure tolerance using software diversity and stringent checking of I/O, data, and commands.[2] Defensive programming techniques include[1]:

- Plausibility and range checks on inputs and intermediate variables that affect physical parameters of the system
- Regular automatic checking of the system and software configuration to verify that it is correct and complete
- Plausibility and range checks on output variables
- Monitoring system state changes
- Checking the type, dimension, and range of parameters at procedure entry

Benefits: Defensive programming results in a more robust system architecture and protection from software design errors and failures in the operational environment.

Limitations: Defensive programming increases the complexity of software supportability.

References:

1. IEC 61508-7, Functional Safety of Electrical/Electronic/Programmable Electronic Safety-Related Systems, Part 7: Overview of Techniques and Measures.
2. NASA GB-1740.13.96, *Guidebook for Safety-Critical Software — Analysis and Development*, NASA Glenn Research Center, Office of System Safety and Mission Assurance, 1996.
3. Storey, N., *Safety-Critical Computer Systems*, Addison-Wesley, 1996.

B.2.9 Degraded-Mode Operations, Graceful Degradation

Purpose: To ensure that critical system functionality is maintained in the presence of one or more failures.[1]

Description: High-integrity, mission-critical systems can rarely cease operation when an error situation is encountered; they must maintain some minimum level of functionality, usually referred to as degraded-mode operations or graceful degradation of service. During the design and development of high-integrity, mission-critical systems, this minimum required set of functionality should be identified, along with the conditions under which the system should transition to this mode. Degraded-mode operations should include provisions for the following items at a minimum[2]:

- Notifying operational staff and end users that the system has transitioned to degraded-mode operations
- Error handling
- Logging and generation of warning messages
- Reduction of processing load (execute only core functionality)
- Masking of nonessential interrupts
- Signals to external world to slow down inputs
- Trace of system state to facilitate post-event analysis
- Specification of the conditions required to return to normal operations

Systems should be designed to ensure that the specified functionality set will be operational in the presence of one or more failures. A maximum time interval during which a system is allowed to remain in degraded-mode operations should be defined.

Benefits: Degraded-mode operations provides an intermediate state between full operation and system shutdown. This allows the minimum priority system functionality to be maintained until corrective action can be taken.

Limitations: Degraded-mode operations only provides a temporary response to system or component failures.

References:

1. IEC 61508-7, Functional Safety of Electrical/Electronic/Programmable Electronic Safety-Related Systems, Part 7: Overview of Techniques and Measures.
2. NASA GB-1740.13.96, *Guidebook for Safety-Critical Software — Analysis and Development*, NASA Glenn Research Center, Office of System Safety and Mission Assurance, 1996.
3. Storey, N., *Safety-Critical Computer Systems*, Addison-Wesley, 1996.

B.2.10 Digital Signatures

Purpose: To provide reasonable evidence of the true sender of an electronic message or document.

Description: A digital signature is a unique block of data that is generated according to a specific algorithm and then attached to an electronic document or message. The block of data is associated with a particular individual.

Therefore, the recipient or an independent third party can verify the sender. Digital signatures establish the source of a message or document, and provide a reasonable degree of nonrepudiation. Digital signatures are created using public key encryption, such as a RSA hashing function. A signature generation algorithm and a signature verification algorithm are involved. The initial Digital Signature Standard (DSS) was established in FIPS PUB 186 in May 1994.[2]

Benefits: Digital signatures, while not 100 percent foolproof, provide a reasonable degree of confidence about the true sender of an electronic message or document.

Limitations: Digital signatures help to establish the identity of a sender of a document or message. However, they do not necessarily prove that the sender created the contents of the document or message.[1] For example, it is very easy to edit forwarded e-mails. Digital signatures consume additional system resources and require that a reliable key management process be followed.

References:

1. Denning, D., *Information Warfare and Security*, Addison-Wesley, 1999.
2. FIPS PUB 186, Digital Signature Standard (DSS), National Institute of Standards and Technology (NIST), U.S. Department of Commerce, May 1994.
3. Ford, W. and Baum, M., *Secure Electronic Commerce: Building the Infrastructure for Digital Signatures and Encryption*, Prentice-Hall, 1997.
4. ISO/IEC 9796(1991-09), Information Technology — Security Techniques — Digital Signature Scheme Giving Message Recovery.
5. Rozenblit, M., *Security for Telecommunications Network Management*, IEEE, 1999.

B.2.11 Diversity

Purpose: To enhance IA integrity by detecting and preventing systematic failures.

Description: Diversity is a design technique in which multiple different means are used to perform a required function or solve the same problem. Diversity can be implemented in hardware or software. For software, this means developing more than one algorithm to implement a solution. The results from each algorithm are compared and, if they agree, the appropriate action is taken. Depending on the criticality of the system, 100 percent agreement or majority agreement may be implemented; if the results do not agree, error detection and recovery algorithms take control.[4] Diversity can be implemented at several stages during the life cycle[1]:

- Development of diverse designs by independent teams
- Development of diverse source code in two or more different languages
- Generation of diverse object code by two or more different compilers
- Implementation of diverse object code by using two or more different linking and loading utilities

Benefits: Diversity limits the potential for common cause and systematic failures.

Limitations: Diversity may complicate supportability issues and synchronization between diverse components operating in parallel.[1]

References:

1. DEF STAN 00-55, Requirements for Safety-Related Software in Defence Equipment, Part 1: Requirements, U.K. Ministry of Defence (MoD), August 1, 1997.
2. DEF STAN 00-55, Requirements for Safety-Related Software in Defence Equipment, Part 2: Guidance, U.K. Ministry of Defence (MoD), August 1, 1997.
3. IEC 61508-7, Functional Safety of Electrical/Electronic/Programmable Electronic Safety-Related Systems, Part 7: Overview of Techniques and Measures.
4. Herrmann, D., *Software Safety and Reliability: Techniques, Approaches and Standards of Key Industrial Sectors*, IEEE Computer Society Press, 1999.
5. Leveson, N., *Safeware: System Safety and Computers*, Addison-Wesley, 1995.
6. Storey, N., *Safety-Critical Computer Systems*, Addison-Wesley, 1996.

B.2.12 Encryption

Purpose: To provide confidentiality for information while it is stored and transmitted.

Description: Encryption provides one layer of protection to sensitive data by making the data unintelligible to all but the intended recipients. Encryption consists of a mathematically based algorithm, which specifies the steps involved in transforming the data, and a key, which represents a specific instance of the algorithm. The keys may be public/private (asymmetric) or secret (symmetric), and are changed frequently; in contrast, the algorithm remains constant. Encryption can be implemented in hardware or software and through the use of block or stream ciphers. Encryption predates computers and can be implemented manually. A variety of different encryption algorithms with varying key types and lengths are available today. The goal is to select the encryption algorithm and mode appropriate for the specific application, operational environment, and level of confidentiality/protection needed (see Chapter 6, Exhibits 19 and 20).

Benefits: Given that the Internet is basically a big party-line, encryption provides one means of protecting the confidentiality of information that traverses it. One challenge is to determine the correct layer(s) in the ISO OSI and TCP/IP reference models in which to implement encryption.

Limitations: Encryption consumes additional system resources. Effective implementation requires staff training and following a reliable key management process. Note, however, that encryption provides temporary confidentiality because all encryption algorithms and keys can be broken — it is just a matter of time. With today's rapid increases in processing power, the times are getting shorter and shorter. Also, encryption does not ensure data integrity.

References:

1. Denning, D., *Cryptography and Data Security*, Addison-Wesley, 1982.
2. ISO/IEC 9797(1994-04), Information Technology — Security Techniques — Data Integrity Measures Using a Cryptographic Check Function Employing a Block Cipher Algorithm.
3. ISO/IEC 9798-2(1994-12), Information Technology — Security Techniques — Entity Authentication Mechanisms — Part 2: Mechanisms Using Symmetric Encipherment Algorithms.

4. ISO/IEC 9798-3(1993-11), Information Technology — Security Techniques — Entity Authentication Mechanisms — Part 3: Entity Authentication Using a Public Key Algorithm.
5. ISO/IEC 9798-4(1995-03), Information Technology — Security Techniques — Entity Authentication Mechanisms — Part 4: Mechanisms Using a Cryptographic Check Function.
6. ISO/IEC 10118-1(1994-10), Information Technology — Security Techniques — Hash Functions — Part 1: General.
7. ISO/IEC 10118-2(1994-10), Information Technology — Security Techniques — Hash Functions — Part 2: Hashing Functions Using an n-bit Block Cipher Algorithm.
8. ISO/IEC 11770-1(1997-01), Information Technology — Security Techniques — Key Management — Part 1: Framework.
9. ISO/IEC 11770-2(1996-04), Information Technology — Security Techniques — Key Management — Part 2: Mechanisms Using Asymmetric Techniques.
10. Menezes, A., Van Oorschot, P., and Vanstone, S., *Handbook of Applied Cryptography*, CRC Press, 1996.
11. Kippenhahn, R., *Code Breaking: A History and Exploration*, Overlook, 1999.
12. Schneier, B., *Applied Cryptography: Protocols, Algorithms, and Source Code in C*, 2nd ed., John Wiley & Sons, 1995.
13. Stallings, W., *Cryptography and Network Security*, 2nd ed., Prentice-Hall, 1998.

B.2.13 Error Detection/Correction

Purpose: To increase data integrity.

Description: Error detection/correction algorithms are used to increase data integrity during the transmission of data within and among networks and system integrity during execution of application software. At the network level, error detection/correction algorithms examine data to determine if any data was **accidentally** corrupted or lost, and to discover if any unauthorized changes were **intentionally** made to the data.[3] These errors are compensated for by self-correcting codes at the receiving end or requests for retransmission. At the application software level, error detection/correction algorithms detect anomalous or illegal modes/states, parameters, etc. and initiate the appropriate error handling routines. It is unlikely that corrective action will be implemented for all potential error conditions due to program size, response time, and schedule and budget constraints; hence, the focus should be on IA-critical and IA-related functions/entities.

Benefits: The severity of the consequences of an error, fault, or failure is minimized by early detection and recovery. Automated error detection and correction is faster and generally more reliable than that which involves humans.

Limitations: The effectiveness of this technique is directly proportional to the thoroughness by which potential error conditions have been identified and compensated for by the design.

References:

1. IEC 61508-7, Functional Safety of Electrical/Electronic/Programmable Electronic Safety-Related Systems, Part 7: Overview of Techniques and Measures.
2. Knight, J., Elder, M., and Du, X., Error recovery in critical infrastructure systems, *Computer Security, Dependability, and Assurance: From Needs to Solutions*, IEEE, 1999, 49–71.

3. Morris, D., *Introduction to Communications Command and Control Systems*, Pergamon Press, 1977.
4. Storey, N., *Safety-Critical Computer Systems*, Addison-Wesley, 1996.

B.2.14 Fail Safe/Secure, Fail Operational

Purpose: To ensure that a system remains in a known safe and secure state following an irrecoverable failure.

Description: Fail safe/secure and fail operational are IA design techniques that ensure that a system remains in a known safe and secure state following an irrecoverable failure. To fail safe or secure means that a component automatically places itself in a safe and secure mode/state in the event of a failure. In many instances, known safe and secure default values are assumed. Then, the system is brought to a safe and secure mode/state by shutting it down. To fail operational means that a system or component continues to provide limited critical functionality in the event of a failure; in some instances, a system cannot simply shut down.

Fail safe/secure and fail operational ensure that a system responds predictably to failures by making proactive design decisions. The first step is to identify all possible failure modes. This is done by developing transaction paths and using IA analysis techniques such as FTA, FMECA, and HAZOP studies. Next, the appropriate response to each failure is specified so that the system will remain in a known safe and secure state.

Benefits: Planning for and implementing provisions for fail safe or fail operational modes reduces the likelihood that unplanned events will occur.

Limitations: A comprehensive set of potential failure modes must be identified, particularly those that effect IA-critical and IA-related functions and entities.

References:

1. Bishop, P. and Bloomfield, R., *The SHIP Safety Case Approach*, Adelard, 1995.
2. Herrmann, D., *Software Safety and Reliability: Techniques, Approaches, and Standards of Key Industrial Sectors*, IEEE Computer Society Press, 1999.
3. Leveson, N., *Safeware: System Safety and Computers*, Addison-Wesley, 1995.
4. McDermid, J., Issues in the development of safety-critical systems, *Safety Critical Systems*, Chapman & Hall, 1993, 16–42.
5. Storey, N., *Safety-Critical Computer Systems*, Addison-Wesley, 1996.

B.2.15 Fault Tolerance

Purpose: To provide continued correct execution in the presence of a limited number of hardware or software faults.[1–5]

Description: Fault tolerance is a category of IA design techniques that focuses on containing and mitigating the consequences of faults, rather than preventing them. There are three types of fault tolerance: system fault tolerance, hardware fault tolerance, and software fault tolerance. Hardware fault tolerance is usually implemented through redundancy, diversity, power-on tests, BIT, and other monitoring functions. The concept is that if a primary component fails, a secondary component will take over and continue normal operations. Software fault tolerance is usually implemented through block recovery, diversity, error detection/correction, and other IA design techniques. The basic premise of software fault tolerance is that it is nearly impossible to develop software that is 100 percent free of defects; therefore, IA design techniques should be employed to detect and recover from errors while minimizing their consequences. System fault tolerance combines hardware and software fault tolerance, with software monitoring the health of both the hardware and the software. System fault tolerance should be employed for IA-critical and IA-related functions.

Benefits: Fault tolerant design is an effective method to increase system reliability and availability.

Limitations: Fault tolerance potentially increases the size, weight, and power consumption of a system that may conflict with specified constraints.

References:

1. IEC 60880(1986-09), Software for Computers in Safety Systems of Nuclear Power Stations.
2. IEC 61508-7, Functional Safety of Electrical/Electronic/Programmable Electronic Safety-Related Systems, Part 7: Overview of Techniques and Measures.
3. Levi, Shem-Tov and Agrawala, A., *Fault Tolerant System Design*, McGraw-Hill, 1994.
4. Lyu, M. (Ed.), *Software Fault Tolerance*, John Wiley & Sons, 1995.
5. Storey, N., *Safety-Critical Computer Systems*, Addison-Wesley, 1996.

B.2.16 Firewalls, Filters

Purpose: To block unwanted users, processes, and data from entering a network while protecting legitimate users, sensitive data, and processes.

Description: A firewall functions as a security gateway between two networks. A firewall can be implemented in software or a combination of hardware and software. It uses a variety of techniques, such as packet filtering, application level gateways, and circuit level gateways to prevent unauthorized users, processes, and data from entering the network. At the same time, a firewall protects legitimate users, processes, and data and allows them to interact with resources outside the firewall. In effect, a firewall implements access control between networks. The main functions of a firewall are[3,4]:

- Performing access control based on sender/receiver addresses
- Performing access control based on the service requested
- Hiding the internal network topology, addresses, and traffic from the outside world
- Checking incoming files for viruses
- Performing authentication based on traffic source
- Logging internet activities
- Blocking incoming junk e-mail and outgoing connections to objectional Web sites

Firewalls should be tested against potential threats, known vulnerabilities, content-based attacks, and specified protection profiles.[4]

Benefits: Firewalls are useful for preventing accidental or malicious intentional traffic from entering a network. The usefulness of firewalls in preventing intentional malicious traffic from entering a network appears to be more in the area of delaying its entry than preventing it altogether.[4] Consequently, firewalls must be used in conjunction with other defensive design features.

Limitations: Firewalls provide one layer of protection for IA-critical and IA-related systems and data. However, they are not 100 percent foolproof.

References:

1. Chapman, D. and Zwicky, E., *Building Internet Firewalls*, 1st ed., O'Reilly & Associates, 1995.
2. Cheswick, W. and Bellovin, S., *Firewalls and Internet Security*, Addison-Wesley, 1994.
3. Denning, D., *Information Warfare and Security*, Addison-Wesley, 1999.
4. Gollmann, D., *Computer Security*, John Wiley & Sons, 1999.

B.2.17 Formal Specifications, Animated Specifications

Purpose: To ensure correctness, consistency, completeness, and unambiguousness of the requirements and design for IA-critical and IA-related functions.

Description: Formal methods describe a system and its intended properties and performance using a fixed notation based on discrete mathematics, which can be subjected to mathematical analysis to detect incompleteness, inconsistencies, incorrectness, and ambiguousness.[6] The description can be analyzed by computer, similar to the syntax checking of a source program by a compiler, to display various aspects of system behavior.[6,7] Most formal methods provide a capability for stating assertions for pre- and post-conditions at various locations in a program.[3,4,8] Some of the more common formal methods used today include: B, calculus of communicating systems (CCS), communicating sequential processes (CSP), higher order logic (HOL), language for temporal ordering specification (LOTOS), OBJ, temporal logic, Vienna development method (VDM), and Z (see Chapter 6, Exhibit 21).

Benefits: The rigor imposed by formal methods exposes many gaps and inconsistencies in specifications and designs that would not be as visible when using other techniques. The animated models that can be developed from the specification and design help to clarify requirements and facilitate communication among different stakeholders.[7]

Limitations: The design team must be thoroughly trained in the formal method to implement it correctly. The use of an automated tool is required. Development life-cycle costs are equivalent to traditional development methods; however, more resources are used earlier in the life cycle. Given that more errors are found earlier in the life cycle with formal methods, when it is easier and cheaper to fix them, overall life-cycle costs are less.

References:

1. Bowen, J. and Hinchey, M., *High Integrity System Specification and Design*, IEEE Computer Society Press, 1999.
2. DEF STAN 00-55, Requirements for Safety-Related Software in Defence Equipment, Part 1: Requirements, U.K. Ministry of Defence (MoD), August 1, 1997.

3. Diller, A, *Z: An Introduction to Formal Methods*, 2nd ed., John Wiley & Sons, 1994.
4. Harry, A., *Formal Methods Fact File: VDM and Z*, John Wiley & Sons, 1996.
5. Heitmeyer, C. and Madrioli, D., *Formal Methods for Real-Time Computing*, John Wiley & Sons, 1996.
6. Herrmann, D., *Software Safety and Reliability: Techniques, Approaches and Standards of Key Industrial Sectors*, IEEE Computer Society Press, 1999.
7. IEC 61508-7, Functional Safety of Electrical/Electronic/Programmable Electronic Safety-Related Systems, Part 7: Overview of Techniques and Measures.
8. Ince, D., *An Introduction to Discrete Mathematics, Formal System Specification, and Z*, Oxford University Press, 1992.
9. Storey, N., *Safety-Critical Computer Systems*, Addison-Wesley, 1996.

B.2.18 Information Hiding

Purpose: To (1) prevent **accidental** access to and corruption of software and data, (2) minimize introduction of errors during maintenance and enhancements, (3) reduce the likelihood of CCFs, and (4) minimize fault propagation.

Description: Information hiding is an IA design technique developed by Dr. David Parnas that minimizes the interdependency or coupling of modules and maximizes the independence or cohesion of modules.[3] System functions, sets of data, and operations on that data are localized within a module. The interface to each software module is designed to reveal as little as possible about the module's inner workings.[4] This is accomplished by making the logic of each module and the data it utilizes as self-contained as possible.[3] In this way, if it is necessary to change the functions internal to one module, the resulting propagation of changes to other modules is minimized.

Benefits: The likelihood of common cause failures is reduced, fault propagation is minimized, and future maintenance and enhancements are facilitated.[3] Object-oriented designs are well suited for information hiding.[1,2]

Limitations: Information hiding requires more time up-front to analyze the design of modules and precise module and interface specifications.

References:

1. DEF STAN 00-55, Requirements for Safety-Related Software in Defence Equipment, Part 1: Requirements, U.K. Ministry of Defence (MoD), August 1, 1997.
2. DEF STAN 00-55, Requirements for Safety-Related Software in Defence Equipment, Part 2: Guidance, U.K. Ministry of Defence (MoD), August 1, 1997.
3. Herrmann, D., *Software Safety and Reliability: Techniques, Approaches and Standards of Key Industrial Sectors*, IEEE Computer Society Press, 1999.
4. IEC 61508-7, Functional Safety of Electrical/Electronic/Programmable Electronic Safety-Related Systems, Part 7: Overview of Techniques and Measures.
5. Parnas, D., On the criteria to be used in decomposing systems into modules, *Communications of the ACM*, December, 1053–1058, 1972.

B.2.19 Intrusion Detection and Response

Purpose: To recognize and respond to a security breach either as it is happening or immediately afterward.

Description: Intrusion detection is a design feature that takes over where firewalls leave off to provide another layer of protection for IA-critical and IA-related functions and data. Intrusion detection and response software looks for both insider and outsider attacks. Three types of algorithms are used to implement intrusion detection[3]:

1. **Statistical anomaly detection** analyzes audit trail data for abnormal system or user behavior.
2. **Rules-based detection** analyzes audit trail data for patterns that match known attack profiles.
3. **Hybrid detection** employs a combination of statistical and rules-based detection algorithms.

Intrusion detection algorithms search for indications of unusual activity that point to past, present, or impending misuse of system resources. Audit trails, keystroke trapping, traffic source, login history, and packet sniffers are employed to assist intrusion detection. Another approach to intrusion detection is to set up decoy servers and LANs that legitimate users would never access (*see also* Audit Trail).

Benefits: Intrusion detection and response systems, while not 100 percent foolproof, provide an extra layer of protection beyond firewalls, access control, and authentication. Intrusion detection and response systems serve as an early warning system, alerting operators and systems so that action can be taken quickly to prevent an attack or minimize its damage.

Limitations: Intrusion detection systems consume additional system resources. Care should be exercised in selecting the events to be monitored. The accuracy of the "normal" profiles determines the percentage of false positives and false negatives generated from statistical anomaly detection. Only known attack profiles are intercepted with rules-based detection.

References:

1. Escamilla, T., *Intrusion Detection: Security Beyond the Firewall*, John Wiley & Sons, 1998.
2. Gollmann, D., *Computer Security*, John Wiley & Sons, 1999.
3. Herrinshaw, C., Detecting attacks on networks, *Computer* (IEEE Computer Society), 30(12), 16–17, 1997.
4. Lehtinen, M. and Lear, A., Intrusion detection: managing the risk of connectivity, *IT Professional*, 1(6), 11–13, 1999.

B.2.20 Partitioning

Purpose: To enhance IA integrity by preventing non-IA-related functions/entities from **accidentally** or **intentionally** corrupting IA-critical functions/entities.

Description: Partitioning is an IA design technique that can be implemented in hardware or software. In the case of software, partitioning can be logical or physical. IA-critical and IA-related functions/entities are isolated from non-IA-related functions/entities. Both design and functionality are partitioned to prevent accidental and intentional interference, compromise, and corruption originating from non-IA-related functions/entities. Partitioning is often referred to as separability in the security community. Several national and international standards either mandate or highly recommend the use of partitioning.[1–7]

Benefits: Well-partitioned systems are easier to understand, verify, and maintain. Partitioning facilitates fault isolation and minimizes the potential for fault propagation. Partitioning helps to identify the most critical components so that resources can be more effectively concentrated on them.

Limitations: Partitioning requires complete interface specifications.

References:

1. CE-1001-STD Rev. 1, Standard for Software Engineering of Safety Critical Software, CANDU Computer Systems Engineering Centre for Excellence, January 1995.
2. DEF STAN 00-55, Requirements for Safety Related Software in Defence Equipment, Part 1: Requirements, U.K. Ministry of Defence (MoD), August 4, 1997.
3. EN 50128:1997, Railway Applications: Software for Railway Control and Protection Systems, The European Committee for Electrotechnical Standardization (CENELEC).
4. Development Guidelines for Vehicle Based Software, The Motor Industry Reliability Association (MISRA™), November 1994.
5. Herrmann, D., *Software Safety and Reliability: Techniques, Approaches, and Standards of Key Industrial Sectors*, IEEE Computer Society Press, 1999.
6. IEC 61508-7, Functional Safety of Electrical/Electronic/Programmable Electronic Safety-Related Systems, Part 7: Overview of Techniques and Measures.
7. NASA GB-1740.13.96, *Guidebook for Safety-Critical Software — Analyses and Development*, NASA Glenn Research Center, Office of Safety and Mission Assurance, 1996.

B.2.21 Plausibility Checks

Purpose: To enhance IA integrity by verifying the validity and legitimacy of critical parameters before acting upon them; detect errors early in the execution cycle to prevent them from progressing into system failures or compromises.

Description: Plausibility checks are an IA design technique. The basic approach is simple: checks are performed on parameters, before critical operations are performed, to verify that the value of the parameters are plausible and legal. Plausibility checks can be used to enhance safety, security, and reliability. Examples of checks that can be performed to enhance safety and reliability include[1,4]:

- Parameter size (number of bits, bytes, digits, etc.)
- Array bounds
- Counter values
- Parameter type verification
- Legitimate called from routine
- Timer values
- Assertions about parameter value, operational mode/state, and pre- and post-conditions
- Range checks of intermediate results

The specific parameters checked will vary by application. However, all parameters that affect IA-critical and IA-related functions/entities should be checked.

Benefits: Plausibility checks enhance the operational integrity of the system.

Limitations: None.

References:

1. DEF STAN 00-55, Requirements for Safety-Related Software in Defence Equipment, Part 1: Requirements, U.K. Ministry of Defence (MoD), August 1, 1997.
2. DEF STAN 00-55, Requirements for Safety-Related Software in Defence Equipment, Part 2: Guidance, U.K. Ministry of Defence (MoD), August 1, 1997.
3. Herrmann, D., *Software Safety and Reliability: Techniques, Approaches and Standards of Key Industrial Sectors*, IEEE Computer Society Press, 1999.
4. IEC 60880(1986-09), Software for Computers in Safety Systems of Nuclear Power Stations.
5. SEMSPLC Guidelines, Safety-Related Application Software for Programmable Logic Controllers, IEE Technical Guidelines 8:1996.

B.2.22 Redundancy

Purpose: To enhance hardware reliability and system availability.

Description: Redundancy is a fault tolerance design technique in which redundant hardware components are employed to increase hardware reliability and system availability. Secondary or redundant components function as hot or cold standbys, ready to assume primary functionality should the primary component fail or exhibit anomalous behavior. Redundancy is employed at the level and to the extent that is meaningful and practical for a given system and the criticality of its operation. This may include redundant memory, disk drives, servers, printers, processors, etc. Many real-time process control operations, especially those involving PLCs, employ triple modular redundancy (TMR).

Benefits: Redundancy helps to eliminate single points of failure.

Limitations: (1) Redundancy does not compensate for design flaws inherent in a component; all redundant components will contain the same error. (2) Redundancy is not applicable to software; the same design errors are simply replicated. Instead, diversity is employed.[2,3,6] (3) Care should be taken to ensure that redundant components are not subject to common cause failure modes.

References:

1. DEF STAN 00-41/Issue 3, Reliability and Maintainability, *MoD Guide to Practices and Procedures*, U.K. Ministry of Defence (MoD), June 25, 1993.
2. Herrmann, D., *Software Safety and Reliability: Techniques, Approaches, and Standards of Key Industrial Sectors*, IEEE Computer Society Press, 1999.
3. Leveson, N., *Safeware: System Safety and Computers*, Addison-Wesley, 1995.
4. O'Connor, P., *Practical Reliability Engineering*, 3rd ed., John Wiley & Sons, 1991.
5. SEMSPLC Guidelines, Safety-Related Application Software for Programmable Logic Controllers, IEE Technical Guidelines 8:1996.
6. Storey, N., *Safety-Critical Computer Systems*, Addison-Wesley, 1996.

B.2.23 Reliability Allocation

Purpose: To distribute reliability and maintainability requirements, derived from IA goals, among system entities.

Description: Reliability requirements are generally specified at the system level early in the life cycle. During architectural analysis, system reliability requirements are allocated to individual system components, including hardware, software, and communications equipment. It is usually necessary to perform trade-off studies to determine the optimum architecture that will meet reliability requirements. This may involve reassigning functionality between hardware and software components. FTA, FMECA, HAZOP studies, and reliability block diagrams provide input to the reliability allocation process. Where appropriate, separate reliability requirements may be specified for different types and consequences of failure[1]:

- The severity of the consequences of the failure
- Whether or not recovery from the failure is possible without operator intervention
- Whether or not a failure causes corruption of software or data
- The time required to recover from a failure

Benefits: If sufficient analysis is conducted to support the reliability allocation, the likelihood that reliability requirements will be met is greater. Also, it is more cost-effective to analyze and allocate reliability requirements early in the life cycle than to wait until after a system is developed to find out that it does not meet reliability requirements.

Limitations: The distinction between random hardware failures and systematic software failures must be maintained when allocating reliability requirements.

References:

1. DEF STAN 00-41/Issue 3, Reliability and Maintainability, *MoD Guide to Practices and Procedures*, U.K. Ministry of Defence (MoD), June 25, 1993.
2. DEF STAN 00-42, Reliability and Maintainability Assurance Guides, Part 2: Software, U.K. Ministry of Defence (MoD), September 1, 1997.
3. O'Connor, P., *Practical Reliability Engineering*, 3rd ed., John Wiley & Sons, 1991.

B.2.24 Secure Protocols

Purpose: To enhance the confidentiality of distributed data communication.

Description: A variety of protocols have recently been developed or are under development to enhance the confidentiality of information exchanged among distributed systems. Some examples include IPSec, NLS, PEM, PGP, S/MIME, SET, SSL3, and TLS1. IPSec and NLS provide network-level security. PEM, PGP, and S/MIME provide e-mail security. SSL3 and TLS1 provide security for distributed client/server applications. SET provides e-Commerce security. Each of these protocols is designed for a specific function and environment.

Benefits: These protocols provide an extra level of confidentiality for Internet transactions. The robustness of the protocols and the level of confidentiality provided vary.

Limitations: None of these protocols is 100 percent secure; they are too new and still evolving. The seamlessness with which these protocols can be implemented within an existing communications architecture varies.

References:

1. Doraswamy, N. and Harkins, D., *IPSec: The New Security Standard for the Internet, Intranet, and Virtual Private Networks*, Prentice-Hall, 1999.
2. Garfinkel, S., *PGP: Pretty Good Privacy*, 1st ed., O'Reilly & Associates, 1994.
3. Kaufman, E. and Newman, A., *Implementing IPSec*, John Wiley & Sons, 1999.
4. Merkow, M., Breithaupt, J., and Wheeler, K., *Building SET Applications for Secure Transactions*, John Wiley & Sons, 1998.
5. Oppliger, R., *Internet and Intranet Security*, Artech House, 1998.
6. Rozenblit, M., *Security for Telecommunications Management*, IEEE, 1999.
7. www.setco.org.

B.2.25 Virus Scanners

Purpose: To automatically detect and remove computer viruses before they are activated.

Description: Virus scan software scans boot sectors, memory, and computer files, looking for the presence of potentially malicious hidden code; for example, executables hidden in document files. Virus scanners look for known viruses and patterns that resemble potential viruses. Most scanners have the option of marking or cleansing files suspected of being infected. On occasion, the cleansing operation may not be successful; the virus is not contained or the original file is not recoverable.

Benefits: If virus scan software is executed frequently and kept up-to-date, a reasonable degree of protection is provided against known viruses.

Limitations: (1) Virus scanners only detect the presence of known viruses or patterns that resemble potential viruses; a new virus strain may go undetected. (2) Virus scan software must be updated constantly. (3) Most users consider themselves too busy to run or update virus scan software; they cannot be relied upon to do so. Hence, the execution and updating of virus scan software must be automatically linked to external events: power-up, time of day, receipt of foreign files, etc.

References:

1. Cohen, F., *A Short Course on Computer Viruses*, 2nd ed., John Wiley & Sons, 1994.
2. Slade, R., *Guide to Computer Viruses*, Springer-Verlag, 1994.
3. http://service.symantec.com.
4. www.mcafee.com.

B.3 IA Verification Techniques

B.3.1 Boundary Value Analysis

Purpose: To identify software errors that occur in IA-critical and IA-related functions/entities when processing at or beyond specified parameter limits.

Description: During boundary value analysis, test cases are designed that exercise the software's parameter processing algorithms. The system's response to specific input and output classes is evaluated, such as:

Exhibit 4 Information Assurance Verification Techniques

			Life-Cycle Phase in which Technique is Used		
IA Verification Techniques	*C/R*	*Type*	*Concept*	*Development*	*Operations*
Boundary value analysis	C3	All		x	x
Cleanroom	C3	All		x	
Control flow analysis[a]	C3	All		x	x
Data or information flow analysis[a]	C3	All		x	x
Equivalence class partitioning	C3	All		x	x
Formal proofs of correctness	C3	SA, SE	x	x	x
Interface testing	C3	All		x	x
Performance testing	C3	All		x	x
Probabilistic or statistical testing	C3	All		x	x
Regression testing	C3	All		x	x
Reliability estimation modeling	C3	RE		x	x
(IA) requirements traceability	C3	All	x	x	x
Review IA integrity case[a]	C3	All	x	x	x
Root cause analysis[a]	C3	All		x	x
Safety/security audits, reviews, and inspections	C3	SA, SE		x	x
Stress testing	C3	All		x	x
Testability analysis, fault injection, failure assertion	C3	All		x	x
Usability testing	C3	All		x	x

[a] These techniques can also be used during accident/incident investigation.

Source: Adapted from Herrmann, D., *Software Safety and Reliability: Techniques, Approaches and Standards of Key Industrial Sectors,* IEEE Computer Society Press, 1999.

- Parameter below minimum specified threshold
- Parameter at minimum specified threshold
- Parameter at maximum specified threshold
- Parameter over maximum specified threshold
- Parameter within specified minimum/maximum range

Zero or null parameters tend to be error-prone. Specific tests are warranted for the following conditions as well[1]:

- Zero divisor
- Blank ASCII characters
- Empty stack or list
- Full matrix
- Zero entry table

Boundary value analysis should be used to verify processing of authentication parameters, parameters that control IA-critical and IA-related functions, and potential buffer overflow conditions. Boundary value analysis complements plausibility checks.

The intent is to verify that the software responds to all parameters correctly, so that the system remains in a known safe and secure state. Error handling routines are triggered if a parameter is out of the specified range or normal processing continues if a parameter is within the specified range. Boundary value analysis can also be used to verify that the correct data type is being used: alphabetic, numeric, integer, real, signed, pointer, etc.

Benefits: Boundary value analysis enhances IA integrity by ensuring that data is within the specified valid range before operating upon it.

Limitations: None.

References:

1. IEC 61508-7, Functional Safety of Electrical/Electronic/Programmable Electronic Safety-Related Systems, Part 7: Overview of Techniques and Measures.
2. IEC 61704(1995-06), Guide to Test Methods for Dependability Assessment of Software.
3. Storey, N., *Safety-Critical Computer Systems*, Addison-Wesley, 1996.

B.3.2 Cleanroom

Purpose: To prevent defects from being introduced or remaining undetected in IA-critical and IA-related functions/entities through an evaluation of the completeness, consistency, correctness, and unambiguousness of requirements, design, and implementation.[1,2]

Description: Cleanroom is a full life-cycle verification process that supports the measurement and analysis of pre-release software reliability. Cleanroom analysis emphasizes the prevention of errors rather than their detection.[3] This approach takes a holistic view of software development by promoting top-down, stepwise refinement of the total design, with the correctness of that design being verified at each step.[3]

Benefits: The cleanroom process is cost-effective; it promotes the prevention and early detection of errors.

Limitations: Cleanroom analysis does not determine if performance and response time requirements will be met.

References:

1. DEF STAN 00-42/Issue 1, Reliability and Maintainability Guides, Part 2: Software, U.K. Ministry of Defense (MoD), September 1, 1997.
2. Dyer, M., *The Cleanroom Approach to Quality Software Development*, John Wiley & Sons, 1992.
3. Herrmann, D., *Software Safety and Reliability: Techniques, Approaches and Standards of Key Industrial Sectors*, IEEE Computer Society Press, 1999.
4. Prowell, S., Trammell, C., Linger, R., and Poore, J., *Cleanroom Software Engineering — Technology and Process*, Addison-Wesley, 1999.

B.3.3 Control Flow Analysis

Purpose: To uncover poor and incorrect program logic structures that could compromise IA integrity.

Description: Control flow analysis is a static analysis technique that examines the logical structure of a program. A digraph is used to represent the control flow through a software system. Unconditional jumps, unused and unreachable code, all of which could be used as an opening for an attack, are uncovered. The digraph is also reviewed for opportunities to optimize program structure and thereby enhance its maintainability. The emphasis is on verifying correct control flow to, from, and within IA-critical and IA-related functions/entities. Control flow analysis should be used in conjunction with data flow analysis to substantiate noninterference claims.

Benefits: Control flow analysis uncovers implementation errors before a product is tested or fielded. Inconsistencies between designs and implementations are also highlighted.

Limitations: Control flow analysis does not verify timing, capacity, or throughput requirements.

References:

1. IEC 61508-7, Functional Safety of Electrical/Electronic/Programmable Electronic Safety-Related Systems, Part 7: Overview of Techniques and Measures.
2. Storey, N., *Safety-Critical Computer Systems*, Addison-Wesley, 1996.

B.3.4 Data or Information Flow Analysis

Purpose: To uncover incorrect and unauthorized data transformations and operations that could compromise IA integrity.

Description: Data flow analysis is a static analysis technique that examines the access and change sequence of critical data elements. Using the digraph developed for control flow analysis, each distinct operation performed on a data element and each distinct transformation of that element are evaluated. Actual data flow is compared to required data flow to detect erroneous conditions and potential leakage, which could lead to a system compromise or failure. Examples of items to check during data flow analysis include[1,2]:

- Variables that are read before they are assigned a value
- Variables that are written more than once before they are read
- Variables that are written but never read
- Variables that are accidentally or intentionally overwritten
- Variables that are accidentally or incorrectly read (framing, addressing errors, etc.) or modified

The emphasis is on verifying correct data flow to, from, and within IA-critical and IA-related functions/entities. Data flow analysis should be used in conjunction with control flow analysis to substantiate noninterference claims.

Benefits: Data flow analysis uncovers incorrect and unauthorized data transformations and operations before a product is tested or fielded. Inconsistencies between designs and implementations are also highlighted.

Limitations: Data flow analysis does not verify timing, capacity, or throughput requirements.

References:

1. IEC 61508-7, Functional Safety of Electrical/Electronic/Programmable Electronic Safety-Related Systems, Part 7: Overview of Techniques and Measures.
2. Storey, N., *Safety-Critical Computer Systems*, Addison-Wesley, 1996.

B.3.5 Equivalence Class Partitioning

Purpose: To identify the minimum set of test cases and test data that will adequately test each input domain.

Description: During equivalence class partitioning, the set of all possible test cases is examined to determine which test cases and data are unique or redundant, in that they test the same functionality or logic path. The intent is to obtain the highest possible test coverage with the least possible number of test cases. Input partitions can be derived from the requirements and the internal structure of a program.[1] In the IA domain, at least one test case should be taken from each equivalence class for IA-critical and IA-related functions/entities.

Benefits: Testing activities are more efficient when equivalence class partitioning is employed.

Limitations: A thorough understanding of the system design and its functionality are needed to perform equivalence class partitioning. Several standard algorithms have been developed to assist this process.

References:

1. IEC 61508-7, Functional Safety of Electrical/Electronic/Programmable Electronic Safety-Related Systems, Part 7: Overview of Techniques and Measures.
2. IEC 61704(1995-06), Guide to Test Methods for Dependability Assessment of Software.

B.3.6 Formal Proofs of Correctness

Purpose: To prove that the requirements, design, and implementation of IA-critical and IA-related functions/entities are correct, complete, unambiguous, and consistent.

Description: Formal mathematical proofs are developed from formal specifications to prove that the specifications and corresponding design and implementation are correct, complete, unambiguous, and consistent. The proofs demonstrate that a program transfers pre-conditions into post-conditions according to the set of specified logical rules. System behavior under normal, abnormal, and exception conditions is verified. The completeness of specifications in regard to logic states, data definitions and operations, timing, termination, etc. is demonstrated. Formal proofs are developed for IA-critical and IA-related functions/entities. For example, formal proofs could be developed to demonstrate that the access control rules do not allow any unintended inferred access control privileges or information flow. (As a historical note, the *Orange Book* required formal proofs of correctness for evaluation class A-1 systems.) The structure of the proof will correspond to the formal method chosen.

Benefits: Formal proofs are a comprehensive ongoing verification activity and provide evidence for the IA integrity case.

Limitations: The thoroughness and accuracy of the proof determines its effectiveness. An automated tool must be used in most cases.

References:

1. Bowen, J. and Hinchey, M., *High Integrity System Specification and Design*, IEEE Computer Society Press, 1999.
2. Diller, A., *Z: An Introduction to Formal Methods*, 2nd ed., John Wiley & Sons, 1994.
3. Harry, A., *Formal Methods Fact File: VDM and Z*, John Wiley & Sons, 1996.
4. Heitmeyer, C. and Mandrioli, D., *Formal Methods for Real-Time Computing*, John Wiley & Sons, 1996.
5. IEC 61508-7, Functional Safety of Electrical/Electronic/Programmable Electronic Safety-Related Systems, Part 7: Overview of Techniques and Measures.
6. Ince, D., *An Introduction to Discrete Mathematics, Formal System Specification, and Z*, Oxford University Press, 1992.
7. Storey, N., *Safety-Critical Computer Systems*, Addison-Wesley, 1996.

B.3.7 Interface Testing

Purpose: To verify that interface requirements are correct and that interfaces have been implemented correctly.

Description: Interface testing verifies that hardware/software, system software/application software, and application software/application software interfaces work correctly, as specified. Interface testing is used to verify that the interfaces between IA-critical, IA-related, and non-IA-related functions/entities are correct, especially if the design incorporates partitioning or information hiding. Different types of parameters are passed under varying system loads and states. Snapshots of pre- and post-conditions are examined. Examples of items to evaluate during interface testing include[2]:

- Detection and handling of failure modes
- Response to out-of-range values
- Response to not receiving a specified input
- Handling of time-out conditions
- Response to inputs that are received too early, too late, or out of sequence
- Responses to minimum and maximum input arrival rates
- Responses to masked or disabled interrupts
- Responses to outputs that are produced faster than specified
- Responses to inputs that are received during initialization, shutdown, or while a system is offline

Benefits: System integration errors are detected prior to a system being fielded.

Limitations: Interface testing must be conducted in the operational environment or a simulated operational environment to yield valid results.

References:

1. DEF STAN 00-55, Requirements for Safety-Related Software in Defence Equipment, Part 1: Requirements, U.K. Ministry of Defence (MoD), August 1, 1997.

2. DEF STAN 00-55, Requirements for Safety-Related Software in Defence Equipment, Part 2: Guidance, U.K. Ministry of Defence (MoD), August 1, 1997.
3. IEC 61508-7, Functional Safety of Electrical/Electronic/Programmable Electronic Safety-Related Systems, Part 7: Overview of Techniques and Measures.
4. System Safety Society, *System Safety Analysis Handbook*, 2nd ed., July 1997.

B.3.8 Performance Testing

Purpose: To verify whether or not a system will meet stated performance requirements and that these requirements are correct.

Description: Performance testing exercises a system under varied loads and operational modes/states to determine if response time, capacity, and throughput requirements will be met. That is, the successful implementation of nonfunctional requirements and the absence of resource contention (memory, processor speed, capacity, I/O buses, communications bandwidth, storage, etc.) is verified. Items evaluated include[1,2]:

- Interactions between system processes
- Resource usage by each process
- Distribution of demands placed upon the system under average and worst-case conditions
- Mean and worse-case throughput and response times for individual system functions
- Real-time response time and throughput tests

Not meeting response time, capacity, and throughput requirements can have a major impact on IA integrity, such as causing a system failure or compromise. Hence, the emphasis in performance testing should be on IA-critical and IA-related functions/entities. Performance testing complements response time, memory, and constraint analysis and should be supplemented by stress testing.

Benefits: Performance shortfalls that may contribute to safety, security, and reliability failures are identified prior to a system being fielded.

Limitations: Performance testing must be conducted in the operational environment or a simulated operational environment to yield valid results.

References:

1. DEF STAN 00-42/Issue 1, Reliability and Maintainability Guides, Part 2: Software, U.K. Ministry of Defense (MoD), September 1, 1997.
2. IEC 61508-7, Functional Safety of Electrical/Electronic/Programmable Electronic Safety-Related Systems, Part 7: Overview of Techniques and Measures.

B.3.9 Probabilistic or Statistical Testing

Purpose: To provide a quantitative assessment of operational IA integrity; verify design integrity against operational profiles.

Description: During probabilistic or statistical testing, test cases are developed from operational profiles which reflect how different classes of users will use a system, the type and frequency of transactions performed, the anticipated system loading, etc. That is, test cases are statistically similar to or mimic the in-service environment. Parameters and conditions that activate IA-critical and IA-related functions/entities, in particular fault tolerant, fail safe/secure, and fail operational features, are exercised. Continuous-mode and demand-mode functions are tested.[4] Test cases are designed to catch random and systematic failures.[3] The test interval must be several times longer than the estimated MTBF to yield valid results.[2] Probabilistic testing should be supplemented by simulation and specification animation.

Benefits: Probabilistic testing yields reliability measures that correspond to how a system is expected to be used. Greater weight is given to the correct operation of transactions that are performed frequently and considered essential than those that are performed infrequently and are not essential. This approach contrasts with typical software reliability models, which treat all errors equally. Other values can be derived from these measures as well, including[3]:

- Probability of failure free operation
- Probability of system survival
- System availability
- (Updated) MTBF
- Probability of safe and secure operation

Limitations: Effective probabilistic testing is dependent on an accurate and complete set of operational profiles.

References:

1. BS5760 Part 8, Guide to the Assessment of Reliability of Systems Containing Software, British Standards Institution (BSI), October 1998.
2. DEF STAN 00-42/Issue 1, Reliability and Maintainability Guides, Part 2: Software, U.K. Ministry of Defense (MoD), September 1, 1997.
3. IEC 61508-7, Functional Safety of Electrical/Electronic/Programmable Electronic Safety-Related Systems, Part 7: Overview of Techniques and Measures.

B.3.10 Regression Testing

Purpose: To verify that changes and enhancements have been implemented correctly and that they do not introduce new errors or affect IA integrity.

Description: After a change or enhancement is implemented, a subset of the original test cases is executed. The results are compared with the original results to ensure stable and predictable system behavior after the change. In particular, regression testing should verify that changes and enhancements have not had an adverse effect on threat control measures. Regression testing should be performed in conjunction with change impact analysis.

Benefits: Regression testing minimizes the potential for unexpected system behavior following changes and enhancements.

Limitations: Test cases must be selected carefully so that both local and global effects of the changes or enhancements are verified.

References:

1. Beizer, B., *Software Testing Techniques*, International Thomson Press, 1990.
2. Kaner, C., *Testing Computer Software*, 2nd ed., John Wiley & Sons, 1993.
3. Kung, D., Hsia, P., and Gao, J., *Testing Object-Oriented Software*, IEEE Computer Society Press, 1998.
4. NASA GB-1740.13.96, *Guidebook for Safety-Critical Software — Analysis and Development*, NASA Glenn Research Center, Office of System Safety and Mission Assurance, 1996.
5. Perry, W., *Effective Methods for Software Testing*, 2nd ed., John Wiley & Sons, 1999.

B.3.11 Reliability Estimation Modeling

Purpose: To estimate software reliability for the present or some future time.

Description: A generic ten-step process is followed for estimating software reliability; the process uses the outputs of several IA analysis (Exhibit 2) and verification techniques:

1. Identify the software application being evaluated.
2. Derive the reliability requirement for this software component from the system reliability allocation.
3. Define failure modes and conditions.
4. Define operational environment and profiles.
5. Define test cases and procedures that correspond to the operational environment and profiles.
6. Select appropriate software reliability models.
7. Collect data from test results.
8. Estimate parameters from historical data.
9. Validate the model.
10. Use the model to estimate reliability for this software component.

Some of the more common reliability estimation models include: Duane, general exponential, Musa basic, Musa logarithmic, Littlewood/Verrall, and Schneidwind.

Note that software reliability is necessary to achieve IA integrity. Software must be reliable for security and safety functions to perform correctly.

Benefits: These models are useful in estimating how much maintenance and support will be required once a product is fielded.

Limitations: All of these models are used late in the life cycle; the software must be operational. Several of them assume that no new faults are introduced during maintenance activities, which is rarely the case. None of these models accommodate data derived from qualitative assessments or static analysis techniques.

References:

1. ANSI/AIAA R-013-1992, Recommended Practice for Software Reliability.
2. BS5760 Part 8, Guide to the Assessment of Reliability of Systems Containing Software, British Standards Institution (BSI), October 1998.

3. DEF STAN 00-42, Reliability and Maintainability Assurance Guides, Part 2: Software, U.K. Ministry of Defence, 1998.
4. IEEE Std. 982.1-1988, IEEE Standard Dictionary of Measures to Produce Reliable Software.*
5. IEEE Std. 982.2-1988, Guide for the Use of the IEEE Standard Dictionary of Measures to Produce Reliable Software.
6. Lyu, M. (Ed.), *Handbook of Software Reliability Engineering*, McGraw-Hill, 1996.

B.3.12 (IA) Requirements Traceability

Purpose: To verify that (1) all safety, reliability, and security requirements derived from IA goals are correct; (2) verify that all safety, reliability, and security requirements have been implemented correctly; and (3) verify that no additional unspecified or unintended capabilities have been introduced.

Description: Requirements traceability demonstrates that all requirements have been satisfied at each milestone during the life cycle. Requirements traceability is bidirectional; one should be able to (1) trace each requirement forward to its implementation in the design and source code, and (2) trace backward from the source code through the design to the requirements specification. Requirements traceability is generally captured in a tabular format. Backward traceability analysis is useful for finding unspecified or unintended functionality that has been accidentally implemented, while forward traceability analysis identifies specified requirements that have not been implemented or are incorrect, incomplete, or inconsistent.

Benefits: Requirements traceability helps to ensure that the product delivered is the product specified. Requirements traceability facilitates the development of test cases, other verification activities, and change impact analysis.

Limitations: The use of an automated tool is required. The degree of specificity in citing design and source code modules that implement a given requirement determines the effectiveness of the traceability analysis.

References:

1. DEF STAN 00-55, Requirements for Safety-Related Software in Defence Equipment, Part 1: Requirements, U.K. Ministry of Defence (MoD), August 1, 1997.
2. DEF STAN 00-55, Requirements for Safety-Related Software in Defence Equipment, Part 2: Guidance, U.K. Ministry of Defence (MoD), August 1, 1997.
3. Kotonya, G. and Sommerville, I., *Requirements Engineering: Processes and Techniques*, John Wiley & Sons, 1998.
4. Sommerville, I. and Sawyer, P., *Requirements Engineering: A Good Practice Guide*, John Wiley & Sons, 1997.
5. Thayer, R. and Dorfman, M., *Software Requirements Engineering*, 2nd ed., IEEE Computer Society Press, 1997.

B.3.13 Review IA Integrity Case

Purpose: To determine if the claims made about IA integrity are justified by the supporting arguments and evidence.

* Note that this standard began an update cycle in late 1999.

Description: The IA integrity case demonstrates that all IA goals and requirements have been achieved or that appropriate progress is being made toward achieving them. Evidence is reviewed to verify that it is complete, accurate, and current, including:

- Results from safety and security audits
- Results from vulnerability and threat analyses
- Reviews of critical threat zones in relation to threat control measures
- Results from static analysis activities
- Results from statistical testing based on operational profiles
- Results from performance testing
- Claims based on previous in-service experience
- Analysis of the impact on IA integrity from ASICs and reused software[1]

Evidence is reviewed to verify that the system and software engineering process is appropriate, such as[1,2]:

- Claims made that the methods, techniques (Exhibits 2, 3, and 4), and procedures used were followed correctly and are adequate
- Claims made that the analysis and interpretation of results from static and dynamic analyses are correct
- Justification for the OS, utilities, compiler, and automated tools used
- Justification of personnel competency
- Justification of the adequacy of IA verification activities

The IA integrity case is evaluated throughout the life cycle, as evidence is accumulated, to monitor that progress is being made toward meeting IA goals or identify the need for corrective action (*see also* Develop IA Integrity Case).

Benefits: The formality of reviewing an IA integrity case helps system designers and developers be more thorough when addressing IA integrity issues. Organized and complete IA integrity cases help Certification Authorities perform a more effective and thorough assessment.

Limitations: IA integrity cases must be succinct and organized in a logical manner to be useful.

References:

1. DEF STAN 00-42, Reliability and Maintainability Assurance Guides, Part 2: Software, U.K. Ministry of Defense (MoD), September 1, 1997.
2. DEF STAN 00-55, Requirements for Safety-Related Software in Defence Equipment, Part 1: Requirements, U.K. Ministry of Defence (MoD), August 1, 1997.
3. DEF STAN 00-55, Requirements for Safety-Related Software in Defence Equipment, Part 2: Guidance, U.K. Ministry of Defence (MoD), August 1, 1997.
4. Herrmann, D. and Peercy, D., Software reliability cases: the bridge between hardware, software, and system safety and reliability, *Proceedings of the Annual Reliability and Maintainability Symposium (RAMS'99)*, IEEE, 1999, 396–402.
5. JA 1002, Software Reliability Program Standard, Society of Automotive Engineers (SAE), 1998.

B.3.14 Root Cause Analysis

Purpose: To identify the underlying cause(s), events, conditions, or actions that individually, or in combination, led to an accident/incident; determine why the defect was not detected earlier.

Description: Root cause analysis is an investigative technique used to determine how, when, and why a defect was introduced and why it escaped detection in earlier phases. Root cause analysis is conducted by examining a defect, then tracing back step by step through the design and the decisions and assumptions that supported the design to the source of the defect. Root cause analysis supports defect prevention, continuous process improvement, and accident/incident investigation.

Benefits: The process of conducting root cause analysis may uncover defects in other areas as well.

Limitations: Root cause analysis can be time-consuming on large complex systems.

References:

1. Latino, R. and Latino, K., *Root Cause Analysis: Improving Performance for Bottom Line Results*, CRC Press, 1999.
2. *Root Cause Analysis Handbook*, ABS Group, Inc., 1000 Technology Drive, Knoxville, TN 37932-3369, 1999.
3. System Safety Society, *System Safety Analysis Handbook*, 2nd ed., July 1997.

B.3.15 Safety and Security Audits, Reviews, and Inspections

Purpose: To uncover errors and mistakes throughout the life of a system that could affect IA integrity.

Description: Safety and security audits, reviews, and inspections comprise a static analysis technique that is used to find errors of commission and errors of omission. Requirements, designs, implementations, test cases, test results, and operational systems can be subjected to safety and security audits. Unlike other audits and reviews, these focus solely on issues that impact safety and security; for example, verifying that fault tolerance has been implemented correctly, access control rules have been specified correctly, or operational security procedures are being followed correctly. Checklists, in the form of a set of questions intended to stimulate a critical appraisal of all aspects of safety and security, can be used to guide the audits.[5] Any open issues or discrepancies are assigned a severity and tracked through resolution. Internal and independent audits should be conducted regularly. Safety and security audits complement IA requirements traceability.

Benefits: Communication among all stakeholders is facilitated. More and different types of errors are detected, due to the involvement of multiple stakeholders.

Limitations: Safety or security audits must yield repeatable results if their validity is questionable; objective criteria need to be evaluated.[1] Adequate preparation time is necessary.

References:

1. Gollmann, D., *Computer Security*, John Wiley & Sons, 1999.